D1784894

A FEMINIST CRITIQUE OF EDUCATION

A Feminist Critique of Education provides a valuable route map to the development of thinking in gender and education over the last 15 years. It includes 21 seminal articles from the journal *Gender and Education*, written by many of the leading authors in the field, from the UK, the USA, Australia and Europe.

Compiled by the current editors of the journal to show the development of the field, the book is divided into seven sections:

- Gender Identities
- Theoretical Debate
- Education Policy and Management
- History
- Sexuality
- Ethnicity
- Social Class

The specially written Introduction by the editors contextualises the selection and introduces students to the main issues and current thinking in the field.

In one, easy-to-access place, this authoritative reference book provides a collection of articles that have led the field, including 'Voice, Harmony and Fugue in Global Feminism' and 'Spice Girls, Nice Girls, Girlies and Tomboys'. It should find a place in every library and on every departmental bookshelf.

This volume is from the Education Heritage series. For details of other titles in this series, please go to the Education website at www.routledge.co.uk

Christine Skelton is Professor of Education at Roehampton University. **Becky Francis** is Reader in Education at London Metropolitan University.

Education Heritage series

Other titles in the series:

A Feminist Critique of Education
15 years of gender education
Edited by Christine Skelton and Becky Francis

From Adult Education to the Learning Society
21 years from the International Journal of Lifelong Education
Peter Jarvis

A FEMINIST CRITIQUE OF EDUCATION

15 years of gender education

Edited by Christine Skelton and Becky Francis

Routledge
Taylor & Francis Group

LONDON AND NEW YORK

First published 2005
by Routledge
2 Park Square, Milton Park, Abingdon, Oxon OX14 4RN

Simultaneously published in the USA and Canada
by Routledge
711 Third Avenue, New York, NY 10017

Routledge is an imprint of the Taylor & Francis Group

First issued in paperback 2011

Typeset in Sabon by
Newgen Imaging Systems (P) Ltd, Chennai, India

British Library Cataloguing in Publication Data
A catalogue record for this book is available from the British Library

Library of Congress Cataloging in Publication Data
A catalog record for this book has been requested

ISBN 978-0-415-50946-6

CONTENTS

ACKNOWLEDGEMENTS

We should like to thank all those involved with *Gender and Education* journal over the years. This includes all the editors and board members; the various administrators; the publishers at Carfax and now Taylor & Francis; and of course the authors of articles – who have all contributed to make the journal the strong, respected and vigorously feminist journal it is today. Particularly, we thank June Purvis and others involved in the journals' inception, and hope they can be proud of the continued role the journal plays in articulating important research findings and feminist debates in the field of education. The support of Graham Hobbs and Ian White (Taylor & Francis) has also been invaluable in facilitating the journal's development.

Finally, we should like to express our gratitude to Nathan Fretwell of IPSE, whose administrative work in bringing together the various papers for this collection is greatly appreciated.

Christine Skelton and Becky Francis
Editors, *Gender and Education*

INTRODUCTION

Christine Skelton and Becky Francis

Gender and Education journal has provided a venue for the dissemination of feminist research in education since 1989. This collection aims to represent key themes and debates in the field since the journal's inception, drawing together papers which particularly represent these. In this way, it is intended that the book will provide readers with an insight into the ways in which feminist research in education has developed over the years, and a point of reference for high-quality research findings and feminist theory in relation to education.

Gender and Education journal

The emergence of *Gender and Education* in 1989 reflected the impact of feminist research in education, which had developed as a result of the 'second-wave' feminist movement in the 1970s. Investigations and considerations of the area had developed on an international scale in both depth and diversity since the 1970s. In the United Kingdom (UK), the successful passage of the Sex Discrimination Act (1975) marked a significant staging post in the work of those academics and teachers who, in the wake of second-wave feminism were critiquing patriarchal schooling processes (Arnot and Weiner, 1987). Key feminist studies of the classroom in the late 1970s and early 1980s made a major contribution in challenging dominant assumptions about educational practice and experience, and caused ripples in the research community.

The creation of the journal highlighted the feminist contribution in education, and its existence (both in demonstrating a market for it, and in its dissemination of feminist research) insisted that this body of research be taken seriously.

The journal's first editor, June Purvis, together with an editorial board consisting of other leading educational feminists, devised a publication that would give added momentum to the work of feminist educators, who were trying to redress inequalities in girls' and women's educational experiences. At the same time, feminist investigations into gender and education were undertaken by researchers from a variety of discipline backgrounds who had an investment in different theoretical traditions, many of which challenged each other. The journal was not simply to provide a platform for feminist voices to be heard, but to allow a venue through which feminist educationalists could debate various feminist perspectives on, and reconceptualisations of, categories, theories and explanations used in educational analyses.

Our selection of articles for the book

In identifying 21 articles from the 362 that the journal has published to date, we sought the views of all those who had served on the editorial board since 1989. We asked them to identify two articles that they had found particularly influential in terms of developing their own thinking or in their teaching. The responses reflected the diversity of feminist interests in education but there were also several key articles that appeared on more than one person's list. As (current) journal editors, we also sought to represent key themes which have been represented and developed in the journal. At the same time, due to page constraints, inevitably, the content can represent only a snapshot of the journal's diversity and output. In looking through the journal content over the years, we should have liked to illustrate the trajectories in the development of ideas in different subject areas, but the publishing constraints have forced us to focus primarily on representing contemporary themes and theories. The themes predominating the authors' interests and reflected in the contents of this book are: femininities and masculinities; theory and method; education policy and management; history; sexuality; ethnicity and social class. This is not to say that papers are not submitted on any other topic or theme, as a reading of the contents list of any one volume will indicate.

Given the previous comments, inevitably readers will observe that some themes or issues are not represented here.[1] This is particularly pertinent in relation to articles from different countries. There is far greater representation of Western countries in the journal, notably Australia, New Zealand, Canada and the UK. However, articles appearing in *Gender and Education* are contributed by authors located across the world. With the inclusion of *Gender and Education* on the Social Science Citation Index in 2000, the number of submissions from the United States of America (USA) has increased substantially, but this 'late interest' means that papers from the USA do not feature significantly in this collection. Moreover, many articles in the journal over the years have represented case studies exploring specific issues in particular countries – this is particularly true of articles from researchers in developing countries. Examples of these are not included here on the basis that, whilst interesting and of crucial importance in documenting the situation in particular countries, they are often too country-specific to appeal to a wide readership.

Our selection of articles reflects how some topics and themes have received more consideration by authors than others. The dominant concerns for many have been to do with gender identities, and theory and method, and, more recently, educational policy and management, and these therefore comprise the largest sections of the book. What we have attempted to do here is put together articles within these themes that illustrate the way in which ideas are debated and developed in the journal. The remaining themes are represented by two papers in each section although this is not an altogether accurate indication of how well they have been represented in the journal. For example, there have been relatively few articles on ethnicity but many on history. Each of the selected themes will be discussed briefly in order to put the articles into context.

Gender identities

The fact that many now talk of femininity and masculinity in the plural (femininities and masculinities) indicates the shifts in thinking that have taken place since the time when the journal started. In the early articles appearing in *Gender and Education*, it was more common to find discussions that concentrated on differences between men/women and girls/boys than intra-gender differences, for example, explorations of gender differences between females. In those earlier days, there was a recognition of diversity created through social class and ethnicity (Deem, 1980; Brah and Minhas, 1985) but only a few writers recognised the importance of looking at differences between, for example, working-class girls (for exceptions see Sharpe, 1976; Anyon, 1983). To understand the reasons for this is to understand the theories that were available and the major concerns that were occupying the efforts of educational feminists.

The main belief underpinning second-wave feminism was that women were globally oppressed by men and something needed to be done about it (Gordon, 1979). However, the notion that all women shared similar experiences of oppression was increasingly criticised, particularly by black women and by white-working class and/or lesbian women, who pointed out that middle-class white feminists were able to (and do) exercise power over other women. There were also differences between feminists in terms of their aims and the theoretical perspectives in which these aims were contextualised.

In terms of education there were initially three very clear perspectives: liberal feminism, radical feminism and Marxist-socialist feminism, and these were joined in the 1980s by black feminism. All four of these perspectives focused to greater and to lesser extents on structural injustices and inequalities, for example, the unequal career opportunities of women academic staff (Cann *et al.*, 1991) or of gay and lesbian teachers (Squirrell, 1989). At this point, notions of 'difference' were related mainly to structural differences with liberal feminists arguing that sex role socialisation and legislation lay at the root of gender inequalities; Marxist-socialist feminists seeing the reproduction by schools of social-class divisions as the major factor; and radical feminists identifying male power as the cause of female educational experiences. It was the increasing articulation of the concept of 'difference' as espoused in identity politics that brought about greater attention to the various ways in which individuals went about constructing identities (Weiner *et al.*, 1997). The articles in this part of the book signal recent progressions in these ways of looking at gender identities. Here, we can see the recognition and engagement with pluralistic notions of masculinities and femininities including discussions of the ways in which gender is intersected by other variables such as ethnicity, culture, social class, able-bodiedness and so forth, in shaping personal identities.

A glance at the popular press in the UK towards the millennium (but also in other countries such as Australia, North America and Northern Europe) demonstrates a heightened interest and concern for boys and education. This concern is articulated in terms of a 'crisis of masculinity' and 'boys' underachievement (the latter mainly on the basis of boys' comparative underachievement at literacy and languages, see OECD PISA research, 2003; Francis and Skelton, 2005). A popularist argument was that the attention given to girls and the inequalities they experienced at school had brought about a situation where boys had been forgotten and marginalised in the classroom. Therefore, so the thinking went, the result was that boys were underachieving due to a combination of their lack of motivation for education, disaffection with schooling and teachers' inabilities to recognise and respond to the differing needs of boys (see Martino and Meyenn, 2001; Skelton, 2001; Lingard, 2003 for discussion and critique of such claims). However, as articles appearing in early issues of *Gender and Education* signify, authors have long been providing empirical research and raising important questions about the ways in which schools reproduce culturally dominant modes of masculinity which boys negotiated, challenged and/or imitated. Indeed in one issue of *Gender and Education* published in 1991, three out of the six articles were about the significance of schools as cultural sites of the reproduction of masculinities (volume 3, issue 3). Yet the understandings that this research and discussions provided with regard to 'boys and schooling' were spectacularly ignored by policy makers in the mid-1990s when schoolboys became a focus of attention due to the publication of public examination results indicating that girls were (in many areas) outperforming boys. Furthermore, this research was ignored on an international plane with governments in the UK, Australia and North America rushing to find practice-based explanations of and solutions to 'boys' problems with schools' (Weaver-Hightower, 2003). More recently, there is evidence to indicate that the gap between theoretically oriented research on masculinities and practice-based initiatives which challenge stereotypical notions of boys' learning identities is being bridged with governments funding projects and setting up official inquiries which draw on both approaches (Warrington and Younger, 2003; Martino *et al.*, 2004).

While many feminist and pro-feminist researchers in education are engaged with analysing these debates around boys and achievement, others are returning to work on femininity in response to the contemporary preoccupation with masculinity. For this reason, 2003 saw a Special Issue of *Gender and Education* published on 'Diverse working class femininities in education' (two articles from which are included in this collection). Close attention to the ways in which gendered identities are constructed and inscribed have been a feature of this contemporary work on femininities and masculinities. Hence, this work has developed theoretical perspectives that encourage greater reflection on the links between the social, the cultural and the 'personal'.

Theory and method

Feminist theories and methodologies have occupied, in recent years, far more space in *Gender and Education* than in the early days of the journal. This is indicative of the fact that feminist research is increasingly concerned with epistemological and methodological matters in contrast to earlier feminist research studies of education where the emphasis was on methods. As was indicated earlier, the various feminist perspectives informed where gender inequalities in schooling were seen as located and there was, certainly in the early years of second-wave feminism, a general acceptance that qualitative methods were more appropriate to feminist research than quantitative. With the emergence of identity politics and the greater recognition of 'difference' and 'otherness' came the opportunity to explore in far more nuanced ways how 'woman'/'girl'/'feminine' has been socially constituted in terms of what 'man'/'boy'/'masculine' is not (and vice versa) (Ramazanoglu and Holland, 2002). At the same time, post-modern and particularly post-structuralist theory have posed a major challenge to identity politics, deconstructing 'truth claims' and the apparent cohesion of groups such as 'women'. The impact of post-structuralism on feminist thinking has been quite profound and not least because, as the papers in this collection indicate, of the questions and challenges it creates for feminism. In spite of these, poststructuralist theory has been enthusiastically taken up by many feminists as a radical theory which offers the potential to engage with complex power differences.

Given the constraints of length of this book, we are unable to adequately represent all the diverse theoretical approaches that have been adopted by contributors. As post-structuralism has been debated most frequently, we have chosen to represent a strand of this argument in the theory part to illustrate how ideas are debated and developed within the journal. The articles chosen here reflect the extent of engagement with, and challenges of, post-structuralism for feminist researchers.

Education policy and management

There have undoubtedly been huge steps forward in many Western countries in the development of policies addressing issues of inequality. As Kate Myers (2000, p. 218) has pointed out, 'much of what we now take for granted is due to pioneers who went before' but this is not to suggest that social justice has now been achieved. The articles in this part point to how the introduction of 'new managerialism' in globalised economies has led to an increasing masculinisation of organisational practices. Briefly, 'new managerialism' is where the principles associated with ways of working in business and industry in a market economy have been incorporated into the public sector. These 'new managerialist' processes place emphasis on the three Es – economy, efficiency and effectiveness (Pollitt, 1993). The consequence of these for teachers and academics is that their research and teaching is scrutinised and measured through public accountability measures such as school and university inspections (such as Office for Standards in Education (OfSTED), the Research Assessment Exercise (RAE) and Quality Assurance Agency (QAA) inspections in the UK). It also impacts on day-to-day practices and resourcing, via increased institutional scrutiny, competition and 'belt-tightening'.

The literature on teachers and women academics and the impact of 'new managerialist' practices in education encompasses three quite distinct viewpoints. There is the argument that new managerialism offers a means of challenging the masculine hierarchies of schools and universities (Hearn, 1998; Harley, 2003). In contrast, there is the view put forward, mainly by feminist authors and represented in the articles in this section, that new managerialism has had a negative impact on the working lives of teachers and academics. Some of these authors also show how this approach has had a pernicious impact on the work of women who are committed to democratic styles of leadership and whose research centres around social justice (see also Blackmore, 1999; Morley, 1999). Then there is a smaller body of work indicating that the consequences of new managerialist practices minimise gender differences in that both male and female academics articulate similar negative consequences (Currie et al., 2000). The authors of this latter body of work are at pains to explain that gender inequities in the schools and the academy have not disappeared but have been marginalised in a system where 'everyone's work is calculated in market terms' (Currie et al., 2000, p. 288).

This marketisation of education touches upon the lives of all involved and not just teachers and academics in universities. As the article by Amy Stambach indicates, in the language of 'school choice' parents are 'consumers' of education but the reality is that mothers who become involved in the setting up and administration of a school 'run the risk of being seen as stepping out of their roles as consumers and caregivers' (2001, p. 199).

The article concluding Part III, Chapter 8 of this volume by Nelly Stromquist (2000), draws together feminist concerns and voices across the globe and considers these in the light of contemporary theoretical positions, notably post-structuralist approaches. She discusses the continued impact and importance of social policy for gender relations, alerting feminists (and she appears to be speaking to Western feminists in particular) not to get caught up with 'ivory tower' contemplation when women in developing countries are still having to fight for rights such as access to a basic education for girls.

History

The subsequent four sections on history, sexuality, ethnicity and social class are each represented by two or more articles. History is probably the most well-represented category of articles that have appeared in *Gender and Education*. Inevitably, the content of the history papers is diverse and in order to bring some coherence to the selection here, two have been chosen which represent nineteenth-century women and the politics of education, and reflect some of the diversity of representation even within this area.

Sexuality, ethnicity and social class

Whilst we have grouped the articles into sexuality, ethnicity and social class it is evident from the titles that they might easily have been put into earlier or other categories. Indeed, some of the articles in other parts deal with these issues quite explicitly. This is a clear illustration of how researching into identity and social justice issues calls on the myriad structural, physiological and psychic factors that make up an individual's personal experiences. However, we have also endeavoured to represent these themes as parts of their own, as they are (particularly in the case of sexuality) strong themes in *Gender and Education*. That being said, especially in the case of research on ethnicity (which is relatively under-represented in the journal), we should like to encourage the development of these strands further. The articles represented here reflect the nuance lent by theories of difference and social constructionist/post-structuralist approaches, while still firmly illustrating the social and material consequences of 'difference' for people's lives.

Concluding comments

In this collection, we have attempted to highlight the key themes and concerns that have engaged the attention of authors from the inception of the journal through to the present day. It is worth reminding readers that we have only touched upon the topics that *Gender and Education* has covered in the last 15 years which have enlivened debate and stimulated interest. The aim has been to provide some indication of the developments, discussions and debates in relation to theory and policy and how these have influenced feminist research and thinking in recent years. We will await with interest the next collection of *Gender and Education* papers in 15 years' time to see what progress has been made regarding these long-standing issues and debates.

NOTE

1   Readers may note the absence of sections on pedagogy, on teaching and learning processes and practices; and on disabilities.

REFERENCES

Anyon, J. (1983) 'Intersections of gender and class: accommodation and resistance by working-class and affluent females to contradictory sex-role ideologies', *Gender, Class and Education* (Lewes, Falmer).

Arnot, M. and Weiner, G. (1987) *Gender and the Politics of Schooling* (London, Unwin Hyman).

Blackmore, J. (1999) *Troubling Women* (Buckingham, Open University Press).

Brah, A. and Minhas, R. (1985) 'Structural racism or cultural difference: schooling for Asian girls', in G. Weiner (ed.), *Just a Bunch of Girls* (Milton Keynes, Open University Press).

Cann, J., Jones, G. and Martin, I. (1991) 'Behind the rhetoric: women academic staff in colleges of higher education in England', *Gender and Education*, 1(1): 15–30.

Currie, J., Harris, P. and Thiele, B. (2000) 'Sacrifices in greedy universities: are they gendered?', *Gender and Education*, 20(3): 269–291.

Deem, R. (ed.) (1980) *Schooling for Women's Work* (London, Routledge & Kegan Paul).

Francis, B. and Skelton, C. (2005) *Reassessing Gender and Achievement* (London, RoutledgeFalmer).

Gordon, L. (1979) 'The struggle for reproductive freedom: three stages of feminism', in Z. Eisenstein (ed.), *Capitalist Patriarchy and the Case for Socialist Feminism* (New York, Monthly Review Press).

Harley, S. (2003) 'Research selectivity and female academics in UK universities: from gentleman's club and barrack yard to smart macho', *Gender and Education*, 15(4): 377–392.

Hearn, J. (1998) 'Men managers and management: the case of higher education', in S. Whitehead and R. Moodey (eds), *Transforming Managers: Engendering Change in the Public Sector* (London, Taylor & Francis).

Lingard, B. (2003) 'Where to in gender policy in education after recuperative masculinity politics', *International Journal of Inclusive Education*, 7(1): 35–56.

Martino, W. and Meyenn, B. (2001) *What About the Boys?* (Buckingham, Open University Press).

Martino, W., Lingard, B. and Mills, M. (2004) 'Addressing the educational needs of boys: a question of teacher threshold knowledges', *Gender and Education*, 16(4): 435–454.

Morley, L. (1999) *Organising Feminisms: The Micropolitics of the Academy* (Basingstoke, Macmillan).

Myers, K. (ed.) (2000) *Whatever Happened to Equal Opportunities in Schools?* (Buckingham, Open University Press).

Organisation for Economic Cooperation and Development (2003) *Literacy Skills for the World of Tomorrow* (OECD/Unesco).

Pollitt, C. (1993) *Managerialism and the Public Service: Cuts or Cultural Change in the 1990s* (Oxford, Blackwell) (2nd edn).

Ramazanoglu, C. and Holland, J. (2002) *Feminist Methodology* (London, Sage).

Sharpe, S. (1976) *'Just Like a Girl': How Girls Learn to be Women* (Harmondsworth, Penguin).

Skelton, C. (2001) *Schooling the Boys* (Buckingham, Open University Press).

Squirrell, G. (1989) 'Teachers and issues of sexual orientation', *Gender and Education*, 1(1): 17–34.

Stambach, A. (2001) 'Consumerism and gender in and era of school choice: a look at US charter schools', *Gender and Education*, 13(3): 199–216.

Warrington, M. and Younger, M. (2003) ' "We decided to give it a twirl": single-sex teaching in English comprehensive Schools', *Gender and Education*, 15(4): 339–350.

Weaver-Hightower, M. (2003) 'Crossing the divide: bridging the disjunctures between theoretically oriented and practice-oriented literature about masculinity and boys at school', *Gender and Education*, 15(4): 407–423.

Weiner, G., Arnot, M. and David, M. (1997) 'Is the future female? Female success, male disadvantage and changing gender patterns in education', in A. Halsey, H. Lauder, P. Brown and A. Stuart Wells (eds), *Education: Culture, Economy, Society* (Oxford, Oxford University Press).

PART I

GENDER IDENTITIES

ONE

PUPILS, RESISTANCE AND GENDER CODES: A STUDY OF CLASSROOM ENCOUNTERS

Sheila Riddell

Source: 'Pupils, resistance and gender codes: a study of classroom encounters',
Gender and Education, 1(2): 183–197, 1989.

Introduction

This paper is based on work undertaken for a doctoral thesis which addresses the problem of how schools aid in the reproduction of gender and class inequalities. It focuses on the part played by the process of subject option choice. The research is set in two rural comprehensive schools in the south-west of England. The first school, where I had previously worked as a full-time teacher, is referred to as Millbridge. The second school, where I had no pre-established reputation, is known as Greenhill. Observation, semi-structured interviews and questionnaires were all used during the research. One of my central concerns was to understand why girls appear to concur in a process which is likely to ensure the perpetuation of the sexual division of labour in the labour market and the family. In this paper, the mechanisms by which this happens, particularly through the reproduction and legitimation of traditional gender codes, are explored through the use of data gathered during periods of fieldwork in the two schools.

The length of the fieldwork was an important factor in the research because it enabled option choice to be seen as the outcome of an extended process and not as an isolated moment. I want to argue that while the school and teachers clearly channelled pupil choices, and pupils' families also had a say, nevertheless girls and boys themselves played an active part in the maintenance of the sex-stereotyped curriculum through the negotiation of their gender identities. A better understanding of this process is essential to the success of future equal opportunities policies in schools.

Methods

At Millbridge, I spent a term and a half, from March to July 1983, observing a third-year mixed-ability group and at Greenhill I carried out observation from September 1984 to July 1985. I found it easier to establish a confiding relationship with teachers at Millbridge because I had previously worked in the school, but this residual teacher identity imposed limitations on my relationship with pupils. The problems which I encountered in attempting to distance myself from the teachers were similar to those encountered by Hargreaves (1967) when he tried to shake off the teacher role and then the Inspector role. At Greenhill, on the other hand, I entered the institution with no previously established identity and was thus able to form much closer relationships with pupils – although this also meant that I tended to be mistrusted by teachers. Like Hammersley (1984), I found the lack of a clear identity quite disorientating at times. As I have already indicated, my overall aim was to explore the part played by individual choices in reproducing gender and class divisions. I used the triangulation methods outlined by Hammersley and Atkinson (1983) in order to cross-check my own observations against the accounts offered by teachers and pupils.

The involvement of teachers and pupils in the reproduction of traditional gender codes

A number of writers, for instance Davies (1984) and Woods (1979), have seen the classroom in terms of a power struggle between pupils and teachers. For many pupils, education is experienced as a form of repression (Corrigan, 1979). I will argue that this struggle for power is often worked out through manipulation of traditional gender codes and struggles over competing gender codes. This happens in two ways. First, teachers base their coping strategies and sanctions on their typifications of male and female pupils. Second, pupils base their resistance to schooling on the exploitation of the contradictions and inconsistencies of traditional gender codes, and sometimes challenge them outright. I will argue that both teachers' attempts to maintain their authority in the classroom, and pupils' resistance to this power generally reinforce rather than undermine traditional gender codes. Some girls, however, do engage in activities which challenge traditional constructions of masculinity and femininity, and I will also consider these. In order to clarify this account, I shall arrange my discussion under the following headings: teachers' typifications of male and female pupils, teachers' coping strategies, boys' and girls' resistance through the manipulation of traditional gender codes.

Teachers' typifications of male and female pupils

Clarricoates (1980) found that many teachers, when they were asked whether there were any differences in the behaviour and attitudes of boys and girls in the third year, said that it was possible to identify clear differences. My own data support her view. Usually, girls were described in terms of maturity, neatness and conscientiousness. Data from Millbridge teachers emphasised these themes.

All the teachers I spoke to commented on the maturity of the girls relative to the boys. One female English teacher, for instance, had this to say:

> Boys are much much more aggressive and immature. I find the girls quite amenable, you can talk to them on quite a normal level, whereas I find the boys, and I always have, very silly and childish, and that tends to carry on until the beginning of the fourth year.

The 'maturity' of the girls, which generally seemed to mean that they were better behaved and quieter, was often attributed to their more rapid physical development. For instance, the head of science told me: 'When you look at the girls most of them have been or are going through their growth spurt. Half the boys in the class are still little boys – some of them in mentality are still two years behind.' Many teachers, it seemed, were attributing girls' maturity not to any qualities they had worked hard to achieve, but rather to some quirk of biological development.

It is significant, however, that 'maturity' was immediately linked with some other quality and often it was a negative one: '...the girls are more sensible but perhaps more petty – well, girls tend to be like that for another year or two – "she's not speaking to me" sort of thing' (Female head of house at Millbridge).

It is also interesting to note that girls' supposed maturity was used to excuse boys' poorer academic performance. One of the boys attending an options interview at Millbridge was told by the head of physics: 'Your grades are a bit low now, but research shows that boys tend to be a bit behind at this stage and then catch up later, so you should be all right.'

Two other qualities which both male and female teachers frequently attributed to girls were their neatness and conscientiousness. In biology and geography, for instance, the teachers felt that the girls' neatness accounted for their success. A male geography teacher at Millbridge said:

> A bright girl will not only produce work that's correct but a map, say, will always be meticulously neat. They seem to be capable of doing this, whereas very few boys will spend the time necessary to produce a very neat map.

Again, it is significant that 'neatness' was not seen as an unqualified advantage for the girls' academic progress. A Millbridge maths teacher told me that one girl presented her work so beautifully that he never liked to put any marks on it. In fact, far from being seen in positive terms, girls' neatness and hard work were seen as evidence of an attempt to hide their intellectual inferiority:

> I think some of the boys have got behind the girls lower down through lack of discipline probably and the girls have been naturally hard working and have tended to get ahead. And in maths, as long as you've got a modicum of intelligence you can get a very long way... But when it comes to seeing through a problem, where a bit of flair is needed, then I think the boys have an edge. When it's just a routine approach – you know, you do one on the board and they do the others with just a few small variations – then the girls, by virtue of following carefully what you've done, and taking it down neatly and reading about it and so on, they do better. I think the boys, if you wanted to devise another way of doing the problem, other than the one you've shown them, I think I would plump for a boy finding that.
>
> (Millbridge male deputy head)

Walden and Walkerdine (1982, 1985), in their study of discontinuity in girls' performance in maths between primary and secondary school, encountered a similar phenomenon. Girls were believed to be 'naturally' good at the more routine approaches to mathematics, but less skilled in higher level problem-solving and lacking in 'flair'. They describe this as a 'Catch 22' situation: 'If they fail at mathematics they lack true intellect but are truly female. If they succeed they are only able to do so by following rules and if they conquer that hurdle then they become somehow less than female.'

The qualities attributed to girls, then, of neatness, hardwork and maturity were decidedly double-edged. It would be easy to argue, as some researchers such as Clarricoates (1980) have done, that teachers impose their gender codes on to passively receptive pupils, but my data indicate a further process is at work. As data presented later in this paper suggest, pupils are also in many ways actively involved in the process of gender construction.

It was clear that girls were indeed quieter in the class than boys, and in this respect my data support the findings of other researchers such as Kelly (1986). However, teachers' explanation of the reasons, for this, in terms of biological development and inherent intellectual inferiority, suggests that they were interpreting objective reality within a cultural framework which did not take account of the circumstances in the classroom producing this response. In the following sections, I will argue that gender construction in the classroom was an essentially dialectical process. Teachers based their coping strategies (see Hargreaves, 1978, for further discussion of this concept) on their typifications of male and female pupils, and in this way transmitted traditional conceptions of masculinity and femininity. Pupils responded either by conforming, or by resisting teachers' authority through the parody and contradiction of these gender codes. Much of this resistance, however, was ultimately hegemonic.

Teachers' coping strategies

I will now consider how teachers' coping strategies are based on their typifications of male and female pupils and reinforce traditional gender codes. Specifically, I will examine how teachers attempt to win the consent of boys to their authority by allowing them to control the physical space of the classroom, the attention of the teacher and the content of lessons. I will also look at how male camaraderie is established in the classroom through the use of humour and the verbal denigration of women. The control of girls through teachers' use of traditional notions of femininity will be examined, and the establishment of female solidarity in feminine areas of the curriculum will also be discussed.

(a) *Teacher authority, noisy boys and quiet girls*   Although most teachers said they thought that they spent an equal amount of time with girls and boys in the classroom, observation of many lessons showed that teachers were forced to spend the majority of their time with boys simply to preserve some semblance of order (see also Ebbutt, 1981). I will describe an art lesson with Lois Roughton at Greenhill School to show the strategies employed by boys to maximise their share of teacher attention, and the strategies which the teacher is forced to adopt to deal with their behaviour. The purpose of the lesson is to paint an ordinary object such as a Mars bar wrapper in a subtly different form. Boys and girls sit at different tables and early on a group of boys attract the teacher's attention by making racist comments which the teacher does not challenge directly, but tells them to get on with their work. Ben Hayter gives a lengthy monologue about a brilliant idea which he had for his homework. It eventually transpires that it was too complicated for him to actually carry out. Later on, when Miss Roughton is talking to me, he calls, 'Miss, Miss', across the classroom in a voice which is almost, a whine, rather like a small child. She breaks off the conversation immediately and goes across to him. Shortly afterwards, she becomes annoyed with Ben and Justin who have been wandering round the classroom making loud comments on other pupils' work, and shouts at them. Ben insists on having the last word in this exchange, 'Oh Miss, we were just having an intellectual discussion.'

The lesson continues with the teacher responding rapidly to the boys' demands, which often seem to reflect the belief that as a woman she is there to service their needs and receive their complaints: 'The paint runs,' 'The sink's not working,' 'I don't like painting, Miss.'

Ben gives the teacher advice on how to deal with his friends: 'I'd keep the packet of crisps Miss.' Another boy walks round the class with a pencil stuck through his jumper pretending it is a nipple, and is told to sit down. At the end of the lesson, a group of boys get up, and start to walk out in the middle of the teacher's explanation of homework, and Justin is kept behind at the end for an individual telling off. By way of contrast, the girls have almost no disciplinary contact with the teacher, even though many are not doing much work either. At one point Miss Roughton walks over to a table where a group of girls are quietly chatting about a teacher at the middle school who is splitting up from his wife. She says: 'This sounds more like a mothers' meeting than an art lesson.' And to me, 'This is where I get all my inside information from.'

Later, Miss Roughton tells me that the boys in the group are able but immature, whereas the girls can be relied on to work quietly by themselves. This lesson provides a clear example of how the boys' behaviour, and the teacher's interpretation of it, has forced her to adopt a particular coping strategy. She rewards their demands for attention with her time, and allows the girls to chat quietly rather than get on with their work simply because she does not have enough time and energy to insist that they do this. Were she to focus more attention on the girls, the boys threaten that their behaviour might get completely out of hand. Her actions are understandable in view of the enormous pressure on teachers to keep classes quiet at all costs (Denscombe, 1980). However, it is also important to recognise that the way in which she justifies this division of her time, in terms of fulfilling the boys' needs, prevents her from examining her actions critically. In this example, we can see how the gender codes which girls and boys bring to the classroom shape their behaviour, and call forth a particular response in the teacher which is then justified by her conception of natural male and female behaviour.

(b) *Lesson content*   At both schools it was apparent that the content of lessons was often shaped to hold the attention of potentially disruptive boys. A history teacher at Millbridge, for instance, was giving a talk on twentieth-century history and spent the entire lessons describing in graphic detail the sort of deaths which men experienced in the trenches during the First World War. He read one account of a man's head being blown off while this body continued to run forward, and when one girl complained that she did not want to hear any more of this, she was told that she must listen because this was how history was created. Boys, on the other hand, made a great show of enjoying these accounts.

In English lessons, almost all the books which were used featured boys as the main characters, often dealing with the problems of the male adolescent. When I discussed this with one particular English teacher she said that this had never occurred to her before, but it was clearly not fair: 'We certainly wouldn't expect boys to put up with listening to stories about girls all the time, but we do expect girls to do it.'

When teachers did make an attempt to appeal to girls, this sometimes also reinforced sexist stereotypes. An extreme example of this was provided by Mr Stanhope's history lessons at Greenhill. Mary's persecution of Protestants, he told them, was due to the fact that she had had a very unfulfilled life because she had not been allowed to marry for political reasons. The girls in the class were asked to imagine her situation:

> When you leave school you may have a career and you may want to return to it afterwards, but still at the heart of your lives will be getting married and having children. It's the most natural thing in the world despite what some feminists might like to say.

Another blatant example of the reinforcement of traditional gender codes through lesson content was provided in a physics lesson at Greenhill. The physics teacher, Mr Lill, was explaining electricity by asking the class to imagine that positive charges were girls and negative charges were boys. They all knew, he said, that girls tended to run after boys, but were nasty to other girls, and of course boys did not like each other unless they were queer. This analogy was used for several weeks, interspersed with comments about queers and fruity boys, and was even extended to the description of an ammeter as a dirty old man standing on the street corner counting girls going by. Mr Lill explained his strategy thus:

> I always try to get rid of the abstract terms in physics. That's why I talk about girls and sex. I say it's the girls who do most of the running round and the boys are interested but quite lazy.

Quite apart from the fact that his explanation was rather inappropriate given the fact that most girls and boys preferred single-sex friendship groups, it did not occur to him that aspects of this explanation were sexist, not to mention heterosexist, and therefore might be less than useful in undermining the masculine image of science.

The examples which have been used here are of a rather extreme nature, and the content of the majority of lessons which I observed was more neutral than this. In many lessons, the masculine bias was fairly subtle, for instance, science lessons would often draw on examples from boys' experience, and deal with subjects with which boys were likely to be familiar such as electricity and magnetism. There were also many lessons which could not be said to be aimed specifically at either boys or girls, for instance, geography lessons which dealt with the development of communication routes. A small minority of lessons actually challenged traditional gender codes, for instance, one drama lesson involved an entire class acting out a space fantasy where they landed on a planet on which gender roles were reversed. This idea was conveyed to pupils in a very interesting way. The teacher, who was also in role, demanded to be taken to the group's leader, and became very angry when a boy was picked for this part, saying that the space travellers were clearly joking. It took some time for the class to realise that a girl had to be picked as leader, and the boys were clearly reluctant to relinquish their leadership role. Overall, however, a significant number of lessons were based on very traditional conceptions of boys' and girls' interests, and it was apparent that at times the teacher was deliberately appealing to the supposed attraction of violence for boys to hold the attention of a group of potentially disruptive male pupils.

(c) *Humour and the derogation of women* Some male teachers dealt with the threat of boys' potentially disruptive behaviour by attempting to establish an atmosphere of male camaraderie based on sexual joking. I asked Mr Broughton, a woodwork teacher at Millbridge, who was also head of house, whether it made any difference having girls in the classes he taught, and he described how he used the supposed universal appeal of the dirty joke in all boys' groups, which was not possible if girls were present:

> All boys enjoy a dirty joke – I do myself as long as it's clever as well. And if it's all boys you can get them to remember things with it. For instance, you see those pipes over there, well the joints you call male or female for obvious reasons and we have a bit of a laugh over that. That's the nice thing about having all boys – if you've got girls there you can't really do that and you've got to watch your language.

Some of the male teachers' joking specifically involved the derogation of women, for example, at the end of a metalwork lesson boys were told that if they forgot their aprons again they would be issued with frilly aprons and bras and panties. At other times jokes were told or comments made which were based on cruelty or vulgarity. A number of girls expressed their dislike of this type of joking, for instance, Mary Roundhay at Greenhill objected to her physics teacher's references to nose picking.

Humour, lesson content and allocation of teacher time, then, were all ways in which teachers created an ethos of masculinity in the classroom, which formed an essential part of their strategy for the containment of boys.

(d) *The establishment of female solidarity* Just as male teachers appealed to shared notions of masculinity as a central part of their classroom coping strategies, so women teachers in female areas of the curriculum drew on a culture of femininity to win girls' co-operation in the classroom. In art/textiles at Greenhill, for instance, Lois Roughton mingled with the girls as they engaged in a whole range of activities such as dyeing clothes which they brought in from home, screen printing large covers for floor cushions and making clothes from newspaper patterns. The atmosphere of this lesson, as girls tried clothes on and talked about boys, parents, friends and teachers, was more like a cosy chat in a bedroom than a school lesson. Clearly, these lessons were a welcome escape from the confrontational atmosphere of much of the school day, but also represented a strange contradiction. In some ways they challenged male power through the establishment of that female solidarity which underlies feminist consciousness. In other ways, however, these lessons were reinforcing the idea of the appropriateness of domesticity for women.

(e) *Gender and coercive sanctions* When attempts to win the consent of boys to teachers' authority failed, then male teachers would use physical violence as a sanction, drawing on notions of the acceptability of male aggression as a means of control. Mr Broughton said that it was because of the availability of this sanction that he found boys easier to control:

> The boy thinks he might get a smack either round the ear or up the backside or whatever, whereas the girl knows you won't do it. I think there is this built in thing that boys can be beaten into submission at home or at school. It's historical more than at present.

This teacher was not typical of male teachers at Millbridge, but since he was head of house he had considerable influence, being responsible for the discipline of a quarter of the children in the school. The symbolic power of the cane as the ultimate sanction against male pupils was clearly demonstrated at Greenhill. Shortly after the start of the autumn term, three boys who had been involved in feuding between the different middle schools were caned, and Mr Flanders, the head of year, held an assembly for the boys in which he displayed the cane and said that the boys who had been caned were really cowards. Many teachers said they supported this show of toughness because it showed the power of those in authority in the school.

Sanctions used by male teachers in the control of boys, then, reinforced traditional notions of the legitimacy of male control through the use of violence. Similarly, traditional meanings of femininity were drawn upon in the control of female pupils. For some teachers, this was a consciously formulated strategy, for instance, Mr Jones, the head of biology at Millbridge said, 'I certainly use sex in the way I teach. I tease girls much more than boys – with quiet girls it's the only way to get them to say anything. It's one of my teaching weapons'. Many male teachers referred to girls as 'love' or 'dear', and allowed 'the ladies' to leave the class before the boys. Cajoling or humouring was often used by male teachers as ways of avoiding confrontation with girls. Pat Rennick, a Greenhill pupil, was sent out of religious education (RE) for shouting at a teacher, and this is her account of what happened:

> He says, "Get out, I'm not having you shouting like this in my lesson. Come back when you're better behaved". And then when he comes out he turns it into a joke. He's laughing and says, "There's no need to get like that". And I says, "It's my dad and that...I'm so used to my dad keeping on to me, you know he teases me, I just crack up in the end, I can't help it".

Pat is able to escape responsibility for her rudeness by drawing on the teacher's sympathy for her emotional state. Buswell (1984) describes similar incidents where male teachers control girls by appealing to their emotionalism. Ultimately, she says, this is against girls' interests because they are learning how to survive through the use of manipulative strategies in relationships with men which are fundamentally unequal. Girls' exploitation of traditional gender code as a form of contestation will be discussed later. Control strategies aimed at the control of both girls and boys, then, were often based on traditional gender codes and in their turn reinforced these conceptions of masculinity and femininity.

So far, then, it has been argued that both male and female teachers appealed to traditional notions of masculinity and feminity in controlling girls and boys in the classroom. Sometimes similar strategies were used by both male and female teachers, but some were only accessible to either men or women because of their predication on shared gender identity and understandings. However, the establishment of teachers' authority in the classroom through the reinforcement of traditional gender codes was not automatically achieved for two reasons. First, pupils were able to contest teachers' power by adopting modes of behaviour which apparently conformed to, but in reality parodied, these gender codes. Second, pupils brought their own conceptions of masculinity and femininity with them to the classroom, which did not necessarily conform to those of teachers, and the contradictions between competing gender codes could be used by pupils in their resistance to education. I will now consider exactly what form this resistance took, and whether it represented effective challenging to broader gender divisions, or whether it was simply a manifestation of individualised contestation without radical implications.

Boys' resistance through manipulation of traditional gender codes

(a) *Boys and macho culture*   In the previous section it has been argued that male teachers appealed to a shared culture of masculinity based on acceptance of violence, sexual bravado, and derogation of women in their attempts to win the consent of boys to their authority in the classroom. However this was not always successful. Some boys accepted this definition of masculinity, but far from seeing it as a legitimation of teacher authority, used it to challenge this very authority. It is interesting that this was most apparent at both schools in metalwork lessons, where traditional masculinity was presented in its crudest form in order to contain the most disaffected working-class pupils.

A description of one particular metalwork lesson at Greenhill will perhaps give some idea of the general atmosphere. In many ways the workshop felt like a factory, with very high-noise levels caused partly by the work and partly by pupils kicking bits of metal around and shouting to each other above the din. Boys showed a great deal of physical aggression to each other, and sometimes hammered each other's work destructively. Sexual imagery was used in a less than subtle way. One boy walked round with a bit of metal tubing between his legs pretending that he had an erection. Confrontation with the teacher was almost continuous, who shouted at them several times that this was 'a man's workshop, not a little kid's workshop'. The atmosphere between the teacher and one particular boy, Desmond Rawlinson, was almost electric. Desmond crashed around the room muttering: 'I hope he punches me and then I'll punch him back.' Ultimately, the head of year was sent for, causing great excitement and anticipation: 'I bet he gets caned.' Although not popular with the other boys, who regarded him as a bit of a bighead, Desmond was also looked on with a certain amount of admiration: 'He's a nutter, he doesn't care what he says to anyone.'

This particular pupil was clearly challenging the teacher's claim to a monopoly on the use of violence and aggression, and other boys followed his example in a less extreme form. Appeals to Desmond to behave like a man were wasted, since his behaviour was a logical extension of the code of masculinity which operated in this classroom. The sanctioning of macho behaviour was a particular problem for women teachers who were not able to use the threat of violence as a means of control. Carol Runyard, a woman RE teacher at Millbridge, talked about this:

> The boys can ride their motorbikes through the social area and it really does not matter. I think that makes life very difficult for women teachers because the law of the jungle starts to apply. The men who can actually assert them-selves physically and be menacing are just fine, and the individuals who can't do that not only suffer because some individuals can do that but because you can't do it yourself. You fall back on methods of discipline that I don't approve of, and I wouldn't want to implement even if I could, which I can't.

Encouragement of a code of masculinity based on the legitimacy of male aggres-sion was a dangerous strategy, then, in that it could be used to undermine as well as uphold teachers' authority.

(b) *Sexual harassment of women teachers*   Another way in which boys exploited accepted notions of masculinity was through the sexual harassment of women teachers. Walkerdine (1981) has observed that liberal educational philoso-phy legitimises any expression of male sexual aggression as natural and normal, and this allows boys to contest the authority of women teachers. Examples of the sexual harassment of women teachers were found at both schools. At Greenhill, for instance, three boys persistently abused their home economics teacher. In one lesson, she was called a wanker and told to fuck off by one of the boys, but instead of rebuking him for these comments, he was told to make less noise. On another occasion, James made a piece of dough into a penis and followed the teacher round the room with this. Again, the sexual implications of his behaviour were ignored, and he was told to get on with his work. Perhaps these boys felt that their gender identity was compromised by their presence in a female area of the curriculum, and therefore felt the need to assert their masculinity in this exaggerated form.

Boys, then, challenged teachers' authority by assuming an exaggerated form of masculine behaviour which was legitimised by the established gender code of the classroom. I will now consider how girls, too, manipulated traditional gender in order to challenge teacher power.

Girls' resistance through the manipulation of traditional gender codes

(a) *The exploitation of the code of femininity*   Just as boys manipulated traditional constructions of masculinity to resist teachers' authority, so girls frequently parodied the accepted code of femininity in their contestation of schooling. Almost all girls were involved in this to some extent. For instance, uniform would be subverted by accompanying it with red lacy fingerless gloves or many dangly earrings. At Greenhill, a little make-up was allowed to be worn by girls because this was considered to be attractively feminine, but some girls would wear a large amount of punk-style make-up clearly exploiting the fact that it was impossible to draw a clear line between the conventional and subversive forms of feminine style. In almost every lesson, girls could be seen doing hair, and in some cases this was taken to the limits of absurdity. One maths lesson, Helen Downes produced a large make-up kit, with a mirror which illuminated when the lid was open. She proceeded to spread out the cosmetics on the desk top as if it were a dressing table, and apply the make-up, asking for comments from the girls nearby. Amazingly, the male teacher completely ignored what was going on.

Other examples of girls' exploitation of the code of femininity were their use of male teachers' reluctance to confront (see earlier description of this particular coping strategy). This conversation with Suan Piper provides a vivid illustration.

S.R.: D'you think girls can get away with more with male teachers?
SUSAN: Yes. Like Mr Fison said to me the other day, 'cos I didn't hand my homework in and he gave the boys that didn't a mouthful and he says to me he goes, 'You hand it in to me on Monday morning'. He goes, 'You bat your eyelids and it melts my heart'. So we put on our sweet and innocent look.

Particularly in masculine areas of the curriculum such as physics, girls exploited the assumption of helplessness by withdrawing and doing very little work at all. A few male teachers at both schools said they were aware of this strategy, but were unsure of how to deal with it:

I know one or two girls say things like, 'Oh, it's probably me. I seem to get most things wrong'.... Sort of like, 'Oh women, they're the weaker sex. They don't get things right, they get things wrong. Therefore I've got this thing

wrong. Therefore don't be cross with me. It's wrong. If you'd helped me...'
That's the kind of inference. And I'm sure some of them turn on a bit of charm
or whatever to take the edge off things.

(Male geography teacher at Millbridge)

Girls, then, were able to use the assumption that females were quiet, helpless,
emotional and very conscious of their appearance to avoid aspects of school that
they found boring or difficult.

(b) *Girls' expropriation of male characteristics*   A further way in which girls
were able to resist schooling was by directly challenging the prevailing code of
femininity with there own cultural meanings. As we have already noted, the naturalness of girls' maturity, seen as synonymous with quietness and good behaviour,
was assumed by most teachers. In both schools, recognisable groups of girls totally
confounded these expectations. At Millbridge, for instance, one group of girls
would exasperate the teacher by talking in just audible voices, making funny
noises, pulling each other's hair, reading magazines under the table and always
being on the wrong page. Julie explained their behaviour like this:

> We really hate Mr Pinkerton because he won't explain anything to us. But the
> lessons are quite good fun because we really wind him up. He really lost his
> temper with me once and hit me. He looked ever so funny.

Far from gaining status in the girls' eyes, this teacher lost credibility even further
by resorting to physical violence, a sanction which they knew transgressed the
accepted code of femininity. The teacher himself felt confused about the way in
which the behaviour of these girls deviated from his idea of appropriate feminine
behaviour. He expressed this by referring to them as 'that posse of girls' and calling them by their surnames like the boys.

As we have already seen, sexual joking and allusions were taken to be perfectly
normal for boys but unacceptable for girls. During one physics lesson, Helen
Downes and Susan Piper openly challenged this norm. A diagram on the board
showing a hand holding a metal bar elicited the following comment from Susan:
'Cor, I can think of something better to have your hand round.'

Later, when the girls were told to hurry up with their work, Helen reminded
Mr Savage of the accepted code of femininity: 'You've got to be gentle with us sir.'

When the class were gathered round the front bench listening to the teacher's
explanation of an experiment, Susan repeated in a clearly audible voice: 'Undo
your trousers. Undo your trousers.' Mr Savage was clearly embarrassed and
ignored her for several minutes. Finally, he told her to go and stand in a corner
without telling her why. When she demanded an explanation:

SAVAGE: Because you keep on saying 'Undo your trousers'.
SUSAN: It's only a joke.

This incident is very similar to the behaviour of the boys in the home economics
lesson described earlier. However, whereas such behaviour was quite common
among boys, it was very rare among girls, and clearly caused the teacher a great
deal of consternation. Part of the shock value of Susan's behaviour was that it confounded expectations of female sexual passivity and ignorance. On several other
occasions, these girls used similar strategies of resistance, for instance, performing

an elaborate striptease when asked to take off a coat in an RE lesson. But even though Susan and Helen's behaviour might be seen as a challenge to the traditional code of femininity, this was undermined by their other actions. They described female teachers as 'bitchy' and used sexually derogatory language such as 'dog' and 'slag' against other girls. Cowie and Lees (1981), reporting work they carried out in a London comprehensive school, describe similar examples of boys using sexually derogatory language against girls, and girls themselves using it against each other. Even though Susan and Helen expressed a great deal of loyalty to each other, they clearly felt no solidarity towards other women and girls, and were taking on a male role in attacking them. Interestingly, girls who were less likely to challenge teachers' authority in the classroom were much more likely to be offering radical resistance to established gender relations. Catherine Thomas, for instance, a working-class Greenhill pupil, was determined to gain access to areas of work and leisure restricted to males, and was actively critical of traditional female spheres of activity. Although she said she loved 'making havoc in a class where the teacher was really pathetic', she also believed in 'work time and playing-in time'. Disrupting lessons through the challenging of gender codes would not have assisted her in her ambition to become a doctor, and she was dismissive of girls who wasted time in physics and metalwork. Other girls were involved in negotiating their right to be both sexually attractive and intellectual, and it is perhaps these sorts of activity which are genuinely productive of radical change rather than the more dramatic acts of resistance that have been described.

Conclusion

Recent work in the sociology of education, reacting to over-deterministic functionalist and Marxist accounts of schooling, has tended to stress the problematic nature of social reproduction, and has highlighted pupils' resistance to many elements of compulsory schooling. A number of writers, for instance Willis (1977) and Anyon (1983), have argued that resistance to schooling may ultimately reinforce rather than undermine traditional class and gender codes. Anyon has pointed out that resistance to the ideology of femininity 'is often a defensive action (no matter how creative) that is aimed not at transforming patriarchal or other social structures, but at gaining a measure of protection within these'. Hargreaves (1982) has pointed to the problem of discriminating between actions which challenge social relations, and those which merely represent a negative response to education. Aggleton and Whitty (1985), in an interesting discussion of middle-class children's 'resistance' to schooling, maintain that a distinction must be made between individualised contestation and effective resistance to prevailing patterns of class and gender relations. One of the problems of making such a distinction is that it is impossible to know the long-term effects of pupils' resistances, nor to have complete access to their intentions. However, despite these problems of interpretation, it was apparent in my study that much of the parodying and contradiction of traditional gender codes supported rather than undermined patriarchal relations. In their exaggerated displays of masculinity and femininity, pupils were locking themselves firmly into restricted gender roles. Even girls who deliberately rejected the conventional notion of femininity in their opposition to schooling were strengthening gender divisions by uncritically adopting male modes of behaviour, and sometimes oppressing other women.

In this paper, then, analysis of particular incidents in the classroom has been used to illustrate the way in which male social dominance was achieved. Teacher coping strategies, based on their typifications of male and female pupils, were identified as a central means by which traditional constructions of masculinity and femininity were conveyed to pupils. Pupils' resistance to schooling was often based on the manipulation of these gender codes, either by adopting them in an exaggerated form or, in the case of some girls, by assuming modes of behaviour normally associated with boys. Far from weakening existing gender divisions, it was argued that these resistances actually strengthened them. Girls who were not totally rejecting schooling, but attempting to use it for their own ends, were likely to be more successful in subverting the traditional code of femininity.

Acknowledgements

I would like to thank Dr Sandra Acker for her helpful comments on an earlier draft of this paper. The work reported here was funded by an ESRC studentship.

REFERENCES

Aggleton, P.J. and Whitty, G. (1985) 'Rebels without a cause? Socialisation and subcultural style among the children of the new middle classes', *Sociology of Education*, 58: 60–72.

Anyon, J. (1983) 'Intersections of gender and class: accommodation and resistance by working class and affluent females to contradictory sex-role ideologies', in S. Walker and L. Barton (eds), *Gender, Class and Education* (Lewes, Falmer Press).

Buswell, C. (1984) 'Sponsoring and stereotyping in a working class secondary school in the north of England', in S. Acker, J. Megarry, S. Nisbet and E. Hoyle (eds), *World Yearbook of Education 1984: Women and Education* (London, Kogan Page).

Clarricoates, K. (1980) 'The importance of being Ernest...Emma...Tom...Jane', in R. Deem (ed.), *Schooling for Women's Work* (London, Routledge & Kegan Paul).

Corrigan, P. (1979) *Schooling the Smash Street Kids* (London, Macmillan).

Cowie, C. and Lees, S. (1981) 'Slags or drags', *Feminist Review*, 9.

Davies, L. (1984) *Pupil-Power: Deviance and Gender in School* (Lewes, Falmer Press).

Denscombe, M. (1980) 'Keeping 'em quiet', in P. Woods (ed.), *Teacher Strategies* (London, Croom Helm).

Ebbutt, D. (1981) 'Girls' science: boys' science revisited', in A. Kelly (ed.), *The Missing Half* (Manchester, Manchester University Press).

Hammersley, M. (1984) 'The researcher exposed: a natural history', in R.G. Burgess (ed.), *The Research Process in Educational Settings: Ten Case Studies* (Lewes, Falmer Press).

Hammersley, M. and Atkinson, P. (1983) *Ethnography: Principles in Practice* (London, Tavistock).

Hargreaves, A. (1978) 'The significance of classroom coping strategies', in L. Barton and R. Meighan (eds), *Sociological Interpretations of Schooling and Classrooms: A Reappraisal* (London, Nafferton Books).

Hargreaves, A. (1982) 'Resistance and relative autonomy theories: problems of distortion and incoherence in recent Marxist sociology of education', *British Journal of Sociology of Education*, 3: 107–26.

Hargreaves, D. (1967) *Social Relations in a Secondary School* (London, Routledge & Kegan Paul).

Kelly, A. (1986) 'Gender differences in teacher–pupil interactions: a meta-analytic review', paper presented at the 1986 *BERA Conference*, University of Bristol.

Walden, R. and Walkerdine, V. (1982) *Girls and Mathematics: The Early Years*, Bedford Way Papers 8 (London, University of London Institute of Education).

Walden, R. and Walkerdine, V. (1985) *Girls and Mathematics: From Primary to Secondary Schooling*, Bedford Way Papers 24 (London, University of London Institute of Education).
Walkerdine, V. (1981) 'Sex, power and pedagogy', *Screen Education*, spring, pp. 14–24.
Willis, P. (1977) *Learning to Labour: How Working Class Kids Get Working Class Jobs* (London, Saxon House).
Woods, P. (1979) *The Divided School* (London, Routledge & Kegan Paul).

TWO

'GIRLIES ON THE WARPATH': ADDRESSING GENDER IN INITIAL TEACHER EDUCATION

Amanda J. Coffey and Sandra Acker

Source: '"Girlies on the warpath": addressing gender in initial teacher education',
Gender and Education, 3(3): 249–261, 1991.

Introduction

That gender influences the teaching and learning processes can no longer be disputed, given the accumulation of sociological and feminist research. However, it remains a difficult task to initiate and achieve significant change in school practices. Many teachers appear hesitant to endorse anti-sexist initiatives and projects (Whyte, 1986; Joyce, 1987; Acker, 1988; Riddell, 1989). Indeed Thompson (1989) describes teachers' reactions as some way between tolerant amusement and genuine antagonism.

What impact does teacher education have on challenging or confirming teachers' views on gender and anti-sexism? Several studies (Skelton, 1985; Thompson, 1986; Hanson, 1987; Equal Opportunities Commission (EOC), 1989a) conclude that gender occupies only a marginal position within the initial training of teachers. The EOC (1989a) sent questionnaires to institutions providing initial teacher education, and followed them up with visits and discussion. Although the questionnaire responses suggested attention to gender issues was widespread, many institutions were unable to provide evidence that this was so. For example, few institutions attempted to assess students on teaching practice using equal opportunities criteria. The EOC sum up the prevailing mode as 'benign apathy'. This reflects Skelton's (1985) findings. Gender issues were not a priority on the teacher education course she studied. Conventional images and stereotypes continued to operate at a 'hidden curriculum' level, conveying messages to novice teachers which reinforced the status quo.

Our task in this paper is to explore why gender issues are given such low key treatment within initial teacher education. We consider how certain features of teacher education, and of teaching itself, work against the development of a framework sympathetic to change, both in a broad sense and with regard to initiating a critical gender analysis. However, not to be unduly pessimistic we also describe how some feminists are creating their own space within the teacher training scenario.[1]

Informing teacher education

What informs, influences, guides initial teacher education is a question deserving of attention because it sets into context the relationship between gender, teachers and teacher training. Four main factors or sets of factors seem particularly relevant to the analysis of initial teacher education. We label these as follows: official guidance; teacher ideologies; teaching as women's work; and classroom survival.

Official guidance

As with the education system generally, teacher education in England and Wales has undergone dramatic changes in the past few decades (Furlong *et al.*, 1988; Edwards, 1990; Gosden, 1990). Institutions have been closed, contracted, absorbed, merged and reconstituted as multi- rather than single-purpose organisations. Changes have occurred not only in structure and control but also in curriculum and ethos. Teacher education is highly vulnerable both to its demographic and economic context (how many teachers do we need to produce?), and to politically inspired fluctuations in educational policy.

State control over education has greatly increased under the Conservative Government of the 1980s and early 1990s. The establishment in 1984 of CATE – the Council for Accreditation of Teacher Education – was one manifestation of this trend. CATE assesses initial teacher education programmes, using criteria which pertain to selection procedures for students, characteristics of tutors, length of course and content of curriculum. Teacher education institutions undergoing scrutiny – including, in a departure from tradition, universities – have been visited by Her Majesty's Inspectors as well as asked to submit documentation to the Council.

One might imagine gender equity could be a key criterion in such reviews. CATE is not unaware of the issue, but has not really prioritised it. This is indicative of the more general government response. Circular 24/89, the 1989 revision of the CATE criteria, refers to equal opportunities as an example (along with multicultural education and personal and social education) of a cross-circular dimension which student teachers should be able to incorporate into their teaching of the National Curriculum (DES, 1989). Students are also to be prepared for teaching 'the full range of pupils' with their diversity of 'ability, behaviour, social background and ethnic and cultural origin'. The document also states that 'students should learn to guard against preconceptions based on the race, gender, religion, or other attributes of pupils' and should 'understand the need to promote equal opportunities' (p. 10).

Gender is 'commatised' here (O'Brien, 1984) – that is, inevitably accompanied by a list of other social divisions (gender-comma-race-comma-class), rather than prioritised or dealt with in its own right. However, there are more references to gender here than in earlier CATE guidelines, perhaps as a result of advice from the EOC (EOC, 1989a,b). The EOC's formal investigation report (EOC, 1989a) revealed that overall commitment to equal opportunities was low. Despite the need for gender awareness being recognised by most teacher training institutions, the EOC found little evidence of any systematic promotion. For example, 75% of the institutions did not have any comprehensive strategy for preparing students to consider and appraise the role of equal opportunities during teaching practice.

It is important to be aware that the functions of providing initial training, in-service work and furthering educational research are generally combined in the same institutions. Thus, shifts in expectations or provision of teacher education or research will influence the capacities and priorities of such institutions. Circular 24/89 supports an emphasis on the vocational aspects of teacher 'training' rather than the theoretical, social science, research base. For example, teacher educators themselves must have recent and regularly renewed school teaching experience. This has enormous consequences for the hiring policies of institutions and their capacity to contribute to educational scholarship and research *as well as* to teacher training. In-service teacher education has also undergone profound alterations in recent years, again in the direction of practice and away from theory (Gosden, 1990; McNamara, 1990).

The central Government now sets national in-service priorities which receive more funding than other topics. Gender has not been among these. Thus, there is increasingly little incentive for universities and polytechnics to develop courses on gender, unless there is local demand.

In both initial and in-service education for teachers, we see 'a rapid retreat from the disciplines of education' (Edwards, 1990, p. 187). Sociology has been especially vulnerable, and in many one-year Postgraduate Certificate of Education (PGCE) courses it has practically disappeared. To the extent it is a subject ideally suited to the critical consideration of gender and of other social divisions, it is another impediment to reform of the sort we are advocating. It is, of course, possible to teach about gender without drawing upon a social science base, but we would argue that a deeper understanding is thereby avoided.

Even educational research shows signs of altering in the direction of practical, small scale, school-based efforts on the one hand, and government-commissioned policy-oriented evaluations and test-development on the other. It is more difficult to find funding for 'basic' research with a traditional base in the disciplines. Much of the money available is tightly tied to policy purposes (Edwards, 1990, p. 190).

The 'rapid retreat' has been accelerated by a barrage of criticism of teacher training from the Right (e.g. O'Hear, 1988; Hillgate Group, 1989). The teacher education curriculum has been accused of being left-wing, overly theoretical and preoccupied with fads and frills (like anti-racism and anti-sexism), instead of being focused on basic teaching skills and knowledge in the core subjects of the school curriculum. These accusations are not based on scholarly research, despite the tendency for them to be described as 'reports' by politicians and journalists; in fact, as McNamara (1990) comments, little in teacher education policy *is* so based. The 'reports' take their place in a climate where even the friends of teacher education have raised similar questions over the years (Universities Council for the Education of Teachers (UCET), 1979). This tide of criticism serves to make teacher training institutions, despite some spirited efforts at self-defence, anxious about their survival and cautious about their public image.

Teacher education institutions are being pushed to adapt and survive. Not only do they need to develop their initial and in-service teacher education provision along lines described earlier, they need to seek additional sources of funding (e.g. by recruiting overseas students on to advanced courses). If they are in the university sector, they must keep up their publications output and research grant attainment to receive a reasonable rating from the Universities Funding Council, which in turn affects their income. Similar pressures are visible in the polytechnics and colleges of higher education. But as Edwards remarks, 'entrepreneurial and academic spirits are not always easily corked in the same bottle' (1990, p. 189). Moreover, departments of education in universities and polytechnics have been hit by the same destabilising forces affecting all of higher education in the past decade, which makes long-term planning of staffing and courses hazardous (Gosden, 1990, p. 84), and we might add, limits innovation to directions which promise to enhance, not threaten, survival.

Some of these trends could actually raise the profile of gender issues. For example, small-scale teacher research or courses linked to school-based activity could easily focus on gender. However, unless gender is prioritised in guidance from central government or local education authorities, and highlighted in official criteria for the teacher education curriculum, such work is likely to stay on the margins of research endeavour and teacher consciousness. Overemphasis on school practice may hamper the dissemination of the large body of theoretical and empirically grounded scholarship on gender and encourage instead a process whereby existing practice (good and bad) is reproduced through generations of teachers. Faced with so many severe and often contradictory pressures and little real outside pressure to innovate in the equal opportunities area, it is not surprising that many institutions, as the EOC (1989a) reported, pay only lip service to equal opportunities or anti-sexism. Or in the words of one of the educators interviewed for our research: 'We do have an equal opportunities policy on paper, but few of us seem to have the time or enthusiasm to implement it fully or effectively'. There appears little scope at present for institutions to take radical stands, although individuals may do so, as we shall show later in the paper.

Ideologies

There is no reason to expect that teachers will be immune to sexist and racist currents within the wider society. However, we have seen that teacher education by and large fails to provide an effective challenge to the dominant discourses. In addition, there are pervasive, traditional teacher ideologies (Alexander, 1984), which may be reinforced by the ethos encountered in colleges, polytechnics and universities (Bell, 1981). Among these are commitments to child-centred learning, political neutrality and professionalism. In the absence of concomitant commitments to opposing systemic injustice and inequality, these ideologies may impede attempts at reform.

Child-centredness   Of the 14 teacher educators interviewed for this study, all but two agreed that a child-centred line was emphasised on the courses taught in their institutions. Several questioned its effectiveness in resolving sexism in schooling. One tutor said: 'It's a shame that such an innovative approach, as it was in the 1960s and 1970s, has led to the failure, more or less, to tackle the real problem of gender inequality'.

How might child-centredness block attention to gender? Skelton (1985, 1989) provides an example. Students on a primary postgraduate certificate course were encouraged to emphasise children's individual needs and differences. They tended to take this stance one step further and resisted *any* categorisation of children, including one based on gender. In another study (Thompson, 1989), students and tutors on a primary BEd course lacked awareness of the structural nature of gender divisions and believed that there was no problem provided they avoided stereotyping in the classroom. Consequently, they could not see why they should study gender issues when there were more pressing and relevant skills to be learned. Riddell (1988) found secondary school teachers also uncomfortable with categorisation by gender, and Carrington and Short (1987) make a similar argument to explain teachers' resistance to anti-racist strategies. Skelton (1989) also makes the point that commitments to 'individualism' can hamper efforts at reform. This is the subtle assumption that the task of teacher education is simply to prepare an individual teacher with appropriate skills and knowledge to carry out the work of teaching. In the process of stressing the teacher's individual responsibility, this model tends to de-emphasise the social and political context in which teaching takes place.

Neutrality Another ideological theme, similarly problematic, is 'neutrality'. Pratt (1985), Riddell (1988) and Whyte (1986) found teachers preferred to remain neutral on issues such as gender rather than venture into controversial political territory. 'Neutrality' may take the form of so-called 'gender-blindness' (Wormald, 1985). One of the women interviewed for our study commented: 'We are supposed to produce impartial, balanced teachers ... but so often this means blind teachers.'

The irony of a 'gender-blind' or 'gender-free' approach is that it qualifies as a form of equal opportunity. Not to pay undue attention to differences can be a strategy for improving things for girls and women in certain cases. One of the great problems facing feminism is whether to stress equality (sameness) or difference (specialness) when compared to men (Snitow, 1990). Many people believe that to make special provision for women or girls is a form of reverse discrimination and may even be insulting in its hint that being female somehow requires compensation. Nevertheless, the practical outcome of such thinking may be a systematic disadvantage for women and girls.

A neutral stance that simply ignores gender considerations can have discriminatory consequences, despite intentions to the contrary. It is not easy to find alternatives, and is well worth remembering that teachers' beliefs in neutrality also incline them to resist becoming uncritical transmitters of right wing political views (Acker, 1988). So as with child centredness, there is virtue here too. What might be helpful would be for student teachers to role-play or discuss dealing with complex dilemmas such as these. We believe they need to be raised to the level of conscious reflection rather than simply ignored.

Professionalism Intricately related to the themes discussed so far is the ideology of professionalism (Ginsburg, 1987). Many teachers, and certainly those who speak for teachers in the public arena, regard themselves as professionals. This issue of professionalism may have implications for innovation within teaching and teacher education.

There are furious debates over the definition and value of 'the professional' (see for example discussions in Hoyle 1980; Dunleavy, 1981; Wilding, 1982; Ginsburg, 1987). Being 'professional' can be taken to mean doing one's job competently. It also has connotations of neutrality, detachment, being uncontroversial and protective of occupational autonomy – and perhaps being masculine as well (Ozga and Lawn, 1988). In the conditions of the late 1980s when England and Wales has seen a series of government-imposed innovations seriously weakening teachers' autonomy (Grace, 1987; Acker, 1990a), professionalism may be seen as an especially desirable attribute.

Clearly professional ideology can be used *against* teachers, as when the public rejects their attempts at industrial action as unprofessional (Burgess, 1986). It may also encourage caution vis-à-vis radical innovations which threaten the standing of the profession. The identification of gender equity in Britain with fringe social and political movements (as opposed to North America where there are prominent and respected liberal feminist organisations with great input into the political process) may mean that 'professions' or occupations which consider themselves to be such will be reluctant to embrace such a goal.

On the other hand, it may be possible to build upon some of the contradictions in the ideology (Ginsburg, 1987), for example, the entrusting of teachers with responsibility for the future of the nation, whilst treating them as basically incompetent and in need of close direction. Whitty *et al.* (1987) suggest that student teachers will themselves sense the contradictions between the ideology of professionalism and the declining material conditions and teacher morale they encounter in the schools. The emphasis placed by the training institutions, following CATE, on school-based rather than college-based experience brings this contradiction to the fore. This may create opportunities for radical teacher educators to encourage students toward critical reflection on wider social issues, including gender equity.

Teaching as women's work

It was suggested earlier that the ideology of professionalism is linked to gender divisions in teaching. The division of labour between women and men within teaching should by now be a familiar tale (Acker, 1989; DeLyon and Migniuolo, 1989). DES figures show that in 1985 78.1% of nursery and primary school teachers were women, compared to 46% of secondary teachers. While most head teachers in nursery and infant schools (i.e. in schools catering for ages up to 7) were women, men held 69.4% of the headships of combined infant/junior schools (age range 5–11) and 83.8% of secondary school headships (Acker, 1989, p. 10).

What are the consequences of these realities? One outcome of the identification of teaching as a majority-female field is – ironically – that gender bias is *less* likely to be seen as an educational problem. Teaching is manifestly unlike engineering or printing or other male crafts which have traditionally excluded or discouraged women from entry. Interviews with women primary school teachers for another project (Acker, 1990b) showed teachers adopting a fatalistic, rather than feminist, stance in response to inequalities they encountered (see also Cogger, 1985). They were aware that men were preferred for promotion, but saw a rationale behind it: in the interests of 'balance' in the staffroom and male role models for the children, schools wanted a share of the few men available; to secure them, they had to offer the carrot of fast-track promotion opportunities.

Many of the women teachers shouldered heavy domestic burdens of housework and childcare, as well as aiming for high standards in their work. If they felt that increased responsibilities of promotion were too much 'on top', it seemed a rational response. Although they resented certain aspects of this unequal situation, few responded with an overtly feminist stance. To do so would have likely been counter-productive; it would simply have made them angry and demoralised and risked rejection in the staffroom for being aggressive or oversensitive. What they lacked was collective support from others who saw matters with a feminist perspective. That such support was unavailable is itself a consequence of the status of feminism in Britain more generally, where there is a low public acceptability and few opportunities to influence that political process (Gelb, 1989). Given all the constraints and barriers in other occupations, teaching was still seen as a relatively 'good job for women', rather than one riddled with bias against them.

Men certainly manage teacher education. In universities in Britain in 1988–89, among wholly university-funded academic staff, there were 3852 men, and 113 women, who were professors, the highest grade. In university departments of education (UDEs) specifically, there were all of nine women professors. Only 27 women held readerships or senior lectureships, the promoted posts below professorships. In contrast, education professorships were held by 77 men and readerships or senior lectureships by 219 (University Funding Council (UFC), 1990). Although the numbers of female lecturers and contract researchers in education are greater than in some other fields, women are seldom in a position to dictate UDE policy.

The dominance of men in management roles in schools beyond infant school level and in higher education diminishes the chances of anti-sexism being placed high on the agenda. Several studies suggest women teachers as a group, especially those in secondary schools, lack power and influence (Cunnison, 1985; Riddell, 1988). Interviews conducted for this study make the point repeatedly for institutions of teacher education. Hanson's (1987, p. 82) comment that sexual harassment was viewed by many teacher educators in her study as 'nothing more than a petty irritation by a minority of females' is indicative of the generally dismissive attitude within teacher education to feminist concerns reported by our interviewees.

One lecturer talked about the antagonism and difficulties she had encountered. She found male students particularly hostile to positive discrimination measures which 'distorted the truth'. For example, where science posters showing mainly female scientists were displayed in a teaching laboratory, the male students, and indeed some of the females, complained of unfairness. In another department, there were only 4 women on a staff of over 20. Gender issues had difficulty making any impact here. One woman spoke of her frustration at being constantly referred to as 'on her hobby horse'. Her efforts to mention gender issues at meetings seemed only to result in typecasting herself, not in effectively challenging the prevailing orthodoxy. Another tutor described the constant battle to ensure women were fairly represented on interview panels and departmental committees as 'an uphill struggle where you never seem to even see the summit'.

Survival in the classroom

Finally, it is likely that teachers' conditions of work are a factor in resistance to gender equality initiatives (Acker, 1988). These conditions include a lack of time, low morale, understaffing and new pressures that imposed reforms, such as new examinations, teacher appraisal, local management of schools and the National Curriculum, bring. Whether or not these trends constitute a form of proletarianisation (Densmore, 1987), it is easy to see how 'survival' becomes a prominent goal, displacing ideas about innovation in 'optional' areas like anti-sexism.

Also relevant are conditions of work within institutions which prepare teachers to teach. Initial teacher education courses, in particular the one-year PGCE, but also the four-year bachelor degree in education, have been criticised for being too short to include all that is desirable as well as all that is required, for example, by the CATE guidelines. This was true even before the tasks of 'delivering the national curriculum' made the pressures greater. Staff interviewed complained of a lack of physical and mental time and space on the courses. Inevitably both students and lecturers have to prioritise some aspects of the courses to the detriment of others.

Skelton and Hanson (1989) suggest that what initial teacher education prioritises is how to 'survive' in the classroom. Classroom-based activities are often perceived by both staff and students as the most valuable, and as we pointed out earlier, there are government directives encouraging this orientation. Postgraduate students are often keen to move away from the modes of study featured in their undergraduate courses to a more practical vocational style. Their preferences reinforce the tendencies outlined earlier which downgrade the more theoretical parts of training courses, those most likely to deal with broader contextual issues like gender.

Survival in the classroom does not necessarily mean a sensitivity to gender issues. Menter's (1989) research suggests the opposite, that students on teaching practice become fearful of 'rocking the boat'. Even where race and gender issues had been raised in lectures, such concerns only rarely surfaced during teaching practice. Given current pressures on teachers and teacher educators, it would not be surprising if there were a preference for simple, non-controversial strategies (Shah, 1989). Survival may seem a more adaptive goal than developing a critical perspective on classroom practices.

Feminist challenges: 'girlies on the warpath'[2]

In the preceding sections of this paper we have concentrated on identifying barriers to anti-sexism becoming a mainstream feature of teacher education. There is little or no lead from government on the issue, although teacher education institutions are faced with a barrage of other directives. A combination of teacher ideologies and material conditions of work incline towards downgrading gender equity issues and the prioritising of survival rather than innovative strategies. Institutions of teacher education share many features with the schools and are experienced as discouraging environments by feminists within them. Nevertheless, there is evidence in our interviews of efforts made by teacher educators to meet these challenges.

Gender days

Several of the women interviewed had been successful in helping to organise 'gender days' as part of initial teacher education programmes. These days had mainly consisted of workshop and seminar type sessions, often with guest speakers. The main aim of the day was three-fold: to increase general awareness of gender issues, to facilitate discussion and debate, and to allow personal and professional feelings about gender relations and sexism to be worked through in a non-threatening environment. In all cases, the days had been optional for both staff and students. In two instances, the event took place on Saturday and in only one case was official funding available. Our interviewees were worried that the optional status and lack of official backing for 'gender days' might convey the message that the topic was of little importance to the institution. A genuine commitment might be shown by following the day with school visits and input from classroom teachers, with outcomes monitored and evaluated as Shah (1989) describes for multicultural/anti-racist issues. Concern was also voiced about the low numbers of men attending such events, suggesting that gender days were therefore insufficient to alter male views, awareness, perceptions or actions. Despite these concerns, the lecturers who had been involved in gender days were positive about what had been achieved. They believed that for those (women) attending, the exercise had been worthwhile, providing a comfortable environment to explore issues.

One interviewee commented: 'You feel successful for just getting a gender day off the ground. I know it's not the only answer but any chance to raise awareness and be listened to has got to be good.'

Links with women's studies

Another strategy involved building links with women in other departments. Many of the tutors taught on inter-departmental women's studies courses and brought their experience from such courses back to their teacher education programmes. Some had attempted, with varying degrees of success, to establish 'women only' seminar groups, and to hold joint PGCE/Women's Studies workshops. Anxiety was raised as to whether these had much impact on teacher education as a whole. And again, male attitudes, both staff and student, were not being challenged by women-only seminar groups. We would add that women-only groups may also increase the isolation and marginalisation feminist women educationalists experience within their departments.

Working with feminist teachers

An interesting initiative reported by one woman teacher educator involved establishing working relationships with feminist teachers in schools. She had recently embarked on a joint project, with a small group of feminist teachers, to develop an assessment schedule for use on teaching practice. The aim was to give more emphasis and thought to the ways gender relations and sexism permeate teaching practice. However, the lecturer concerned was not hopeful that the proposal would gain institutional support. She had already been informed by a male colleague that feminists joining forces did not worry him!

These initiatives serve as examples of the work the teacher educators who were interviewed had embarked on. Other work included role-play exercises to explore gender relations, examining educational histories of staff and students, and producing statistical material to show how gender pervades school life.

Responses

Most of those interviewed revealed their frustration and anger at being constantly referred to as a 'lefty, feminist' or a 'women's libber'. It was not necessarily the stereotyping to which they objected, but the result that their initiatives and arguments were often not taken seriously.

One tutor described a conversation overheard between a male colleague and a group of male students. Urging the students to attend the 'gender and education' course, he described the course as a bit of a bore, but suggested their attendance would ensure the female tutor in question did not make a fuss and begin lobbying for widespread male castration!

Several of the teacher educators described their battles to establish staff training, in order to specifically address gender and other salient issues. One was told by her head of department that teaching is a sexless occupation and should be preserved as such. Another staff member was more pragmatically informed that due to significant competition for time and resources, efforts should be concentrated on the 'important matters'. One comment from a female teacher educator succinctly summarises these experiences:

> If we ask for time and space for ourselves we are told there isn't any. If we ask for commitment to an equal opportunities policy, we are informed that the best we can hope for is 10 minutes at the end of some meeting or other. If we so much as suggest we are not addressing gender in teacher training we are accused of insulting the whole profession. Quite frankly, we are made to feel stupid and marginal. It's a wonder we don't just run out of steam.

This seems particularly pertinent considering the EOC's recommendations to increase staff training and programmes of action (EOC, 1989a).

It proved to be both refreshing and frustrating to hear women teacher educators talk of their work: refreshing because it showed that those who sought to put gender on the teacher education agenda were persistent and resilient in their actions and challenges; frustrating because so much good work was being done without the institutional and official support that could make all the difference.

Concluding comments

As a discipline, education seems slower to change in feminist directions than some others (Dubois *et al.*, 1985), perhaps because of its conserving and reproducing functions. But there is a parallel between women's studies pedagogy and radical or progressive styles of educating which could be exploited if the connection were made. Both, for example, emphasise participation and democracy. The social science disciplines which in the past have informed teacher training offer points at which gender issues could be integrated into the teacher education curriculum. Maher and Rathbone (1986) give a number of examples such as considering the gender biases of philosophies of education or questions of sex differentials in cognitive abilities and development. Essentially they are arguing for an infusion of women's studies perspectives into teacher education. Laird (1989) looks carefully at what a feminist pedagogy – a concept and practice widely discussed in the United States – might mean for teacher education. For example, the gendered nature of the teaching occupation itself could become a focus for critical reflection and reconceptualisation.

These proposals touch on a wider debate in education, between 'balance' and advocacy. Critical education perspectives, as developed by writers such as Aronowitz and Giroux (1985), Weiler (1988) and McLaren (1989), require taking a stand on social and political issues. A curriculum such as Maher and Rathbone's, or critical reflections such as Laird advocates, needs such an outlook. As noted earlier, teacher education in Britain tends to avoid controversy rather than seek it, and its timidity has been exacerbated by its vulnerability.

On balance it seems we have identified more impediments than stimulants to reform. But even opening up a debate may help, as the gender regimes (Kessler *et al.*, 1985) of teacher education have received little attention compared with those of schools. There is an Anti-Racist Teacher Education Network (ARTEN) – why not an Anti-Sexist one? Wouldn't such a strategy of organisation be a good start?

Sharing of feminist scholarship and practice is essential if teacher education is to break down its gendered barriers. It is also essential to give heart to those at present labouring alone to challenge the prevailing patterns within teacher education.

NOTES

1   Interviews with these teacher educators were carried out by Amanda Coffey for a masters thesis. Sandra Acker was the supervisor for the thesis. This article represents a blending of our ideas and is written collaboratively.
2   The subtitle is taken from a conversation one of us (Coffey) had with a male colleague. After describing her interest in feminist challenges in teacher education, she was met with the response that in his department, too, 'the girlies were on the warpath'.

REFERENCES

Acker, S. (1988) 'Teachers, gender and resistance', *British Journal of Sociology of Education*, 9(3): 307–322.

Acker, S. (ed.) (1989) *Teachers, Gender and Careers* (Lewes, Falmer Press).

Acker, S. (1990a) 'Teachers' culture in an English primary school: continuity and change', *British Journal of Sociology of Education*, 11: 257–273.

Acker, S. (1990b) 'Women teachers at work', paper presented to the Canadian Teachers' Federation Conference, *Women in Education*, Vancouver, BC, November.

Alexander, R.J. (1984) *Primary Teaching* (London, Holt, Rinehart & Winston).

Aronowitz, S. and Giroux, H. (1985) *Education Under Seige* (South Hadley, MA, Bergin & Garvey).

Bell, A. (1981) 'Structure, knowledge and the social relationships in teacher education', *British Journal of Sociology of Education*, 2: 3–23.

Burgess, R. (1986) *Sociology, Education and Schools* (London, Batsford).

Carrington, B. and Short, G. (1987) 'Breakthrough to political literacy: political education, antiracist teaching and the primary school', *Journal of Education Policy*, 3: 1–13.

Coffey, A.J. (1990) 'Addressing gender in initial teacher education', Unpublished MSc thesis, University of Bristol.

Cogger, D. (1985) 'Women teachers on low scales', Unpublished MEd thesis, University College, Cardiff.

Cunnison, S. (1985) 'Making it in a man's world: women teachers in a senior high school', *Occasional Paper No. 1* (Hull, University of Hull, Department of Sociology and Social Anthropology).

Delyon, H. and Migniulo, F. (eds) (1989) *Women Teachers: Issues and Experiences* (Milton Keynes, Open University Press).

Densmore, K. (1987) 'Professionalism, proletarianization and teachers' work', in T. Popkewitz (ed.), *Critical Studies in Teacher Education* (Lewes, Falmer Press).

Department of Education and Science (1989) *Initial Teacher Training: Approval of Courses*, Circular No. 24/89 (Circular No. 59/89 Welsh Office) (London, HMSO).

Dubois, E., Kelly, G., Kennedy, E., Korsmeyer, C. and Robinson, L. (1985) *Feminist Scholarship* (Urbana, IL, University of Illinois Press).

Dunleavy, P. (1981) 'Professions and policy changes: notes towards a model of ideological corporatism', *Public Administration Bulletin*, 36: 3–16.

Edwards, T. (1990) 'Schools of education – their work and their future', in J.B. Thomas (ed.), *British Universities and Teacher Education: a Century of Change* (Lewes, Falmer Press).

Equal Opportunities Commission (1989a) *Initial Teacher Training in England and Wales*, Formal Investigation Report (Manchester, NH, EOC).

Equal Opportunities Commission (1989b) *Gender Issues: Implications for Schools of the Education Reform Act* (Manchester, NH, EOC).

Furlong, V.J., Hirst, P.H., Pocklington, K. and Miles, S. (1988) *Initial Teacher Training and the Role of the School* (Milton Keynes, Open University Press).

Gelb, J. (1989) *Feminism and Politics* (Berkeley, CA, University of California Press).

Ginsburg, M. (1987) 'Reproduction, contradiction and conceptions of professionalism: the case of pre-service teachers', in T. Popkewitz (ed.), *Critical Studies in Teacher Education* (Lewes, Falmer Press).

Gosden, P. (1990) 'The James report and recent history', in J.B. Thomas (ed.), *British Universities and Teacher Education: a Century of Change* (Lewes, Falmer Press).

Grace, G. (1987) 'Teachers and the State in Britain: a changing relationship', in M. Lawn and G. Grace (eds), *Teachers: the Culture and Politics of Work* (Lewes, Falmer Press).

Hanson, J. (1987) 'Equality issues, permeation and a PGCE programme', Unpublished MEd dissertation, University of Sheffield.

Hillgate Group (1989) *Learning to Teach* (London, Claridge Press).

Hoyle, E. (1980) 'Professionalization and deprofessionalization in education', in E. Hoyle and J. Megarry (eds), *World Yearbook of Education 1980: Professional Development of Teachers* (London, Kegan Paul).

Joyce, M. (1987) 'Being a feminist teacher', in M. Lawn and G. Grace (eds), *Teachers: the Culture and Politics of Work* (Lewes, Falmer Press).

Kessler, S., Ashendon, D., Connell, R.W. and Dowsett, G.W. (1985) 'Gender relations in secondary schooling', *Sociology of Education*, 5: 34–48.

Laird, S. (1988) 'Reforming "women's true profession": a case for "feminist pedagogy" in teacher education?', *Harvard Educational Review*, 58: 449–463.

McLaren, P. (1989) *Life in Schools: an Introduction to Critical Pedagogy in the Foundations of Education* (New York, Longman).

McNamara, D. (1990) 'Research on teacher training: the case of Britain in the late 1980's', in R.P. Tisher and M.F. Wideen (eds), *Research in Teacher Education* (Lewes, Falmer Press).

Maher, F. and Rathbone, C. (1986) 'Teacher education and feminist theory: some implications for practice', *American Journal of Education*, 94: 214–235.

Menter, I. (1989) 'Teaching practice stasis: racism, sexism and school experience in initial teacher education', *British Journal of Sociology of Education*, 10: 459–473.

O'Brien, M. (1984) 'The commatization of women: patriarchal fetishism in the sociology of education', *Interchange*, 15: 43–60.

O'Hear, A. (1988) *Who Teaches the Teachers?* (London, Social Affairs Unit).

Ozga, J. and Lawn, M. (1988) 'Schoolwork: interpreting the labour process of teaching', *British Journal of Sociology of Education*, 9: 323–336.

Pratt, J. (1985) 'The attitudes of teachers', in J. Whyte, R. Deem, L. Kant and M. Cruickshank (eds), *Girl Friendly Schooling* (London, Methuen).

Riddell, S. (1988) 'Gender and option choice in two rural comprehensive schools', Unpublished PhD dissertation, School of Education, University of Bristol.

Riddell, S. (1989) 'It's nothing to do with me: teachers views and gender divisions in the curriculum', in S. Acker (ed.) *Teachers, Gender and Careers* (Lewes, Falmer Press).

Shah, S. (1989) 'Effective permeation of race and gender issues in teacher education courses', *Gender and Education*, 1(3): 309–318.

Skelton, C. (1985) 'Gender issues in a PGCE teacher training programme', Unpublished MA thesis, University of York.

Skelton, C. (1989) 'And so the wheel turns; gender and initial teacher education', in C. Skelton (ed.), *Whatever Happens to Little Women?* (Milton Keynes, Open University Press).

Skelton, C. and Hanson, J. (1989) 'Schooling the teachers: gender and initial teacher education', in S. Acker (ed.), *Teachers, Gender and Careers* (Lewes, Falmer Press).

Snitow, A. (1990) 'A gender diary', in M. Hirsch and E. Fox Keller (eds), *Conflict in Feminism* (London, Routledge).

Thompson, B. (1986) 'Gender issues in a primary BEd teacher training programme', Unpublished MA thesis, University of York.

Thompson, B. (1989) 'Teacher attitudes: complacency and conflict', in C. Skelton (ed.), *Whatever Happens to Little Women?* (Milton Keynes, Open University Press).

Universities Council for the Education of Teachers (1979) *The PGCE Course and the Training of Specialist Teachers for Secondary Schools* (London, UCET).

Universities Funding Council (1990) *University Statistics 1988–89, Vol. 1, Students and Staff* (Cheltenham, Universities Statistical Record).

Weiler, K. (1988) *Women Teaching for Change* (South Hadley, MA, Bergin & Garvey).

Whitty, G., Barton, L. and Pollard, A. (1987) 'Ideology and control in teacher education: a review of recent experience in education', in T. Popkewitz (ed.), *Critical Studies in Teacher Education* (Lewes, Falmer Press).

Whyte, J. (1986) *Girls into Science and Technology: the Story of a Project* (London, Routledge & Kegan Paul).

Wilding, P. (1982) *Professional Power and Social Welfare* (London, Routledge & Kegan Paul).

Wormald, E. (1985) 'Teacher training and gender blindness', *British Journal of Sociology of Education*, 6(1): 112–116.

THREE

MASCULINITY, VIOLENCE AND SCHOOLING: CHALLENGING 'POISONOUS PEDAGOGIES'

Jane Kenway and Lindsay Fitzclarence

Source: 'Masculinity, violence and schooling: challenging "poisonous pedagogies"',
Gender and Education, 9(1): 117–133, 1997.

Introduction

Violence is one of the major social problems of our times and so should be one of the major issues in current debates about education. As people have become more aware of the extent and consequences of domestic violence, childhood sexual abuse, sexual harassment, homophobia and racial vilification, our understanding of violence has become more nuanced and the definition of violence has widened. It is increasingly understood that violence occurs along a continuum and involves physical, sexual, verbal and emotional abuses of power at individual, group and social structural levels. Kelly (1987) argues that violence involves 'a continuous series of elements or events that pass into one another and cannot be readily distinguished' but that, nonetheless, these different events 'have a basic common character' (1987, p. 48). Our particular focus in this paper is on physical violence (sexual and other assault and homicide). However, the backdrop to our understanding is the Kelly continuum. In this context of understanding, many social institutions and cultural forms have become implicated in discussions about both the causes of violence and its prevention. One such institution is the school.

There are several bodies of research literature which support the following contentions: that violence is widespread in schools, that most often such violence is perpetrated by males and can thus be understood as a violent expression of certain types of masculinity, that schools are implicated in the making of masculinities and that consequently they can be involved in the unmaking of the types of masculinity which are implicated in violence. It is increasingly accepted that schools have an important role to play in the prevention of violence. However, the connections between the matters noted and the exact role of the school with regard to the prevention of violence and how it might best be carried out are not at all clear. These are the difficult issues which we will begin to address.

Violence and masculinity, marginality, sexuality, intimacy and age

Let us continue with a little evidence to support some of the assertions we have made thus far, drawing from the situation in Australia. The Report of the National Committee on Violence (Australian Institute of Criminology, 1990, p. 3) reached the following general conclusions.

> Violent offenders in Australia are overwhelmingly male, primarily between the ages of 18 and 30 and predominantly from blue collar backgrounds.
>
> Victims of violence most commonly tend to fall into two broad categories: men who become engaged in altercations with other men; and women and children who suffer at the hands of men with whom they have been living.
>
> Men, especially those who are young, single and unemployed, are at far greater risk of becoming victims of all forms of violence than are women, except for the categories of sexual assault and domestic violence.
>
> The majority of victims of violence, like perpetrators, come from relatively disadvantaged backgrounds. Homicide risk, in particular, varies inversely with occupational status.
>
> Aboriginal Australians face a much greater risk of becoming the victims of violence than do members of the general Australian population, possibly up to ten times greater in the case of homicide.
>
> A considerable number of violent crimes never come to police attention; foremost in this 'dark figure' are the majority of sexual assaults and incidents of domestic violence.
>
> (Australian Institute of Criminology, 1990, p. 3)

Masculinity, marginality, sexuality, familiarity or intimacy and age are central to these generalisations and suggest that a holistic understanding of violence is crucial if we are to develop adequate approaches to anti-violence education in schools (Fitzclarence, 1995a). This, therefore, implies that an analysis of causes and suggestions for solutions must factor in gender and sexuality and the other asymmetrical relationships of power involved in race and social class dynamics and those between adults and children/adolescents.

What do analyses with such foci tell us? First, they suggest that given that such stark, broad patterns of violence exist, violence cannot simply be understood as related to the deviance or deficiency of the personality of the perpetrator or victim or to the 'dysfunctions' of the particular family, culture or subculture involved – although these may well be relevant. Second, such analyses tell us that violence cannot be understood as an occasional social aberration. Third, they tell us that a broader socio-cultural and a more refined psychoanalytic analysis is required; one which attends to dominant and subordinate cultures and to the ways in which these are represented in the psyche. We will begin our attempt at such an analysis by focusing on masculinity. Given that males are the main perpetrators of violence, this is not an arbitrary decision.

Masculinity

It is now fairly well understood that the social, cultural and psychic construction of masculinity is related to violence and that some kinds of masculinity are more directly associated with violent behaviour than are others. It is less well understood that particular types of masculinity are related to particular types of violence. Which masculinity is most associated with such physical violence as sexual and other assault and homicide and what are its key features? Answers to this question must be placed in the context of our current understandings of the construction of masculinity itself and its relationship to the politics of gender between males and females and between males alone.

The most convincing discussions of the construction of masculinities, and it is difficult to go past Connell (1995) here, make the following points. First, they argue that masculine identities are not static but historically and spatially situated and evolving. They arise through an individual's interaction with both the dynamisms and contradictions within and between immediate situations and broader social structures – gender regimes and gender orders if you like. It is this understanding which allows Connell to talk about masculinity as a life *project* involving the making and remaking of identity and meaning. It also allows us to understand the social and psychic complexity and fragility of masculinity. An appreciation of such complexity and fragility is essential to an understanding of male violence. It points to the vulnerable underbelly of all masculinities, to the driving force of such emotions as confusion, uncertainty, fear, impotence, shame and rage and to their expression in what Nayak and Kehily (no date) call masculine *performances*. These performances displace such emotions at the same time as they allow the performer to claim power and potency (Fitzclarence, 1992).

A second point arising from our best knowledge to date is that although there are many masculinities, these can be clustered on the basis of general social, cultural and institutional patterns of power and meaning and are built in relationship to each other. Connell (1995, ch. 3) calls these *hegemonic, subordinate, complicitous and marginal*. The concept 'hegemonic masculinity' is now widely used in discussions of masculinity and refers to those dominant and dominating forms of masculinity which claim the highest status and exercise the greatest influence and authority. It structures dominance and subordinate relations across and between the sexes and legitimates the broad structure of power known as patriarchy. Hegemonic masculinity makes its claims and asserts its authority through many cultural and institutional practices – particularly the global image media and the state, and although it does not necessarily involve physical violence it is often underwritten by the threat of such violence. Subordinate masculinity stands in direct opposition to hegemonic masculinity and is both repressed and oppressed by it. Indeed, as Connell (1995, p. 79) says, it is 'expelled from the circle' of masculine legitimacy. Gay masculinities feature in this category. Also represented are any forms which draw most elements of their core identity from beyond the core of the hegemonic. Any major attachment to 'the feminine' is likely to propel its owner into this category and to subject him to various forms of violence. Hegemonic masculinity is the standard-bearer of what it means to be a 'real' man or boy and many males draw inspiration from its cultural library of resources. Nonetheless, few men can live up to its rigorous standards. Many may try and many may not, but either way, according to Connell, they benefit from the '*patriarchal dividend*; the advantage men in general gain from the overall subordination of women ... without the tensions or risks of being the front line troops of patriarchy'

(1995, p. 79). In this sense, he says, in the politics of gender, they are complicitous with hegemonic forms of masculinity even if they fail to live up to and do not draw moral inspiration from its imperatives.

Connell (1995, p. 80) says that the three masculinity dynamics mentioned so far are 'internal to the gender order. The interplay of gender with other structures such as class and race creates further relationships between masculinities'. In order to explain the dynamics going on here, he argues that there are masculinities associated with the dominant and subordinate or *marginal* races and classes. He further notes that these marginalised masculinities, which are associated with subordinate social groupings, may draw both inspiration and legitimacy from hegemonic forms but only wield structural power to the extent that they are *authorised* by the dominant class/race (e.g. Magic Johnson in the USA). Thus, while marginal masculinities may not be marginal within their own patch, they are unlikely to exert power beyond it without some sort of sponsorship by and only within the tolerance limits of the dominant. In summary, what we see here is the ebb and flow of masculinities in concert and contest.

It is commonly accepted that masculinities cannot be fully understood without attending to their relationship to femininities within the broader scope of patriarchy. It is therefore important to identify the sorts of femininities which unwittingly underwrite hegemonic masculinity. The literature suggests that this particular version of femininity involves compliance and service, subservience and self-sacrifice and constant accommodating to the needs and desires of males. This indicates that anti-violence education is not a boys' only matter.

This emphasis on the fragile and fluid nature of masculinities in the context of dynamic power politics between males and females and between males points to the uncertainty of settlements about what constitutes masculinity in a given person, time and place and between and within groups. It also suggests that some masculinities may be more 'at risk' than others. Such settlements are challenged both intentionally and unintentionally by an array of life forces. The social movements associated with feminism, gay and lesbian movements and anti-racism are amongst such forces, but so too are other and perhaps bigger historical sweeps associated with such major economic and cultural shifts as post-modernity. In turn this means that many masculinities are constantly on the offensive and the defensive and in need of regular maintenance, renewal, repair and adjustment (Kenway, 1995). Nonetheless, when insecure, masculinity is likely to 'lash back', to reinvent itself and to try to shore up either its old or new foundations.

It is now possible to make some specific points about masculinity and violence. Some potential flashpoints should already be evident. If we consider the ongoing *project* of sustaining male power and masculine identity, and the individual and group performances, repressions, oppressions and contests that this may 'require', then we can see why violence is mobilised. What also becomes evident is the general interest that compliant masculinity has in the violence which helps to sustain male/female power relations. An understanding of the why is crucial to an understanding of the role of schools in both producing and challenging violence. Let us now consider the characteristics most associated with physical violence.

Predictably and in very general terms, it is the characteristics most associated with hegemonic masculinity which are most likely to be articulated with violence, but not in the obvious way that simplistic discussions of 'macho values' might suggest. At this stage of Western history, hegemonic masculinity mobilises around physical strength, adventurousness, emotional neutrality, certainty, control, assertiveness, self-reliance, individuality, competitiveness, instrumental skills, public knowledge, discipline, reason, objectivity and rationality. It distances itself from physical weakness, expressive skills, private knowledge, creativity, emotion, dependency, subjectivity, irrationality, co-operation and empathetic, compassionate, nurturant and certain affiliative behaviours. In other words, it distances itself from the feminine and considers the feminine less worthy. Violent males draw selectively from this repertoire, exaggerate, distort and glorify these values, attributes and behaviours and blend them into potent combinations. For example, rather than distance themselves from the feminine they might avoid and even fear it; rather than look down upon the feminine they might hold it in contempt and despise it; rather than consider women and children their inferior, they may regard them as less than human and more as objects and possessions to be used and discarded at will. To take some more quick examples, assertiveness may be exaggerated to become aggression, physical strength to toughness associated with physically beating others, bravery to bravado and cruelty, adventurousness to extreme risk-taking, self-discipline to disciplining others as well, self-reliance to isolation – preferably from earlier, emotional neutrality to emotional repression on the one hand and to extremes of rage and shame on the other, competitiveness to hostility, rationality to the rationalisation of violence, sexual potency to control over and contempt for women's bodies and so on.

Violent cultures, be they in the family, the school, the locker room, the pub, the workplace or the street, draw from, distort and exaggerate discourses from the discursive field of hegemonic masculinity. Nonetheless, their emotional underbelly remains characterised by identity uncertainty, anxiety and fear; with unfortunate consequences. The consequences involve what Miller (1987a) labels a complicated psycho dynamic mechanism of splitting off from uncomfortable feelings and of projecting such feelings on to an externalised object or other person. Such splitting and displacement are key features of violence. Miller (1987b, pp. 88–89) uses the notion of the *vicious circle of contempt* to explain how emotions that cause discomfort are projected on to others. She describes the process thus: 'Contempt for those who are smaller and weaker thus is the best defence against a breakthrough of one's own feelings of helplessness: it is an expression of this split-off weakness.' Let us now consider some more specific examples of violence – male to male, male to female and adult male to child.

Male/male violence

The literature on boys and schooling is replete with examples of school boy tribalism and tribal rivalry. It shows that groups develop a distinctive style either in line with or against the criteria mentioned earlier. Boy groups offer their members peer friendship, pleasure and pride, identity development, excitement and status resources and goals. However, there is often a price to pay for both the individual and the group.

In and out of school life for many adolescent boys is characterised by constant attempts to sort out identity issues and dominance relations (Weisfeld, 1994, p. 56). Dominance performances and contests occur at the individual and the group level, may revolve around issues of toughness, athletic ability, strength, popularity with girls, sexual achievements, risk-taking, fearlessness and fighting prowess. These will often include harassing girls, teachers and other boys, particularly those identified as 'gay'. Sexual harassment and homophobic violence can be seen to arise from the gender politics, hetero/sexist politics (Epstein, in press) and the fear of the feminine noted earlier. Such performances are directed towards reputation, towards being seen as strong, cool and in control and towards saving face, avoiding humiliation. Often dominance displays will involve a calculated rejection of school achievement and an anti-authority stance.

Male dominance/subordination relations are often worked out through the use of legitimate (sport) and illegitimate (brawling, bashing) physical violence. Again, such violence is premised on beliefs about the importance of aggressive and violent acts for gaining and maintaining status, reputation and resources in the male group, to sustain a sense of masculine identity and as a form of 'self' protection. Studies of violent older boys in the school and in out-of-school gangs show that much time is spent seeking respect and striving for positional power which is recognised by the group. However, power here is unstable and those who achieve positional power must work hard to sustain it. As a consequence, such groups often are characterised by intense male to male competition for dominance. Taking risks and fighting over drugs, territory, honour, girls, perceived insults and ethnic tension can readily transform into assaults and homicides when access to alcohol, drugs and weapons is readily available and involved (Goldstein, 1994).

The boys and men from racial and class minorities who subscribe to the beliefs about violence outlined earlier and who use various forms of violence to demonstrate their power and potency may find that it pays off in group leadership, popularity, pride, friendship and excitement and other resources which may not be available to them in other settings outside, say, the group or gang. Indeed, there is an argument which suggests that it is the groups of boys who are most marginalised by society and by the school who are most prone to violence and who subscribe to such values and who, paradoxically, are victims of such values. They are Connell's 'shock troops'; those who do the dirty work of patriarchy.

The argument goes that for boys who are in poverty, from racial and ethnic minority cultures, who are educationally disadvantaged, homeless, unemployed, risky and violent behaviour provides almost the only way of obtaining status and cultural resources. In other words, physical violence may well be most pronounced among those who have more to gain and little to lose (in the short term at least), most likely to occur amongst those outside the mainstream of education, employment and stable relationships. Such behaviour provides 'an opportunity to exercise personal power under conditions of minimal structural power . . . a mode of influence of last resort' (Archer, 1994, p. 317). What we see in these examples is the consequences for individuals of belonging to groups with less structural power and status and the ways in which a lack of power and status at the structural level can result in the exercise of violence at the individual and group level. What we also see are the consequences of the failure of society and its institutions to integrate all its members. This is not to suggest that males from other social groupings are non-violent, rather it is to offer an explanation for the relatively high levels of violence among disadvantaged groups. However, the role of the privileged should not be overlooked in this context, as Giroux points out with regard to the US experience:

> Beneath the growing culture of violence, both real and simulated, there lies a deep-seated racism that has produced what I want to call a white moral panic. The elements of this panic are rooted, in part, in a growing fear among the white middle class over declining quality of social, political, and economic life that has resulted from an increase in poverty, drugs, hate, guns, unemployment, social disenfranchisement, and hopelessness.
>
> (1996, p. 66)

It is *young* men who are most likely to be violent and to be victims of violence. What is it, in particular, about young men that makes them prone to violence? There are many theories put forward and those of particular pertinence relate to the nature of adolescence itself. Adolescence is a time of striving for independence, searching for and experimenting with identity, challenging authority and focusing away from the family to peer and sexual relationships. Exaggerated hegemonic values are likely both to appeal to adolescent boys and to spill over into violence for many possible reasons. These include the following. First, as a function of their move from childhood to adulthood and their resultant push against authority and search for autonomy adolescent boys may be drawn to risk-taking. Second, the exercise of power is most likely to erupt into overt violence when status and identity are uncertain. Third, inter-male competition is most pronounced when an interest in sexual activity is highest; at later adolescence it may become particularly pronounced due to the intensification of sexual activity and sexual competition.

Male/female violence

Violence by males against females most commonly takes the form of rape and sexual assault, domestic violence and verbal and physical harassment. Most violence against women and girls occurs within relationships of one sort or another. Intimate relations and settings are more likely to result in violence than are stranger relations and public spaces, although clearly violence erupts there too. Even so, there is overwhelming evidence to show that verbal and physical harassment, teasing and taunting relating to sexuality or gender against girls and women is rife in schools. Most boys either engage in this or comply with it.

The literature indicates that the males who are most likely to resort to serious physical violence against females subscribe to traditional and patriarchal views of male power and supremacy, traditional gender roles and to the view that violence is an acceptable way of resolving conflict. They believe that men are superior to women and have natural rights over them and natural dues from them. These include the following: the male's right to regard the woman as property and legitimately to control her through violence; the belief that it is legitimate to use physical violence when the rights and dues are not fulfilled and to resolve interpersonal conflict through the use of violence. When the male's status or power is threatened in some way, violence is regarded as an appropriate way of restoring the right and proper order – of keeping women in a subservient position. In this view, the male's sense of his masculine identity is caught up in the exercise of power over women through violence.

Sex and sexuality are key features of this scenario. Misogyny easily translates into sexual violence. Denigrating women and girls legitimates such violence and allows violent males selectively to interpret their own behaviour around, for example, 'only joking' motifs and to ignore the feelings of others. Violent males' reputations may be based on obtaining sexual access to women but their self-worth is often caught up in the sexual dominance and exploitation of women. Callous sexual attitudes are a common feature of the conversation of young males in schools, as are conceptions of sexual violence as manly – this is how 'real men' treat women (Wood, 1984). Belonging to a sexually exploitative peer group is more than likely to predispose a young man towards violence against girls and women. There are many generally accepted social beliefs which develop a cultural tolerance of rape and other sorts of violence against women and girls. These are called *rape myths* and prepare the male for his rape or harassment activities through a cultural library of excuses to forgive his misdemeanours.

There is a literature which argues that males and females have different orientations to aggression and violence. This suggests that to males, violence is instrumental to obtaining tangible or abstract benefits. As Anne Campbell says:

> men see aggression as a means of exerting control over other people when they fell the need to reclaim power and self esteem. Women see aggression as a temporary loss of control caused by overwhelming pressure and resulting in guilt.
>
> (1993, p. 411)

To women violence represents an emotion and not coping rather than an exercise of power. This literature also suggests that men and women have different orientations to intimacy. It suggests that men who subscribe to traditional versions of masculinity find intimacy terrifying as it represents the feminine values about which they are so fearful. It 'makes' them feel vulnerable and puts their sense of control at risk. For women, intimacy is more the natural order of things and they find it difficult to understand and deal with such men's distancing behaviour with regard to it. When one brings these understandings to the issues of violence between males and females in relationships, we see a fundamental clash of styles and understandings with explosive potential. Further, as Jenkins (1990, p. 37) argues: 'males have an exaggerated sense of entitlement and status in relation to females and children, an avoidance of social and emotional responsibility and a reliance on others (especially females) to take social and emotional responsibilities'.

Adult male/child violence

Childhood sexual abuse/assault is more difficult to explain than the other forms of violence discussed earlier. Nonetheless, it is not too difficult to extrapolate from those values associated with violence against females – particularly those associated with entitlement and emotional irresponsibility. Most cases involve adult males aged between 35 and 40 years of age; however, as Andrews (1994) reports, they have no agreed profile. Even so, many have cognitive distortions about the acceptability of their behaviour, which often has traumatic consequences for survivors leading to severe psychological problems and next generation offences. This inter-generational process is well explored and explained by Alice Miller, formerly a practising psychoanalyst for over 20 years and currently a strong critic of both psychoanalytic theories and methods.

Miller's (1987a,b, 1990) basic thesis is that from generation to generation the practices of child-rearing privilege the needs of adults over those of children. Based on her many years of counselling she argues that this often involves various forms of abuse – some obvious, some not so. Either way, the processes involved are aimed at breaking the will of the child in order that he or she can be controlled. Miller argues that when children are abused in this way they are 'trained' to be abusive and that as a result they learn, subconsciously, how to 'train' others in turn. Miller calls this process *poisonous pedagogy*. She observes that the effects of this abuse are destined to be repeated by victims at a later time in their lives unless they have had an opportunity to acknowledge what has happened and to work through the associated feelings. The absence of such a conscious acknowledgement of the powerful feelings associated with abuse leads, she says, to the ongoing return of repressed anxieties and frustrations and this can sometimes lead to violent and destructive behaviours. Such behaviour is often rationalised in the perpetrator's mind and thus made 'legitimate'. This in turn leads to further repressions, and to the cyclical repetition of the behaviour. In order for a person to break out of the cycle and avoid violent and abusive behaviour, he/she has to be able both to acknowledge the situation and to understand and integrate anger/ fear/frustration as part of him/her.

'Schooling the violent imagination'[1]

What does all of this imply about school education? Here are the hard truths as we see them based on our preceding analysis. If schools implicitly subscribe to and endorse hegemonic versions of masculinity, particularly in their more exaggerated forms, then they are complicit in the production of violence. If they fear 'the feminine' and avoid and discourage empathetic, compassionate, nurturant and affiliative behaviours and emotional responsibility and instead favour heavy-handed discipline and control then they are complicit. If they seek to operate only at the level of rationality and if they rationalise violence then they are complicit. If they are structured in such a way as to endorse the culture of male entitlement and indicate that the needs of males are more important than those of females then they are complicit. If they are repressive in their adult/child relations and do not offer adolescent students in particular opportunities to develop wise judgements and to exercise their autonomy in responsible ways then they are complicit. If they operate in such a way as to marginalise and stigmatise certain groups of students then they are complicit. The following remark speaks volumes in this regard:

> It is easier for politicians, educators and service providers to manage racism when it is defined in terms of visible, face-to-face incidents. What this implies is that the only perpetrator of racism is the racist aggressor and it exempts Australian systems, structures and institutions. It leaves invisible racism and racist structures in place and untouched. Common sense, day-to-day practises are never questioned, therefore we continue to offer services to all Australians without any thought of how, through these structures, we are reproducing inequality.

> (Indigenous Australians, 1995, p. 8)

It is our view that interventions which do not attend to all these matters will be limited in their effects and conversely that whatever schools do to address the issue of violence must attend to them (Fitzclarence *et al.*, 1995). However, how schools might best do this is not at all clear. We do not know as much as we need to know about schooling and violence, let alone about making gender and related matters central components of educational challenges to it. That aside, the main difficulty in all of this is first that *gender, age and marginality* are central structuring features of school cultures and education systems, and second that *emotional neutrality and hyper-rationality* are core structuring values. Hence, to attend to the matters mentioned is to go right to the heart of school culture (Fitzclarence, 1995b).

Attending to school culture is not a popular approach in anti-violence programmes in schools. Most approaches draw their insights from psychology. This has meant that they have concentrated on the personal and interpersonal and the small scale. The dominant tendency here has been to individualise and pathologise and indeed infantilise the violence which occurs within schools and/or to blame the peer group, family and/or the media for violence both in schools and beyond. Such approaches have not encouraged schools to see themselves as amongst the many institutions which are complicit in the production of violent behaviour. More recently however, the focus has shifted, at least in some quarters.

This shift has resulted from insights developed in educational sociology and feminism. According to this view, the school is not the innocent victim of isolated incidents of violence, neither is it the safe haven for victims of outside violence; violence is embedded in its culture and power relationships. In many obvious and subtle ways schools model, permit and shape violent attitudes and behaviours, they encourage students to accept that certain levels and orders of violence are normal and natural. This means that violence often goes unrecognised and unaddressed. This set of perspectives has encouraged 'whole school' approaches to addressing violence at the level of administration and curriculum (see Salisbury and Jackson, 1996).

This general approach provides a necessary corrective to those which focus on the psychology of the individual or group. Clearly, an adequate understanding of patterns of violence in schools requires a holistic perspective. However, it is not clear to us that even the socio-cultural or the psychological perspectives *together* offer such a perspective. As we have implied throughout it is not a matter of putting the big picture alongside the small, it is a matter of seeing how each is represented in the other. It is also our view that the socio-cultural perspective does not attend sufficiently to what we have identified earlier as the central components of violence. Indeed, we would go so far as to say that some of the approaches contribute to the very problems that they seek to eradicate. How could this possibly be? Some examples from the research into gender reform and education in schools by one of us will serve to illustrate the point. Further details of the research are provided in Kenway *et al.* (1997) so suffice it to say that case, cameo and survey data were gathered in many schools which were selected because they were undertaking some sort of gender reform. The schools ranged over various types and locations and included students of different social and cultural catchments. This choice of example is apt as gender reform should be a central component of anti-violence programmes.

We categorised strategies for gender reform in our research schools into two broad camps, one which demonstrated elements of authoritarianism and the other, elements of therapy. In the first instance, the tendency was to ignore altogether the world of feelings and to resort to highly rationalistic and even authoritarian policies and pedagogies. Hyper-rationalistic solutions were offered to deeply emotive issues. In many cases, these subverted their intentions and alienated many students and staff. Alternatively, when they did attend to such matters, it was often the case that the approach was more therapeutic than educational. Ensuring that students and colleagues enjoyed themselves and/or felt good about their gender became more important than helping them to become critical, informed and skilled advocates for a better world. Usually for the people on the receiving end, either too much or too little was demanded and at stake. In both cases gender reform in our schools was a heady emotional cocktail. The feelings which were mobilised included discomfort, uncertainty, inadequacy, defensiveness, anxiety, envy, insecurity, stress, anger, resentment, rejection, contempt, fear, grief, loss, pain, blame, shame, betrayal and abandonment. They also included feelings of pleasure, courage, yearning, security, strength, comfort, amusement, delight, connectedness, excitement, gratification and even gusto, but, to be honest, less often. As a result the effects of gender reform were not easy to predict (Kenway *et al.*, 1996). Nonetheless, on the basis of this research it is possible to make some points which pertain to anti-violence education.

This research suggests that approaches which preach rather than teach and which are destructive rather than deconstructive and reconstructive do not work. Adolescents do not like to be told and they particularly do not like to have the things they do and value criticised by older generations. Peer relations are generally considered far more important than teacher–student relations. The implication here is that a socially critical/deconstructive *negotiated* curriculum is preferable; one which guides and encourages students both to discover their own truths about gender, marginality and age and violence and to develop their own responsible preventative practices. This should be a curriculum which is oriented towards action. It should treat students as agents of rather than passive recipients of anti-violence reform. There is another implication here about discipline. As we indicated earlier, repressive practices help to produce violence and also prevent victims/survivors from addressing its consequences for them as individuals.

Equally counter-productive in our research schools were approaches which failed to recognise that adolescence is a time at which young people are shaping up their identities in the context of individual, and indeed economic and cultural uncertainty and instability. Destabilising gender can be very disruptive, particularly for those who have invested heavily in particular types of masculinity or femininity. This has implications for those anti-violence programmes which seek to encourage students to rewrite their gender identity through pedagogies which attend to the emotions. Arguably, it has particular implications for those boys who fear 'the feminine' and who see no worthwhile investment in emotional reworking; indeed, who may well see such work as risky in the context of the pecking order of schoolboy culture. Clearly a *pedagogy of the emotions* needs to be carefully thought through. It must attend to the ways in which the big picture is represented in students' emotional worlds and it also must help them develop the 'emotional intelligence' (Goleman, 1996) to understand the implications of their emotions for the ways they behave. We will offer some suggestions for such a pedagogy shortly.

A final point to be made about the socio-cultural perspective is that despite its sociological insights, this set of approaches generally fails to attend to one set of school practices which is particularly complicit in producing violence. We refer to the relations of power between adults and children, a particular feature of schooling, and particularly to the verbal, emotional and sometimes physical violence associated with certain disciplinary practices. Such understandings of violence are likely to make teachers and policy-makers uncomfortable. But let us take a closer look to see why.

Poisonous pedagogy

Alice Miller's work offers new insights into the relationship between schools and violence. Generally, her ideas suggest that mass education, with its penchant for order and control and for privileging the rational and the instrumental over the relational and affective provides a fertile seed-bed for advancing the culture of violence through 'poisonous pedagogy'. Sendak commenting on Miller's (1987a) work says: 'She makes chillingly clear to the many what has been recognised only by the few: the extraordinary pain and psychological suffering inflicted on children under the guise of conventional child rearing practices.' Miller's studies raise questions about the dominant idea that teacher–student relationships are based principally on care. The idea of breaking the will of the child by force or by connivance in order that he or she can be controlled is no stranger to education, which is structured around the power relationships between adults and children. Indeed, school organisation depends upon such control and almost invariably the needs of the organisation and the teachers take precedence over those of the child. In a sense then, schools repeat the poisonous pedagogies that many children have been exposed to in the home.

Miller's ideas also question the extent to which it is wise for schools to move down the late twentieth-century path of increasingly rational curriculum development encouraged by our economically rationalist curriculum policy-makers. Let us consider this issue a little more closely.

The structures and discourses of contemporary education are built on a foundation of rationality. Built into the organisation of learning is an overwhelming faith in the orderly pattern of human affairs. This extends from the dominant ideas about intelligence through to methods for teaching particular subjects. This faith is also reflected in approaches to violence. Take two examples. Some schools have relied on pedagogies of authority in an attempt to control 'outbreaks of violence'. Strict codes of behaviour have been enforced inspired by the regimes of discipline used in industry and the military. Other schools have used counselling methods designed to effect conflict resolution via approaches involving 'talking through the problems'. While apparently different, this draws on the same underlying faith in rationality. However, when it comes to issues of violence, this faith in human rationality becomes unstable (Fitzclarence, 1992).

For Scheff and Retzinger (1991) any adequate interpretation of patterns of violence involves a consideration of complex emotional responses such as shame, rage, alienation, humiliation and repression and revenge. However, such a lexicon is hardly the conceptual material of 'rational' education discourses. Indeed it is alien to them. Nonetheless, the absence of an adequate pedagogy of the emotions has serious consequences. Miller's ideas imply that the replacement of the expressive and creative aspects of the curriculum with instrumental, cognitive-based regimes may actually *reduce* the capacity of education to break what Miller (1987) describes as the 'vicious circle of contempt' which characterises inter-generational patterns of violence. To ignore the emotional world of schooling and of students and teachers is to contribute to the repressions which recycle and legitimate violence.

Miller's work thus raises doubts about professional development and a curriculum on violence which only appeals to people's rationality and which assumes that teachers and students have rational control over their behaviours. Her work points to the probability that such reforms on violence are likely to touch deep psychic sensitivities and investments, particularly for certain students and teachers; victims, survivors, perpetrators and those who are complicit and in different ways draw on the patriarchal dividend. It thus casts some doubt on those reforms which overlook the powerful role of emotion in the teaching/learning process and suggests that we may well rely too heavily on students' and teachers' goodwill and rationality in attempts to effect change. The challenge here, then, is to work with and through the emotions and to look to other fields of inquiry which may help us to do this. This quest has led us to turn to therapy for ideas; not, we stress, to the sort of self-absorbed, ahistorical and culturally decontextualised therapy which Connell (1995, pp. 206–212) critiques as 'masculinity therapy', in what he scathingly describes as 'Books about Men'. Instead we have turned to narrative therapy in order to explore its implications for pedagogy.

Narrative therapy and its implications for anti-violence pedagogy

In an attempt to get beyond the limitations of social and psychological theories that are not sensitive enough to the reflexive and dynamic nature of humanity and social life, White and Epston (1990) have turned to narrative and have developed narrative therapy in their counselling practice at the Dulwich Centre in South Australia. They use the 'story' metaphor to explore the perpetual process of identity construction through meaning making. Their following statement explains this perspective:

> In striving to make sense of life, persons face the task of arranging their experiences of events in sequences across time in such a way as to arrive at a coherent account of themselves and the world around them. Specific experiences of events of the past and present, and those that are predicted to occur in the future, must be connected in a lineal sequence to develop this account. This account can be referred to as a story or self narrative.
>
> (White and Epston, 1990, p. 10)

According to White (1992, p. 123), people live and shape their lives by stories. These stories, he argues, 'have real, not imagined effects'; they 'provide the structure of life'.

Narrative therapy offers individuals and groups a means for remaking the dominant storylines which have governed their lives. It encourages them to search for alternative stories – to search for accounts that contradict or resist the dominant individual and socio-cultural stories through which their lives have been constructed and through which they have constructed their lives. This involves a process of 'externalising' the problem with its attendant feelings through the use of story and also of identifying critical moments which tell a different story. Through such a process it becomes possible for the dominant narrative to be resisted. White refers to such moments as 'unique outcomes'. He describes these moments when an invitation to retell the dominant story of a particular problem is resisted and a new meaning is established. In the case of perpetrators of violence, this process also encourages them to accept responsibility for their actions and for the consequences of previous behaviours. In turn, this becomes a process of shaping a new and alternative story-line through which to rebuild identity and relationships. The following example is derived from an exchange between a therapist and a violent offender. It highlights the start of a restorying process designed to facilitate new action.

> Can you remember a time when you took action to stop/prevent violence yourself? Can you remember a time when you made a stand against your own violence and did not expect your partner to do it for you? How did you do it?
>
> (Jenkins, 1990, p. 87)

In our view there are several advantages to be gained in using ideas drawn from narrative therapy to address the problems of violence in schools. First, as Kehily and Nayak (no date) vividly demonstrate, storying is a key feature of schooling and of students' and teachers' ways of making meaning about their place in schools. Second, the indeterminate nature of storytelling suggests that collective and individual stories and identities are fluid and can therefore be rewritten or retold – albeit not easily. For both perpetrators and victims of violence, alternative stories point to the possibility of changing direction. To make the link to violence in education more concrete, consider the following self-narrative of Adam from one of the research schools referred to earlier.

I have been harassed at eleven schools now. At every school I have been to I have been the ten pound weakling. Like, I am the only kid I know with backwards elbows! And, like, because in my job in the school I deal with the locker grills and all that. I get harassed guaranteed at least every morning. They just feel like throwing rocks at me, pushing me around, shoving me, throwing me into walls.

Adam's story is one of a good-humoured victim. But what might it look like if he rewrote it and himself as a courageous survivor and emphasised the strengths he has had to draw on to maintain his sense of humour? A word of caution is necessary here. This is not to suggest that tangible, material practices can be simply thought or talked out of existence. Adam's story makes clear that stories of violence represent harsh realities. It is to say, however, that he is able to see himself differently in this context.

A third advantage of the narrative approach is that it enables a person's experience to be considered within wider frameworks of meaning. It encourages them to consider the impact on their lives and relationships of wider cultural and social power relations. For example, a personal story can be linked to a more general cultural story. This helps to develop an appreciation of the ways in which a person is situated within the dominant storylines of a culture or a society. Let us take some other examples of this process. The following 'story' of 15-year-old Colin contains some identifiable socio-cultural themes.

Being big is great. [Laughter] No, I just walk down the road and people dodge out of your way, 'cause they think I'm going to hit them. Sometimes I do if they get too close to me. So they let me go first, unless there's a girl, I let her go first. It's better than being one of those school kids that keep getting pushed around you see. I save the rest of them, so when they get pushed around, I just grab the other kid and smack him against the wall or something.

The storylines represented in Colin's self-narration have widespread currency. 'Big is best' and 'take control by force and fear' are cultural themes that apply in the world of business and in law enforcement systems. Quite possibly, Colin has modelled his behaviour on one of the current stock of independent law enforcers depicted in Steven Segal or Sylvester Stallone warrior movies. This next example shows how a teacher of a single-sex class of 'tough' boys and two members of that class formed an alliance around exaggerated hegemonic masculinity. In commenting on his relationship with the class, the teacher notes that:

When I'm there and I'm relaxed I'm also one of the boys. You know if you had an inexperienced man or an effeminate man or a bloke who's too academically inclined or something like that, then that might not work. You might end up with a 'them and me' situation.

In turn Ben, a student, comments, 'I can swear more' (referring to having no girls in the class) and Matthew, referring to how it might be different if they had a female teacher, says:

But if say a nice woman walked past, like we couldn't say 'Ooh, look at her' cause she'd look at us and say 'That's sexism' and all this. But Mr Kennedy, he'd just laugh and say 'I'd buy that for a dollar'.

Again we see represented some of the features of violence which we mentioned in the first part of the paper. What has narrative therapy to offer in these instances? At a minimum it would help Colin, Mr Kennedy, Ben and Matthew to identify the entitlement storylines they are living their lives by and would also invite them to search for others that are more socially and emotionally responsible. Let us consider further the implications of narrative therapy for school's anti-violence education programmes.

While narrative therapy has been pioneered by therapists working primarily outside of the education system, the possibility of adaptations for work in school is now being recognised – but not of course by the hyper-rationalists who drive school systems. At this stage, the suggestions for pedagogy which we think have the most potential are those developed and employed by Sydney's *Men Against Sexual Assault Group* (MENSA). Their approach also builds on the strengths but avoid the weaknesses of the authoritarian and the therapeutic approaches we outlined earlier. It also operates outside of the rationalist frameworks which we mentioned earlier and seeks to work with and through the anxieties of young males in particular. Without going into detail, in an environment characterised by respect and support rather than by blaming and shaming, it explores with students their experiences of violence and encourages them to identify the dominant narratives which have shaped such violence (rape myths, e.g.) and to unpack the cultural library of excuses which are used to justify it. However, this approach does not stop there. It then assists students to find some positive counter-narratives; to draw out and upon alternative sources of strength and status and to build new communities of support for alternative ways of being male and female. Witness the following example.

David Denborough's (1996) work on narrative therapy has been used in working with male students in a programme designed to address emerging problems in junior secondary schools. The process, designed to address issues of sexual harassment/violence and by implication power relations and contested identities, demonstrates a whole-class approach for working through issues that are clearly embedded in the dynamics of society more generally. The process includes mapping experiences of violence, naming the effects, inviting an articulation of the need to change and naming a counter-plot. In more specific detail, the approach which Denborough advocates can be summarised as follows:

■ Beginnings – considering notions of respectful practice; a game of sex and lies; addressing the climate.
■ Mapping the extent of the violence in their lives.
■ Eliciting an articulated invitation to discuss these ideas.
■ Identifying the gendered nature of violence. Identifying messages and beliefs about the dominant masculinity and exploring why it is that men are the ones who are violent in the vast majority of instances. Looking at some key-gendered messages and how boys are encouraged and coerced into positioning themselves within them.
■ Naming this dominant plot, for example, 'being tough'.
■ Mapping the effects of this dominant plot on different social groupings.
■ Inviting an articulation of the need for change.
■ Finding exceptions – exploring what it means to exist in terms of hope and in terms of what it says about them.
■ Naming the counter-plot.

- Asking for an articulation that moving towards this counter-plot, a plot of resistance, would be a good thing (for men, women – hetero- and homosexual, young people, children).
- Building on exceptions: building on strengths – exploring how they did it; building on histories – instances in the past that would support thinking of themselves in this new way; building communities of support – who supported them, how they could find other support.
- Reflecting on strengths: what it says about them; what significant others would think.
- Broadening the responsibility – taking their suggestions as to how they could be supported in their attempts to move towards 'being themselves', by staff, the school, families and the local community.

The approach outlined here is part of a layered pedagogy. This involves discussions at a number of different levels in the school and including parents and community members. Of particular relevance is the focus on developing respectful dialogue between boys and girls.

> We need to work with our boys *and* our girls – together. They have much to learn from each other, we have much to learn from all of them. The potential for programs in which boys and girls listen to one another's experiences, and develop strategies to work together against out-dated notions of gender, are perhaps the most exciting of all.
>
> (Denborough, 1996, p. 26)

As we see it, the goal of anti-violence education is a future in which males and females, males and males and adults and children can live alongside each other in safe, secure, stable, respectful and harmonious ways and in relationships of mutual life-enhancing respect.

NOTE

1 This title is taken from Schostak (1986).

REFERENCES

Andrews, B. (1994) 'Family violence in a social context: factors relating to male abuse of children', in J. Archer (ed.), *Male Violence*, pp. 195–210 (London, Routledge).

Archer, J. (1994) 'Power and male violence', in J. Archer (ed.), *Male Violence*, pp. 310–332 (London, Routledge).

Australian Institute of Criminology (1990) *Violence: Directions for Australia: Report of the National Committee on Violence* (Canberra, Australian Capital Territory).

Campbell, A. (1994) *Out of Control* (London, Pandora).

Connell, R.W. (1995) *Masculinities* (Sydney, Allen & Unwin).

Denborough, D. (1996) 'Step by step: developing respectful and effective ways of working with young men to reduce violence', in C. McKean, M. Carey and C. White (eds), *Men's Ways of Being*, pp. 91–117 (Denver, CO, Westview Press).

Epstein, D. (in press) 'Keeping them in their place: hetero/sexist harassment, gender and the enforcement of heterosexuality', in J. Holland and L. Adkins (eds), *Sex, Sensibility and the Gendered Body* (London, Macmillan).

Epstein, D. and White, M. (1992) *Experience, Contradiction, Narrative and Imagination*, selected papers of David Epston and Michael White, 1989–1991 (Adelaide, Dulwich Centre Publications).

Fitzclarence, L. (1992) *Shame: The Emotional Straw that Breaks more than Backs*, paper presented at the *Australian Association for Research in Education Conference*, November (Geelong, Deakin University).

Fitzclarence, L. (1995a) 'Beyond adrenalin, testosterone and repressed memories: the search for an holistic perspective on violence in schools', *Australian Association for Research in Education Conference*, Hobart, 26–30 November.

Fitzclarence, L. (1995b) 'Education's shadow? Towards an understanding of violence in schools', *Australian Journal of Education*, 39: 22–40.

Fitzclarence, L., Warren, C. and Laskey, L. (1995) 'Schools, sexuality and violence: a case for changing direction', in L. Laskey and C. Beavis (eds), *Schooling and Sexualities: Teaching for Positive Sexuality* (Geelong, Deakin University Centre for Education and Change).

Giroux, H. (1996) *Fugitive Cultures: Race, Violence, and Youth* (New York, Routledge).

Goldstein, A.P. (1994) 'Delinquent gangs', in J. Archer (ed.), *Male Violence*, pp. 87–105 (London, Routledge).

Goleman, D. (1996) *Emotional Intelligence: Why it can matter more than I.Q.* (London Bloomsbury Publishing).

Indigenous Australians Addressing Racism in Education: a conversation with Lester Rigney in Schooling and Education, Exploring new possibilities, *Dulwich Centre Newsletter*, 1995, 2–3: 5–15.

Jenkins, A. (1990) *Invitations to Responsibility* (Adelaide, Dulwich Centre Publications).

Kehily, M.J. and Nayak, A. (no date) 'Narrative of oppression: pupil cultures and story telling forms', unpublished paper, CEDAR, University of Warwick.

Kelly, L. (1987) 'The continuum of sexual violence', in J. Hanmer and M. Maynard (eds), *Women, Violence and Social Control*, pp. 46–61 (London, Macmillan).

Kenway, J. (1995) 'Masculinity – under siege, on the defensive, and under reconstruction', *Discourse*, 16: 59–81.

Kenway, J., Blackmore, J. and Willis, S. (1996) 'Beyond feminist authoritarianism and therapy in the curriculum?', *Curriculum Perspectives*, 16: 1–12.

Kenway, J., Willis, S., Blackmore, J. and Rennie, L. (1997) *Answering Back, Remaking Girls and Boys in Schools* (Sydney, Allen & Unwin).

Miller, A. (1987a) *For Your Own Good: The Roots of Violence in Child-rearing* (London, Virago Press).

Miller, A. (1987b) *The Drama of Being a Child* (London, Virago Press).

Miller, A. (1990) *For Your Own Good: Hidden Cruelty in Child-rearing and the Roots of Violence* (New York, The Noonday Press).

Nayak, A. and Kehily, M.J. (no date) 'Playing it straight: masculinities, homophobias and schooling', unpublished paper, CEDAR, University of Warwick.

Salisbury, J. and Jackson, D. (1996) *Challenging Macho Values: Practical Ways of Working with Adolescent Boys* (London, Falmer Press).

Scheff, T. and Retzinger, S. (1991) *Emotions and Violence* (Lexington, MA, Lexington Books).

Schostak, J. (1986) *Schooling the Violent Imagination* (London, Routledge & Kegan Paul).

Weisfeld, G. (1994) 'Aggression and dominance in the social world of adolescent boys', in J. Archer (ed.), *Male Violence*, pp. 12–70 (London, Routledge).

White, M. (1992) 'Deconstruction and therapy', in D. Epston and M. White (eds), *Experience, Contradiction, Narrative and Imagination*, selected papers of David Epston and Michael White, 1989–1991 (Adelaide, Dulwich Centre Publications).

White, M. and Epston, D. (1990) *Narrative Means to Therapeutic Ends* (New York, London, W.W. Norton & Co.).

Wood, J. (1984) 'Groping towards sexism: boys' sex talk', in A. McRobbie and M. Nava (eds), *Gender and Generation* (Basingstoke, Macmillan).

FOUR

'SPICE GIRLS', 'NICE GIRLS', 'GIRLIES' AND 'TOMBOYS': GENDER DISCOURSES, GIRLS' CULTURES AND FEMININITIES IN THE PRIMARY CLASSROOM

Diane Reay

Source: '"Spice girls", "nice girls", "girlies" and "tomboys": gender discourses, girls' cultures and femininities in the primary classroom', *Gender and Education*, 13(2): 153–166, 2001.

Introduction

This article attempts to demonstrate that contemporary gendered power relations are more complicated and contradictory than any simplistic binary discourse of 'the girls versus the boys' suggests (Heath, 1999). Although prevailing dominant discourses identify girls as 'the success story of the 1990s' (Wilkinson, 1994), this small-scale study of a group of 7-year-old girls attending an inner London primary school suggests that, particularly when the focus is on the construction of heterosexual femininities, it is perhaps premature always to assume that 'girls are doing better than boys'. While girls may be doing better than boys in examinations, this article indicates that their learning in the classroom is much broader than the National Curriculum and includes aspects that are less favourable in relation to gender equity. Although masculinities are touched on in this article, this is only in as far as they relate to girls. This deliberate bias is an attempt to refocus on femininities at a time when masculinities appear to be an ever-growing preoccupation within education.

However, although the subjects of this research are 14 girls, the position the article takes is that femininities can only be understood relationally. There is a co-dependence between femininities and masculinities which means that neither can be fully understood in isolation from the other. The article therefore explores how a particular group of primary-aged girls is positioned, primarily in relation to dominant discourses of femininity but also in relation to those of masculinity. There is also an attempt to map out their relationships to transgressive but less prevalent discourses of femininity, which in a variety of ways construct girls as powerful. The findings from such a small-scale study are necessarily tentative and no generalised assertions are made about girls as a group. Rather, the aim is to use the girls' narratives and their experiences in school and, to a lesser extent, those of the boys, to indicate some ways in which the new orthodoxy, namely that girls are doing better than boys, does not tell us the whole story about gender relations in primary classrooms.

The last decade has seen a growing popular and academic obsession with boys' underachievement both in the UK and abroad (Katz, 1999; Smithers, 1999). However, as Lyn Yates points out, much of the 'underachieving boys' discourse fails either to deal adequately with power or to see femininity and masculinity as relational phenomena (Yates, 1997). For instance, within the explosion of concern with masculinities in academia, there has been little focus on the consequences for girls of 'boys behaving badly'. As Gaby Weiner and her colleagues argue: 'new educational discourses have silenced demands for increased social justice for girls and women characterised by increasing resistance to policies and practices focusing specifically on them' (Weiner et al., 1997, p. 15).

Jill Blackmore describes attempts by some male academics in Australia to develop programmes for boys which seek to depict boys as powerless in the face of the progress and success of feminism and girls, and, indeed, as victims of their own male psychology (Blackmore, 1999). Jane Kenway writes more broadly of 'the lads' movement' in Australia; a general resurgence of concern that boys and men are getting an unfair deal (Kenway, 1995). In Britain, there has been a growing alarm about 'boys doing badly' that preoccupies both mainstream and feminist academics alike (Epstein et al., 1998). What gets missed out in these current concerns is the specificity of the 'failing boy' and the ways in which other groups of males continue to maintain their social advantage and hold on to their social power (Arnot et al., 1999; Lucey and Walkerdine, 1999). It is within this context of contemporary preoccupation with boys that this article attempts to problematise issues surrounding gender equity and, in particular, to challenge the view that in millennial Britain it is boys rather than girls who are relatively disadvantaged.

The research study

The article is based on data from a 1-year study, conducted over the academic year 1997–98, of children in a Year 3 class in an inner-city primary school. 3R comprised 26 children, 14 girls and 12 boys. There were 5 middle-class children, 3 girls and 2 boys, all white apart from Amrit who was Indian. The 21 working-class children were more ethnically mixed. As well as 1 Somalian and 2 boys of mixed parentage, there were 4 Bengali children, 3 boys and 1 girl. The social class attribution of the children was based on parental occupations but was also confirmed by information provided by the class teacher. Fifteen of the children were entitled to free school meals. The school is surrounded by 1960s and 1970s public housing estates from which most of its intake is drawn, and indeed, 14 of the children in 3R lived on one of these 5 estates.

I spent one day a week over the course of the year engaged in participant observation in both the classroom and the playground, amassing over 200 pages of field notes. Additionally, I interviewed all the children, both individually and in focus groups. I also carried out group work activities in which children both wrote and drew on a range of topics from playground games to best friends. As James *et al.* (1998, p. 189) point out: 'Talking with children about the meanings they themselves attribute to their paintings or asking them to write a story allows children to engage more productively with our research questions using the talents which they possess.'

The unequal relationship between researcher and researched is compounded when the researcher is an adult and the researched a child. In order to mitigate at least some of the power differentials I organised workshops for the children in which I taught simple questionnaire design and interviewing techniques. The children then compiled their own questionnaires so that they could interview each other. These interviews, as well as those I conducted, 84 overall, were tape-recorded and transcribed. The class teacher and I also collected sociogram data, which enabled us to map out the children's friendship networks and work relationships.

Gender discourses

Many writers on education have attempted to provide a variety of conceptual tools in order to understand educational contexts and processes (Ball, 1994; Maclure, 1994). A key debate amongst educational researchers has been between structuralist and post-structuralist approaches. Although often these two conceptual approaches are seen as opposing perspectives, in this article, I use and combine what I perceive to be the strengths of both positions to illuminate the ways in which girls both construct themselves, and are constructed, as feminine (see also, Walkerdine, 1991, 1997; Williams, 1997; Walkerdine *et al.*, 2000 for similar approaches). As Davies *et al.* (1997) assert, power is both located in the structural advantage of individuals and also exercised partly through the construction of discourses.

Multiple discourses contribute not only to how researchers appreciate the conditions of childhood but also to how children come to view themselves (James *et al.*, 1998). Post-structuralist feminists have explored extensively the ways in which different discourses can position girls (Davies, 1993; Hey, 1997; Walkerdine, 1997). It is important to recognise that there are many competing gender discourses, some of which have more power and potency than others for particular groups of girls (Francis, 1998). Such processes of discursive recognition, of feeling a better fit within one discourse than another (Francis, 1999), are influenced by social class. Similarly, gender discourses are taken up differentially by different ethnic groupings. It is also important to stress that girls can position themselves differently in relation to gender discourses according to the peer group context they find themselves in. For example, it soon became evident in my research that girls assume different positions depending on whether they are in single- or mixed-sex contexts. As Gee and his colleagues assert:

> There are innumerable discourses in modern societies: different sorts of street gangs, elementary schools and classrooms, academic disciplines and their sub-specialities, police, birdwatchers, ethnic groups, genders, executives, feminists, social classes and sub-classes, and so on and so-forth. Each is composed of some set of related social practices and social identities (or positions). Each discourse contracts complex relations of complicity, tension and opposition with other discourses.
>
> (Gee *et al.*, 1996, p. 10)

I found similar 'complex relations of complicity, tension and opposition' in relation to the nexus of gender discourses that these girls draw on. Yet, any local discursive nexus is framed by a wider social context within which, as Valerie Hey (1997) points out, there is a lack of powerful public discourses for girls, leaving them caught between schooling which denies difference and compulsory hetero-sexuality which is fundamentally invested in producing it. If this gives the impression of a fluid situation in relation to how contemporary girls position themselves as female, there is also substantial evidence of continuities in which, at least for the girls in this research, conformist discourses continue to exert more power than transgressive or transformative ones.

Masculinities in the classroom: setting the context

Although the main focus of this article is how gender discourses position girls at school, in order to understand femininities in this primary classroom, the ways in which masculinities are being played out cannot be ignored. I want to start with two short excerpts from boys. Josh and David, two white, middle-class, 7-year-old boys, interviewed each other about what they like most and least about being a boy:

JOSH: David, what do you like most about being a boy?
DAVID: Well, it must be that it's much easier to do things than being a girl, that's what I think. You get to do much better things.
JOSH: So you think you find being a boy more interesting than being a girl? Is that what you're saying?
DAVID: Yes because it's boring being a girl.
JOSH: OK, and what do you like least about being a boy?
DAVID: Well, I don't know, I can't think of anything.
JOSH: Well, can't you think really – there must be something.
DAVID: I'll think [long pause]. Well, it's easier to hurt yourself.
DAVID: OK, What do you like most about being a boy?
JOSH: I'd probably say that it's better being a boy because they have more interesting things to do and it's more exciting for them in life I find.
DAVID: Yes, I see. What do you like least about being a boy?
JOSH: Ohh, I'd probably say not being so attractive as girls probably I'd say they're much more attractive than boys.

Josh and David were the only middle-class boys in a Year 3 class of predominantly working-class children. Existing research has found that the culturally exalted form of masculinity varies from school to school and is informed by the local community (Skelton, 1997; Connolly, 1998). These two boys were adjusting to a predominantly working-class, inner-city peer group in which dominant local forms of masculinity were sometimes difficult for both to negotiate, but in particular, for David (for one thing, he did not like football). They both also found the low priority given to academic work among the other boys problematic. Even so, they were clear that it was still better being a boy.

Both boys, despite their social class positioning, were popular among the peer group. In particular, Josh commanded a position of power and status in the peer group which was virtually unchallenged (see also Reay, 1990). Sociogram data collected from all the children in the class positioned him as the most popular child, not only with the working-class boys in the class but also with the girls. David's positioning is more difficult to understand. His particular variant of middle-class masculinity was far less acceptable to his working-class peers than Josh's. He was studious and hated games. In the exercise where children drew and described their favourite playground activity, David sketched a single figure with a bubble coming out of his head with 'thoughts' inside. He annotated it with 'I usually like walking about by myself and I'm thinking'. However, within the confines of the classroom, for much of the time, he retained both status and power, paradoxically through a combination of being male and clever. When the girls were asked to nominate two boys and two girls they would most like to work with, David was the second most popular male choice after Josh. However, he was the most popular choice with the other boys. The complex issues as to why these two boys were popular when their masculinities did not fit the dominant one within the male peer group are beyond the brief of this article. Rather, what is salient is the relevance of their positioning within the peer group for the group of girls who are the article's main protagonists.

Although the focus has been on 'the others' within masculinity, black and white working-class boys (Willis, 1977; Sewell, 1997), it is the association of normativity with white, middle-class masculinity that seems most difficult for girls to challenge effectively. Disruptive, failing boys' behaviour has given girls an unexpected window of opportunity through which some variants of femininities can be valorised over specific pathologised masculinities, particularly within the arena of educational attainment. Both girls and boys were aware of discourses which position girls as more mature and educationally focused than boys and regularly drew on them to make sense of gender differences in the classroom (see also Pattman and Phoenix, 1999). What seems not to have changed is the almost unspoken acceptance of white, middle-class masculinity as the ideal that all those 'others' – girls as well as black and white working-class boys – are expected to measure themselves against. Popular discourses position both masculinity and the middle classes as under siege, suggesting an erosion of both male and class power bases (Bennett, 1996; Coward, 1999). While there have been significant improvements in the direction of increasing equity, particularly in the area of gender, the popularity of Josh and David, combined with the uniform recognition among the rest of the peer group that they were the cleverest children in the class, suggests that popular discourses may mask the extent to which white, middle-class male advantages in both the sphere of education and beyond continue to be sustained.

However, 10 of the 12 boys in 3R were working class. The 'failing boys' compensatory culture of aggressive 'laddism' (Jackson, 1998) had already started to be played out at the micro-level of this primary classroom. The working-class, white and mixed race boys were more preoccupied with football than the academic curriculum (see also Skelton, 1999). When they were not playing football in the playground, they would often be surreptitiously exchanging football cards in the classroom. Alongside regular jockeying for position within the male peer group, which occasionally escalated into full-blown fights, there was routine, casual labelling of specific girls as stupid and dumb. The three Bengali boys at the bottom of this particular male peer group hierarchy compensated by demonising, in particular, the three middle-class girls. Their strategy echoes that of the subordinated youth in Wight's (1996) study, where in order to gain the approval and acceptance of their dominant male peers, they endeavoured to become active subjects in a sexist discourse which objectified girls.

Sugar and spice and all things nice?

3R had four identifiable groups of girls – 'the 'nice girls', the 'girlies', the 'spice girls' and the 'tomboys' (see Figure 4.1).

The latter two groups had decided on both their own naming as well as those of the 'girlies' and the 'nice girls', descriptions which were generally seen as derogatory by both girls and boys. 'Girlies' and 'nice girls' encapsulate 'the limited and limiting discourse of conventional femininity (Brown, 1998), and in this Year 3 class, although there was no simple class divide, the 'nice girls' were composed of Donna, Emma and Amrit, the only three middle-class girls in 3R, plus a fluctuating group of one to two working-class girls. The 'nice girls', seen by everyone, including themselves, as hard-working and well behaved, exemplify the constraints of a gendered and classed discourse which afforded them the benefits of culture, taste and cleverness but little freedom. Prevalent discourses which work with binaries of mature girls and immature boys and achieving girls and underachieving boys appear on the surface to be liberating for girls. However, the constraints were evident in the 'nice girls'' self-surveillant, hypercritical attitudes to both their behaviour and their schoolwork; attitudes which were less apparent amongst other girls in the class. It would appear that this group of 7-year-old, predominantly middle-class girls had already begun to develop the intense preoccupation with academic success that other researchers describe in relation to middle-class, female, secondary school pupils (Walkerdine *et al.*, 2000).

Contemporary work on how masculinities and femininities are enacted in educational contexts stresses the interactions of gender with class, race and sexuality (Mac an Ghaill, 1988; Hey, 1997; Connolly, 1998). Sexual harassment in 3R (a whole gamut of behaviour which included uninvited touching of girls and sexualised name-calling) was primarily directed at the 'girlies' and was invariably perpetuated by boys who were subordinated within the prevailing masculine hegemony either because of their race or social class. However, while sexual harassment was an infrequent occurrence, identifying the 'nice girls' as a contaminating presence was not. In the playground, the three working-class Bengali boys were positioned as subordinate to the white and Afro-Caribbean boys; for example, they were often excluded from the football games on the basis that they were not

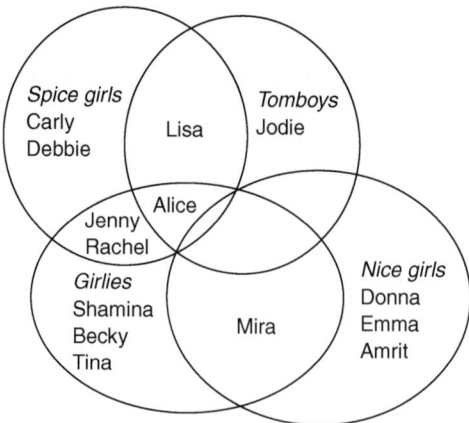

Figure 4.1 Girl groups in 3R.

skilful enough. These three boys constructed the 'nice girls' as a polluting, contagious 'other'. They would regularly hold up crossed fingers whenever one of these girls came near them. As a direct result, the 'nice girls' began to use the classroom space differently, taking circuitous routes in order to keep as far away from these boys as possible. Barrie Thorne (1993) found similar gender practices in which girls were seen as 'the ultimate source of contamination'. Like the girls in Thorne's research, the 'nice girls' did not challenge the boys but rather developed avoidance strategies which further circumscribed their practices.

Being one of the 'nice girls' had derogatory connotations for working-class girls as well as working-class boys. Alice, in particular, was adamant that she could not contemplate them as friends because they were 'too boring', while in one of the focus group discussions, Jodie, Debbie and Carly all agreed that 'no one wants to be a nice girl'. Their views reflect the findings of feminist research which position 'being nice' as specific to the formulation of white, middle-class femininity (Jones, 1993; Griffin, 1995; Kenway et al., 1999). For a majority of the working-class girls in the class, being a 'nice girl' signified an absence of the toughness and attitude that they were aspiring to.

This is not to construct the 'nice girls' as passive in relation to other groups in the class. They often collaborated with Josh and David on classwork and were vocal about the merits of their approach to schoolwork over those of other girls in the class:

EMMA: The other girls often mess around and be silly, that's why Alice and Lisa never get their work finished.
DONNA: Yes we're more sensible than they are.
EMMA: And cleverer.

However, the dominant peer group culture in the classroom was working class and, while this had little impact on the popularity of Josh and David, it did have repercussions for the status and social standing of the 'nice girls' within the peer group.

'The limited and limiting discourse of conventional femininity' also had a powerful impact on the 'girlies', a group of three working-class girls (two white and one Bengali). Kenway et al. (1999) write about 'the sorts of femininities which unwittingly underwrite hegemonic masculinity' (p. 120). Certainly, the 'girlies', with their 'emphasised femininity' (Connell, 1987, p. 187), were heavily involved in gender work which even at the age of 7 inscribed traditional heterosexual relations. Paul Connolly (1998) describes the ways in which sexual orientation and relations defined through boyfriends and girlfriends seems to provide an important source of identity for young children. This was certainly the case for the 'girlies'. These girls were intensely active in the work of maintaining conventional heterosexual relationships through the writing of love letters, flirting and engaging in regular discussions of who was going out with whom. They were far more active in such maintenance work than the boys.

Both the 'girlies' and the 'nice girls' were subject to 'discourses of denigration' circulating among the wider peer group (Blackmore, 1999, p. 136). In individual interviews, many of the boys and a number of the other girls accounted for the 'nice girls'' unpopularity by describing them as 'boring' and 'not fun to be with', while the 'girlies' were variously described by boys as 'stupid' and 'dumb'. While the boys were drawing on a male peer group discourse which positioned the 'girlies' as less intelligent than they were, the 'girlies' were far from 'stupid' or 'dumb'. Although not as scholarly as the 'nice girls', they were educationally productive and generally achieved more highly than their working-class male counterparts. Rather, the working class discourse of conventional femininity within which they were enmeshed operated to elide their academic achievement within the peer group.

Discourses of conventional femininity also seemed to have consequences for the two Asian girls in the class. Amrit, who was Indian, was from a middle-class background while Shamina was Bengali and working class. Yet, both girls, despite their class differences, shared a high degree of circumscription in relation to the range of femininities available to them in the school context. As Shamina explained, 'the spice girls and the tomboys are naughty. I am a good girl'. In contrast to the other girls in the girls' focus group discussion, who all claimed to enjoy playing football, both Shamina and Amrit asserted that 'football was a boys' game', and Amrit said, 'It's not worth bothering with football. It's too boring. Me and my friends just sit on the benches and talk'.

Heidi Mirza (1992) argues that the cultural construction of femininity among African-Caribbean girls fundamentally differs from the forms of femininity found among their white peers. In the case of Amrit and Shamina, there were substantial areas of overlap rather than fundamental differences. However, neither managed to carve out spaces in which to escape gender subordination from the boys in the ways that the 'spice girls' and the 'tomboys', both all-white groups, did. Racism and its impact on subjectivities may well be an issue here. Although it is impossible to make generalisations on the basis of two children, ethnicity, as well as class, appears to be an important consideration in the possibilities and performance of different femininities.

Membership of the 'spice girls' revolved around two white, working-class girls, Carly and Debbie. Jenny, Rachel, Alice and Lisa were less consistently members of the group. Lisa and Alice would sometimes claim to be 'tomboys' while Jenny and Rachel, when playing and spending time with the 'girlies', and especially when Carly and Debbie were in trouble with adults in the school, would realign themselves as 'girlies'. Very occasionally, when she had quarrelled both with Carly and Debbie, and with Jodie, the one consistent tomboy among the girls, Alice too would reinvent herself as a 'girlie'.

Although there were many overlaps between both the practices and the membership of the 'girlies' and the 'spice girls', aspects of the 'spice girls'' interaction with the boys appeared to transgress prevailing gender regimes, while the 'girlies' behaviour followed a far more conformist pattern. Yet, the 'spice girls' were, for much of the time, also active in constructing and maintaining traditional variants of heterosexuality. Their espousal of 'girl power' did not exclude enthusiastic partaking of the boyfriend/girlfriend games. There was much flirting, letter writing, falling in and out of love and talk of broken hearts. However, they also operated beyond the boundaries of the 'girlies' more conformist behaviour when it came to interaction with the boys. Debbie and Carly, the most stalwart members of the 'spice girls', both described the same activity – rating the boys – as their favourite playground game. As Carly explained, 'you follow the boys around and give them a mark out of ten for how attractive they are'.

The 'spice girls'' adherence to so-called girl power also allowed them to make bids for social power never contemplated by the 'girlies' or the 'nice girls'. During a science lesson which involved experiments with different foodstuffs, including a bowl of treacle, Carly and Debbie jointly forced David's hand into the bowl because, as Carly asserted, 'he is always showing off, making out he knows all the answers'. This incident, which reduced David to tears and shocked the other children, served to confirm the class teacher in her view that the two girls 'were a bad lot'. The 'girls with attitude' stance that Carly and Debbie so valued and their philosophy of 'giving as good as they got' were reinterpreted by adults in the school as both inappropriate and counterproductive to learning. Paul Connolly (1998) points out that girls' assertive or disruptive behaviour tends to be interpreted more negatively than similar behaviour in boys, while Robin Lakoff (1975) has described how, when little girls 'talk rough' like the boys do, they will normally be ostracised, scolded or made fun of. For the 'spice girls', 'doing it for themselves' in ways which ran counter to traditional forms of femininity resulted in them being labelled at various times by teachers in the staffroom as 'real bitches', 'a bad influence' and 'little cows'. The tendency Clarricoates found in 1978 for girls' misbehaviour to be 'looked upon as a character defect, whilst boys' misbehaviour is viewed as a desire to assert themselves' was just as evident in teachers' discourses more than 20 years later.

Debbie and Carly were doubly invidiously positioned in relation to the 'girls as mature discourse'. They were perceived to be 'too mature', as 'far too knowing sexually' within adult discourses circulating in the school but they were also seen, unlike the boys and the majority of the girls in 3R, as 'spiteful' and 'scheming little madams' for indulging in behaviour typical of many of the boys. There were several incidents in the playground of sexual harassment of girls by a small group of boys. Most of the adults dismissed these as 'boys mucking about'. However, Carly and Debbie's attempts to invert regular processes of gender objectification, in which girls are routinely the objects of a male gaze, were interpreted by teachers as signs of 'an unhealthy preoccupation with sex'. Their predicament exemplifies the dilemma for girls of 'seeking out empowering places within regimes alternatively committed to denying subordination or celebrating it' (Hey, 1997, p. 132). In this classroom, girls like Carly and Debbie seemed to tread a fine line between acceptable and unacceptable 'girl power' behaviour. Overt heterosexuality was just about on the acceptable side of the line but retaliatory behaviour towards the boys was not.

Valerie Walkerdine (1997) describes how playful and assertive girls come to be understood as overmature and too precocious. Girls like Debbie and Carly, no less than the girls in Walkerdine's advertisements, occupy a space where girls have moved beyond being 'nice' or 'girlie'. Rather, as sexual little women, they occupy a space where they can be bad. As Walkerdine points out, while it is certainly a space in which they can be exploited, it provides a space of power for little girls, although one which is also subject to discourses of denigration. The forms that denigration takes are very different to those experienced by the 'nice girls' or the 'girlies' but become apparent in teachers' judgements of the two girls' behaviour.

'It's better being a boy' – the tomboys

The most intriguing case in my research was that of the 'tomboys'. The 'tomboys' in Becky Francis's research study were depicted by another girl in the class as traitors to girlhood:

> Rather than rejecting the aspiration to maleness because it is 'wrong' or 'unnatural', Zoe argues that 'girls are good enough', implying that her girlfriends want to be boys because they see males as superior, and that she is defending girlhood against this sexist suggestion.
>
> (Francis, 1998, p. 36)

As I have touched on earlier in the article, in 3R, there was a general assumption among the boys that maleness, if not a superior subject positioning, was a more desirable one. While, in particular the 'spice girls', but also at various times both the 'girlies' and 'nice girls' defended girlhood against such claims, their stance was routinely undermined by the position adopted by the tomboys.

Jodie was the only girl in the class who was unwavering in her certainty that she was not a girl but a 'tomboy', although a couple of the other girls in the class for periods of time decided that they were also 'tomboys':

JODIE: Girls are crap, all the girls in this class act all stupid and girlie.
DIANE: So does that include you?
JODIE: No, cos I'm not a girl, I'm a tomboy.

On the one hand, Jodie could be viewed as a budding 'masculinised new woman at ease with male attributes' (Wilkinson, 1999, p. 37). Yet, her rejection of all things feminine could also be seen to suggest a degree of shame and fear of femininity. Jodie even managed to persuade Wayne and Darren, two of the boys in the class, to confirm her male status. Both, at different times, sought me out to tell me Jodie was 'really a boy'. It is difficult to know how to theorise such disruptions of normative gender positionings. Jodie's stance combines elements of resistance with recognition. She clearly recognised and responded to prevailing gender hierarchies which situate being male with having more power and status. Jodie appears to operate at the boundaries where femininity meets masculinity. She is what Barrie Thorne calls 'active at the edges'.

However, while Thorne reports that it was rarely used among her fourth and fifth graders, the term 'tomboy' is frequently used in 3M as a marker of respect by both boys and girls. Being a 'tomboy' seems to guarantee male friendship and male respect. Several of the working-class girls in the class, like Alice, appeared to move easily from taking up a position as a 'tomboy' through to assuming a 'girls with attitude' stance alongside Debbie and Carly to becoming a 'girlie' and back again. One week Alice would come to school in army fatigues with her hair scraped back, the next, in lycra with elaborately painted nails and carefully coiffured hair. However, Alice was unusual among the girls in ranging across a number of subject positions. For most of the girls, although they had choices, those choices seemed heavily circumscribed and provided little space for manoeuvre.

The regulatory aspects of the 'girlies' and the 'nice girls'' self-production as feminine were very apparent, yet the conformity of the 'tomboys' to prevailing gender regimes was far more hidden. While it is important to recognise the transgressive qualities of identifying and rejecting traditional notions of femininity in Jodie's behaviour, the empowering aspects of being a 'tomboy' also masked deeply reactionary features embedded in assuming such a gender position. Implicit in the concept of 'tomboy' is a devaluing of traditional notions of femininity, a railing against the perceived limitations of being female. This is particularly apparent in Jodie's comments:

JODIE: I don't really have any friends who are girls cos they don't like doing the things I like doing. I like football and stuff like that.
DIANE: Don't girls like football?
JODIE: Yeah, some of them, but they're no good at it.

Perhaps, in part, it is Jodie's obsession with football that contributes to her contradictory gender positionings. As Christine Skelton (1999) points out, there is a close association between football and hegemonic masculinities and, therefore, if Jodie is to be seen as 'a football star', she needs to assume a male rather than a female subject positioning.

But there is another possible reading in which Jodie's preoccupation with football facilitates, rather than is the cause of, her flight from femininity. Michelle Fine and Pat Macpherson define girls' identification with football as 'both a flight from femininity...and an association of masculinity with fairness, honesty, integrity and strength (Fine and Macpherson, 1992, p. 197). The girls in their study would call each others boys as a compliment: 'Girls can be good, bad or – best of all – they can be boys' (p. 200) and this was definitely a viewpoint Jodie adhered to. Jodie's individualised resistance can be set alongside Carly and Debbie's joint efforts to disrupt prevailing gender orders among the peer group. Yet, paradoxically, Jodie, no less than the 'girlies', seemed engaged in a process of accommodating the boys. The means of accommodation may differ but the compliance with existing gender regimes remains. Madeline Arnot (1982) writes of the ways in which boys maintain the hierarchy of social superiority of masculinity by devaluing the female world. In 3R, Jodie was also involved in this maintenance work. Although her practices are not rooted in subordination to the boys, she is still acquiescent in prevailing gender hierarchies. Her practices, no less than those of the 'girlies' and the 'nice girls', are confirmatory of male superiority.

Connell writes that 'it is perfectly logical to talk about masculine women or masculinity in women's lives, as well as men's' (Connell, 1995, p. 163). However, so-called 'masculine' girls do not seem to disrupt but rather appear to endorse existing gender hierarchies. All the girls at various times were acting in ways which bolstered the boys' power at the expense of their own. Even Jodie's performance of a surrogate masculinity works to cement rather than transform the gender divide. As a consequence, the radical aspects of transgressive femininities like those of Jodie's are undermined by their implicit compliance with gender hierarchies. Being one of the boys seems to result in greater social power but it conscripts Jodie into processes Sharon Thompson (1994) identifies as 'raging misogyny'. In my field notes, there are 16 examples of Jodie asserting that 'boys are better than girls'. Jodie's case is an extreme example of the ways in which girls' ventriloquising of the dominant culture's denigration of femininity and female relations can serve to disconnect them from other girls (Brown, 1998).

Conclusion

Performing gender is not straightforward; rather, it is confusing. The seduction of binaries such as male:female, boy:girl often prevents us from seeing the full range of diversity and differentiation existing within one gender as well as between categories of male and female. Both the girls and boys in 3R were actively involved in the production of gendered identities, constructing gender through a variety and range of social processes (Kerfoot and Knight, 1994). Yet, within this 'gender work', social and cultural differences generate the particular toolkit of cultural resources individual children have availablity to them. There is a multiplicity of femininities and masculinities available in this primary classroom. But this is not to suggest that these children have myriad choices of which variant of femininity and masculinity to assume. They do not. Class, ethnicity and emergent sexualities all play their part, and constrain as well as create options.

Pyke argues that:

> Hierarchies of social class, race and sexuality provide additional layers of complication. They form the structural and cultural contexts in which gender is enacted in everyday life, thereby fragmenting gender into multiple masculinities and femininities.
>
> (Pyke, 1996, p. 531)

Yet, despite the multiple masculinities and femininities manifested in 3R, there is evidence of hegemonic masculinity in this classroom no less than outside in the wider social world. Within such a context, it makes sense for girls to seek to resist traditional discourses of subordinate femininity. Yet, attempting to take up powerful positions through articulation with, and investment in, dominant masculinities serves to reinforce rather than transform the gender divide. As a consequence, the prevailing gender order is only occasionally disrupted, in particular by the 'spice girls' through their sex play and objectification of a number of the boys and also, paradoxically, through their working-class status. Unlike the 'nice girls' whose activities are circumscribed through being positioned by the boys as a contagious, polluting other, the 'spice girls'' positioning as 'rough' in relation to sensitive middle-class boys allows them to take up a 'polluting' assignment (Douglas, 1966) and use it as a weapon to intimidate the boys.

The girls' struggle to make meaning of themselves as female constitutes a struggle in which gendered peer group hierarchies such as those in 3R position boys as 'better' despite a mass of evidence to show they are neither as academically successful nor as well behaved as girls in the classroom. Peer group discourses constructed girls as harder working, more mature and more socially skilled. Yet, all the boys and a significant number of the girls, if not subscribing to the view that boys are better, adhered to the view that it is better being a boy. There are clearly confusions within the gender work in this classroom. To talk of dominant femininity is to generate a contradiction in terms because it is dominant versions of femininity which subordinate the girls to the boys. Rather, transgressive discourses and the deviant femininities they generate like Jodie's 'tomboy' and Debbie and Carly's espousal of 'girl power' accrue power in both the male and female peer group, and provide spaces for girls to escape gender subordination by the boys.

On the surface, gender relations in this classroom are continually churned up and realigned in a constant process of recomposition. But beneath, at a more subterranean level of knowing and making sense, both boys and girls seem to operate with entrenched dispositions in which being a boy is still perceived to be the more preferable subject positioning. Despite the contemporary focus, both within and without the classroom, on 'girl power' (Arlidge, 1999), as Jean Anyon (1983) found almost 20 years ago, it appears that girls' subversions and transgressions are nearly always contained within, and rarely challenge, the existing structures. For much of the time, girls are 'trapped in the very contradictions they would transcend'. Girls' contestation may muddy the surface water of gender relations, but the evidence of this classroom indicates that the ripples only occasionally reach the murky depths of the prevailing gender order. Within both the localised and dominant discourses that these children draw on, being a boy is still seen as best by all the boys and a significant number of the girls.

Children may both create and challenge gender structures and meanings. However, for much of the time for a majority of the girls and boys in 3R, gender either operates as opposition or hierarchy or most commonly both at the same time. As Janet Holland and her colleagues found in relation to the adolescents in their study, the girls just as much as the boys in this class were 'drawn into making masculinity powerful' (Holland *et al.*, 1998, p. 30).The contemporary orthodoxy that girls are doing better than boys masks the complex messiness of gender relations in which, despite girls' better educational attainment, within this peer group, the prevalent view is still that it's better being a boy.

Despite the all-pervading focus on narrow, easily measured, learning outcomes in British state schooling, learning in classrooms is much wider than test results suggest. While test results indicate that girls are more successful educationally than boys, it appears that in this primary classroom girls and boys still learn many of the old lessons of gender relations which work against gender equity. Sue Heath (1999, p. 293) argues that there is a need for school-based work that sensitively addresses issues of gender identity and masculinities within a pro-feminist framework. There is also an urgent need for work that addresses the construction and performance of femininities.

REFERENCES

Anyon, J. (1983) 'Intersections of gender and class: accommodation and resistance by working-class and affluent females to contradictory sex-role ideologies', in S. Walker and L. Barton (eds), *Gender, Class and Education* (Lewes, Falmer Press).

Arlidge, J. (1999) 'Girl power gives boys a crisis of confidence', *Sunday Times*, 14 March.

Arnot, M. (1982) 'Male hegemony, social class and women's education', *Journal of Education*, 16: 64–89.

Arnot, M., David, M. and Weiner, G. (1999) *Closing the Gender Gap: Postwar Education and Social Change* (Cambridge, Polity Press).

Ball, S.J. (1994) *Educational Reform* (Buckingham, Open University Press).

Bennett, C. (1996) 'The boys with the wrong stuff', *Guardian*, 6 November.

Blackmore, J. (1999) *Troubling Women: Feminism, Leadership and Educational Change* (Buckingham, Open University Press).

Brown, L.M. (1998) *Raising Their Voices: The Politics of Girls' Anger* (Cambridge, MA, Harvard University Press).

Clarricoates, K. (1978) 'Dinosaurs in the classroom – a re-examination of some aspects of the "hidden" curriculum in primary schools', *Women's Studies International Forum*, 1: 353–364.

Connell, R.W. (1987) *Gender and Power* (Sydney, Allen & Unwin).

Connell, R.W. (1995) *Masculinities* (Cambridge, Polity Press).

Connolly, P. (1998) *Racism, Gender Identities and Young Children* (London, Routledge).

Coward, R. (1999) 'The feminist who fights for the boys', *Sunday Times*, 20 June.

Davies, B. (1993) *Shards of Glass* (Sydney, Allen & Unwin).

Davies, P., Williams, J. and Webb, S. (1997) 'Access to higher education in the late twentieth century: policy, power and discourse', in J. Williams (ed.), *Negotiating Access to Higher Education* (Buckingham, Open University Press).

Douglas, M. (1966) *Purity and Danger: An Analysis of Concepts of Pollution and Taboo* (London, Routledge & Kegan Paul).

Epstein, D., Elwood, J., Hey, V. and Maw, J. (1998) *Failing Boys? Issues in Gender and Achievement* (Buckingham, Open University Press).

Fine, M. and Macpherson, P. (1992) 'Over dinner: feminism and adolescent female bodies', in M. Fine (ed.), *Disruptive Voices: The Possibilities of Feminist Research* (Ann Arbor, MI, University of Michigan Press).

Francis, B. (1998) *Power Plays: Primary School Children's Construction of Gender, Power and Adult Work* (Stoke-on-Trent, Trentham Books).

Francis, B. (1999) 'Modernist reductionism or post-structuralist relativism: can we move on? An evaluation of the arguments in relation to feminist educational research', *Gender and Education*, 11: 381–394.

Heath, S. (1999) 'Watching the backlash: the problematisation of young women's academic success in 1990's Britain', *Discourse*, 20: 249–266.

Hey, V. (1997) *The Company She Keeps: An Ethnography of Girls' Friendship* (Buckingham, Open University Press).

Holland, J., Ramazanoglu, C., Sharpe, S. and Thomson, R. (1998) *The Male in the Head: Young People, Heterosexuality and Power* (London, Tufnell Press).

Gee, J.P., Hull, G. and Lankshear, C. (1996) *The New Work Order* (London, Allen & Unwin).

Griffin, C. (1995) 'Absences that matter: constructions of sexuality in studies of young women friendship groups', paper presented at the *Celebrating Women's Friendship Conference*, Alcuin College, University of York, 8 April.

Jackson, D. (1998) 'Breaking out of the binary trap: boys' underachievement, schooling and gender relations', in D. Epstein, J. Elwood, V. Hey and J. Maw (eds), *Failing Boys? Issues in Gender and Achievement* (Buckingham, Open University Press).

James, A., Jenks, C. and Prout, A. (1998) *Theorising Childhood* (Cambridge, Polity Press).

Jones, A. (1993) 'Becoming a "girl": post-structuralist suggestions for educational research', *Gender and Education*, 5: 157–166.

Katz, A. (1999) 'Crisis of the "low can-do" boys', *Sunday Times*, 21 March.

Kenway, J. (1995) 'Masculinities in schools: under siege, on the defensive and under reconstruction', *Discourse*, 16: 59–79.

Kenway, J., Willis, S., Blackmore, J. and Rennie, L. (1999) *Answering Back: Girls, Boys and Feminism in Schools* (London, Routledge).

Kerfoot, D. and Knight, D. (1994) 'Into the realm of the fearful: identity and the gender problematic', in H.L. Radtke and H.J. Stam (eds), *Power/Gender: Social Relations in Theory and Practice* (London, Sage).

Lakoff, R.T. (1975) *Language and Woman's Place* (New York, Harper & Row).

Lucey, H. and Walkerdine, V. (1999) 'Boys' underachievement: social class and changing masculinities', in T. Cox (ed.), *Combating Educational Disadvantage* (London, Falmer Press).

Mac an Ghaill, M. (1988) *Young, Gifted and Black: Student–Teacher Relations in the Schooling of Black Youth* (Buckingham, Open University Press).

Maclure, M. (1994) 'Language and discourse: the embrace of uncertainty', *British Journal of Sociology of Education*, 15: 283–300.

Mirza, S.H. (1992) *Young, Female and Black* (London, Routledge).

Pattman, R. and Phoenix, A. (1999) 'Constructing self by constructing the "other": 11–14 year old boys' narratives of girls and women', paper presented at the *Gender and Education Conference*, University of Warwick, 29–31 March.

Pyke, K.D. (1996) 'Class-based masculinities: the interdependence of gender, class and interpersonal power', *Gender & Society*, 10: 527–549.

Reay, D. (1990) 'Working with boys', *Gender and Education*, 2: 269–282.

Sewell, T. (1997) *Black Masculinities and Schooling: How Black Boys Survive Modern Schooling* (Stoke-on-Trent, Trentham Books).

Skelton, C. (1997) 'Primary boys and hegemonic masculinities', *British Journal of Sociology of Education*, 18: 349–369.

Skelton, C. (1999) '"A passion for football": dominant masculinities and primary schooling', paper presented to the *British Educational Research Association Conference*, University of Sussex, 2–5 September.

Smithers, R. (1999) 'Self-esteem the key for macho boys who scorn "uncool" school', *Guardian*, 16 March.

Thompson, S. (1994) 'What friends are for: on girls' misogyny and romantic fusion', in J. Irvine (ed.), *Sexual Cultures and the Construction of Adolescent Identities* (Philadelphia, PA, Temple University Press).

Thorne, B. (1993) *Gender Play: Girls and Boys in School* (Buckingham, Open University Press).

Walkerdine, V. (1991) *Schoolgirl Fictions* (London, Verso).

Walkerdine, V. (1997) *Daddy's Girl: Young Girls and Popular Culture* (London, Macmillan).

Walkerdine, V., Lucey, H. and Melody, J. (2000) 'Class, attainment and sexuality in late twentieth-century Britain', in C. Zmroczek and P. Mahony (eds), *Women and Social Class: International Feminist Perspectives* (London: UCL Press).

Weiner, G., Arnot, M. and David, M. (1997) 'Is the future female? Female success, male disadvantage and changing gender patterns in education', in A.H. Halsey, P. Brown, H. Lauder and A. Stuart-Wells (eds), *Education: Culture, Economy and Society* (Oxford, Oxford University Press).

Wight, D. (1996) 'Beyond the predatory male: the diversity of young Glaswegian men's discourses to describe heterosexual relationships', in L. Adkins and V. Merchant (eds), *Sexualising the Social: Power and the Organisation of Sexuality* (London, Macmillan).

Wilkinson, H. (1994) *No Turning Back: Generations and the Genderquake* (London, Demos).

Wilkinson, H. (1999) 'The Thatcher legacy: power feminism and the birth of girl power', in N. Walters (ed.), *On the Move – Feminism for a New Generation* (London, Virago).

Williams, J. (ed.) (1997) *Negotiating Access to Higher Education* (Buckingham, Open University Press).

Willis, P. (1977) *Learning to Labour: How Working Class Kids Get Working Class Jobs* (Farnborough, Saxon House).

Yates, L. (1997) 'Gender equity and the boys debate: what sort of challenge is it?', *British Journal of Sociology of Education*, 18: 337–348.

FIVE

REPRODUCING TRADITIONAL FEMININITIES? THE SOCIAL RELATIONS OF 'SPECIAL EDUCATIONAL NEEDS' IN A GIRLS' COMPREHENSIVE SCHOOL

Shereen Benjamin

Source: 'Reproducing traditional femininities? The social relations of "special educational needs" in a girls' comprehensive school', *Gender and Education*, 14(3): 281–294, 2002.

Introduction

MEERA: When I got, when I got, when I did my SATs (standard assessment tasks) and I got Level 2 my Mum, she cried, well, she didn't cry, she was like 'Oh no' and I, and people think, and I think like when you can't read, like 2 on your SATs, I think, people think like you're dumb...And when you go in your secondary school, at first you're like, 'this is gonna be easy' and you like put your hand up all the time in class, you're like 'Miss, Miss pick me' and then you like – when like you still ain't good in reading, like still, um, still 2 on your SATs, when Miss, you're like all the time with your arm over your work when Miss goes past, um, you're like hiding, 'cause when Miss sees you, she's like, um, she *might* tell you off, or she's like 'You poor thing, I'll help you' and then everyone, like, everyone sees, and they're all like 'Meera's dumb', like 'Meera can't read and Miss has to help her' so you're with your arm over your work, you're all hiding like Miss doesn't see, and sometimes Miss doesn't see you.

Current schooling policy in the UK and elsewhere foregrounds the raising of student achievement to normative levels as measured by examination performance (Slee *et al.*, 1998; Carrington, 1999; Department for Education and Employment

(DfEE), 1999a,b; Bines, 2000). How is this emphasis on normative levels of attainment lived by school students to whom those levels of attainment are inaccessible? And how are other indices of difference – including those of class, ethnicity and gender/sexuality – articulated in that lived experience? This article uses some of the findings of a larger ethnographic study to examine aspects of the 'identity work' of a group of girls in their first year (Year 7) at secondary school. These 11 and 12-year-olds had all been identified as having 'special educational needs' (SEN) and they had all failed to perform according to the 'expected standard for their age' (DfEE, 1999a,b) in the statutory tests taken at the end of their primary schooling. As I will show, these students do not recognise, or apply to themselves, the much-critiqued SEN terminology. Nevertheless, in its production of what staff routinely refer to as 'special needs students', the school constructs a specific subject position that the girls are required to inhabit. The production of this subject position is associated with the identification of individual 'difficulties' and their conversion into 'needs' that can be met. Its production also serves to separate and hierarchise young people according to their perceived academic ability. This article looks at how nine girls actively negotiate the identity resources prescribed and proscribed through their inscription as 'special needs students'. It looks in particular at the links between certain traditional versions of femininity and the charity/tragedy model of disability, and their implications for the girls' identity work.

Meadway School for Girls (not its real name) is a comprehensive school in an English city. It is in many ways a successful school, performing well in local league tables of school performance, and popular with its local multi-ethnic community. It has a strong tradition of work in equal opportunities, and its staff are proud of the school's anti-sexist and anti-racist ethos and initiatives. I had worked at Meadway as a learning support teacher for two years before embarking on ethnographic research in the school, and I had become increasingly concerned that the students with whom I worked – known in the staffroom as the 'special needs students' – occupied a difficult position. They had to find a way to negotiate the school's overt promises that 'girls can do anything' alongside the hard evidence of their own failure in norm-referenced examinations. This article examines how the standards agenda of current policy, Meadway's own micro-politics, student micro-cultures and the wider systemic politics of class, gender and ethnicity combine to produce the identity resources used by the girls. I look at three of the identifications on offer to the girls as they perform their identity work, and show how these are very clearly linked, through notions of vulnerability and dependence, to some very traditional versions of 'femininity'.

The production of 'special needs students'

SHAZIA: Why do you want to know what we think, Miss? I mean, 'cause we don't know nothing, we're just all the stupid girls, we don't know nothing to say, there's lots of girls in my class, they know what to think, you should talk to them.

SB: I'm interested – I really am – I think you've got lots of, um, interesting things to say, I do.

FOZIA: Why did you, why did we get choosed?

SB: Well, um, you know when Mr Elliott wrote to your parents saying you were on the special needs register, that you would get extra help, I decided I wanted to talk to some girls who were on the school special needs register, and see what they thought about the school.

FOZIA: What's special needs register? I ain't never heard of it.

SHAZIA: It's for all the stupid girls, so you can take a register like in registration, only not, so you know who is all the stupid girls, so they can all go like on one side, when you take a register of all the dumb girls.

Since 1994, schools in England and Wales have been required to identify those of their students who are considered to have 'SEN', and to compile registers of such students for their own use and for official statistics (DfEE, 1994). Fozia and Shazia appear to have the haziest of notions about that register and its functions. This in part speaks to an adult reluctance to use the designation 'special educational needs' – which, as Corbett notes, 'is becoming a most unacceptable term' (1996, p. 2) – in front of the girls so designated. Since its inception (Warnock, 1978) and its establishment in the UK in the 1981 Education Act, the terminology of 'special needs' has become saturated with the shame and fear associated with perceived intellectual disability (Skrtic, 1995; Corbett, 1998; Slee, 1998). This shame and fear takes a particular form in relation to current school policy, and to Meadway's aspirations for itself and its students. The position of 'special needs student' implicitly refers to failure to make academic progress according to the norms constructed by the standards agenda. These are the students who enter the school having already failed to reach the 'expected standard for their age' (DfEE, 1999a,b) and who will not achieve the 'good' results in external examinations at age 16 on which Meadway's top place in the league tables depends. But such failure cannot be named, especially in a school such as Meadway with its emphasis on 'success for all'.

Since inscription into discourses of 'SEN' is so irretrievably shameful, and so difficult to voice, Meadway's teachers tend to confine the term itself to staffroom use. Outside of the staffroom, the 'special needs student' is awkwardly and uncomfortably euphemised as the 'student who needs extra help'. Riddell and her colleagues argue that no positive identification exists for people considered to have learning difficulties (Riddell et al., 1998), and that the rationale behind the practices that group such people together is hidden from them. 'Special needs students' in school likewise have no positive identifications available. They have to make some sort of sense of their inscription into the discursive practices of SEN out of the silences and euphemisms that characterise the discourse. Whilst I agree with the many critiques of 'special' terminology that exist, I would want to retain the term in specific contexts, for the strategic purposes of illuminating the continuing reproduction of material and relational inequalities in which it plays a part.

The apparently much more pejorative 'stupid' and 'dumb' seem to make much more sense to Fozia and Shazia, and to be more useful to them, than does the apparently neutral 'SEN' terminology. But what looks at first like straightforward misunderstanding could also indicate that, on some levels, Shazia has uncovered some of the reactionary purposes underlying that supposed neutrality. One reading of Shazia's interpretation of the special needs register would suggest that she is aware of how she is positioned as part of a deviant group, its deviance subject to heightened adult surveillance. In the SEN context, as in many others, surveillance contains a cocktail of meanings related to both governmentality and care.

Allan (1999) argues that 'surveillance of pupils with special needs enables professionals to show their concern for their welfare and acquire knowledge about their condition and the progress they are making. It also constructs them as objects of power and knowledge' (p. 21). This process – of constructing the 'special needs student' through her inscription into psycho-educational discourses of intrinsic need and professional benevolence – is thoroughly gendered. Into the production of the 'special needs student' is encoded her dependence on a professional (or group of professionals) who can operate the technical machinery of identification and assessment from a position of caring for the needy. This link between 'neediness' and governmentality is important, especially in the current schooling context. The educational 'needs' of a girl who has been identified as having SEN must (according to prevailing understandings of schooling) be managed more carefully than those of other students through the rational (and therefore traditionally masculine) apparatus of monitoring and target-setting. But the framework for meeting those needs is the traditionally feminine realm of care and compassion for the vulnerable. The two combine to produce a version of dependence that is almost impossible to resist.

The Year 7 'special needs students' are thus offered a subject position that is highly problematic from the outset. It is a position that inscribes the girls within a bureaucratised regime of governmentality legitimated through benevolent humanitarianism (Tomlinson, 1982; Slee, 1995). Whilst they can and do refuse to recognise the label 'special needs student', and whilst all members of the school community can and mostly do refuse to address them as such within their hearing, the girls nevertheless have to position themselves in relation to the discursive practices that produce them as 'special needs students'. To understand how these work with traditional versions of femininity, it is necessary to look to the charity/tragedy model of disability (Stone, 1995; Ervelles, 1996; Allan, 1999; Biklen, 2000). The association of intellectual disability with helplessness, dependence and childlikeness resonates strongly with those understandings of femininity that have positioned generations of women as helpless, dependent and childlike, and have helped to hold in place hetero/patriarchal relations of domination and subordination. It is in the identity work of girls and young women who have been institutionally identified as 'special needs students' that we can see these notions of perpetual vulnerability working to reproduce similarly reactionary relations and practices.

'Sweet little girls'

For the eight Year 7 girls who took part in this study, their inscription into SEN discourses and their experience of failure according to the dominant standards agenda has been central in shaping the sets of identity resources to which they have had access. But these resources can only be understood in the context of their articulation with other axes of difference, most notably those of class, ethnicity, gender/sexuality and physical appearance. All of the Year 7 participants in this study are invested, to some extent, in producing themselves as compliant, hardworking students. None of them overtly rejects what she perceives to be the academic or disciplinary aims of the school. Already, however, they are beginning to be recognisable as members of one of three distinct categories: 'sweet little girls', 'big bad girls' or 'lazy girls'. I would want to introduce a note of caution here, though. In using this well-worn sociological device of identifying distinct pupil cultures, I would not want to suggest that the positions I have delineated are fixed or immutable, or that any of the participants had a completely unitary or uncontested position within any one of them. They are 'tendencies' rather than inevitabilities.

Fozia, Shazia and Ambrine tend to produce themselves as the 'sweet little girls' of the group. All are of Asian origin and are observant Muslims. In his work with young children, Connolly (1998) notes the tendency for boys and girls of South Asian origin to be infantilised, and referred to by teachers and others as 'little'. This tendency would appear to be working with their gender, physical appearance and perceived intellectual ability to interpellate these three girls into the hyper-feminine 'sweet little girl' subject position. All three are physically small for their age, and they code themselves as childlike. They wear shoes with low or no heels, they do not use make-up, and they specialise in a shy version of a smile, whilst looking down at the floor to suggest submission and eagerness to please. Like many of the Muslim students, they wear shalwar kameez, and Fozia also covers her head. But whereas many of the Muslim girls at Meadway manage to play with the dress code, these girls present themselves as completely desexualised, and, in both interviews and informal conversations, made clear the distance between themselves and the hetero/sexualised Other girls.

The 'sweet little girl' position is in many ways an obvious one for 'special needs girls' to take up. The official version of 'special needs student' overlaps with the charity/tragedy discourse of disability to construct them as people who are child-like, vulnerable and 'needy' of help. Given the infantilisation of Asian students, the likelihood that an Asian 'special needs student' will be recognised by teachers and other girls as a 'sweet little girl' is strong. This is not to say that *only* Asian girls can be recognised as such, or that this is the only position available to Asian 'special needs students' but that Asianness nuances and shapes the identity resources available to and desirable by girls of varying ethnic backgrounds.

Student microcultures are an important site for the production of the 'sweet little girl'. Many of these girls find the hurly-burly of the microcultural work that goes on amongst their peers difficult to understand and often frightening:

FOZIA: They shouldn't let you out of lessons. There's some girls, they go out, they say they have to go out to the toilet, and then they go out and meet their friends and they do their hair, and talk about who's got what boyfriend. They didn't want to go to the toilet, but they're in there, and when you have to go, yeah, like if you really want to go to the toilet, and you got out of lessons, and they're all in there, and when they're doing their hair, you go in there, and it's sort of embarrassing, and you're all like 'Oh no, I don't wanna be in here'.

SHAZIA: And you think they're all looking at you, like, 'What are you doing in here?' yeah, and, um, when I went out of maths that time, and I was really like, I really needed to go, and I didn't even dare go in, and I was waiting round the corner, um, in the students' bit, you know, and I'm thinking like, I don't know what to do – um . . .

FOZIA: And you wish a teacher would come and um, and tell them they have to go to their lessons. It would be better if they didn't let you out, 'cause some girls, they just do their hair, and, you know, um, talk about their boyfriends, and like where they're going after school, um, and it makes you scared to be in there.

High-speed, high-volume and heterosexually coded ways of doing girl, associated variously with 'girl power' and with transgression against authority, appear to make these girls afraid. Such practices are also in conflict with the values of honour and respect that they hold dear (Bhatti, 1995, 1999). In the accounts of these students, theirs is an altogether gentler, more childlike and apparently more passive version of femininity (Walkerdine, 1989, 1997), and one that positions teachers as powerful allies who will protect and defend them. But this apparent passivity can conceal the fact that the girls have to work actively at producing themselves as 'sweet little girls'.

AMBRINE: In humanities, Sir, he sometimes says, 'Get in groups' and we have to choose, but you can't have more than five 'cause he thinks we'll all be argue, and if you've got like six friends, you're looking at the floor 'cause you want to be with the people what helps you, and me and Asma this time, in humanities, when we was doing about the castles, when Sir said to go in groups, we was both trying to look all sad, and looking at the floor, 'cause it's Gulshan who's in charge, who's always in charge, and she would, um, would only let the person stay who was all sad and who needed help, and if you didn't have needed help, you would have to go in another group, but it was all right because Sir he came over and we was both looking at the floor, me and Asma, we was both looking all sad, and Sir he said we could both stay, me and Asma, if we all did what Gulshan said.

Skeggs (1997) notes that the young women who participated in her study 'usually "did" femininity when they thought it was necessary' (p. 116). It is likely that something similar is happening here. The position of 'sweet little girl' is not without a certain power. These three girls (and others whom I witnessed deploying similar strategies in classrooms) have developed an effective means of eliciting and retaining adult and peer help, which in many instances is crucial if they are to be able to participate in routine classroom activity. But in doing so they are also inscribing themselves into hyperfeminine discourses of vulnerability and dependence.

'Big bad girls'

Kerry and Cheryl, the 'big bad girls' of the group, are both very tall for their age, and both are physically strong and athletic. They wear shoes with high heels, and they flout the school's rules on make-up as openly as they dare, wearing nail polish and transparent or pale lipstick. Both have a reputation for making a lot of noise in class: they are frequently told off for talking or playing about, and moved away from their friends for failing to get on with their work. The position of 'big bad girl' that they are trying to achieve is an oppositional one, resistant of the school's academic ethos and its imperatives to work hard and allow others to work hard at all times. It is, additionally, a hetero/sexualised position, involving students in producing themselves as hetero/sexually active and attractive.

Cheryl and Kerry tend to act in ways that often have disruptive effects on their classes. Kerry comes from an indigenous white working-class background, and Cheryl from a materially impoverished African–Caribbean family. Given that most of the school's teaching staff are white, institutionally positioned as middle class, and academically successful, there are few identifications that Kerry and Cheryl can make with their teachers. They are the Others of the dominant official discourses through which Meadway produces its youngest students: they are Other to the construction of incrementally developing, target-reaching student which Meadway strives to make available and desirable to its students (Walkerdine and Lucey, 1989). They are also Other to the construction of endearing, vulnerable little girl, as they cannot easily be recognised as vulnerable or childlike.

Kerry and Cheryl's positioning as 'big bad girls' is highly unstable, however. It is especially precarious for Cheryl, who, as an autistic girl,[1] does not have access to the microcultural resources that would be necessary to produce herself as hetero/sexually active and attractive. Her position as 'big bad girl' has been achieved more through misrecognition of her intentions than by her active insertion of herself into the discourse. Kerry, too, is unwilling to abandon altogether the possibility of becoming a 'successful' student. She is aware that there may be costs, as well as benefits, in taking up an oppositional position in relation to the school's official agenda. But hers is not a rational analysis of the costs and benefits. During a paired interview, I asked her to role-play a 'failing student'. In this role-play, she presented the 'big bad girl' as both the dangerous and undesirable Other, and as a natural option for a 'girl like me'. Later in the interview, she talked through the decisions she had made in the course of the role-play:

KERRY: My girl was called Anne, and she was wearing a black mini-skirt, a black mini-skirt all the way up to here [indicates and grimaces, apparently indicating distaste], and black tights, and shoes with heels like this [indicates]. And lipstick, loads of lipstick, she puts it on after line-up. She's bad [grimaces again]. She was in English, and she wasn't listening to what the teacher said, she was all the time writing, but it wasn't English, it was to her friend, it was about their boyfriends that evening and after school. And her friend, she wanted to listen to what the teacher was saying, but she couldn't because Anne kept on writing to her a note and saying like, 'Take it, take it', and her friend would have been scared if she hadn't've taked it.

SB: What did she do at lunchtime?

KERRY: In lunchtime, um, she went outside of the gates, and she made her friend go with her, even though her friend didn't want to go, and she said, 'Do we have to' and Anne said, 'Yes you have to come with me to where our boyfriends is'. And Anne's friend she was all scared because she wanted to go to her lessons and she didn't know where their boyfriends worked – did I say that, did I tell you their boyfriends, they worked in – um – they – um, their boyfriends was out at work in, um, somewhere down the High Street. And Anne and her friend, they goes out of the gate when the teacher wasn't looking. Well, the teacher was looking, it was Ms Rivers, but Anne didn't care but her friend she didn't want to get in trouble, she said, 'We can't go, Ms Rivers will see us' but Anne said, 'Yeah, we've got to, the boys are expecting us'. 'Cause Anne had phoned them on her mobile phone, even though you're not supposed to, and she'd said, 'We'll come and see you this afternoon, down the High Street, at where you work'. And so they walked up to the gates and just walked out, and Anne's friend she was like, 'Oh no, Ms Rivers has seen us, and she'll tell the other teachers, and it's science, my favourite subject this afternoon and I wanna go to it' but Anne, she didn't care, like she didn't care who saw her, and missing science, and going to their boyfriends. Even though it's a girls' school and her Mum thought she wouldn't have a boyfriend. And her friend, she didn't want to miss science, and, um, maths, it was maths last lesson, but Anne she didn't care...

SB: Why did you, I mean, why do you think Anne doesn't care?

KERRY: Um, well I think she does care a bit, only she, what she really cares about is her boyfriend, and, um, don't know if I can say this [giggles], she, um, she wants to [pause] *it*, you know, Miss [giggles]. It's not like she doesn't care *at all* about school, but, um, it's her first time and she wants to do *it* with her boyfriend. Ms Rivers isn't going to hear this is she?

SB: No, no, I'm not playing the tape to anyone at school, don't worry. So what I'm wondering, is, if Anne cares a bit about school, well, can you say a bit more about the things she cares about?

KERRY: She does care a bit, but only a bit, and, well, when she was in Year 7, she was just a girl like me, she was just a girl like me, you couldn't tell she was failing, except she was a bit scruffy like me, but then when she got in Year 8 she got fed up of all the teachers going, 'Blah, blah, you aren't getting no better at science, you have to work more harder, you have to do good for your exams, blah, blah' like that. And it just, I dunno, it got on her nerves, 'cause she'd been working hard, she did work hard, well not very hard, but a bit hard, and she just said, 'Well, I ain't gonna do good in exams, 'cause I've been all the time trying, and so I'll just get a boyfriend'. And she just did, and that's all, and that's how she got like she didn't care. But in Year 7, when she was in Year 7 she was just a normal girl like me.

The 'SEN' discourse is one place in which the notion of child-in-danger meets with the notion of child-as-danger (Boyden, 1990; Hunt and Frankenburg, 1990; Walkerdine, 1997). The child-as-danger (as well as the child-in-danger) is a thoroughly classed, gendered and racialised subject: Boyden (1990) shows that one important strategy in the global export (and imposition) of the Western bourgeois version of childhood is the presentation of street children (violent boys and sexually promiscuous girls) as a threat to their communities. Walkerdine (1997) argues that:

> The little working-class girl, produced by and consuming popular culture, becomes a central object of social and moral concern. She is one of the figures (along with the violent boy) who most threatens the safe pastures of natural childhood, a childhood free from adult intervention and abuse, a childhood so carefully constructed as a central fiction of the modern order, the childhood which will ensure the possibility of a liberal democracy.
>
> (p. 4)

Current definitions of 'SEN' seek to encompass both understandings. The child-in-danger is primarily the child with learning difficulties, who can be constructed as vulnerable. The child-as-danger is the student with 'emotional and behavioural difficulties': the student whose effect on classrooms can be disruptive, and who risks becoming 'socially excluded'. Complex elisions and distinctions are made between the two groups at different times in Meadway. But it seems fair to say that staff and students alike go to considerable lengths to avoid recognising Year 7 students as 'child-as-danger'. Ainscow (1999) notes that the current move towards inclusion features a group of pupils and students who would previously have been educated at segregated special schools entering mainstream schools by the front door, whilst others are being bundled out of the back. It is the child-as-danger who finds herself in this second group, although at Meadway, the rate of permanent exclusions is very low. Pressures on schools not to exclude students, teachers' desires not to fail any student and the students' desires for a measure of success in the schooling endeavour combine to make it very problematic for a Year 7 student to take up a 'big bad girl' position. Where the younger girls are concerned, formal identification as child-in-danger tends to override formal identification and informal (mis)recognition as child-as-danger. For a Year 7 'special needs student' who has been identified as having what the school terms 'learning as a primary cause for concern', any oppositional activity will tend to be formally interpreted as proof of further neediness, and will often trigger further offers of support. Kerry and Cheryl are thus simultaneously positioned as child-in-danger and needful of help, and as child-as-danger, and threat to all things traditionally feminine and childlike.

Kerry's ambivalent and problematic investment in doing 'big bad girl', containing as it does something of the quality of a moth flying around a candle flame, also appears to contain the knowledge that she has not fully achieved recognition as a 'big bad girl', and that the act of working to produce herself as such will involve some intensive changes for 'a normal girl like me'. In her description of the role-play she had invented, it could be argued that she identifies both with 'Anne', who once was like her, and with Anne's friend, who is more obviously invested in achieving academic success, and who is even able to find lessons pleasurable. Anne appears to contain the unknown and unknowable desires which only a complete disinvestment from academic endeavour makes accessible. She inhabits a world of dangerous femininities. Anne's friend, on the other hand, contains the longing for the safety provided by investment in the rationally knowable and (so the story goes) controllable world of working for and achieving academic targets. Her world is the traditionally masculine realm of reason and order, whose 'safe pastures', as Walkerdine puts it, are threatened by Anne's disruptions.

The two are irreconcilable: to remain friends with Anne, the unnamed girl must abandon – literally walk out on – her desire for academic success. And she must take a step into what is the complete unknown for both imaginary girls, the enigmatically and euphemistically-coded 'it' of hetero/sexual intercourse in a venue whose precise location remains unspecified. 'Somewhere down the High Street' implies a world that is both more public and more adult than the world of school. The setting is prosaic and everyday, but the ambiguity that surrounds the exact location renders it exotic and mysterious. In Kerry's account, Anne takes with her to the High Street not only her own desires for the exotic and adult world of hetero/sexual activity, but also her friend's desires for academic success. The episode Kerry imagines has something of the quality of a modern-day Cinderella story, a story in which a cocktail of compliance with and rebellion against unreasonable authority brings rescue, romance and fortune. Like Hey's (1997) working-class girl who is able to imagine the public sites of domestic labour as the setting for potential romantic encounters, 'Anne' and her 'friend' make the exotic and adult world of heterosexual activity geo-socially accessible through locating it in working-class female territory (Hey, 1997). But her concluding comments, in which 'Anne' gives up on academic achievement and gets a boyfriend instead, suggest that Kerry does not easily position herself within such a world, viewing it as both second-best to the world of academic achievement, and as mysterious and frightening. Her investment in producing herself as 'big bad girl' is thus configured through an intricate blend of (often contradictory) fears and desires, in relation to a number of equally contradictory discourses of childhood, academic success and femininity, worked through the material conditions of white working-class girlhood. And the context of her investment is a reality in which the discursive practices of 'SEN' pull her away from the dangerous 'big bad girl' version of femininity towards versions that are more dependent and thereby more governable.

'Lazy girls'

Sunna and Meera tend to position themselves as 'lazy girls' (their self-description, shared by many teachers). They are increasingly disconnected from what they perceive as the academic goals of the school. Unlike the 'big bad girls', they do not act in ways that can be interpreted as oppositional to the school's formal agenda and authority, and their effect on classrooms is not disruptive. They are both observant Muslims, and dress in shalwar kameez, but unlike the 'sweet little girls', they augment their uniforms with discreet make-up, and they wear shoes with heels. When speaking to adults, they usually make eye contact, so their general demeanour does not code submission. Josephine, however, does code herself as more submissive, customarily looking at the floor, and appearing to welcome adult support, characteristics more associated with the 'sweet little girls'. However, I would tend to include her in this group for three reasons. First, she describes herself as 'lazy'. Second, she deploys a 'rescue' discourse when talking about her academic struggles. Third, teachers perceive her as 'lazy', although this is often euphemised as a problem of 'low self-esteem'. All three are from materially impoverished backgrounds, though Josephine's class position is complicated, as her West African family were once comparatively wealthy and powerful. For all three of these girls, the material rewards of academic success are located elsewhere, and this plays an important role in their identity work.

Students who take up positions as 'lazy girls' do something very complex with the connotation of helplessness and vulnerability that attends the SEN discourse. On the one hand, they appear to refuse such a connotation, and narrate their struggles as arising from their recalcitrance, or an untenable situation, rather than from any lack of ability. Meera, interviewed with Ambrine (a 'sweet little girl'), uses the unsatisfactory secondary school set-up, and her habit of procrastination, to account for the poor academic performance that is worrying her:

MEERA: It's more, it's, it's more, it's like there's more to worry about 'cause you like get all this homework in one day, and you just worry about more things.

SB: Do you worry about homework?

MEERA: Yeah.

AMBRINE: I can't sleep – if I've forgotten to do something, I can't sleep, I'm like twisting and turning and I end up watching TV.

SB: Does that happen often?

AMBRINE: It used to, it used to.

SB: What is it that stops you doing something? I mean, you say it's when you've forgotten to do something?

MEERA: I'm a loafer – I procrastinate.

SB: [laughs] What do you mean when you say you procrastinate?

MEERA: I was supposed to do something yesterday, and I end up – and I'm supposed to be doing something and I end up doing something else. It's like, say you're, it's a really sunny day, and you can't be bothered to sit in your house and do your homework, so you like go on a bike ride or something, and you're like, 'Oh no, I forgot to do my homework', it's like nine o'clock in the night.

But whilst Meera and the other 'lazy girls' appear to resist the helplessness of the SEN discourse, they are inscribing themselves in a different version of passivity and helplessness. Alongside references to themselves as lazy, and therefore exercising intentionality and agency in relation to their academic struggles, the girls suggest that 'rescue' is the only solution and the only way to attain the academic success they all appear to want. All three of them express their disappointment that taking up a place in Meadway School has not, in itself, been enough to effect the rescue. Meadway promotes itself as a successful school, deploying in that promotion the fiction that academic success can be attained by everyone. These girls appear to have believed (or at least to have wanted to believe) in the promise:

JOSEPHINE: I was all excited on the first day, on the first day when I come, and I was putting on my uniform, and I was all excited. And you had to go in the hall when they read out your form group, and I was in 7T, and Ms Cashmere, I didn't listen, not the whole time. And Ms Cashmere, she was talking about Meadway, and how you all do good when you come here, and how you all get good in your work and she was saying you all get good in your work, and in your reading and your maths. And my Mum says it's a good school here, but I've been here two terms, and it's just like in primary school, like in Year 6 but it's just like Year 6. The only thing what's better is there isn't any boys, 'cause in Year 6 they used to throw things, but anyway it's just like Year 6.

The 'lazy girls' accounts draw also on a version of the entitlements discourse that is daily becoming more prevalent in the educational landscape of the UK: the notion that it is schools and teachers who must be held responsible, and held to account, for 'pupil performance' (Barber, 2000). The 'lazy girls' deployment of this discourse in this way constructs their own 'poor academic performance' (Barber, 2000) as something shameful that must be blamed on someone. Just as the material rewards for successful performance are located elsewhere for these three girls, so the sanctions for failure are similarly displaced. Their accounts are replete with people and systems which appear as culprits: teachers, boring lessons, unviable quantities of homework and other students who distract them. Sometimes these culprits are aspects of themselves, such as Meera's loafing, but there is a sense in which these aspects of themselves somehow float free and they are not responsible for them.

For Meera, Sunna and Josephine, poor performance connotes failure and deficiency, in which blame necessarily inheres, and which must be displaced onto someone else or a distant and disembodied part of themselves. And so the 'lazy girls' refusal of the SEN discourse and its attendant suggestions of helplessness and passivity appears to be inscribing them in another version of helplessness and passivity. In this version they wait to be rescued, with what appears to be a decreasing belief that rescue is possible. The accounts of the 'lazy girls' imply a deeply contradictory impasse, in which they simultaneously believe, and refuse to believe, in the possibility of rescue. Like the 'sweet little girls', their identity work interpellates them into some very traditional versions of femininity, with the rescue motif inscribing them further into cycles of neediness and dependence. Whilst they describe themselves as needy of rescue, they also produce themselves as beyond it.

This may in part be an intricate way of working out what it is possible and realistic to want (Bourdieu, 1984), as the girls go about negotiating the contradictions in which they are embedded: caught between the promise that they, too, can get good examination results if they work hard enough, and the reality that those examination results are out of their reach. While the 'sweet little girls' produce themselves and are read as inherently dependent, and the 'big bad girls' try to resist that production of inherent dependence head-on, the 'lazy girls' take up positions of socially produced dependence. In practice, this brings them close to 'victim' versions of femininity, passively awaiting rescue, and resentful of the powerful princely rescuer who never turns up (Walkerdine, 1990). But it is difficult to see what other choices they have, since the promises of academic success that

Meadway – and the standards agenda – constantly hold out to them have always, in their experience, been withheld.

Conclusion

In this article I have discussed the identity work of eight students in their first year at a girls' comprehensive school. The perceived neediness and dependence that inhere in traditional versions of both femininity and disability work with current policies – especially those that foreground normative achievement – to produce specific identity resources for these students. These resources are further nuanced by class, ethnicity and by other, less 'categorical', indices of difference such as physical appearance. The girls have some room for manoeuvre in their negotiation of these resources, but this has its limits: in particular, none of them can refuse the production of herself as a 'special needs student', with its attendant connotations of dependence and neediness. And those connotations of dependence and neediness contain mechanisms of governance, as well as of care.

The 'sweet little girl' position can most easily be associated with traditional versions of femininity. The position is associated with the power to attract and retain adult and peer help, but its flip side is its very firm association with perpetual vulnerability and neediness. The 'big bad girl' position is closer to 'dangerous' versions of femininity, connoting the resistance to authority and especially the premature hetero/sexual activity that is the opposite of the hyperfeminine childlikeness of the 'sweet little girl'. Such a position is difficult for a Year 7 'special needs student' to sustain, since her attempts at resistance are officially read (and read back to her) as further evidence of 'neediness', and slide her back towards hyperfemininity. The 'lazy girl' also has a complicated relationship with traditional hyperfemininity. She takes up a feminised position as needful of rescue – a rescue arguably necessitated by Meadway's insistence on the universal availability of 'success' in normative terms – whilst simultaneously disbelieving in the possibility of rescue, resulting in a 'victim' version of femininity.

This article has given a flavour of the complex processes through which the girls make sense of themselves as 'special needs students'. I have looked at how the participants negotiate identity resources, emphasising the ways in which traditional, inegalitarian versions of femininity and disability work together to produce students as vulnerable and needy. I want to end by turning outwards again, from Meadway School to the wider political context. Whilst this article has focused on the social relations of schooling, I would not want to ignore their material consequences. The 1999 Labour Force Survey, cited by the National Advisory Council for Education and Training Targets (NACETT) in their recommendations for school target-setting beyond 2002 (NACETT, 2000), shows that people without educational qualifications earn on average one-third of the salaries of people educated to degree level, and that unqualified women earn half as much as unqualified men. Girls such as those in this study, who will emerge from school with few, if any, credentials, may accordingly face severe material deprivation in the future. The inscription of these girls into traditional, dependent versions of femininity and disability cannot then be understood as a 'merely' cultural phenomenon. The context of that cultural phenomenon is the continuing reproduction of social and material disadvantages for specific groups of girls.

Acknowledgement

I am grateful to the Economic and Social Research Council (ESRC) for the award of a PhD studentship which enabled me to carry out this research.

NOTE

1   Cheryl has been formally identified as having Asperger's Syndrome (an Autistic Spectrum Disorder). Her position as 'big bad girl' is especially problematic: unlike the other girls in this study, she can claim a recognisably disabled identity, which intensifies her positioning within the tragedy/charity discourse, and makes repositioning especially difficult.

REFERENCES

Ainscow, M. (1999) *Understanding the Development of Inclusive Schools* (London, Falmer Press).

Allan, J. (1999) *Actively Seeking Inclusion: Pupils with Special Needs in Mainstream Schools* (London, Falmer Press).

Barber, M. (2000) 'High expectations and standards for all – no matter what', *Times Educational Supplement*, 7 July, 22–24.

Bhatti, G. (1995) 'A journey into the unknown: an ethnographic study of Asian children', in: M. Griffiths and B. Troyna (eds), *Antiracism, Culture and Social Justice in Education* (Stoke-On-Trent, Trentham Books).

Bhatti, G. (1999) *Asian Children at Home and at School* (London, Routledge).

Biklen, D. (2000) 'Constructing inclusion: lessons from critical, disability narratives', *International Journal of Inclusive Education*, 4: 337–353.

Bines, H. (2000) 'Inclusive standards? current developments in policy for special educational needs in England and Wales', *Oxford Review of Education*, 26: 21–33.

Bourdieu, P. (1984) *Distinction: A Social Critique of the Judgement of Taste* (London, Routledge & Kegan Paul).

Boyden, J. (1990) 'Childhood and the policy makers: a comparative perspective on the globalization of childhood', in A. James and A. Prout (eds), *Constructing and Reconstructing Childhood: Contemporary Issues in the Sociological Study of Childhood* (Basingstoke, Falmer Press).

Carrington, S. (1999) 'Inclusion needs a different school culture', *International Journal of Inclusive Education*, 3: 257–268.

Connolly, P. (1998) *Racism, Gender Identities and Young Children: Social Relations in a Multi-ethnic, Inner-city Primary School* (London, Routledge).

Corbett, J. (1996) *Bad-Mouthing: The Language of Special Needs* (Bristol, Falmer Press).

Corbett, J. (1998) *Special Educational Needs in the Twentieth Century: A Cultural Analysis* (London, Cassell).

Department for Education and Employment (1994) *Code of Practice on the Identification and Assessment of Special Educational Needs* (London, Department for Education and Employment).

Department for Education and Employment (1999a) *Excellence in Cities* (London, Department for Education and Employment).

Department for Education and Employment (1999b) *National Learning Targets for England for 2002* (Sudbury, Department for Education and Employment).

Ervelles, N. (1996) 'Disability and the dialectics of difference', *Disability and Society*, 11: 519–538.

Hey, V. (1997) *The Company She Keeps: An Ethnography of Girls' Friendship* (Buckingham, Open University Press).

Hunt, P. and Frankenburg, R. (1990) 'It's a small world: Disneyland, the family and the multiple rerepresentations of American childhood', in A. James and A. Prout (eds), *Constructing and Reconstructing Childhood: Contemporary Issues in the Sociological Study of Childhood* (Basingstoke, Falmer Press).

National Advisory Council for Education and Training Targets (NACETT) (2000) *Aiming Higher: NACETT's report on the National Learning Targets for England and Advice on Targets Beyond 2002* (Sudbury, NACETT).

Riddell, S., Wilkinson, H. and Baron, S. (1998) 'From emancipatory research to focus group: people with learning difficulties and the research process', in L. Barton and P. Clough (eds), *Articulating with Difficulty: Research Voices in Inclusive Education* (London, Paul Chapman).

Skeggs, B. (1997) *Formations of Class and Gender* (London, Sage).

Skrtic, T. (1995) *Disability and Democracy: Reconstructing (Special) Education for Postmodernity* (New York, Teachers College Press).

Slee, R. (1995) *Changing Theories and Practices of Discipline* (London, Falmer Press).

Slee, R. (1998) 'High reliability organizations and liability students – the politics of recognition', in R. Slee, G. Weiner and S. Tomlinson (eds), *School Effectiveness for Whom? Challenges to the School Effectiveness and School Improvement Movements* (London, Falmer).

Slee, R., Weiner, G. and Tomlinson, S. (1998) 'Introduction: school effectiveness for whom?', in R. Slee, G. Weiner and S. Tomlinson (eds), *School Effectiveness for Whom? Challenges to the School Effectiveness and School Improvement Movements* (London, Falmer Press).

Stone, S.D. (1995) 'The myth of bodily perfection', *Disability and Society*, 10: 413–424.

Tomlinson, S. (1982) *A Sociology of Special Education* (London, Routledge and Kegan Paul).

Walkerdine, V. (1989) 'Femininity as performance', *Oxford Review of Education*, 15: 267–279.

Walkerdine, V. (1990) *Schoolgirl Fictions* (London, Verso).

Walkerdine, V. (1997) *Daddy's Girl: Young Girls and Popular Culture* (Basingstoke, Macmillan).

Walkerdine, V. and Lucey, H. (1989) *Democracy in the Kitchen: Regulating Mothers and Socialising Daughters* (London, The Women's Press).

Warnock, M. (1978) *The Concept of Educational Need: The Charles Gittins Memorial Lecture* (Dyfed, Gomer Press).

PART II

THEORETICAL DEBATE

SIX

TEACHING POST-STRUCTURALIST FEMINIST THEORY IN EDUCATION: STUDENT RESISTANCES

Alison Jones

Source: 'Teaching post-structuralist feminist theory in education: student resistances', *Gender and Education*, 9(3): 261–269, 1997.

In 1993 I published an article in *Gender and Education* entitled 'Becoming a "girl": post-structuralist suggestions for educational research' (Jones, 1993).[1] I argued that theoretical concepts such as 'positioning' and 'subjectivity' allow a more intricate understanding of how we are/become gendered, and that these ideas are particularly useful for educational research.

After 3 years of teaching undergraduate education students this material, I am struck by our recurring difficulties with it. Instead of becoming key words in a more complex conceptualisation of the re/production of gender, terms such as 'subjectivity', 'positioning', 'subject positions' have been taken up by students in confused and unwittingly contradictory ways.

It seems that the students have been introduced to this new post-structuralist language without adequate knowledge of its underlying philosophical premises; hence they struggle with its meanings. Or, to put it another way, terms such as 'subjectivity' are regularly interpreted via a particular, humanist discourse which education students typically bring to their studies. And this interpretation, often unrecognised, leads to real problems in my attempts to teach (and their attempts to understand) within an anti-humanist, or post-structuralist frame. There is amongst education students a lack of understanding of relevant aspects of structuralism which means they encounter *post*-structuralism, or its language, if not in a theoretical vacuum, then certainly without the theoretical building blocks necessary for a basic understanding of ideas increasingly popular in feminist education studies. As a result, many of them are prevented from exploring the interesting conceptual spaces opened by aspects of post-structuralist discussion.

Socialisation

What the students *have* learned is to question some simplistic aspects of socialisation which posit girls (and boys) as blank slates on which an appropriate and uniform gender is more or less successfully inscribed. They see that girls might be understood as actively 'taking up' their gender, rather than being simply its passive recipients. And they have become critical of an easy invoking of 'girls' as a unitary group; they accept that the category 'girls' is problematic due to cultural and social differences amongst girls. That is, they understand girls (and boys) as *becoming* gendered, and that gender is *socially constructed* in a range of ways.

Construction metaphors have been readily taken up by educationists. Due to their implications of passivity and uniformity, and neglect of social and cultural context, phrases such as 'sex role socialisation' have been largely replaced by the language of 'social construction'. Education and schooling are seen as very much about how girls/boys/citizens/workers are 'made', or shaped. Instead of simply learning their appropriate gender roles, girls are seen as actively formed and form-ing themselves within the (patriarchal, racist...) social structures into which they are born. They are 'constructed' through, say, parent and teacher practices which reward and punish children on the grounds of cultural assumptions about gender. In turn, girls construct and reconstruct the social world through their (changing) understanding of it, and through their practices. Education is a key to such understanding, and to conceptual and material change.

Despite the new language, the subject of earlier 'socialisation' theories remains intact. The irreducible 'real person' who is 'made' (becomes a girl), or who 'makes' the world, is at the heart of this view of social construction. And it is this human-ist subject which is immovably present in students' reception of post-structuralist theory – theory which is predicated on an *anti*-humanist subject.

Agency and the subject

Post-structuralist conceptions of the subject have appealed to many because they seem to offer a way through an apparent tension in notions of 'social construc-tion': how do we speak about people as constructions of the social order on the one hand, and as constructing agents or actors on the other, without erring on either side? Those 'social constructionist' accounts of schooling and socialisation which accentuated the determining effects of the social structure and ideology had been unattractive not only due to their inherent pessimism, but also for the ways in which they seemed to obliterate the 'real' thinking person who can choose to resist, change and 'make a difference'. On the other hand, accounts which emphasised 'agency' and change were too often voluntarist, in danger of assuming an individ-ual able to act and think independently of the social structure and its ideologies.

In terms such as 'subjectivity', students see the possibilities for getting away from the endless ping-pong of this dualist agency–structure framework. As one popular text puts it:

> 'Subjectivity' can be defined as that combination of conscious and unconscious thoughts and emotions that make up our sense of ourselves, our relation to the world and our ability to act in that world...(T)he concept of subjectivity can capture the notion of people as intentional subjects – actors in the world – and at the same time as subject to forces beyond their conscious control.
>
> (Crowley and Himmelweit, 1992, p. 7)

The doubled sense of 'subject' (subject/ed *to*, and subject *of* action) apparently allows for an individual who is socially produced, *and* 'multiply positioned' – neither determined nor free, but both simultaneously.

The terms 'subject' and 'subjectivity' are central to post-structuralist theory, and in this context, as Chris Weedon (1987, p. 32) points out, they 'mark a crucial break with humanist conceptions of the individual'. While humanist accounts pre-suppose an already existing individual who is socialised, who becomes 'a girl', post-structuralism proposes 'a subjectivity which is precarious, contradictory and in process, constantly being reconstituted in discourse each time we think or speak' (Weedon, 1987, p. 32).

In other words, the doubled/complex sense of 'being (a) subject' is understood in post-structuralist theory through the foregrounding of language (discourse/ meaning). At centre stage is not a real person ('us') who is 'made into a subject (girl)', but the meaning systems which *produce* what counts as girls. Yet students in education tend to resist this centring of language and meaning – for several reasons.

One is that individuals – 'me', this girl, the boys in my school – remain the focus for most feminist and other education students whose legitimate concern is with 'real people', their experiences and with institutional structures. Real people seem dissolved in the post-structuralist takeover by language and meaning; indeed, it appears that 'words alone [have] the power to craft bodies from their own linguistic substance' (Butler, 1993, p. x). It seems we are thrown back into determinism; everything is determined – not by social structures this time, but by language.

In addition, and perhaps most important, we all *experience* ourselves as humanist subjects; we *do* 'consider our options', choose and think critically, act on our ideas. Our everyday language is suffused with a pronoun grammar which expresses our experience as active, independent subjects. From a post-structuralist perspective we experience ourselves as humanist subjects precisely *because* we are produced as such via the assumptions of our everyday language. However, the evidence of our seemingly common-sense and 'natural' experience makes the centring of language difficult indeed.

It is perhaps because of the self-evident truth of experience that the language needed to talk about the productivity of language is often so complex. Students understandably baulk at the way comfortingly straightforward accounts of the world are undermined by attempts to explain how 'language produces us' which seem to leave us with a hard-to-grasp, shifting and murky complexity. Metaphor and allusion abound as theorists wrestle to speak within/against the obvious, in the gaps and spaces, boundaries and margins – romancing/fictioning/troubling, fragmentary, volatile and illusory. For some this language is exciting, and offers opportunities for new conceptualisations. For most, it is simply too slippery in an environment like the university where formal requirements for a kind of prosaic clarity still ensure good grades.

After structuralism

Many of the difficulties students encounter with post-structuralist theory are problems already widely debated in the theoretical literature. However, students can barely begin to follow the debates when they have little sense of the historical development of the ideas they encounter with suspicion. While the notion that language and meaning might *form* 'real people' and their experiences is certainly difficult to grasp, it is far from new. Structuralist thinkers over the last 50 years have debated the constitutive effects of language, and the idea that 'far from the world determining the order of our language, our language determines the order of the world' (Sturrock, 1986, p. 17).

Education students missed out on much of this debate. A form of Marxism which emphasised the determining features of the material world, rather than language or 'consciousness', has dominated educational sociology until recently. Similarly, much feminist research in education has focused on the effects of role modelling, teacher attention, curriculum choice, disadvantage, stereotyping, discrimination and harassment on girls' beliefs and practices – rather than on the effects of the assumptions enshrined in that very language of critique (see Jones and Jacka, 1995).

According to Sturrock's readable text *Structuralism* (1986), 'structuralists' understood society, and language, as made up of timeless, ahistorical structures which did not need reference to the intentional 'real' individual. Such theorists assumed a universal social (or linguistic, or cultural, or unconscious) order, and maintained that this order is 'constructed', 'structured' or interpreted variously through language.

'Humanist' theorists agreed, but whereas they perceived language as a tool with which people *expressed* ideas or experiences of the social order, structuralists (such as Saussure and Levi-Strauss) saw language and culture as expressing itself through us, *forming* or *producing* experience and social reality (and us) in the process. Language and its meaning was something to be understood as largely separated from, but determining, experience and thought. Like culture, society and human experience, language was considered to be structured by underlying universally shared rules, which we could discover.

From a 'humanist' perspective, 'behind' the social order and experience are the human beings who *make* meaning, *have* experiences and so on. Structuralists argue that humans only *think* they make meaning, but it is 'beyond' them (Poster, 1975, p. 316). In other words, structuralists 'decentre' human experience and meaning; the conscious subject is displaced from the centre of understanding. So, while humanists saw the subject (individual) as intentional, choosing and fully conscious, structuralists undermined this, saying that history, culture and language had its own logic beyond individual intention. Studying human life, then, becomes the study of that logic, which Foucault saw in terms of *'the episteme'*, and which has become more popularly known as 'discourse'. Discourse, embodied in the language that people speak, write and enact, including the images they produce and the acts they perform, becomes the focus for social researchers and theorists.

It is this difficult, counter-intuitive notion of 'people' – a notion which displaces the individual, who chooses, thinks and acts intentionally, with a 'subject' who is formed through (produced by, inscribed with...) structures of culture, language and meaning (discourse) – which many students find difficult to comprehend. At the same time, they happily use the language of discourse and subjectivity, without understanding – or even agreeing with – its structuralist tenets.

Post-structuralism, it must be remembered, is a development of structuralism. It seeks critically to 'extend' the insights of structuralism (Sturrock, 1986, p. 137). What *post*-structuralist writers do is to radically foreground language, rather than structures/culture/society – which after all are *interpretations*. Derrida, considered by some to be the 'creator' of post-structuralism, emphasised that we cannot reach outside language; that everything is mediated by language and meaning. Not only that, but we can never *fix* meanings; they are deeply contextual and shifting, endlessly taken from other meanings which are taken from others, and so on. There are a range of historically and culturally specific possible meanings, so researchers/thinkers can never get to the final, 'real' meaning or structure of a society or action or text (although structuralists assume that possibility).

Writers such as Foucault,[2] for instance, have documented the historically specific discourses which produced sexuality. Foucault does not tell 'the real truth' about sexuality, but rather indicates how 'the real' where sexuality is concerned (what sexuality 'is') is a product of the historically specific meaning systems or discourses within which it is enacted and spoken about – or, better, which 'speak' it, or 'produce' it.

Here, 'produce' means something different from the sense of 'construction' referred to earlier. 'Produce' means something like 'comes into existence', rather than 'shaped' or 'made (out of something else)'. Most commonly, the word 'constitute' is used by post-structuralists to capture this sense of language 'producing' us, our experience, the world, the 'real'. I will return to this phrase later; suffice it to say here that the constituted subject is an *anti-humanist* subject – one which does not exist and act in relation to discourse, but rather is 'produced' or 'comes into existence' within discourse. This will also be revisited in the following paragraphs.

Choosing subject

As I discussed in my 1993 article, contemporary feminist writers in education have been interested in the possibilities such post-structuralist conceptions offer for understanding gender, its production and change. They argue that while we (women and girls) can be understood as produced by/within the structures of language and meaning, we are not simply determined by one particular set of meanings...herein lie possibilities for change. In so far as different meanings are mobilised in different contexts, shifting definitions of gender and different possibilities for 'being' women or girls appear in the movement/spaces[3] between meanings. Some theorists, making further use of the spatial metaphor, use the term 'position' and 'positioning' to denote the productive possibilities in discourses for subjects.

It is into this sort of metaphorical, abstracted explanation that a humanist subject easily reappears. There is an easy slippage from meaning or discourse determining possibilities, to 'people' determining them via discourses, especially when our concern is with 'real people'. But how can we talk about real people, and especially the actions and thoughts of real people, when 'real people' are discursive products?

Bronwyn Davies, whose work my students find accessible and interesting, grapples with just such a question in her attempts both to invoke an anti-humanist subject and to talk about real people ('agency') in an educational context. In discussing the impossibility of 'choice' she says: 'We can only ever speak ourselves or be spoken into existence within the terms of the available discourses...choices are understood as more akin to "forced choices", since the subject's positioning within particular discourses makes the "chosen" line of action the only possible action' (Davies, 1991, pp. 42, 46).

This is a very difficult idea, and given the common-sense meaning of 'choice', almost impossible to explain using that term. In her use of the phrase 'forced choice' she inevitably offers a choosing subject to her student readers, despite her intentions. A subject, they read, is someone (a person) who is 'forced' to do one thing rather than another (e.g. choose teaching over airline piloting as a career) due to, say, patriarchal ideologies and practices. Girls can either accept or reject the 'forced choices' by taking up different discourses – say, feminist discourses – which provide them with different possibilities.

In another paper, Davies is more explicit in her attempts to 'have' both a constituted subject and a choosing one too: 'A particular strength of the post-structuralist research paradigm is that it recognises both the constitutive effects of discourse, and in particular of discursive practices, and at the same time recognises that people are capable of exercising choice in relation to those practices' (Davies and Harré, 1990, p. 46).

In education in particular, as I mentioned earlier, this sense of 'choice' makes Davies's 'post-structuralist research paradigm' attractive – it seems that we can have our cake and eat it too; we are both constituted and yet can choose what we might be constituted as. As a result, Davies's work unwittingly encourages education students' confused attempts to take seriously the anti-humanist language of 'post-structuralism' whilst simultaneously invoking a humanist subject (a choosing agent). This shows up in some of my students' essays, when they write:

> Girls can be multiply positioned. They can be powerful, they can be power-less. They can be stroppy or shy. They are active in taking up these different subjectivities; they can position themselves in a range of ways, as tomboys or feminine.
>
> Discourses offer individuals numerous subject positions. In my everyday life as a woman I might take on different, even contradictory, subjectivities...
>
> There are a range of subject positions available to women in engineering textbooks. Some students take up the 'woman engineer' position with alacrity, others struggle with the ambivalence they encounter in other positions which seem to produce the 'woman engineer' as an impossibility.

Indeed, my own writing is littered with similar phrases as I grapple with the subject. In these sorts of sentences, 'subject positions' become just so many available costumes from which prediscursive girls can choose or 'take'. Girls simply act differently, or 'take up' gender differently, depending on how they feel, or the context in which they find themselves. There is an implicit suggestion that girls are 'made' from a sexed subject who becomes gendered in a range of different ways. The prediscursive body is the material of the construction, the 'stuff' which is moulded into shape, the 'I' that 'does' femininity differently.

A similar assumption is made about the relation between the subject and discourse, which are often radically separated in students' writing. Discourse confronts the acting, choosing subject who, in turn, responds to it: 'Women accommodate and resist the power within discourse...Women resist the subordinate position in which they are placed by discourse.'

It is this sort of view which Judith Butler (1990, 1993) has been at pains to criticise from an anti-humanist position. In her attempt to write about how gender 'forms' bodies, she uses the metaphor of performance, which she appears to use interchangeably with 'constitute'. 'Performance', though, is a term full of difficulties in its potential to produce the very subject Butler seeks to problematise.

She cautions: 'If I were to argue that genders are performative, that could mean that I thought that one woke in the morning, perused the closet or some more open space for a gender of choice, donned that gender...such a theory would restore a figure of a choosing subject – humanist – at the centre of a project whose emphasis on construction seems quite opposed to such a notion' (Butler, 1993, p. x). Butler is well advised to be worried about being so misunderstood. The language of performance does seem to imply an 'actor', a pre-gendered choosing subject who enacts the performance of choice.

The notion of 'taking on/up' feminine subject positions (phrases of Davies's) sounds very similar to gender 'performance', invoking assumptions about an active agent or subject for which Judith Butler (1990, p. 8) takes to task de Beauvoir and her famous statement, 'One is not born a woman, but rather becomes one'. Butler's comment is also instructive about the term 'constructed':

> For Beauvoir, gender is 'constructed', but implied in her formulation is an agent, a cogito, who somehow takes on or appropriates that gender and could, in principle, take on another gender [or another subject position]...For Beauvoir there is an 'I' that does its gender, that becomes its gender...On such a model culture and discourse mire the subject, but do not constitute that subject.
>
> (Butler, 1990, p. 143)

Constituted subject

Butler argues that there is no subject who 'takes up' or 'puts on' the various possibilities for being. Rather, it is discourses ('discursive injunctions') which form meanings and thus possibilities in any culture and which 'take on' and produce the subject – and social change. For instance, 'The...injunction to be a given gender takes place through discursive routes: to be a good mother, to be a heterosexually desirable object, to be a fit worker...The convergence of such discursive injunctions produces the possibility of a complex reconfiguration' (Butler, 1990, p. 145). It is not a transcendental, choosing subject who enables action in the midst of such possibilities, says Butler: 'There is no self...who maintains integrity prior to its entrance into this conflicted cultural field. There is only the taking up of the tools where they lie, where *the very "taking up" is enabled by the tool* lying there' (1990, p. 145, my emphasis).

This seems a good description of the constitutive relation. The use of 'taking up' as *constitutive* contrasts with the notion of a (choosing) self taking something up. The taker and the taken are, in a sense, 'the same', mutually determining. The subject 'is' the discursive practices which produce it. So, in other words, there is no 'doer behind the deed'; rather, the 'doer is invariably constructed in and through the deed' (Butler, 1990, p. 142). As such, the doer/subject/person is never fixed, finally a girl or a woman or whatever, but always becoming or being. Becoming a woman or girl is an ongoing discursive practice, in constant reproduction. Butler puts it this way: 'If there is something right in Beauvoir's claim that one is not born, but rather becomes a woman, it follows that woman itself is a term in process, a becoming, a construction that cannot rightfully be said to originate or to end' (Butler, 1990, p. 33).

It is hardly surprising that undergraduate students in education indeed, all of us find this difficult and seek to import the apparent solidity of the 'real' person/girl into our writing and talk. In an attempt to meet such desires as well as illustrate the idea of the ongoing production/constitution/performativity of the subject,

I sometimes use examples taken in the classroom. It is never easy to leap from the abstractions of theory to the actuality of the body, and practice, but... 'Take me, the teacher', I say to my students. 'I am not "a teacher" outside of our collective understanding – I only become a teacher in the performance of certain socially understood acts (discursive practices). And those acts only "make" me a teacher as I am produced by you, the students (people acting as "students" right now). We are all engaged in the performance, the production of the teacher. And this room too is recruited in the process – the inert architecture of the lecture room is alive in "speaking" me the teacher and you the students into existence as we take our sanctioned places in the space. Moreover, what counts as a "teacher" is re-enacted by all of us, including the architecture, in our culturally produced actions in relation to each other and the space. "The teacher" is produced through/in our material bodies in the ways we move, what we wear, who we look at, the gestures we make. All this is "aside" from the "I" of me, or you. The "real" embodied individual is largely irrelevant to the performance (which will be enacted slightly differently depending on personal style). In that the teacher embodies some (culturally meaningful) gender, race, class, sexuality, the whole performance of the teaching and its possibilities are shaped within these intersecting meanings.'

Perhaps the example of being a girl/woman differs to the extent that I can be socially recognised as a woman in any context, whereas I am not recognised as a teacher everywhere. But the idea of production – or performance – is essentially the same. I am produced as gendered, and produce myself as such, through the meaningful actions (discursive practices) of others (and my own) in any context. 'Real people', then, – me as teacher, as a woman, and so on – are themselves products of the collective discursive practices in which they/I engage.

Butler's notion of performance – while containing the uncomfortable possibility of the prediscursive actor who performs – signals gender as existing only and always 'in the act' as it were, (per)forming itself through meaningful actions. 'In this sense, gender is always a doing, though not a doing by a subject who might be said to pre exist the deed...' (Butler, 1990, p. 25).

Being wrong

It is important to understand that I am not suggesting that students are 'wrong' in asserting an acting subject. It is not as though the 'acting subject' does not exist. They (we) reproduce the 'acting subject' through our writing it into existence. Similarly with 'reality' and 'truth'. Contrary to the misunderstanding that 'post-structuralism suggests there is no such thing as truth or reality', what *is* suggested by post-structuralist theory is that 'truth' and 'reality' *do* exist – *because/as we invoke them*. In other words, truth, reality and our acting, choosing selves exist in so far as we refer to them and socially legitimate them. What post-structuralism maintains is that they exist in our discursive practices, not prior to them.

Likewise, it is through the constitutive effects of language that *we understand and experience ourselves* as 'doers behind deeds' or actors who make choices. We *are* 'rational choosing subjects' – we behave as though we are, we run whole social systems on that premise – because we understand ourselves to be so through the meaning systems forming our cultural and social context. Through language we produce ourselves, 'embodied in pronoun grammar in which a person understands themselves as historically continuous and unitary' (Butler, 1990, p. 147) – and, we might add, as choosing actors. In referring to 'me' or 'I', our language continuously produces 'me'; and thus that ongoing 'me'/person/humanist subject 'exists'. Davies reminds us that – as Althusser argued using his notion of interpellation – in order to be a 'person in the modern world' it is necessary for us to (mis)understand ourselves as the authors, and fail to recognise the constitutive force, of the language we speak (Davies, 1990, p. 507).

In the end, I do not mind which discursive framework my students adopt. What concerns me is their (our) invoking of 'post-structuralism' as they (we) write about 'the subject who positions herself...' or when they overlook the discursive tension between a set of words such as 'construct' and 'agency' on the one hand, and 'constitute', 'produce' and 'subject' on the other. My desire is not only to recognise the contradictory ways in which we are positioned, but also to recognise, rather than simply unconsciously engage in, contradictions in our writing and thinking about theory, and our 'experience'.

With the increasing enthusiasm for metaphorical language in feminist social theory, the possibilities for further contradiction, and confusion, seem set to multiply. For instance, the language of *surfaces*, and inscription on surfaces, fails to escape the tendency to assume a prior something that 'becomes' a subject: the surface this time is the prediscursive space on which meaning is written. It looks like a good topic with which to continue the conversation: '*discuss the tension between "writing the body" and "written on the body"*'.

NOTES

1   This article is written in response to Jones (1993) and assumes some prior knowledge of the arguments in that paper.
2   Although Foucault differed from Derrida in his ideas about language, both might be considered to have similar assumptions about its productivity.
3   Spaces and gaps are not 'empty', but might be understood as a 'relation between'.

REFERENCES

Butler, J. (1990) *Gender Trouble: Feminism and the Subversion of Identity* (New York, Routledge).
Butler, J. (1993) *Bodies that Matter: On the Discursive Limits of 'Sex'* (New York, Routledge).
Crowley, H. and Himmelweit, S. (eds) (1992) *Knowing Women: Feminism and Knowledge* (Cambridge, Polity Press and the Open University).
Davies, B. (1990) 'The problem of desire', *Social Problems*, 37: 501–516.
Davies, B. (1991) 'The concept of agency: a feminist poststructuralist analysis', *Social Analysis*, 30: 42–53.
Davies, B. and Harré, R. (1990) 'Positioning: the discursive production of selves', *Journal for the Theory of Social Behaviour*, 20: 43–63.
Jones, A. (1993) 'Becoming a "girl": post-structuralist suggestions for educational research', *Gender and Education*, 5: 157–167.
Jones, A. and Jacka, S. (1995) 'Discourse of disadvantage: girls' school achievement', *New Zealand Journal of Educational Studies*, 30: 165–176.
Poster, M. (1975) *Existential Marxism in Postwar France: From Sartre to Althusser* (Princeton, NJ, Princeton University Press).
Sturrock, J. (1986) *Structuralism* (London, Paladin).
Weedon, C. (1987) *Feminist Practice and Post-structuralist Theory* (Oxford, Basil Blackwell).

SEVEN

THE SUBJECT OF POST-STRUCTURALISM: A REPLY TO ALISON JONES

Bronwyn Davies

Source: 'The subject of post-structuralism: a reply to Alison Jones', *Gender and Education*, 9(3): 271–283, 1997.

I am intrigued both by Alison Jones' exposition of the problems her students face in acquiring post-structuralist discourse, since I see my own students engaging in similar struggles, and by her finding in my writing an (unwitting) incitement of her students to unwanted bouts of confused humanism. Active verbs, such as 'positioning' and 'choice', and terms such as 'agency' incorrectly invoke, according to Jones, a 'prediscursive' humanist subject. The subject as it is understood in post-structuralism, in contrast, can only engage in *apparent* acts of choosing, or positioning, or of experiencing the self as an agent. Such acts do not spring from an essential prediscursive self, but rather are constituted in humanist discourses through which subjects (mis)take themselves to be 'choosing', 'positioning', etc. The terms 'positioning', 'choice' and 'agency' can only be correctly used to describe what subjects do, Jones argues, by students who acknowledge that they are writing humanist discourse and not post-structuralist discourse.

The problematic relationship between the subject as it is constituted through humanist discourses and the subject as it is understood through post-structuralist discourses is one I have explored in detail both in my book *Shards of Glass* (1993, in particular in chapter 2, 'The subjects of childhood') and in the various articles Jones refers to (Davies and Harré, 1990; Davies, 1991). In these texts I do not set up a binary between the humanist subject and the 'anti-humanist subject' (as Jones does in her article), but in part use post-structuralist theory to show how the humanist self is so convincingly achieved, and goes on being achieved, through the inscription of humanist discourses on the one who is *always already* a subject (Althusser, 1984), and who manages indeed to become 'what will always already have been' (Lacan, 1966).

The *point* of post-structuralism is not to destroy the humanist subject nor to create its binary other, the 'anti-humanist subject' (whatever that might be), but to enable us to see the subject's fictionality, whilst recognising how powerful fictions are in constituting what we take to be real. One of Foucault's major contributions has been to enable us to see that what we understand by 'being human' has shifted radically over the ages. His concern was not with individual subjects, but with subjectification. At the same time he was fascinated by the ways in which as writer he constituted himself as individual 'author' (1977), even through the simple act of signing his name to what he had written, rather than signing it as emerging from a particular discursive field. Deconstructive writing has been used by many writers in a complementary way to the writing of Foucault. The textual analysis it makes possible has enabled us to attend to the ways in which language traps us, for example, into binary forms of thought (such as the 'humanist' and the 'anti-humanist' subject). Deconstruction enables us to see that which we normally disattend, not just in the words on the page, but in the texts of 'self' which signify this or that kind of individual subject. Post-structuralist theory draws attention to:

> the signifying matter, which, instead of making itself transparent as it conveys a particular meaning, becomes somewhat opaque like a piece of stained or faceted glass. Thus in the most basic way the reader is invited to look *at* rather than *through* the linguistic surface.
>
> (Levine, 1991, p. xvi)

By looking '*at* rather than *through* the linguistic surface' we can begin to explore how it is that we can think we have, and act as if we have, (and can be required by law to have) a sense of agency, and recognise at the same time that it is in the constitutive force of discourse that agency lies. Deconstructive thought thus requires us to take on board contradictory thoughts and to hold them together at the same time. In my article on agency (1991) I redefine agency as lying in the inscription of some forms of the humanist self (if you are constituted as a powerful agent you may well be able to act powerfully), *and* more significantly, as lying in the reflexive awareness of the constitutive power of language that becomes possible through post-structuralist theory. I have struggled to reclaim this concept for use in post-structuralist theory precisely because, as a feminist, I am not willing to forgo the possibility of conceptualising and bringing about change. So yes, I want my cake and I want to eat it. And as a post-structuralist I do not find that problematic. Linear forms of logic are too constraining for those of us who wish to embrace the rich complexity of life lived through multiple and contradictory discourses.

But for Jones, to talk of agency (she assumes rather than argues) is to insist on a real, prediscursive self. She is troubled by the tension between the constituted subject (which she acknowledges as 'real'), and the post-structuralist foregrounding of the discourse through which 'subjects' are constituted. She argues that correct post-structuralist usage will be taken to have been achieved when: (a) the possibility of the humanist subject cannot be read into the text produced, and in its place an 'anti-humanist' subject is achieved, and (b) it is understood, following Derrida, 'that we cannot reach outside language; that everything is mediated by language and meaning'.

In relation to the first of these requirements, of course the writer is not in control of how the reader brings the written text to life in the reading of it. Reading and writing are deeply interactive processes, and readers will necessarily bring with them to any reading a range of strategies for making meaning out of the marks on the page. For some readers these may well be humanist strategies, and no amount of clever writing will dislodge them. It is this problem that I began work on in *Frogs and Snails and Feminist Tales* (1989).

In relation to the second of Jones's requirements, it is useful to look closely at what Derrida meant by his famous phrase, '*il n'ya pas de hors-texte*' [there's nothing outside the text]. This can be taken to mean that the only thing we can legitimately attend to or talk about is language (or text), *or* it can be seen to mean that everything is text; that is, that *there is no outside*. In other words we can refuse the binary text/not-text, and see all as text. Fuery's analysis of Derrida's meaning is that:

> nothing can exist 'outside' the text because the ideas of 'outsides' and 'centres' are problematic issues in their own right... Textuality consumes all, because in attempting to represent or attribute meaning to something we textualise it. So the act of reading itself becomes part of the text. However, 'reading' is not simply an act anybody might take up; rather, it is the site of a conflict as to who looks, that is, who is authorised to gaze and so has the capacity to read. The act of reading, then, comes to be determined through the act of interpretation.
> (Fuery, 1995, p. 58)

Reading Derrida's words in this way, and thinking about Jones' article as generating a site of conflict, her argument can be read as a claim that I and her students should not be authorised to gaze (at post-structuralist theory), as we do not have the capacity to read/write it. She then elaborates what a correct reading of post-structuralist theory is, proffering Butler as having appropriate authority.

For me this creates an intriguing puzzle. How does she make and sustain this claim? How is she reading my texts and the texts the students create in such a way that she sees the need to de-authorise us?

The 'subject' of post-structuralist theory

The original writers of 'post-structuralist theory' do not always name themselves as such. The writer, for example, whose work is perhaps most drawn on by those who do name themselves post-structuralist is Foucault, yet Foucault himself expressed a wish to distance himself from the label. This is not uncommon when a new theoretical discursive field is being developed. The naming of it, the delineation of its subject matter and the decision as to which authors to include in the discursive field being defined, are not necessarily the same processes as those being undertaken by the writers being recognised. So there are those whose thinking inspires others, who in turn define and delimit what the field is that they are examining. In looking to what the original inspirational writers have to say about the human subject, we can then contemplate what sense we might want to make of the human subject in what we call 'post-structuralist theory'.

The original writers did not want to abandon the human subject, though they made that subject problematic. Foucault claimed that the goal of his work was to make sense of how 'human beings are made subjects', not in the particularity of the lives of individual subjects, but in the processes which shift the meaning of being a subject over time:

> I would like to say, first of all, what has been the goal of my work during the last twenty years. It has not been to analyze the phenomena of power, nor to

elaborate the foundations of such an analysis. My objective instead, has been to create a history of the different modes by which, in our culture, human beings are made subjects... Thus it is not power, but the subject, which is the general theme of my research.

(Foucault, 1983, pp. 208–209)

Derrida is equally clear about the importance of the subject in his work. The subject is, he says, incontrovertibly there, as an *effect* of subjectivity. His interest, though, is in resituating the subject, in moving from a supposed identity which has substance independent of language to the subject inscribed in language:

I have never said that the subject should be dispensed with. Only that it should be deconstructed. To deconstruct the subject does not mean to deny its existence. There are subjects, 'operations' or 'effects' (*effets*) of subjectivity. This is an incontrovertible fact. To acknowledge this does not mean, however, that the subject is what it says it is. The subject is not some meta-linguistic substance or identity, some pure cogito of self-presence; it is always inscribed in language. My work does not, therefore, destroy the subject; it simply tries to resituate it.

(Derrida in Kearney, 1994, p. 125)

And as Butler herself comments, refusing the subject as a starting point for theorising does not mean we can dispense with it altogether:

To refuse to assume... a notion of the subject from the start is not the same as negating or dispensing with such a notion altogether; on the contrary, it is to ask after the process of its construction and the political meaning and consequentiality of taking the subject as a requirement or presupposition of theory.

(Butler, 1992, p. 4)

It is assumed by post-structuralist theorists that the subject is *always already* a discursively constituted subject when s/he encounters the discursive possibilities of post-structuralism. What the encounter with post-structuralism does is to enable the subject to see not just the object it appears to itself to have become, but to see the ongoing and constitutive force of language (with all its contradictions). It is through making that constitutive force visible that the subject can see its 'self' *as* discursive process, rather than as a unique, relatively fixed personal invention. Post-structuralist discourse entails a move from the self as a noun (and thus stable and relatively fixed) to the self as a verb, always in process, taking its shape in and through the discursive possibilities through which selves are made. The 'maker', in this post-structuralist turn, is what would appear to lie at the heart of the difference Jones is arguing between herself/Butler, and me/her students. The maker, for Jones/Butler, is language. For me, it is not some pre-discursive self, as Jones assumes, but an already discursively constituted subject, a subject in process, a subject as verb, a subject who, like post-structuralist writers, can:

■ see the constitutive process;
■ read the texts of their 'selving';
■ recognise the constitutive power of discourses to produce historically located ideas of what it might even mean to be a self, or engage in 'selving';

- look at the contradictions between discourses (and not reject them solely on those grounds); and
- play endlessly with the discursive possibilities that have been made observable through post-structuralist analysis.

As Mellor and Patterson comment:

> While modern linguistics is sometimes referred to as announcing the 'death of the subject', it can be argued, as Foucault (1973) does in *The Order of Things*, that on the contrary, it marks the birth of a modern conception of the subject in which subjectivity is both the effect of 'structures' *and* the ground where this effect will be opened to reflexive knowledge and seen through.
>
> (1996, p. 51)

The subject of post-structuralism, unlike the humanist subject, then, is constantly in process; it only exists as process; it is revised and (re)presented through images, metaphors, storylines and other features of language, such as pronoun grammar; it is spoken and respoken, each speaking existing in a palimpsest with the others. What Jones draws our attention to is that in attempting to reconceptualise the subject as process, we are limited by the images and metaphors we can find to create the new idea. Pronoun grammar is a good example of this. We cannot yet see how to do without it. We see the power of gendered pronouns, for example, to reconstitute the male/female binary every time we speak. We are frustrated to observe pronoun grammar re-creating the binary in the very language we use in our attempts to move beyond gender (Davies, 1989). Similarly, 'I', which signals 'identity', almost inevitably appears in the very same sentences we use to attempt to undo the idea of identity. Some post-structuralist writers adopt 'i' to signal the shift they are attempting to engage in. But the text/discourse relentlessly writes us as existing, even when our intention is to enable the reader to disattend the active subject/writer and to attend to the constitutive force of discourse.

Palimpsest, a metaphor frequently used in post-structuralist writing, is equally problematic. This metaphor is derived from the image of writing on parchment, writing which was only partially erased to make way for new writing, each previous writing, therefore, bumping into and shaping the reading of the next layer of writing. This metaphor is used to explain the ways in which the subject is written and overwritten through multiple and contradictory discourses. It enables us, for example, to imagine how the unitary, essential, pre-discursive self, constructed through humanist discourses, is still there, bumping into and shaping our interpretation of the self-as-process. At the same time, the concept of palimpsest holds the possibility of a conceptual trap. Since the image it may evoke is one in which the *original* writing is on a blank parchment, the metaphor of palimpsest can, without the writer or reader realising it, hold in place the idea that there is an original pre-discursive self that is shaped through discourse. Because the blank parchment can be imagined as visible if we were to rub out all the writing, the pre-discursive self who is free of discourses, and able therefore, freely, to choose amongst discourses, can be said to be 'there' in the metaphor. Nothing can prevent a reader who wants to read the metaphor that way from doing so.

The intention of those who use the palimpsest metaphor is not to invite this reading. Its power as a conceptual tool requires a focus on the multiple layers of writing, and their effect on one another in the reading of them. Foucault works hard to persuade the reader to abandon the binary of surface/depth and to imagine surface as infinitely folded and containing its own depth. Yet a reader who interprets, using binary strategies, can read something behind the surface which they take to be parchment, or prediscursive self, and the meanings the writer is struggling after are lost.

At the same time, any writer using the concepts of 'palimpsest' and 'surfaces' can continue to point out that 'selving' or subjectification can be understood in the intricate folds of reading and writing and that the parchment should not (mistakenly) be equated with either an imagined original self or the body. This is precisely the kind of work that Butler does in her discussion of the metaphor of self as performance. She makes clear that the post-structuralist subject is expressed (formed) in the very act of the performance, and does not exist independent of the performance. At the same time, she carefully explains the dangers of her metaphor if it brings to mind the actor (self) who acts many parts and who is identifiably separate from the part that is being played. Curiously, her warning both is and is not accepted by Jones. While she says 'performance' unacceptably invokes the performer behind the performance, she incorporates 'performance' into her repertoire of acceptable post-structuralist terminology.

Structuralism and post-structuralism

One reading of the text of Jones's argument is that the difference between Butler/Jones and Davies/the students lies in the different possible readings of the relations between structuralism and post-structuralism. Jones's reading of the relationship is that the determinism of structuralism is still there, but it has moved from structures to discourses. My reading has been different. While I have centred discourse, and recognised its constitutive force, I have read subjects as both constituted and constitu*tive*. Indeed, in my earliest attempts at post-structuralist writing (Davies, 1989), I find I took the fundamental difference between structuralism and post-structuralism to be the room for movement that the reflexively aware subject had once the constitutive power of discourses was made visible. I was fascinated by the ways in which the contradictory readings of myself, made so problematic within humanist theory, could become extraordinary resources for exploring the complex and dynamic relations between subjects and the discourses through which they were constituted (e.g. Davies, 1992, 1993).

Interestingly, I have found no two accounts which are in agreement on the precise difference between structuralism and post-structuralism. This is, of course, predictable given the diversity of writings pulled together under the label 'post-structuralism', and given that '...poststructuralism [has] openly sought out and celebrated the inconclusive nature of its own methodologies' (Fuery, 1995, p. 15). Jones' reading of the difference is as legitimate a reading as any other. However, the difference can also be read as Fuery reads it:

> Part of the reason why post-structuralism is designated 'post' is that it claims to have superseded structuralism by challenging two of its foundational claims. One is that structures are present in all spheres of human activity (from anthropology to economics to religion) and that by understanding such structures we gain a sense of 'truth'. The other claim is that the structure of the sign...is the systemic key to all processes of meaning and communication. Post-structuralism challenges these two concepts on the grounds that there can

be no truth or truths...outside the construction of [them];...furthermore, it is imperative not only to reveal the artifices of such social structures but also to develop a more dynamic model of the sign.

(1995, p. 38)

In other words, for Fuery, the important difference is that post-structuralism *rejects* structuralism's absolute certainties. Instead, it takes up and plays with the idea that any truth is constructed (presumably including structuralist and post-structuralist truths) and it seeks a dynamic (rather than a deterministic) under-standing of the way signs/discourses work. Fuery also points out that that dynamism is inherent in post-structuralism itself: 'The folds of post-structuralism – subjectivity, signification, culture, power, self-reflexive analysis and, of course, desire – can never be contained comfortably within any structure or system' (Fuery, 1995, p. 1).

Jones' article, in contrast, appears to seek certainties – a certain 'truth' about post-structuralism. But rather than fall into the trap of attempting to guess at Jones' intentions or desires in the production of the text, it is interesting to look more closely at the text itself, and at the process of analysis engaged in here.

In summary, the argument in the article appears to go as follows.

- Although I have argued (in Jones, 1993) that post-structuralist theory enables us to understand better how we are/become gendered, students 'struggle with its meanings'.
- A major source of their confusion is their lack of understanding of structural-ism. Structuralism introduces the counter intuitive notion 'which displaces the individual who chooses, thinks, and acts intentionally, with a "subject" who [is] formed through (produced by, inscribed with...) structures of culture, language and meaning (discourse)...'
- While students gain some useful insights from post-structuralist theory and they take up some of its language in their writing, they fail to let go of 'the irre-ducible "real person" who is "socially constructed" ...'. In doing so they fail to see that post-structuralist talk is 'predicated on an *anti*-humanist subject'. 'Despite the new language' the humanist subject is 'immovably present in stu-dents' reception of post-structuralist theory'. This immovability is a serious problem.
- Post-structuralist theory is different from structuralist theory in that it 'centres' language: 'At centre stage is not a real person ("us") who is "made into a subject (girl)," but the meaning systems which *produce* what counts as girls...' '...everything is determined – not by social structures this time, but by language'.
- The 'use of the term "position" and "positioning" to denote the productive possibilities in discourses for subjects' creates a 'sort of metaphorical, abstracted explanation' into which 'a humanist subject easily but illegitimately reappears'. Davies, in particular, in her use of the words 'forced choice', for example, feeds the students' belief in the choosing homunculus (or 'prediscur-sive subject'), floating free of discourse prior to making its choice amongst discursive possibilities. The students' confusion is thus fed by Davies who, like them, wanting her cake and eating it, uses the language of post-structuralist theory and yet still wants agency (meaning 'real people').
- Butler's idea of performance may also evoke the humanist subject as the one who chooses what to perform. However Butler clearly states: 'There is no

self...who maintains integrity prior to its entrance into this conflicted cultural field. There is only the taking up of the tools where they lie, where *the very "taking up" is enabled by the tool* lying there'. What this produces for Jones is the clear insight that 'The subject is the discursive practices which produce it'.

■ The active subject does, however, exist because we discursively produce it. If, however, students want to produce a doer behind the deeds, or actors who make choices, or subjects who position themselves, then they cannot legitimately do so within the discursive field of post-structuralist theory. In the final event, it does not matter which discourse they take up, as long as they use it correctly.

In constructing her argument, Jones defines two categories of talk, one which is post-structurally correct and one which she reads as guilty of humanism. For Jones, the humanist subject appears to be the 'real person' behind the surface who makes rational choices between different discourses or different subject positions. *Guilty phrases* which are seen to produce the spectre of this homunculus or pre-discursive self are:

■ 'We can only ever speak ourselves or be spoken into existence within the terms of the available discourses...choices are understood as more akin to "forced choices," since the subject's positioning within particular discourses makes the "chosen" line of action the only possible action' (Davies, 1991).
■ 'A particular strength of the post-structuralist research paradigm is that it recognises both the constitutive effects of discourse, and in particular of discursive practices, and at the same time recognises that people are capable of exercising choice in relation to these practices' (Davies and Harre, 1990).
■ 'Girls can be multiply positioned. They can be powerful, they can be powerless. They can be stroppy or shy. They are active in taking up these different subjectivities; they can position themselves in a range of ways, as tomboys or feminine' (student 1).
■ 'Discourses offer individuals numerous subject positions to take up. In my everyday life as a woman I might take on different, even contradictory, subjectivities...' (student 2).
■ 'There are a range of subject positions available to women in engineering textbooks. Some students take up the "woman engineer" position with alacrity, others struggle with the ambivalence they encounter in other positions which seem to produce the "woman engineer" as an impossibility' (student 3).

It is interesting to contrast these guilty phrases with apparently innocent ones. In this list I include the phrases Jones uses to refer to herself and her students. (This assumes, perhaps incorrectly, that Jones takes herself to be correctly using post-structuralist discourse.) The list also includes phrases from Butler:

Apparently non-guilty phrases:

■ 'terms such as "subjectivity," "positioning," "subject positions," have been taken up by students...' (Jones);
■ 'they struggle with its meanings' (Jones);
■ 'Students often understandably baulk at the way...accounts of the world are undermined...' (Jones);

■ '...students can barely begin to follow the debates when they have little sense of the historical development of the ideas they encounter with such suspicion' (Jones);

■ students 'adopt' discursive frameworks (Jones);

■ 'I am produced as gendered, and produce myself as such, through the meaningful actions (discursive practices) of others (and my own) in any context' (Jones);

■ 'The...injunction to be a given gender takes place through discursive routes: to be a good mother, to be a heterosexually desirable object, to be a fit worker...The convergence of such discursive injunctions produces the possibility of a complex reconfiguration' (Butler, 1990);

■ 'There is no self...who maintains integrity prior to its entrance into this conflicted cultural field. There is only the taking up of the tools where they lie, where *the very "taking up" is enabled by the tool* lying there' (Butler, 1990);

■ 'In this sense gender is always a doing, though not a doing by a subject who might be said to pre-exist the deed...' (Butler);

■ 'Through language we produce ourselves, "embodied in pronoun grammar in which a person understands themselves as historically continuous and unitary" – and, we might add, as choosing actors. In referring to "me" or "I," our language continually produces "me"; and thus that ongoing "me"/person exists' (Jones quoting Butler).

Curiously, it is very difficult to find the textual difference between the guilty phrases and the innocent ones. I use 'choice' while arguing that choice is constitutive. Butler describes scenes which imply that 'choices' must be made (which tool shall I pick up and how shall I use it, how shall I take up the 'possibilities of reconfiguration' made possible through contradictory 'discursive injunctions'?) She does not, however, make the active, choosing subject visible in her text. The invisible hand that takes up the tool in her metaphor reminds me of the invisible women in men's histories of early Australian settlement/invasion, who put the food on the table, who bore the children but were never themselves written about as subjects.

The three 'faulty' quotations from the students are not necessarily as faulty as they might seem on first reading. Jones assumes their faults are self-evident and so did I in my first reading of them. I saw them as struggling with issues more adequately dealt with in liberal feminist discourse rather than in post-structuralist discourse. Individual career choices are not the central subject matter of post-structuralism. But it is interesting to look more closely. Student 1 starts with the passive verb 'positioned', stating, 'Girls can be multiply positioned'. She then elaborates that multiplicity. Following that she tells us that the take-up of subjectivities is an active process and that the range of possible subjectivities can be very different. Her presumed fault? I suppose it is to assume that girls can be active in relation to discourse rather than always and only passive. As teacher, I might want to add: 'Positioning oneself' does always need to be accompanied by the phrase 'being positioned' as well as an understanding of the power of subject positions in that process. Student 2 also emphasises the multiple subject positions available to women in discourse. She imagines that she might in the future take on 'different, even contradictory, subjectivities'. Her presumed fault? Perhaps that she uses the active verb 'take on' instead of the passive verb, 'be taken up by'? Student 3 again begins with a statement about multiple subject positions. Some of these positions are taken up by some 'with alacrity' while others struggle with the ambivalence in the text which rules out an active take-up. It is not at all clear to me that these students intended to evoke a choosing homunculus or pre-discursive subject in what they wrote. Certainly the student writing about engineering seems to be struggling to express how discourses shape perception and desire. Their words could equally be read as attempts to analyse the complex relation between the constitutive force of multiple and contradictory discourses and the subject who is constituted through those discourses.

What is even more interesting, in examining Jones' text, however, is the similarity between the words of the students and the words Jones uses to describe those same students in their partial take-up of post-structuralist theory. In their own words they 'take things up with alacrity' or find a subject position 'produced as an impossibility'. They imagine themselves being 'multiply positioned', offered 'numerous subject positions to take up', actively taking up 'different subjectivities'; seeing that they 'might take on different, even contradictory, subjectivities...'. Jones writes of them as equally active in their relations with discourse: they 'struggle with its meanings', they 'baulk at' it, even though they have 'learned to question', 'to see', 'to become critical', 'to understand', and they 'encounter [certain ideas] with suspicion' and they 'adopt' discursive frameworks. The students thus constituted in Jones' writing certainly do not seem to confirm Butler's claim, 'There is only the taking up of the tools where they lie, where *the very "taking up" is enabled by the tool* lying there' (Butler, 1990). According to Jones' own analysis, the taking up of post-structuralist tools is not enabled simply by them lying there. There are other tools needed (such as structuralism), and, according to Jones, there are other tools getting in the way, having their constitutive effects, occluding the perception of the thing lying there, preventing its taking the student over.

Is Jones saying indirectly, through her choice of words, that she does not agree with Butler, and that she now prefers to engage in humanist analyses? On this point I am not clear. However, she does appear unequivocally to claim the active subject (acting upon discourse) as incompatible with post-structuralist theory. Of course, Jones is not alone in this reading of post-structuralism. There are other readers who define it as ruling out altogether the possibility of a speaking subject. But as Hazel observes in response to one such reader:

> I see no impossible conflict between the practice of a politics of voice and the critical examination of its ground;... 'the experiencing subject' that we all feel ourselves to be and for whom we seek acknowledgement, is not something that can easily be comprehended...[and] despite the relationship we inevitably retain to the humanist subject, this [comprehension] is not an unproblematic goal for feminism.

(1996, p. 315)

And Flax argues, even more strongly, that emancipatory struggle and the post-structuralist subject not only can but must go conceptually hand in hand as:

> Many theorists argue that the decentered/postmodernist forms of subjectivity some critics advocate as replacements for older ones cannot exercise the agency required for liberatory political activity. Are the claims of the Enlightenment philosophers from Kant to Habermas correct? Does emancipatory action – and the very idea and hope of emancipation – depend upon the development of a unitary self capable of autonomy and undetermined self-reflection? Can there be forms of subjectivity that are simultaneously

fluid, multicentered, and effective in the 'outer' worlds of political life and
social relations? Could multicentered and overdetermined subjects recognize
relations of domination and struggle to overcome them? I believe a unitary self
is unnecessary, impossible, and a dangerous illusion. Only multiple subjects
can invent ways to struggle against domination that will not merely recreate it.

(1993, pp. 92–93)

Post-structuralist pedagogy

Jones' observation of her students is that their understanding of post-structuralist
theory is inadequate because it is contaminated by their already constituted selves
through other discourses. What puzzles me is that their attempts are not welcomed
as a stepping off stone which the students can use to reflexively explore the ways in
which they are constituted as subjects through these conflicting discourses. One of
the major difficulties in introducing post-structuralist theory to students is to make
language reflexively visible, that is, not just visible as an object, but visible as an
active force shaping bodies, shaping desire, shaping perception. In my own experience of teaching, the words of post-structuralist theory are not enough. The
students have to be able to catch language in the act of shaping subjectivities. An
examination of their own writing, or of their own storytelling, or of their own acts
of reading can be ideal means by which they can begin to catch the text in the act
of constituting (Davies, 1993, 1996a).

Jones' pedagogical intent with students who engage with post-structuralist
discourse would seem to be, in the final event, that they use it 'correctly', rather
than that they develop the reflexive awareness and competencies that enable them
to engage with the possibilities post-structuralism can open up. She wants them, in
other words, to become competent mimics. She is afraid they have become incompetent to the extent that they are mimicking the wrong person and thus muddling
their discourses, using 'positioned' when they should use 'produced'. Of course it
is always partially true that what we require of our students is that they learn to
mimic the discourses we want them to be able to use (Davies, 1996b). Crane talks
of the dilemma this creates for students who are simultaneously required to be
original and to become 'imposters':

> As a student, I've always hated brownnosers. As a teacher . . . , I've also hated
> them, but only when they've been too 'obvious'; that is, when their perform-
> ance is too easily seen, when their interest in me as a teacher is not 'personal',
> but an act, false, an imposture – which may mean that it seems too personal.
> Yet (true) imposture – unlike impersonation – can't be seen too easily. An
> imposter, after all, relies on acting and seeming genuine, and that label only
> really fits after the ingenuity of the act – that blurring of false and true – has
> been revealed.
>
> (Crane, 1995, pp. ix–x)

It would seem that both Jones and I want our students to become competent in
their use of post-structuralist discourse, though Jones suggests it may indeed be too
hard for many students. She also claims she does not mind 'which discursive
framework' her students 'adopt'. (I am sure she does mind, actually. I cannot
imagine her cheerfully reading an essay using the discursive framework of

members of the Ku Klux Clan, for example, and complimenting the student on how well s/he had taken up the discourse of that group.) She does not mind, she says, as long as they understand that they cannot use (some) active verbs such as 'the subject who positions herself or who chooses, or who struggles after the possibility of agency, and at the same time claim to be using post-structuralist theory. Students must take a pure line in which all signs of an active, individual subject are removed if they want to claim to be using post-structuralist theory'. For me, this sounds worryingly like the correct knowledge of Parsons or Marx or the Bible that students have been required to achieve in the past. Both feminist pedagogy and post-structuralist pedagogy can be less authoritarian and less absolute in their strategies, and thus have quite different effects.

In my own teaching, I do not want my students to become mimics of what they take post-structuralism to be, producing forgeries of 'correct' 'anti-humanist' experiencing of 'themselves' (though I have no doubt some of them will do that). Rather, what I want of them is to learn the skills of finding the texts/discourses they interact with in the act of shaping them and shaping what they see. When these are humanist texts, I want them in particular to be able to see that process, to see why they find those texts desirable and pleasurable, and why the text of themselves as humanist subject is so hard to eradicate from their writing. At the same time, I want them to experience the disruptive/blissful possibilities opened up through the play of post-structuralist practices (Davies, 1994). This requires a particular way of attending to the details of the texts they read and see and hear and the texts they produce (which includes the texts of themselves). The skills of attending to texts in post-structuralist ways are ones which must be struggled after continuously; they are not achievable as a repertoire of specific skills, though there are ways of writing and speaking which are helpful in producing post-structuralist practices.

What seems most powerful to me in post-structuralist theory is precisely the fact that we are taken up/over/under by contradictory discursive practices. As humanists we can engage in quite extraordinary intellectual feats to convince ourselves of our unitariness. As feminists we can use the confusion to sharpen our reflexive gaze and resist our take-up in discourses we find undesirable; as post-structuralists we can find the ways in which the 'injunction to be a given gender takes place' (Butler, 1990). What I encourage my students to do is to take up the possibilities inherent in the complex reconfigurations post-structuralist theory makes possible, and to find where that might take them (Davies *et al.*, 1997). For those who do so, they may well find themselves irreversibly traversed and shaken by new discourses. It is that shaking up that is so fascinating (and sometimes dangerous) for students of post-structuralism:

> Lacan wants us, his readers (his analysands?), to be challenged and changed intellectually through his seminars and writings. This is because at the heart of things, as with the poststructuralist movement overall (if one can speak of it in such terms), is the need to analyse analysis, understand understanding, interpret interpretation. And once such a task is undertaken, one of the consequences is a self-reflexivity that must challenge the very discursive practices in operation.
>
> (Fuery, 1995, pp. 9–10)

And classrooms are, after all, also sites of struggle, struggles that are about existence and about power. As a pedagogical strategy, I do not believe it is appropriate, or even useful, to declare that the familiar sense of self the students have achieved is not only *sous rature* – under erasure, but that it simply does not exist *whilst we are engaging in post-structuralist discourse.* To put something under erasure is to say that it is *a term we still need and use,* but which needs deconstructing and moving beyond. To enable students to move confidently beyond the humanist conception of the subject, students need familiar ground from which to speak and write. The texts of their own speaking and writing can then become the material that they use to acquire the skills of deconstruction. The complexity of this task should not be underestimated, however, and if students need some aspects of familiar discourses in order to continue as speaking, writing subjects while they find their deconstructive feet, then it is important to ensure that they have easy (and eventually reflexively aware) access to them.

REFERENCES

Althusser, L. (1984) *Essays on Ideology* (London, Verso).

Butler, J. (1990) *Gender Trouble: Feminism and The Subversion of Identity* (New York, Routledge).

Butler, J. (1992) 'Contingent foundations', in J. Butler and J.W. Scott (eds), *Feminists Theorize the Political* (New York, Routledge).

Crane, D. (1995) 'A personal postscript, an impostured preface', in J. Gallop (ed.), *Pedagogy. The Question of Impersonation* (Bloomington, IN, Indiana University Press).

Davies, B. (1989) *Frogs and Snails and Feminist Tales. Preschool Children and Gender* (Sydney, Allen & Unwin).

Davies, B. (1991) 'The concept of agency: a feminist poststructuralist analysis', *Social Analysis*, 30: 42–53.

Davies, B. (1992) 'Women's subjectivity and feminist stores', in C. Ellis and M. Flaherty (eds), *Research on Subjectivity: Windows on Lived Experience* (Newbury Park, CA, Sage).

Davies, B. (1993) *Shards of Glass. Children Reading and Writing beyond Gendered Identity* (Sydney, Allen & Unwin).

Davies, B. (1994) *Poststructuralist Theory and Classroom Practice* (Geelong, Deakin University Press).

Davies, B. (1996a) *Power/Knowledge/Desire. Changing School Organisation and Management Practices* (Canberra, Department of Education, Employment and Youth Affairs).

Davies, B. (1996b) 'What makes Australian education strange: Australian education in the Asian context', *Australia in its Asian Context, Occasional Paper Series 1/1996*, pp. 22–30 (Canberra, Academy of the Social Sciences in Australia).

Davies, B. *et al.* (1997) 'Ruptures in the skin of silence: a collective biography', *Hecate*.

Davies, B. and Harré, R. (1990) 'Positioning: the discursive production of selves', *Journal for the Theory of Social Behaviour*, 20: 43–63.

Flax, J. (1993) *Disputed Subjects: Essays on Psychoanalysis, Politics and Philosophy* (New York, Routledge).

Foucault, M. (1977) 'What is an author', in D. Bouchard (ed.), *Language, Counter-memory, Practice*, pp. 113–138 (Ithaca, NY, Cornell University Press).

Foucault, M. (1983) 'The subject and power', in H. Dreyfus and P. Rabinow (ed.), *Michel Foucault: beyond structuralism and hermeneutics* (Chicago, IL, University of Chicago Press).

Fuery, P. (1995) *Theories of Desire* (Melbourne, Melbourne University Press).

Hazel, V. (1996) 'The politics of voice', *Australian Feminist Studies*, 11: 309–316.

Jones, A. (1993) 'Becoming a "girl": post-structuralist suggestions for educational research', *Gender and Education*, 5: 157–167.

Jones, A. (1997) 'Teaching post-structuralist feminist theory in education: student resistances', *Gender and Education*, 9: 261–269.

Kearney, R. (ed.) (1994) 'Jaques Derrida', in *Dialogues with Contemporary Continental Philosophers: The Phenomenological Heritage* (Manchester NH, Manchester University Press).

Lacan, J. (1966) *Ecrits* (London, Tavistock).

Levine, M. (1991) 'Translator's introduction', in S. Weber (ed.), *Return to Freud. Jacques Lacan's Dislocation of Psychoanalysis* (Cambridge, Cambridge University Press).

Mellor, B. and Patterson, A. (1996) 'Reading capacities: foundations or formulae?', *Interpretations*, 29: 46–69.

PART III

EDUCATION POLICY AND MANAGEMENT

EIGHT

EQUAL OPPORTUNITIES: RHETORIC OR ACTION

Sue Lees and Maria Scott

Source: 'Equal opportunities: rhetoric or action', *Gender and Education*, 2(3): 333–343, 1990.

Introduction

The recent Report of the Hansard Society Commission on *Women at the Top* (1990) documents how little change has been achieved in women's access to positions of power in Britain. Between 1975 and 1988, the proportion of women studying in the universities increased from 35% to 42%. However, the proportion of women in senior academic posts is derisory and has scarcely risen. Thus while women form 11% of full-time non-clinical staff, they make up only 3% of university professors (Hansard Society Commission, 1990, p. 65). The report documents discrimination against women in all areas of life, politics, the economy, the law, the universities and business. Barriers continue to block or impede women's careers in politics, universities and public life. As Adrienne Rich pointed out over ten years ago, universities are hierarchical institutions: 'At the top is a cluster of highly paid and prestigious persons, chiefly men, whose careers entail the services of a very large base of ill-paid or unpaid persons, chiefly women' (Rich, 1979).

Equal opportunity (EO) policies challenge this elite, the unrepresentativeness of those at the top and the academic criteria that are used to retain power. It calls on men to step down to make way for less represented groups. It challenges the separation between the public and the private and argues that if women are to obtain EOs, men will have to step out of their ivory towers and take equal responsibility in the servicing of society. This involves taking equal responsibility for housework and child care as well as equal time and opportunities for self development. The separation between work and home will need to be broken down. The radical tone of many of these proposals has meant that they have not even been on the agenda in the university sector. In other institutions of higher education, however, in the last ten years, some of these demands have been voiced and have even led to proposals for action.

It is against this background that it is particularly useful to examine what has been happening in EOs initiatives in higher educational institutions outside the university sector. There are a number of reasons why polytechnics and colleges of higher education should be more open to change than universities. These institutions have always had a concern with providing education for the less privileged and have had more flexible entry requirements for mature students. A higher proportion of their students are female or from ethnic minorities. This is increasingly the case as the number of 18-year olds has declined and the labour force requires more graduates. In addition, polytechnics are more responsive to new developments than the universities.

What does equal opportunities mean?

The first difficulty in evaluating EO is the term itself. Everyone voices support but EOs can mean totally contradictory things to different people. In particular, a distinction can be made between three areas:

1   changing employment practices of staff to make them less discriminatory;
2   encouraging access for non-traditional students and trying to adapt the institution to the needs of those with child care and domestic responsibilities; and
3   changing the curriculum so that it addresses issues of gender.

In practice, EOs' initiatives very often amount to little more than statements of intent. This does not however mean that the potential of these initiatives is not immense. Put into effect they would radicalise institutions, modify their manifest and latent discriminatory policies, change the face of education. EO means challenging the present structure of employment in terms of appointments, promotion and the criteria of expertise. It means democratising the institution and allowing women's voice to be heard within the curriculum. It means breaking down the separation between institutions and the home. In practice, however, change is often slow and fraught. Monitoring change, a vital prerequisite of EO initiatives, is often refused for this very reason. Even EO units set up to monitor initiatives are often not allowed to do so and act as little more than a public relations front. As several investigators have pointed out (see Jewson and Mason, 1986; Webb and Liff, 1987) in attempting to implement EO, the aim is not so concerned with radically changing the practices of institutions as with tinkering with the procedures to ensure that individuals are treated in a standardised way, for example, that women should not be questioned about their child care responsibilities in selection processes, jobs should be advertised widely so that ethnic groups are not excluded. The main concerns are not with changing the employment structure, at present biased towards white males, or with prioritising the provision of adequate child care facilities (a crucial precondition for equal access).

This dominant model described by Jewson and Mason as 'liberal', is based on the assumption, as noted earlier, that equality will be achieved by treating individuals in a standardised way rather than as members of significantly different social groups. Fairness is equated with standard procedures of employment regardless of the *outcome* rather than with politicising employment decisions to change the staff structure and make it more representative of the community which it serves. The emphasis on standardisation within a framework where the composition of panels is overwhelmingly male and white, where the criteria for appointments are biased towards the present structures, and where the barriers to educational access for certain groups is disregarded, precludes the possibility of change. Many do not even see the need for change. Arguments about changing the criteria by which appointments are made are dismissed on the grounds that standards would be lowered. Such arguments overlook the built-in biases of power holders to define criteria that serve to replicate their kind. In practice, the majority of staff within any institution are committed to maintaining the status quo so that any policies that seek to challenge existing practice are likely to be resisted. This is one of the contradictory facets of EO policies. The very power groups who are responsible for adopting the so-called EO policies are the groups that are most likely to lose out and, therefore, most motivated to resist change. This is why institutions have been so reluctant to monitor change and so anxious to redefine what is meant by EO in their own terms.

The painful process of change

It should be remembered that change is often a painful process and is unsettling and threatening to many. When seeking to alter attitudes towards long-established practices, conceptual frameworks or sexist or racist views, the process can be frightening. To disregard this and pretend people are just stubborn or lazy is to be short-sighted and to have no vision of how change can come about. The slowness of progress must be accepted if disillusionment is not to set in: the difficulties should not be underestimated. Look how long it took for women to gain the vote and how little influence that gain has had on their involvement in political processes. Why should it be any easier to gain a voice in decision-making processes in education?

EO initiatives in higher educational institutions

Looking back on the last ten years, a number of institutions of higher education have experienced some grass roots activity by women aimed at changing discriminatory practices. Most institutions have drawn up policies. Some institutions, mainly in the polytechnic sector, have gone further and prioritised EO initiatives. At one polytechnic, it was after the appointment of a new director in 1983, sympathetic to EO policies, that a report on the needs of women in the polytechnic was commissioned which identified and highlighted, for the first time, the disadvantaged position of polytechnic women. Following this initiative, the academic board set up an EO committee which was chaired by an assistant director. Because the EO committee was a committee of the academic board everything proposed was obliged to pass through academic board before going to the governors. A wide range of policies, involving both a publicly stated intention of EO in employment and many positive measures to overcome women's disadvantage were accepted in principle.

Following the report, a series of developments and policies evolved covering such issues as the need for child care facilities, career break, job share, flexitime, EO in employment and academic affairs. Drawing up policy statements was far less of a problem than actually implementing them. Many women ended up feeling that there had been something tokenistic about EO; a lot of noise and not much outcome. Policies were proposed, but did not come into existence; or agreed but not implemented; or any rights women may have gained through this process were not made clear to them.

Often proposals were sent back to be amended and long delays ensued before they got back onto the agenda. Often EO matters were given low priority and 'dropped off the end' of the agenda for lack of time. Some board members effectively opposed proposals. The trade unions represented themselves as favourable to equality but in practice were among the most serious sources of delay. The EO committee did a great deal in raising awareness of the sex equality issue but resigned as a gesture of protest at what it felt to be a lack of genuine commitment on the part of the polytechnic's management to progress and implement EO policies. After the resignation of the committee, a researcher was invited in the spring of 1987 to assess the achievements and failures of the sex equality process. She distributed a questionnaire. More than half the respondents felt that developments had been impeded or slowed down by a number of groups with influence in the polytechnic. The polytechnic council, academic board and their committees were cited most often, followed by 'individual men in authority' and 'middle management in general'. Some women believed the polytechnic to be steeped in individual sexism. Such issues are not unique.

Sheila Quaid, an EO officer, in a paper given at the European Forum Conference of Socialist Feminists at Manchester in 1988 outlined the following prerequisites as necessary for institutional change to occur in regard to EO issues:

1   Examination of existing structures.
2   Training – both to meet the needs of women staff and to extend awareness of the issues for those senior staff with responsibility in relation to implementation.
3   The review and assessment of procedures and practices in employment practice, and provision of a focal point to co-ordinate those with expertise in EO initiatives.
4   The setting up of a support group of women and of a core of people who would act as advocates in cases of complaints.

Unfortunately, in the case study discussed, few of these prerequisites existed. There were, however, some positive achievements. The crèche for 20 children opened in late 1984 was expanded. By 1990, this had been extended to 48 places with facilities for up to 60. Support from the top of the institution, though not enough to meet all demands, did seem to have led to some real advance at least in the provision of child care facilities.

At another higher educational institution progress was made during a short period when EO issues were first raised at grass roots level. Women succeeded in setting up a broadly representative committee which as a subcommittee of the board of governors has some powers of implementation. The management was not at first aware of the radical and potentially 'destabilising' implications of the EO policies put forward. For a short time, women not only had some say in the drawing up of a policy, which had happened in other institutions across the country, but more radically, were also able to have some effect on its implementation. The conflict that ensued is important to consider as it illustrates the contradictions and tensions that can arise between grass roots demands and management who often see change as disruptive.

The involvement of an active group of women staff, concerned with EO initiatives led to far more radical measures being proposed than management had anticipated. An EO (gender) committee with wide representation from staff across the institution was set up, chaired by a single parent governor sympathetic to EO. The strength of this committee lay in its direct link with the governors. Motions passed at the EO subcommittee went directly to the board, preventing interference from committees, the directorate or bureaucracy. This overcame, albeit temporarily, one hurdle to policy implementation. When issues relating to such core questions as the distribution of resources, the monitoring of various employment practices and the questioning of the day to day running of the institution were brought up, it was not long before management moved in, and dissolved the EO subcommittee on the grounds that it had caused delay and duplication.

This was far from true. Progress had only been delayed by the reluctance of the bureaucracy and the management to bring about change. The proposed new structure and the report supporting it were both framed within a particular model of EO implementation, that was a *top-down* approach, where issues of concern are decided at high levels within the institution and a 'pro-active' structure is formed around specifically defined tasks. This model was totally inappropriate for the achievement of EO. An EO programme must allow for members of disadvantaged groups to have a voice in setting the agenda for issues of concern. By necessity this implies a need for a 're-active' structure, where the problems and areas of concern highlighted by representative bodies within the institution can be effectively implemented at senior levels within the management structure. However, this can only be achieved if the senior management is committed to change rather than to their own vested interests within the present status quo. To challenge the bureaucratic hierarchical structure of institutions by the introduction of more democratic structures is the only way of bringing about change. Present EO measures are likely to benefit a few token women and lead to the appointment of a few black staff, but will do little to improve the position of disadvantaged groups within the institution or change the overall composition of staff.

Monitoring and resource implications

All those attempting to introduce EO initiatives have emphasised that they can only be effective if adequately resourced and monitored. In some institutions, policies have been adopted *in principle* but this often means that little can be changed unless there are no resource implications. Bids for funding the implementation of the EO programme in general have to be considered in competition with other similarly agreed objectives. The argument that no resources are available for EO initiatives is frequently put forward. Though it is not possible to fund EO initiatives without resources, imagination could be used to transfer from other areas.

For example, as long as such issues as child care provision are regarded as extras, not vital for the entry of many women into academic life, it will be summarily dismissed. Why is child care provision not as much a priority as the provision of sports facilities or flower beds? It is farcical that institutions can espouse a commitment to EO, yet fail to provide basic facilities to enable women with children to study at all. Yet, the idea of allocating a percentage of the budget to provide adequate facilities is considered quite unrealistic, particularly at a time when higher education is suffering from cutbacks. Governing and academic boards and committees, largely composed of those who have never been responsible for looking after young children, dismiss the demands of women students and staff for prioritising this issue without a qualm. The idea of allocating adequate resources to offer child care facilities as a right is not given serious consideration. At one higher education institution in 1979–80, for example, only 0.01% out of a total budget of £15 m was allocated to the nursery. During the same financial year £20,000 was allocated to the construction of a covered tennis court. At another institution in 1980, only £5000 was allocated to the nursery out of an estimated budget of £17 m. From the same budget £48,700 was set aside for maintenance of athletic facilities and £40,000 for upkeep of gardens. In many institutions no budget is allocated to the nursery, though a shortfall from fees is topped up. Pressure is, however, often put on staff to reduce the extent of the shortfall by running jumble sales etc. Such financial allocations raise fundamental questions about the reality of higher educational institutions commitment to EO for women.

Problems of implementation

Barriers to implementing policies within a bureaucratic institution should not be underestimated. Bureaucratic processes can be used very effectively to block any change even if measures have been agreed by committees. Agreed policies can disappear under a pile of paper. Looking back over the past ten years, let us sum up what has been achieved in those few higher educational institutions where EO has been on the agenda. Taking the three areas which come under the rubric of EO, let us look at how much difference these initiatives have made.

1   In employment, involving both selection and promotion, little change has occurred in the representation of women. At no higher educational institution has there been a formal spelling out or adoption and monitoring of positive action in promotion/regrading of activities or appointments. It was reported at one polytechnic that much misunderstanding and confusion existed. There were allegations, on the one hand, of lack of a positive policy for women and, on the other, of favouritism and counter discrimination against men. Without targets or quotas it is unlikely that whatever procedures are agreed, the inbuilt bias of the present appointment panels will change. If such a policy were adopted, it would only be effective if it were adequately monitored. This requires the availability and constant updating of comparable statistical data on a wide range of indicators. This should be part of a management information activity designed to guide planning and evaluation throughout the polytechnic's management system.

2   A significant expansion in Access courses for Non-traditional students, mainly women, has undoubtedly taken place. This embraces not only Return to Learning courses but Access courses into non-traditional higher educational courses such as Architecture, Electronics, Engineering, Science, Computing and Law. Attempts have been made in some institutions to provide some extra support for these students but little has been done to address their child care needs. The standard of child care provision has improved in some institutions but the provision of child care as a right is far from accepted. Some polytechnics still have no nursery. The argument is one of priorities. By early 1990, at one polytechnic where the child care campaign had led to an improvement in the facilities, the number of nursery places had, however, not increased. When the issue of child care was raised in meetings it was still ignored and considered irrelevant to academic issues.

3   Changing curricula so that issues of gender are addressed is the area of EO that
      has been most effective. The growth of Women's Studies courses in polytechnics
      has been startling over the past decade and is still expanding. Both at under-
      graduate level (at Middlesex Polytechnic, the Polytechnic of East London,
      Polytechnic of North London, Sheffield and Lancashire Polytechnics) and at
      post graduate level (at Middlesex, South Bank, Sheffield, Wolverhampton, East
      Anglia Higher Education College) Women's Studies courses have been set up
      and are flourishing. At universities, too, Women's Studies MA courses have
      proliferated from the first at Kent and Bradford to courses at York, Bristol,
      Exeter and the Institute of Education, to name but a few. Lancashire University
      also has a popular undergraduate programme and Sheffield is extending its
      Certificate course to degree level.

Options in Women's Studies, Sexuality and Feminist Theory are also now an
integral part of many degree courses, from Cultural Studies and the Social Sciences
to vocational courses for social workers. Developments are even taking place in
introducing gender issues into computing and science and technology courses. In
many institutions race, gender and sexual orientation are on the agenda as issues
to be looked at in relation to the curriculum. Progress may seem slow but compared with ten years ago, the climate and awareness of these issues have changed
dramatically. All these developments have rested on the significant expansion of
publishing in the area.

Positive action

There is a contradiction implicit in all EO employment policies in education. The
goal is to achieve a more representative staff but the only effective means of achieving
this goal (positive action) is unacceptable and paradoxically seen as discriminatory.
At the launch of the report *Women at the Top* to the Hansard Annual General
Meeting in April 1990, Lady Howe, when asked by an MP what could be done
about men who objected to women's promotion replied, 'Don't misunderstand me.
I am not in favour of positive action'. A common feature of EO policy implementation is to deny that their effectiveness involves a loss of power to the present
incumbents, a changing of long-standing practices, conflict rather than consensus.
It is when broader issues of disadvantage (in regard to nursery provision and the
processes of appointment and promotion of staff and management structures
themselves) are raised that tension in negotiations with senior management arises.

Achievements of the equal opportunity initiatives

In five years little has changed fundamentally but the climate has changed and EO
in many institutions is now firmly on the agenda. Some have agreed employment
procedures, and staff on appointments panels have to undergo EO training.
However, since this is unmonitored it can easily be ignored. There has probably
been some general improvement in employment practice, but the appointment and
promotion of women has not markedly improved. Ethnic monitoring is gradually
being introduced in many places. It is significant that many of these changes have

been brought about as a result of commitment from the top, often in response to pressure from outside. Curriculum reform is also occurring in many institutions. Access courses have proliferated and such issues as adapting criteria to encompass non-traditional student recruitment are on the agenda. A number of working groups have met and produced useful reports but are hampered by the lack of monitoring and absence of processes of implementation. Disability and gay and lesbian committees have been set up in some places.

Some lessons can be learned from these early attempts at EO Initiatives that arise from the grass roots and are supported by several constituencies, but the constraints disadvantaged groups experience resulting from their responsibilities outside the institution makes it hard for any women's campaign to be sustained.

Many who support EO initiatives face hostility, out of proportion to the issues raised or changes advocated. This indicates how contentious such policies are. In one institution an EO committee was seen as a staff committee 'gone wild', totally unrealistic in its demands and a threat to the 'reasonable' taken for granted processes of the polytechnic. The research projects undertaken by the committee carried out by well established and professionally trained researchers were described as 'biased' even before completion. This was one way of marginalising any recommendations for change. Above all, to be involved in such recommendations is to jeopardise one's progression within the present structure. One member who was in line for promotion in one institution was told by management that she would have to decide 'whose side she was on'. At another institution a few people of both sexes felt the EO Committee to be the tool of an unrepresentative clique of feminists, too militant in their cause, giving EO too high a profile and provoking a backlash. The experience has been very similar to that described by Martin and Rein's (1970) description of positive discrimination initiatives in America in the 1960's where attempts to change government institutions came up against vested interests and resulted in little progress.

Crucial prerequisites for change

Little will be achieved overnight. It is all too easy to become disillusioned and disheartened by the hostility with which demands are met. It is difficult to achieve much unless at least some of the following prerequisities are present:

1   Firm commitment to changing the employment structure of institutions through positive action, the setting of targets or quotas for the selection and promotion procedures, and monitoring of the process.
2   The establishment of an EO committee with wide representation to give a voice to unrepresented groups within the institutions and a commitment to taking notice of what they say.
3   A reappraisal of total resource allocations of the institutions with a view to transferring resources to EO initiatives from elsewhere. This should involve channelling resources to disadvantaged groups themselves.
4   A recognition of the structural sources of inequality and a reassessment of the taken for granted concept of ability or talent in regard to appointments and promotion.
5   A recognition that bureaucratic devices can operate to facilitate the disappearance of EO issues from the institutional agenda, delay action and defuse the energies of women seeking change.

6   A recognition of forms of resistance to implementation. Power groups will usually resist change which means that management will often seek to control and oppose initiatives. Women too who have become part of the male structure will often be pushed to the forefront of resistance tactics, as 'legitimate' obstructors.

7   A commitment to strengthening the identity, culture and organisation of women and disadvantaged groups in order to 'forge a new power base' to 'open up the possibility of greater change' (see Davies, 1988).

8   A commitment to engage men actively in dealing with male attitudes and practices.

Mechanisms of resistance

Cynthia Cockburn in considering the disillusionment of many concerned with EO policies reviewed the potential of such policies for progressive change within organisations (Cockburn, 1989). She criticises the limitations of both the 'liberal' and 'radical' model of change put forward by Jewson and Mason (1986) and instead suggests a 'transformational' strategy. She points out that 'radical' EO, in the sense of positive discrimination for a particular interest group, may be necessary as a first step, but is retrogressive in further dividing the already fragmented powerless groups:

> It lacks many dimensions. It seeks to give disadvantaged groups a boost up the ladder, while leaving the structure of that ladder and the disadvantages it entails as it was before. It fails to address processes in the life of the organisation that, if the on-going changes of all groups are to be equalised and sustained, must be democratised and opened. It does not question the role and purpose of the organisation. It does not change attitudes and cultures. And it does not question the damaging relationship that work currently has to home and private life. It is about gaining power not changing it.
>
> (Cockburn, 1989, p. 217)

She suggests that what emerges from studies of EO policies is an EO agenda of shorter or greater length. At its shortest it involves new measures to minimise bias in procedures such as recruitment and promotion. It is formal and managerial, but nonetheless desirable. At its longest and most ambitious it is a project of transformation for organisations which tackles the nature of power itself, both in the sense of how power is reproduced as residing in the same group and how it is reproduced as the same kind of power.

In considering how power is retained, she isolates from her study of a High Street Retail company five important mechanisms which are equally applicable to educational institutions. First, by continually emphasising the ostensible purpose of the organisation ('We're here to make a profit', 'We're here to provide a service' or likewise, we suggest, 'We're here to provide education'). Second, by defining what is legitimate EO policies (equal chances are OK while positive action to overcome past discrimination is not). Third, by defining when it is and when it is not appropriate for groups to be identified as 'different' (Yes when you want to exploit them, No when it is a matter of autonomous organisation and pressure). Fourth, a consistent refusal by men to take up the provisions for leave of absence, long or short, to look after babies, children and ill relatives. Fifth, the retaining by men of a regime of organisation sexuality which is specifically heterosexual and continually puts women, to say nothing of gays and lesbians, on the defensive. The result of such mechanisms, suggests Cockburn, is that positive action for equality tends to keep the form given it by 'benefactors' at the top, and not to develop into a grass roots movement from below.

Conclusion

The Hansard Society Commission Report on *Women at the Top* (1990) argued that all institutions of higher education should appoint an EO Officer who will produce regular audits on the progress of women within the institution, and that this should be combined with the setting of voluntary targets. It goes on to say:

> These targets would not be given any statutory force. Their function would in part be that of consciousness-raising: and failure to achieve the target would give rise to questions about whether the institution is adopting the right approach to ensure EO becomes a reality.
>
> (Ibid., p. 67)

This statement presumes that inequality is only really a result of failure of present management to realise that women are unrepresented and that the only obstacle to change is ignorance. It fails to take into account the vested interests of power groups who are intent on holding onto power and to recognise that male power is an aspect of women's subordination. It fails to take into account that women are incorporated in different ways into the institution, and that most women staff and students carry a 'double' load. It assumes that change will come about by consensus without conflict. Such an apologetic approach to the introduction of targets needs explanation.

Why do women involved in EO dissociate themselves from the only effective way of bringing about more equality, by an enforceable programme of positive action? EO has always been constrained by the idea that positive action is a discrimination in itself, that to prioritise the appointment of women rather than redressing the inbuilt biases of present appointment practices would be wrong and would lead to a 'lowering of academic standards' and a general decline in academia. The spin-offs from encouraging more women into academic life (not only in providing role models for the increasing numbers of women entering higher education and non-traditional areas of study, but also of breaking down the ivory tower mentality of many educational institutions and transforming the curriculum) are scarcely given any credence at all. Men would benefit too from a breaking down of the gender division though it may take a leap of the imagination for them to appreciate this. With the increase in staff student ratios and the greater pressure of work it is becoming increasingly difficult for women staff with responsibilities outside to survive even at lower levels of the institutional hierarchy. For women students too, the prospect of student loans and financial pressures make it harder and harder to manage.

For EO initiatives to be in any sense meaningful, there must be a clear acknowledgement that change involves conflict and that conflict may arise not only between the demands of the unrepresented and powerful but also between the disadvantaged groups themselves. The progressive aspect of conflict should be recognised. With scarce resources, priorities will need to be set between the needs of teaching versus non-teaching staff, manual versus non-manual workers, black versus white, disabled versus abled and men versus women; this will raise dissension. The challenge to the mono white male culture will also involve making alliances with men who support these initiatives as in every institution there are some men who would welcome change, in spite of the restriction of their privileges. EO initiatives can only be implemented if all concerned have a clear commitment to the policy.

REFERENCES

Cockburn, Cynthia (1989) 'Equal opportunities: the short and the long agenda', *Industrial Relations Journal*, March, pp. 213–225.

Davies, Celia (1988) 'Workplace action programmes for equality for women: an orthodoxy examined', paper presented to the conference, *EO for Men and Women in Higher Education*, University College, Dublin, September.

Hansard Society Commission (1990) *Report on Women at the Top* (London, Hansard Society).

Jewson, N. and Mason, D. (1986) 'The theory and practice of EO policies: liberal and radical approaches', *Sociological Review*, 34: 307–315.

Marris, P. and Rein, M. (1971) *Dilemmas of Social Reform* (London, Penguin).

Quaid, S. (1988) 'Structures and strategies for equality policies in further education', paper presented to the *European Forum Conference of Socialist Feminists*, Manchester, United Kingdom.

NINE

VOICE, HARMONY AND FUGUE* IN GLOBAL FEMINISM

Nelly P. Stromquist

Source: 'Voice, harmony and fugue in global feminism',
Gender and Education, 12(4): 419–433, 2000.

Introduction

At its core, feminism has a dual nature: it is a theory of power relations between women and men, and it is a movement seeking social justice. Its perspectives on social and political life have resulted in a questioning of the normative social order and a new assessment of priorities in state policies. Today, most feminists are sensitive to the complex ways in which gender intersects with other social markers, but diverge in how best to address them. Overall, women's conditions are changing and they reflect improvement; yet, these changes are proceeding slowly and face increasingly contradictory approaches to solving the perceived problems.[1]

A discussion that started in the North with the concept of the 'feminine mystique' (Friedan, 1963) and the 'female eunuch' (Greer, 1971) in the early 1960s has undergone significant theorization and modification to encompass the concepts of 'exploitation' and 'subordination' in the three decades that followed. The key referent moved also, from women to gender. The shift from 'women' to 'gender' has brought greater sensitivity to the importance of men in considering the situation and condition of women. Among most feminist scholars, in both the North and South, 'gender' has been upheld as the 'better' of the two approaches because of its relational and thus dynamic nature, and, unwittingly in some cases, the efforts of many women's groups have been denigrated by some feminist theorists as incomplete, essentialist and unsophisticated.[2] In the industrialized countries today, there are voices that argue that to talk about 'women' is to fall into a position that naturalizes one difference between women and men. In contrast, in the Third World, the changes in the concept of gender are focusing more attention on the link between women and lack of economic and political power and on the interplay between gender and ethnicity and social class, but there is no doubt that 'women' is a fundamental category and that to discuss the conditions of women does not mean diversity among them is forgotten. It is also clear to most feminists in the

Third World that the oppression of most women in those countries is so great that they require special action for human rights and social justice.

This article has an ambitious goal. It seeks to present the voices of four disparate sets of actors in the global gender arena: women in academia (primarily in the North), women in non-government organization (NGOs), the state in both its domestic and international versions, and the diffuse yet influential globalizing market. These voices range from ascribing to women and men fixed, unambiguous identities to placing great emphasis on the differences and diversities between and among women and men. The voices are diverse indeed. The increasingly postmodern academy lives in a world that seldom considers the job market or government policies; it theorizes women but inhabits the space of identities and micro-interactions. NGOs seek to improve the conditions of women but, being challenged by the survival needs of low-income women, they theorize little. Governments and donor agencies tend to ignore intellectual production around them and define the gender problem through minimally incremental doses of equality.

The voices of feminist NGOs and governments tend not to agree with those of the academic world. Outside the university there is a strong position that women constitute an entity. The disagreement between NGOs and governments does not revolve around the existence of 'women' as an identity, but rather what that identity should be. For NGOs, the struggle around one's identity as woman is for social justice and more comprehensive human rights. For governments, the challenge is to incorporate women into existing social and economic frameworks by making their conditions and status marginally better. From the state's perspective, the basic division of labour – and thus identity – should build on women's responsibilities as mothers and wives. Their autonomy as workers and as citizens in a broader sense is recognized only at a superficial level.

To locate my assessment on a theoretical terrain, I will rely on conceptual frameworks proposed by Gramsci, Touraine and Foucault.[3] From Gramsci (1994) I borrow the notion that the construction of ideology is a key function of those who hold hegemonic power in society. I find the construction of 'common sense' fundamental to the understanding of how women and men are perceived in patriarchal society and how women are held to possess intrinsic attributes that are considered not to make them suitable for political or economic positions of value; Gramsci also contributes the idea of counter-hegemony, by which subordinate groups may question received ideas. From Touraine (1989), I borrow the notion that the most important cultural conflicts of our time are conducted by social movements and that even when those movements are uneven and weak, they tend to bring new conceptions of self and society. From Foucault (1977 and 1991), I draw the notion that power exists at all levels. In the case of women, therefore, it is crucial to see how domination occurs also at micro-levels and becomes produced and contested at that level. But, unlike Foucault, I do hold that the state is one of the most powerful institutions in any contemporary society and that it carries crucial importance in efforts to attain redefinitions of gender. The conceptual mantle of social movements, organic intellectuals and micro-power leads me move to examine some recent developments in global feminism as played out by the four actors identified in this introduction.

Voice 1: the endless diversities in postmodernity

Postmodernity is a voice that brings multiple themes and multiple issues within these themes. Postmodernity has become a strong voice within academic feminism, particularly in the North and increasingly so in elite universities in the Third World. I will hold that feminism has received a very ambivalent contribution from postmodernism: the positive contribution has come in terms of ontological reflections and methodological tools. The negative contribution has come in its depoliticizing rhetoric through an exaggerated emphasis on diversity.

Ontologically, postmodernism argues that there is no 'generic' woman: the notion of 'women' is not a concrete reality, but rather an arbitrary figment of our imagination since infinite variation characterizes women (as much as men). Gender is seen by most postmodernists as a system of relations and differentiation, and much less as a system of oppression. Many post-feminist writers like to avoid concepts such as hegemony, domination and oppression on grounds that they do not enable us to perceive the 'highly differentiated, quite fragmentary and continually under negotiation' set of relations in the household and in heterosexual gender difference (Gibson-Graham, 1996, p. 68). According to Butler (1998, p. 278; see also Butler, 1990), ' "women" is merely a discursive formation which has stability and coherence only in the context of the heterosexual matrix'. Postmodern feminists consider identities as multifaceted, fluid and creative (Plotke, 1990–91; Mouffe, 1993; Fraser, 1998a). The extension of this argument leads them to assert that both women and men have multiple memberships across difference and that since individuals occupy multiple social positions and locations, they cannot be forced into a single identity.

In the view of postmodern feminists, the acknowledgement of multiple differences among women is politically helpful (Mouffe, 1993; Fraser, 1998a). Mouffe (1993) sees as a prerequisite to the application of principles of liberty and equality the deconstruction of all essentialisms. She is certain that if we consider the lack of homogeneity in women, we are in a better position to theorize the multiplicity of relations of subordination because gender plays at different levels of intensity depending on the nature of situation. Mouffe's view echoes that of Lyotard, who also argues that difference and multiplicity do not represent an obstacle to emancipation but enlarge the possibilities and varieties of these movements (cited in Cowen, 1996). As does Mouffe, several other postmodernist feminists argue that 'unity is not necessary for political action', as 'certain forms of acknowledged fragmentation might facilitate coalition building precisely because unity of the category women is neither presupposed nor desired' (Butler, 1998, p. 228).

Postmodern thought has contributed in significant ways to the transformation of gender in the university, where women's studies have shifted the centre of gravity from social justice for women to issues of sexuality, sexual desire and sexual orientation. Although gay and lesbian studies began about 20 years after the start of women's studies, in many US universities they dominate the gender discourse. Barrett and Phillips (1992) observe that in the North American academic world in the past 10 years, there has been an extensive 'turn to culture' in feminism, in which the social sciences have lost to the arts, humanities and philosophy. Even feminist sociology examines less social structure than questions of culture, sexuality or political agency (Barrett and Phillips, 1992). With this kind of lens, it is possible, then, to see gender as quite distinct from a study of the conditions of men and women in society.

Feminism has certain principles in common with postmodernism: the intent to use knowledge not to control or predict but to locate and understand social dynamics and their expressions; the urge to explore the conditions and factors that made an action possible or produced a point of view; the modesty to consider the perspective of the communities themselves by becoming familiar with their everyday life and grasping the common sense of social actors. Postmodernity has added a powerful and meaningful vocabulary: the subaltern, the dominance of the grand narrative, the constitutive nature of discourse, the importance of language and representation, the formation of identity, the impossibility of distancing knowledge from subjectivity. Methodologically, postmodernity has the virtue of disrupting single and linear accounts, of deconstructing apparently innocuous texts, of introducing the voices of peoples previously ignored. These emphases are pushing us beyond the use of quantitative methods and even beyond common qualitative methods to highlight more strongly the meaning-making and context in the human experience (Lather, 1992). Many of us are very appreciative of post-structural and postmodernist contributions to our awareness of absences and discontinuities in public discourse and to consideration of how difference and multiplicity have been obscured in several events in our daily lives.

Postmodernity has brought challenges regarding the existence of universals, the fluidity of identity, the absolute certitude regarding scientific and political projects, the implicit domination in totalizing discourses (Buenfil, 1997–98). Where, some feminists and postmodern feminists part ways lies in the latter's tendency to: (1) locate women's movement as a cultural struggle where the fundamental injustice may not be material exploitation but 'cultural misrecognition of group difference' (Fraser, 1998a, p. 98); and (2) equate economic concern with essentialism. I coincide with Ortner's observation that cultural studies may be proposing 'the fantasy that one can understand the working of public cultural representation solely by interpreting/deconstructing the representations' (Ortner, 1998, p. 45). For instance, deconstructing the cultural representation of the welfare mother does not explain why some women become poor and not others or why most women are poorer than men.

Of course, we want a citizenship where sexual differences are irrelevant (Mouffe, 1993). But this new construction is not possible merely through debate; we need political action. And political action needs identities to move on, since identities tend to serve as the rallying notion around which movements coalesce. The notion of identity is further crucial to demonstrate to others how limiting and damaging is the classification of people into two discrete categories. Paradoxically, the feminist movement must use binary categories before it can move to their elimination. Also, for those who may not realize it, it must be said that even minor shifts in the definitions of 'women' and 'men' are heavily contested by the state and its many public institutions. To argue that these categories do not exist is tantamount to saying that there is nothing further to be said. I agree with Young (1998), who defends group identity, when she calls for group representation in democratic government. She advocates group differentiation to improve the organization of the group, to voice analysis of how policy proposals affect group members and to generate their own policies, and to have veto power over negative policies. She says, 'Group representation is the best antidote to self-deceiving, self-interest masked as an impartial or general interest' (Young, 1998, p. 415). Group representation does not preclude possibilities of making rational normative claims (Young, 1990, p. 427).

In short, the voice of postmodernity highlights the large variation among social subjects and the role of discourse in the construction of binary categories but it muddles the questions of exploitation and subordination, and avoids political treatment of issues.

Voice 2: the problem-solving agendas of women in NGOs

It is through organized groups that feminism has made the biggest impact on social structures and practices. NGOs in the feminist movement are best understood in the context of Touraine's dictum: 'Those who oppose social movements to democracy are blind and prepare the destruction of the former by authoritarian power. But those who speak only of institutions and rules of the game are building upon sand' (1989, p. 538).

Molyneux (1998) maintains that women's movements are essentially modern phenomena in as much as they present demands associated with the spread of Enlightenment ideas and institutions about social and economic modernization and political democratization. She observes that not all movements in which women participate are led by either women or feminists. Their forms have been influenced by the cultural context, family norms, political formations, the extent of female solidarity and the character of their civil society. Some movements are autonomous while others are directed by the existing government or party or though women's alliances with political parties or public officials (Molyneux, 1998, p. 221). Here, I will concentrate on women-led NGOs, or those who work to make feminist agendas a concrete reality in their respective societies.

The voice of the NGOs is by and large consensual in recognizing women as an oppressed group it is necessary to address with urgency. Feminist action within NGOs involves an ethical sense of the world – a sense of what is right and wrong. The realization that there is something wrong also calls for identifying the parties behind the undesirable situations; thus, it calls for recognition of oppositional, not just relational, dynamics. Women-led NGOs are fighting for rights and empowerment approaches for women. They seek solutions to serious problems women face concerning literacy, education, employment, health, poverty, violence, human rights and political participation.

Many of those in the feminist movement as crystallized by women-led NGOs have long known that women's gender interests are not always primary in the same way as gender identity is not their sole identity. They have also argued that feminism is more than a case of identity politics characterized by a single issue and particularistic demands. Feminism often defends reproductive choice and goes against domestic violence but it also seeks a wide set of political and ethical principles, such as social justice and the reshaping of state–individual relations. Thus, women-led NGOs see themselves contesting relations of domination beyond gender to include race, religion, class, caste, sexual orientation or 'any other which hinder the development and the expression of views and cultural values of subordinate groups' (DAWN, 1995, p. 2002).

Through the work of women-led NGOs, there is today a new conception of social justice, one not limited to justice for women. Despite the diversity, groups in the feminist movement have in common social and economic modernization ideas. The claims by feminist activists on public policy have been decisive in bringing up new issues. They have tried to abolish the distinction between the public and private spheres and, despite national differences, the feminist movement has transcended national boundaries with new values and common demands (Gelb, 1990). Judging from the positions advocated by feminists in recent international conferences, there is substantial consensus on such issues as poverty, education, health, violence, armed conflict, the economy, decision-making, human rights, communication media, the environment and the situation of girls. These issues are well reflected in the themes adopted at the Fourth World Women's Conference document (United Nations (UN) 1996) signed by governments under the unrelenting lobbying of NGO groups at Beijing in 1995.

Two key challenges, being discovered by many women-NGOs in developing countries, are: (1) how to link the women's demands not only to the family and the community but to national policies; and (2) how to move beyond the situation of poor and marginal women and to infuse these demands into civil society. The serious economic situation of women frequently leads to consideration of practical needs, even though most activists recognize the crucial importance of working toward the solution of strategic needs.[4]

Yet another challenge resides in the failure of many women activists to see the need for coalition building through the creation of a women's political party. Touraine observes, not without regret, that 'Women's action establishes a strong link between private life and social action but penetrates only slightly the world of organized political forces, whether parties or labor unions' (1989, p. 116). Important in the feminist movement has been the collective struggle through small workshops, some public demonstrations, participation in global conferences and the elaboration of governmental agreements and plans of action. These strategies have proved useful but they have clear limitations due to their size and the reliance on distant others for implementation.

From the perspective of NGOs, feminists in universities have not succeeded in incorporating gender issues in the overall training of their professionals and, thus, students graduate having acquired a very limited awareness of gender issues. Moreover, few are the academics that are practical allies of feminists. While academicians critique women-led NGOs for not building upon theory, NGO practitioners counter that academicians do know how to move from theory to practice. A recent call made by various women-led NGOs working on health was to seek ways to make researchers, professionals in reproductive health, women networks and gender trainers work together (Diaz and Spicehandler, 1997). Women-led NGOs maintain that, unlike the university, civil organization is the place where conceptual frameworks and the operationalization of concepts become combined.

The voice of NGOs underscores the concrete and the here and now, particularly issues that conflate gender and class. Their pragmatic approach is clearly focused on 'women', a category which is not disputed by them.

Voice 3: national and foreign states

The paternalistic voices of the national and foreign states reserve for themselves the right to define the real nature of gender in society.

National states

These voices are usually expressed in international conferences, particularly women's conferences, at which time represented governments sign documents promising to take action upon return to their societies.

Women's influence – through the lobbying by NGOs in the North and the presence of northern and southern NGOs at related UN conferences held in large part in response to feminist pressures – has been substantial. Women and gender issues are recognized identified today in governmental political discourse. The voice of government regarding women is that they are important and should be incorporated into the development project. Most states have offices to address women's concerns and many have national plans, though these are typically a symbolic response because the offices are small and the budgets are not independent (Krawcyk, 1998; Stromquist, 1998).[5] Women are becoming accepted in the international arena at the women's meetings they have effectively influenced and in which NGOs have wide acceptance as partners. Governments are signing international documents pertaining to gender and women are pushing for increasingly better monitoring mechanisms at the UN and regional levels, even though staff and budgets of these mechanisms are also limited.

The fulfilment of these governmental promises and the implementation of gender-oriented policies in developing countries tend to be very problematic. Most of the time, the promises are forgotten. When policies are designed, they are hardly contestatory, but rather framed as part of existing conditions (Yates, 1993). When the state recognizes women's needs, it is their practical needs, seldom their strategic needs. A universal characteristic of governments vis-à-vis gender is the links they make between gender and women and between women and poverty. This is dangerous because it reduces gender issues to the problems of poor women and, by implication, denies the existence of problems among women of other social classes.

NGO groups following the progress of implementation of the Cairo and the Beijing agreements notice that the 'most evident expression is the semantic revolution' – the language transformation in the policies and among decision-makers. Today governments speak of gender equity and domestic violence, but women-led NGOs note that reproductive health and issues of autonomy and self-determination for safe abortions are still not realized; 'reproductive health' is often a new term for family planning. International agencies do not support expanding the dialogue to get agreement on implementation issues (DAWN, 1998).

Regarding education, the governmental, voice is clear: 'Let's give girls more access to *basic* education'. Little is said about secondary education, except for some calls for more girls to have access to science and mathematics courses. Higher education, the level of knowledge transmission most likely to prepare people in a critical way and to open the best opportunities for access to positions of power and leadership, is seldom part of the state's agenda when addressing education and gender. In these days of globalization influences on the economy, knowledge that will best command societal recognition and financial reward is most likely to be acquired in universities. Women with basic levels of education will be able to join only lower categories of occupations. While governments support literacy and income-generating programmes target the adult women in need of non-formal education, these programmes tend to have a small-scale and fragmented nature – which renders them incapable of addressing material needs of the large mass of women, much less their gender-consciousness transformation.

A clear example of the myopic view of the state regarding gender and education is reflected in the position of the US government vis-à-vis its own women citizens. In a key document produced after Beijing, it acknowledges in its education section the need to 'remove barriers facing girls and women of different backgrounds, including girls and women with disabilities, those of low income, and those from ethnic and racial minorities' (President's Interagency Council on Women, 1996, p. 17). Barriers are seen only as those that prevent access to further education; nothing is said about the ideology present in educational systems that might be producing and reproducing gender identities. To achieve its narrow aims, the government promises initiatives such as creating a national assembly to discuss girls' and women's education; launching a public awareness campaign to change discriminatory policies and practices; collaborating with other lead agencies to promote girls and women in science, mathematics and technology; combating violence against girls and women; and intensifying efforts to raise the number of employers who encourage family involvement in children's learning. These strategies: (1) do not take aim at the educational system as a target of comprehensive and long-term intervention; and (2) fail to acknowledge the ideological messages of the educational system as transmitted both by curricula and teachers.

Women-led NGOs certainly uphold the importance of the state; however, a minute but vocal group of activists in Latin America, exhausted by the deceptive practices of the state, are calling for autonomy. But, as Plotke asks, autonomy from what and for what? Autonomy might make sense if there were only one social movement challenging the logic of parties, unions and the state; then, autonomy would affirm its identity and ability to create a new civil society (Plotke, 1990–91). But if autonomy means radical separation from other social and political actors, such autonomy is undesirable and probably unlikely.

Women need social and political rights but they need also greater access to institutional power (Molyneux, 1998). Thus, the state in its domestic and international form (through bilateral and multilateral action) must be targeted. Opportunities for co-optation of gender issues are there, if the treatment of women is narrow and reduced to their roles of childbearing and child-raising. Efforts must be undertaken to establish linkages among different sectors, particularly health and education, and to give priority to youth programmes using a gender perspective to deal with sexual and reproductive health. This task is not without problems. Eisenstein, who has been observing the capitalist state's relations towards women, is sceptical and declares: 'Feminist demands uncover the truth that capitalist patriarchal society cannot deliver on its "liberal" promises of equality or even equal rights for women without destabilizing itself' (1982, p. 569).

International development agencies

The voice of international agencies is by and large similar to that of national states, with the exception of the Nordic and Dutch bilateral agencies that demand deeper gender changes. Regarding education, the prevailing international voices state, 'Education is a great social leveller and is women's main tool for access to good jobs'.

Agencies have had a roundabout way of influencing gender. Originally influenced by NGOs in their own countries, some bilateral agencies (notably the Dutch and the Scandinavian) have adopted progressive views about gender and thus strongly influence recipient states to be sensitive to gender issues. But most agencies still hold a very limited view of gender-related intervention in education. This support is circumscribed to the question of participation: having more women be able to attain basic education and increasing the representation of women in fields such as science and technology. Thus, these agencies concentrate work in countries where disparities in enrolment at primary levels are the most dramatic (e.g. Sub-Saharan Africa and South Asia). This emphasis enables them to avoid dealing with more controversial issues such as teacher training in non-sexist education or the questioning of patriarchal values in textbooks and school subjects.

Special mention must be made of the World Bank, the largest institution in international development and unquestionably the most influential organization of its kind. In a very recent position paper by the president of the World Bank, the strategy of an 'integrated development framework' was announced. The new strategy calls for a consideration not only of economic and infrastructural issues but also of human needs, such as education and health (Wolfensohn, 1999). Yet, the discourse about women is painfully brief and describes them primarily as mothers. Thus, the document reiterates the importance of women's education to achieve healthy children.

Fraser (1998b) makes a distinction between affirmative remedies and transformative remedies, the former being 'those aimed at correcting inequitable outcomes of social arrangements without disturbing the underlying framework that generates them', and the latter, 'those that aim at correcting inequitable outcomes by restructuring the underlying generative framework' (p. 443). Affirmative and transformative remedies parallel those that Molyneux calls practical and strategic needs. What Fraser adds to the debate is her argument that affirmative remedies generally promote group differentiation while transformative remedies destabilize or blur it (Fraser, 1998b, p. 446). I think Fraser is right in saying that affirmative remedies may be reproducing women's responsibilities towards the family and children while preventing interjection of ideas about reconfigured societal arrangements. But I would like to emphasize that, without a firm sense of one's identity and group membership, contestation of oppressive practices and ideologies could not take place. This may seen paradoxical, yet, without an initial aggregation of individual wills and mobilization around our identity as women, the movement towards erasing arbitrary boundaries between women and men could not take place.

As can be seen, the voice of the state either in its domestic or foreign (through international development assistance) form recognizes the category of 'women', yet the range of the measures envisaged to help tend to be framed within existing ideological norms regarding women and men's roles.

Voice 4: the unifying realities of globalization and neoliberalism

Through these voices speaks the muddled but sustained view of the market. The fragmented and fluid world of postmodernity collides with the integrated world of globalization. In many developing countries, globalization has coincided with the imposition of structural adjustment programmes. Globalization has also come accompanied by neoliberal economic principles in favour of reducing the state and amplifying the role of markets. In so doing, neoliberalism makes women – especially those of low-income sectors – more aligned with traditional family needs (i.e. providing more services for family members) and vulnerable in terms of social security. At the same time, neoliberalism requires women's availability for low-wage competition in the labour market. With globalization, women are finding employment more easily than men but their situation is not getting better, as they are placed in casual, insecure, and home production jobs which are really new forms of the informal market. While market forces move towards the creation of multiple and innovative products, these forces also encourage conformity vis-à-vis the social status quo. As Blackmore states, 'equity is not a factor in the market' (1997, p. 451).

The new job conditions are damaging for women's economic well-being as economists observe that it is important that women control 'not just their income but also their own labour power, work time, means of production, raw materials, output, and proceeds of output and skill' (Standing, 1998, p. 25). McLaren (1998) notes that postmodern theorists build on questionable assumptions such as 'symbolic exchange taking place outside the domain of value and production' and that they emphasize structures of difference (i.e. diversity among women) over structures of exploitation (p. 443). One of the largest global feminist networks, DAWN, in contrast with the position of feminist postmodernists, has such a strong appreciation of the economic situation that it even argues that currently used economic and social indicators fail to capture the extent of suffering and inequality confronting women:

> Indices of social development cannot be trivialized, softened, or limited only to literacy/education, health or expenditure on social services alone, however important these may be. The prevalence of violence, its promotion in the media, gross inequalities in consumption, the dislocation of children from their homes due to the pressures on their settlements and lives, the unrepresentative character of the institutions associated with political and economic management, should also be considered indicators of social decay.
>
> (1995, p. 2002)

Although postmodern feminists talk about the endless differentiation of women, statistics on participation in the labour force and salaries show marked discrepancies between men and women, as they do in education, particularly at higher levels, in access to property, and in access to managerial and political positions. Judging from the annually reported United Nations Development Programme's (UNDP) Gender Empowerment Measure, absolutely no country offers women equality in power and wealth.[6]

Among women-led NGOs there is great concern with the globalized economy where 'economic growth no longer guarantees poverty alleviation or employment generation' (DAWN, 1995). For DAWN, the situation of women is critical. DAWN seeks a threefold strategy: reclaiming the state for the benefit of the majority; challenging the market to become more socially responsible; and rebuilding institutions to strengthen civil societies, giving special attention to the role of the women's movement (DAWN, 1995, p. 2003). DAWN presents clear proposals: cutting military expenditures, taxing speculative financial transactions, negotiating debt alleviation schemes, establishing more sensible tax structures and drafting a comprehensive plan of land reform (DAWN, 1995, pp. 2003, 2004). These proposals have a tangible beneficiary: women.

For women, globalization has brought greater exposure to values of democratization and women's human rights. At the same time, since globalization has brought a weak state and a spirit of economic competitiveness and consumption, the role of the state in setting up public policies for education and for gender equity in particular will diminish considerably. The voice of globalization does not address gender directly; it does make it increasingly more difficult to consider it given other 'higher' stakes, particularly setting countries and transnational corporations in leading production and marketing positions.

Educational themes in the prevailing voices

From a transformative feminist perspective, a distinction between schooling and education is crucial. Schooling – the learning that occurs through the formal school experience – is an area that most likely will not be very contestatory given the link between schools and the state. Education is best defined as knowledge broader than schooling. The education that goes on in women-led NGOs, being separate and autonomous from the state apparatus, can afford to be different in objective and form.

To be sure, children are socialized by many experiences, ranging from the family, to peers, to media messages. Schools are but an additional element in this array of influences. Nonetheless, to the extent that schools are institutions created ostensibly for the benefit of society, they must be an explicit target in all efforts to improve gender relations. The feminist voice recognizes that formal education, despite the wide areas of knowledge it transmits, has disempowering features for women. As feminism shifts from a needs-based discourse to rights-based issues (Molyneux, 1998, p. 241), it increasingly advocates the creation of democratic cultures and a more moral society. As a consequence of this position, changes should occur in the curriculum so that it includes critical and moral concerns and a redefined notion of democracy.

With globalization, greater importance is assigned to learning the basics while the possibility to question the knowledge students obtain has been reduced. In both the USA and the UK (Millard, 1998), the emphasis on achievement reduces the importance of the relationship of gender and education. The retrenchment of the state will alter the educational labour market not only in terms of the supply (private schools, competitive performance) but also in terms of the demand (a shift from social to private goods) (Blackmore, 1997). Globalization raises the priority for science and technology in the curriculum, that is, knowledge for production of commodities. In this new climate, little attention will be given to questions of ethics and equity, since 'customer satisfaction' will be the ruling slogan.

Referring to the UK context, Millard (1998) observes that, while there has been progress in EO legislation and in our understanding of power relations between men and women, the balance of power in the classroom and in extra-curricular affairs remains dominantly in favour of men. A similar statement could be made for conditions in the USA. So little has happened in gender-sensitive educational policies in the less industrialized countries that this assertion is even more valid there. A very important global-level commission, set up by UNDP, concluded that schooling remains an essential institution in the reproduction and maintenance of modern patriarchies. It also affirmed that the most pervasive inequality in education is that between men and women, over that of social class or ethnicity (Independent Commission, 1996, p. 184).

Intellectual progress has been made in industrialized countries, particularly those of Anglo-Saxon origin, in reframing the issue from sexual stereotyping and role modelling to gender regime and gendered identity (Clark and Millard, 1998). This shift has brought under closer scrutiny the school context in which relationships between girls and boys develop, and the consequences of these interactions for the formation of masculine and feminine identities. For instance, the manner in which male students tend to dominate physical and linguistic space produces for the most part negative consequences for the development of women students' assertiveness and self-esteem.

Feminist educators such as Weiler (1993), Arnot (1993) and Scott-Jones (1991) hold that we need to understand 'specificities' because concepts such as equity, equality, egalitarianism and equality of opportunity are defined differently in different social settings. Elaborating on this notion of specificities, Mac an Ghaill states that 'contemporary models of pupil masculinities and femininities are portrayed as highly complex and contradictory, displaying power, violence, competition, a sense of identity and social support', and that we need to see gender as 'a crucial point of intersection of different forms of power, stratification, desire and subjective identity formation' (Mac an Ghaill and Haywood, 1998, p. 215). Lather (1992) calls for the creation of multivoice, multicentred texts in the schools. She asks, 'How do we deconstruct the ways our own desires as emancipatory inquirers shape the texts we create?' (p. 9). I would reframe this concern by asking, 'How do we deconstruct hegemonic texts so that our emancipatory goals are not lost?'

In an increasing number of countries there are revised and even new textbooks and related educational materials that introduce better coverage of women's roles and a non-sexist language, but no country has developed a gradually gauged curriculum that takes gender issues across the different levels of schooling and ages of students. We have yet to produce a school curriculum that considers gender knowledge in relation to the age of the students and that moves from the basic to the more complex; for instance, from gender-inclusive vocabulary in grade one to consideration of the social relations of sex and partner relations for teenagers.

From the perspective of the feminist movement in the Third World, access to basic education for girls is considered paramount. These feminists generally do not attack content and the gendered nature of schooling, maintaining thus a line similar to their governments and donor agencies.

Feminism has to be attentive to various forms of education and learning. We know education can create critical awareness and autonomy, but efforts must be imbued with a questioning of male-created knowledge and power. Younger female students – those in formal school – need non-sexist and anti-sexist education. So, it is clear that political learning and consciousness-raising about gender can take place primarily with adult women, not children or adolescent girls immersed in an educational system under state surveillance. Mobilization around concrete problems that women, particularly low-income women, must face creates changes in consciousness and vice versa. Despite its many limitations, it is the non-formal and formal education provided by women-led NGOs which may hold the highest promise for contestatory and transformative gender knowledge.

Concluding arguments

The existence of multiple voices represents the differential location of the social actors stating them. From positions of privilege, such as the academy, it is difficult to feel the bite of gender discrimination, particularly when it becomes intertwined with disadvantaged social class. From positions of power, such as those of the state and the neoliberal world, it is tempting to frame gender issues as needing marginal adjustment.

Unquestionably in the academic arena, there has been a shift from positioning women's conditions in terms of exclusion/inclusion to adopting less gender-specific issues such as those exploring homogeneity/heterogeneity, sameness/diversity and universality/difference (Phillips, 1998, p. 15). Postmodernity has introduced a voice that reclaims complexity, high levels of differentiation and constant reshaping of identities. Postmodernity critiques all forms of essentialism – humanism, rationalism, universalism, etc. But, it must be argued that these issues do not constitute aspects of human existence of equal importance. Universalism as a form of uniformity in human expression must be criticized on several grounds, yet the human race should endeavour to become more benign, and reason over sacred beliefs should play a role in our decisions.

Theoretical analysis and political action do not operate at the same level of specificity. Analytically, we have to be sensitive to views – thus, to the importance of voice and voices. Analysis can be much more complex and multilayered than a political strategy for redress. Action, in contrast, calls for simplification. Law – which emerged to produce order and justice – is expressed in relatively broad terms. It certainly needs the interpretation of lawyers and judges as it becomes applied. The point is that prescriptions for action must necessarily be based on simple assertions and referents. Education, as a form that combines both knowledge and action, must recognize the existing of diverse voices in global feminism and elucidate on their points of disagreement and potential agreement, but it also must recognize the current impasse and disconnection.

There is a major contradiction between endorsing a flexible identity and proposing rights. The latter is predicated on the assumed existence of referent groups. In my view, postmodern feminists misinterpret the claim for equality in rights with equality in identities – the assertion that all women are equal. They view equality as a fixed attribute while it is in fact a political goal that will undergo modifications as time and circumstances both allow and call for them. Equality as a political objective and equality as a philosophical discourse are two very different conceptions. With postmodernism, the possibilities for variations of being a 'woman' and a 'man' are endless. Paraphrasing a literary critic's view of a famous novelist, the plots of post-modernity are so intricate that they defy summary. We have to watch out we do not get lost in such complex accounts that no action could possibly follow.

Strategic and tactical alliances between elements of the national and the global civil society need to expand. Women have won several important public spaces but action still lags. Mouffe says that are many feminisms and that the search for the 'true' form of feminist politics should be avoided (1993, p. 88). There might not be a single true form, but there are many weak forms that are not conductive to any political success. Women lack at this point an association or agent that would give the women's movement coherence and stronger political direction. This has occurred, in part, because there is no resolution among women regarding our equality or difference relative to men.

There is something extremely ironic in the notion of multiple voices within feminism. The women's movement started as a rebellion against the established notion that women were all alike and should be alike in their behaviour and life chances (passive; obedient; loyal; mothers; and wives). So women asked for others to recognize not only women's rights but also women's diversity. With the influence of postmodernism, it has been argued that because women constitute such an enormous diversity, we should not treat them as a category. Is not this what we have been saying all along? But why deny the existence of categories when it is precisely categories that serve mechanisms of oppression?

The recognition of multiple forms of femininity and masculinity are important, but let us be sure that our concern with 'complexity' and 'multiple layers of social action' does not lead us into 'ivory tower' contemplation and away from the worldly need to fight poverty, injustice and insecurity faced by millions of women and powerfully visible in national and global statistics.

NOTES

*   Keynote speech presented at the Second International Conference on Gender and Education, University of Warwick, 29–31 March 1999.
1   Moreover, some fields are expanding in some ways that addressing gender is delinked from feminist analysis. For instance, anthropology is trying today to capture gender systems, moving beyond the standard binary dichotomy to the multiple categories in different world cultures, arguing, for example, that the influence of gender on an adolescent girl is different from that of a married woman.
2   Some observers consider that the distinction between the North and the South is misleading for it masks considerable heterogeneity between these regions. My position is that diversity exists indeed, yet economic and social conditions between these sets of countries is dramatic and persistent, with the South characterized by financial crisis, poverty, social exclusion and limited life chances among women.
3   Although these authors are not feminist thinkers, I find their political conceptualizations extremely suitable to an emancipatory project. All three develop analytical frameworks sensitive to the possibility of individual agency and consider notions of resistance to domination.
4   Following Molyneux (1985), I am using the terms 'practical' to refer to actions attempting to solve short-term and basic needs still framed as women's concerns, and 'strategic' to refer to those more explicitly linked to the transformation of the gender system either through questioning of dominant ideologies or promoting pertinent public policy.
5   Most governmental units dealing with women, it must be observed, are funded by international agencies. This reveals the weak priority to women given by national governments.
6   GEM is a composite index that comprises women's representation in parliament, share of managerial and professional positions, participation in the labour force and share of the national income. A score of 1 would indicate women's political and economic power equal to men; only in nine countries (all industrialized) do women have GEM values higher than 0.6. For greater elaboration, see UNDP, 1995.

REFERENCES

Arnot, M. (1993) 'Introduction', in M. Arnot and K. Weiler (eds), *Feminism and Social Justice* (London, Falmer Press).
Barrett, M. and Phillips, A. (1992) *Destabilizing Theory. Contemporary Feminist Debates* (Cambridge, Polity Press).
Blackmore, J. (1997) 'Level playing field? Feminist observations on global/local articulations of the re-gendering and restructuring of educational work', *International Review of Education*, 43: 438–461.
Buenfil, R.N. (1997–98) 'Filosofia de la Educacion, Posmodernidad y Modernizacion Educativa', *La Vasija*, 1: 89–96.
Butler, J. (1990) *Gender Trouble. Feminism and the Subversion of Identity* (New York, Routledge).
Butler, J. (1998) 'Subjects of sex/gender/desire', in A. Phillips (ed.), *Feminism and Politics*, pp. 273–291 (Oxford, Oxford University Press).
Clark, A. and Millard, E. (1998) 'Introduction', in A. Clark and E. Millard (eds), *Gendered in the Secondary Curriculum. Balancing the Books*, pp. 1–8 (London, Routledge).
Cowen, R. (1996) 'Performativity, post-modernity, and the university', *Comparative Education*, 32: 245–258.
DAWN (1995) 'Rethinking social development: DAWN's vision', *World Development*, 23: 2001–2004.
DAWN (1998) 'Sequimiento Cairo + 5', *La Red Va*, Montevideo: REPEM, 56: 2–6.
Diaz, M. and Spicehandler, J. (1997) *Foro Latinoamericano. La Incorporacion del Enfoque de Genero en la Capacitacion, Implementation, Investigation y Evaluation en los Programas de Salud Sexual y Reproductiva* (Washington, DC, International Center for Research on Women and Population Council).

Eisenstein, Z. (1982) 'The sexual politics of the New Right: understanding the "crisis of liberalism" for the 1980s', *Signs*: 7: 567–588.

Foucault, M. (1977) *Discipline and Punish* (London, Penguin).

Foucault, M. (1991) 'Politics and the study of discourse', in G. Burchell, C. Gordon and P. Miller (eds), *The Foucault Effect: Studies in Governmentality* (London, Harvest).

Fraser, N. (1998a) 'A future for Marxism', *New Politics*, 6: 95–98.

Fraser, N. (1998b) 'From redistribution to recognition? Dilemmas of justice in a post-socialist age', in A. Phillips (ed.), *Feminism and Politics*, pp. 430–459 (Oxford, Oxford University Press).

Friedan, B. (1963) *The Feminine Mystique* (New York, Dell).

Gelb, J. (1990) 'Feminism and political action', in R. Dalton and M. Kuechler (eds), *Challenging the Political Order: New Social and Political Movements in Western Democracies*, pp. 137–155 (New York, Oxford University Press).

Gibson-Graham, J.K. (1996) *The End of Capitalism (As We Know It). A Feminist Critique of Political Economy* (Cambridge, MA, Blackwell).

Gramsci, A. (1994) *Letters from Prison* (New York, Columbia University Press).

Greer, G. (1971) *The Feminine Eunuch* (New York, McGraw-Female Hill).

Independent Commission on Population and Quality of Life (1996) *Caring for the Future. Making the Next Decades Provide a Life Worth Living* (Oxford, Oxford University Press).

Krawcyk, M. (1998) 'Algunos elementos para la agenda: mujeres en America Latina y el Caribe a fines de los noventa' (Santiago, Comision Economica para America Latina y el Caribe) draft.

Lather, P. (1992) 'Critical frames in educational research: feminist and poststructural perspectives', *Theory Into Practice*, 31(2): 1–13.

Mac an Ghaill, M. and Haywood, C. (1998) 'Gendered relations beyond the curriculum', in A. Clark and E. Millard (eds), *Gendered in the Secondary Curriculum. Balancing the Books*, p. 225 (London, Routledge).

McLaren, P. (1998) 'Revolutionary pedagogy in post-revolutionary times. Rethinking the political economy of critical education', *Educational Theory*, 48: 431–462.

Millard, E. (1998) 'Endnote', in A. Clark and E. Millard (eds), *Gendered in the Secondary Curriculum. Balancing the Books*, pp. 244–253 (London, Routledge).

Molyneux, M. (1985) 'Mobilization without emancipation: women's interests, the state and revolution in Nicaragua', *Feminist Studies*, 11: 227–245.

Molyneux, M. (1998) 'Analyzing women's movements', *Development and Change*, 29: 219–245.

Mouffe, C. (1993) *The Return of the Political* (London, Verso).

Ortner, S. (1998) 'Generation X: anthropology in a media-saturated world', *Cultural Anthropology*, 13: 414–440.

Phillips, A. (1998) 'Introduction', in A. Phillips (ed.), *Feminism and Politics*, pp. 1–20 (Oxford, Oxford University Press).

Plotke, D. (1990–91) 'What's so new about new social movements?', *Socialist Review*, pp. 81–102.

President's Interagency Council on Women (1996) *Follow-up to Beijing* (Washington, DC, President's Interagency Council on Women).

Scott-Jones, D. (1991) 'From "voice" to "fugue" in females' development', book review of *Making Connections: The Relational Worlds of Adolescent Girls at Emma Willard School* by Carol Gilligan *et al.*, *Educational Researcher*, pp. 31–32.

Standing, G. (1998) 'Transformation of jobs and employment', in Proceedings of workshop on *Gender and Development* (Washington, DC, The World Bank), mimeo, pp. 25–27.

Stromquist, N. (1998) 'The institutionalization of gender and its impact on educational policy', *Comparative Education*, 34: 85–100.

Touraine, A. (1989) *Palavra e Sangue. Politico e Sociedade na America Latina* (Campinas, Trajetoria Cultural).

United Nations (1996) *Platform for Action and the Beijing Declaration* (New York, United Nations).

United Nations Development Program (1995) *Human Development Report 1995* (New York, UNDP).

Weiler, K. (1993) 'Feminism and the struggle for a democratic education: a view from the United States', in M. Arnot and K. Weiler (eds), *Feminism and Social Justice*, pp. 210–225 (London, Falmer Press).

Wolfensohn, J. (1999) 'A proposal for a comprehensive development framework', a discussion draft (Washington, DC, The World Bank).

Yates, L. (1993) 'Feminism and Australia state policy: some questions for the 1990s', in M. Arnot and K. Weiler (eds), *Feminism and Social Justice*, pp. 167–185 (London, Falmer Press).

Young, I. (1990) *Justice and the Politics of Difference* (Princeton, NJ, Princeton University Press).

Young, I. (1998) 'Polity and group difference: a critique of the ideal of universal citizenship', in A. Phillips (ed.), *Feminism and Politics*, pp. 401–429 (Oxford, Oxford University Press).

TEN

MAKING A DIFFERENCE: WOMEN IN MANAGEMENT IN AUSTRALIAN AND CANADIAN FACULTIES OF EDUCATION

Johanna Wyn, Sandra Acker and Elisabeth Richards

Source: 'Making a difference: women in management in Australian and Canadian faculties of education', *Gender and Education*, 12(4): 435–447, 2000.

It would be a thousand pities if women wrote like men, or lived like men, or looked like men, for if two sexes are quite inadequate, considering the vastness and variety of the world, how should we manage with one only? Ought not education to bring out and fortify the differences rather than the similarities?

(Woolf, 1957, p. 91)

The achievement of formal equality does not eliminate social difference, and rhetorical commitment to the sameness of persons makes it impossible even to name how those differences presently structure privilege and oppression.

(Young, 1990, p. 164)

Introduction

In the 70 years that have intervened since Virginia Woolf imagined leaning against the wall of the university that was 'a sanctuary in which are preserved rare types' (1957, p. 8), academic women in Australia and Canada and elsewhere have indeed achieved a greater degree of social equality. Representation of women among full-time faculty has substantially increased compared with figures of 20 or 30 years ago. Women now comprise about a quarter of full-time faculty in Canada (Drakich and Stewart, 1998) and 28 per cent of tenurable faculty in Australia (Probert *et al.*, 1998, p. 21). Predictably, they are less well represented in senior ranks, holding 11 per cent of full professorships in Canada and 12 per cent of positions above senior lecturer level in Australia. Nevertheless, women are indisputably now a significant part of the academic labour force; moreover, they have a presence in the middle ranks and are beginning to appear in the upper levels of university management.

At a structural level, these women do count because they are among the first to obtain the top positions in academic work in any significant numbers. Senior women in education are 'negotiating newly acquired status positions, forms of institutional power and intellectual authority in many different ways' (Luke, 1997, p. 193). Feminists have operated (often uneasily) as change agents in the universities of the last three decades (Morley and Walsh, 1995; Yeatman, 1995; Morley, 1999), through creating women's studies programmes, working to introduce or improve policies along equity lines, staffing equity-oriented positions and, more recently, entering the ranks of senior management. Interestingly, as this cohort of women achieves university management positions, a new genre of feminist-influenced literature wherein senior academic women reflect on their careers has begun to appear (e.g. Doyle Walton, 1996; Eggins, 1997; David and Woodward, 1998; Kolodny, 1998). In view of the fact that autobiographies of women academics are rare, a fact that Dyhouse (1995, p. 154) attributes to their mixed feelings about their own success, these accounts are valuable. But here we go beyond individual personal accounts and discuss the results of a small comparative study of 17 senior women in faculties of education in Canada and Australia. Our objective is to explore the ways in which senior women academics are positioned and position themselves as agents of change within academia. We examine the pathways and strategies adopted by these women in their efforts to make a difference.

'Making a difference' is the phrase that the women in our study often used to describe their contribution. Many strive to make a difference to the institution – by not simply 'fitting in' but by challenging discriminatory and unjust practices and creating new practices. Like the feminist secondary school principals in New Zealand studied by Strachan (1999), these women did not simply respond to demands, but were proactive and creative in their approach to leadership. The article explores the processes and strategies they used to create change. It is also about how women often *make* the difference, by actively *fortifying* women's different ways of being academics, managers and leaders and making their difference count.

We do not equate the role of difference with adopting a framework which essentialises the qualities of women and men as leaders. Within the educational management literature, some writers have emphasised gender differences along the lines of Gilligan's (1982) 'different voices' or Noddings's (1992) plea for (womanly) caring to become the basis of teaching and school organisation (for critiques and extensions, see Marshall, 1997; Sernak, 1998; Acker, 1999a,b; Blackmore, 1999). These approaches have been a needed corrective to the management theories that assumed a male-only world, yet they typically have difficulty in creating a flexible concept of difference. What we try to do, instead, is to focus on what the women in our sample say about their experiences and goals and their *perceptions*, and in a sense, their *politics*, of difference.

In previous articles, we have reported on the marginalisation of women academics (Wyn, 1997) and on their subjective assessment of their work situation (Acker and Feuerverger, 1996). There, we identified the ways in which women felt uneasy in the academic world, outside the mainstream of academic work and a minority in meetings, compelled to undertake the emotional labour that students desire and the housekeeping work that departments require (see also Park, 1996; Blackmore, 1999; Morley, 1999).

Although marginality is a constant and recurring theme in our study, it is complex. As our discussion reveals, marginality itself may be used as a positive strategy (Wyn, 1997; Sinclair, 1998). Other researchers have noted the 'contradictory and tension-filled' experiences of senior women in academia (Luke, 1997, p. 192), or their 'difficult careers' (Dyhouse, 1995), or the 'dynamic contradictions' of universities entrusting major equity related social change functions to an otherwise vulnerable and marginalised group within the institution (Yeatman, 1995, p. 201). Deem and Ozga suggest that concentrating on the 'pessimistic' dimensions of women's situations not only assumes similarity rather than diversity, but misses 'opportunities for pleasure, enjoyment, creativity and transformations' (1997, p. 34). Similarly, Gallop (1995) distinguishes between the hard-working and long-suffering female academic (the 'good-girl feminist') and the women who, while acknowledging their nurturing side, also take pleasure in the power they have through their visibility and their control over knowledge (the 'bad-girl feminist'). Taking issue with this binary view of women academics' experiences, Eagleton (1998) argues that a new understanding needs to be forged that takes account of the simultaneous experience of pleasure, constraint, passion and control in women's negotiation of their place in educational institutions (see also Tamboukou, 1999).

Difference, marginalisation, power and performance provide the organising concepts for the analysis of data reported in this article. Our intent is to explore the contradictory, multilayered and multidimensional nature of women's experiences of management and senior academic work in contemporary times, and to suggest the implications for the theory and practice of leadership in faculties of education.

The research

This article draws on interviews with eight women in Canada and nine in Australia who hold management responsibilities in faculties of education.[1] The Canadian interviews form part of a larger study in which approximately 200 in-depth interviews were conducted between 1995 and 1999 with academics in four professional fields: social work, education, pharmacy and dentistry. Among the 43 women in faculties of education in the larger sample, there were eight with major management responsibilities. These eight women came from three universities, located in three different provinces.

The Australian component of the study was restricted to identifying and interviewing women whose positions would be comparable to those holding senior management responsibilities in the Canadian study. Nine women were interviewed in five universities across three states. The ranks in the two countries are not the same. In Australia, few academics become full professors, while in Canada, that status would be a reasonable expectation for an academic career. All of the Canadian faculty who are featured in this article are full professors, while the Australian academics are associate or full professors, with the one exception being a senior lecturer who had senior management responsibilities. Across the two samples, the women held a variety of management positions, including deanships, associate deanships, department headships, directorships of research centres or responsibilities for major programmes such as graduate studies or pre-service teacher education. These senior participants were all white, reflecting the slowness with which universities have responded to minority groups (see Carty, 1991). Their ages ranged from late 40s to early 60s. In order to protect anonymity, pseudonyms are used; a few details have been changed in some cases; and participants' positions are identified only by vague terms such as 'senior professor'.

All of the interviews were conducted by the co-authors. In both countries, the interviews lasted between 60 and 90 minutes and were taped, transcribed and scrutinised for themes that could be used in analysis. Participants were asked about experiences with procedures such as hiring, tenure and promotion, feelings of centrality or marginality, any incidents of discrimination or harassment, and for details about their teaching, research and other work responsibilities. Questions were also asked about the ethos or culture of the department and faculty, the interface of home and work, health and stress and future career plans. In addition, interviewees filled out a short form documenting the main events in their careers.

The Australian interviews were carried out during the aftermath of a significant restructuring of the higher education sector, which occurred in the late 1980s (Marginson, 1997). Colleges of Advanced Education were amalgamated with universities, bringing together different academic cultures. At that time, staff numbers in many of the newly formed faculties were 'downsized' and the newly formed faculties and schools went through significant reorganisation. The Canadian higher education sector has not undergone such dramatic restructuring across the board (Slaughter and Leslie, 1997). On the other hand, in each university visited, some form of restructuring had taken place or was currently ongoing in response to cutbacks or for other reasons embedded in the individual institutional or provincial policies (see Cassin and Morgan, 1992).

Our interest in understanding how women both challenge and comply with university practices led us to employ a methodology that features narratives. This method gives access to concepts of self as well as understandings of the institution. The following statement could have been used to describe any of the women in our study: 'Hers is a diverse self, shaped in relations of power and dominance in which she is implicated: relationships of connectedness where exclusions and the negation of difference also have to be acknowledged as central' (Johnson, 1993, p. 156). The quotation is taken from Johnson's *The Modern Girl* in which she is writing about Minnie Bruce Pratt's narrative of growing up (Pratt, 1984). She uses Pratt's work 'Identity: skin blood heart' to illustrate how the feminist project of reconceptualising forms of political collectivity can recognise diversity and acknowledge the open-endedness of personal development. It is this openness and the possibilities of change that we wished to capture in our interviews.

Inevitably, the narratives of women reveal contradictions and complex processes. A single phenomenon or event (promotion, e.g.) may be both positive and negative, welcome and problematic, inclusive and marginalising. Reaching positions in which they are relatively powerful and visible creates tensions associated with 'bad girl feminism' (Gallop, 1995). Women in education are having to reconcile nurturing and egalitarian ideals with those of 'power, knowledge and desire' (Davies, 1996). The changing nature of higher education institutions itself creates complexities as women find themselves engaging with institutions that are very different from those which they entered a quarter of a century ago.

Difference, marginalisation and management

In analysing the findings of our research, the concepts of marginalisation and difference are central; they are strong themes in the narratives of the women we interviewed. Echoing a silence in feminist writing, the women were less likely to reflect on what they enjoy about their work. Nevertheless, enjoyment emerges throughout their discussions, often surprisingly and incongruously, and is sometimes associated with the opportunity to exercise (relative) power in the university ('bad-girl feminism').

Difference and marginality

For a majority of the women, a sense of otherness was openly and bluntly reinforced at a point early in their careers. Each of the women had a story about a struggle to gain tenure, promotion or recognition. In some situations, their area of research was seen to be marginal to the central or 'mainstream' concerns of education. For others, discriminatory practices by heads of department and in some cases, deans, were aimed at holding them back. In the cases of Adrienne and Tamara, detailed later, as well as others not reported here, recourse had to be made to a complaints procedure, a new search or an alternative process before they could break through the barriers put before them. For example, Adrienne explained that she applied for the position of associate professor in an Australian university:

> An appointment was made within the faculty for an associate professor on a five-year term and I applied for it. I understood I was the top candidate. When it came to the selection committee the then dean said he would vote against me. So the committee finished in disarray. He said he was voting for somebody else. They brought in somebody and the committee wouldn't accept the other person and the dean wouldn't accept me. And then I was advised to go through the university system, which I did the following year successfully. It really polarised a lot of people. It was a very distressing time. I found it personally very distressing. It was extremely difficult. It looked as if I would never succeed.

A Canadian example is provided by Tamara, who recounted a lengthy story about her struggle to gain a departmental headship:

> What happened was that the committee recommended somebody else [despite support from most of her colleagues]...The dean had accepted the recommendation of the committee and so he was making arrangements to hire this other person...The people in the department complained to the president's advisor on women's issues [and the other appointee was ruled out on a technicality]. I later learned that one of the people on the committee, a male, said he didn't want a woman boss. Another faculty member said that he didn't think that a single mother should be a head. So, then, they did another search and they brought in two outside people, males, and they offered them to each one and they declined...And, so, then...people came to me...I agreed that I would do it.

Some women had to go beyond alternative processes. Oppositional and assertive approaches were necessary in order to survive in a hostile environment. In her early years in a Canadian university, Diana became aware that extra graduate student teaching assistants were being allocated to her male colleagues while none at all had been assigned to her. She found it a difficult position to be in 'because in order to rectify it, you have to put yourself in the position of being confrontational'. She said:

> But I didn't stop there either, because I just felt that this was going to keep happening unless I was vocal about it, so I do confront. I also became more finely attuned. I had my ear to the ground after that. I thought, I have got to look out for myself, nobody else is going to look out for me. I'll just keep working here till I drop dead. And no one's going to give me any help. Because, they'll say, well, she always manages to get it done. At what expense though, right? At what cost?

Others make special efforts to analyse the effects of their contributions and make them work. Catherine (Australia) discovered that an attempt at humour in a meeting where she was the only woman went badly awry when the dean responded in a negative way: 'I just felt devastated. And I haven't been brave enough to crack a joke since then'. Yet, Catherine still manages to be assertive:

> I still do speak out in the committees although I do feel uncomfortable... I think a lot of the men here resent me [but] I partly think that being a woman works for me... [when someone attacks a colleague] I'm appalled by such bad manners that that actually helps me to be able to come back again... I usually come back with one more, usually only one more. And I think I come back sounding reasoned and rational... I think in meetings where I am the only woman... I work at not being emotional.

Assertiveness for women can be double-edged. Aline, in Canada, told a story about how when she was seeking a new academic position, a referee apparently described her as 'aggressive', and she had to do some damage control:

> The dean said to me, well, one of your letters says that you're quite aggressive. And what have you got to say about this? And I immediately made up a reply that there were two kinds of aggression. One was a piece of sandpaper. And the other one was what I consider normal in academe, and that I can defend myself and advance an argument and hold up my end of a discussion. And that I would call assertive... So I'm not a piece of sandpaper, but I can hold up my own. So that satisfied him.

Assertiveness and activism can also take a toll on activists (Yeatman, 1995; Morley, 1999, p. 55). Kolodny comments about her years as dean: 'I never antici- pated the killing hours that my activist agenda would require of me' (1998, p. 8). Some, but not all, of the women in our study expressed feelings of exhaustion and told stories of ill health (Acker and Feuerverger, 1996). It may be that these women are the survivors, the ones with the stamina to cope with the stresses of the acad- emy, and their positioning as senior managers reflects that fact. Yet, for some, the cost has been high. In addition to discussing specific illnesses, some spoke of burn- out and the pressing need to find 'time for me'.

It was not only the women themselves who struggled to gain acceptance. Repeatedly, the women were told that their *work* was not 'in the mainstream' of educational scholarship. Rosalind, in Canada, commented, 'It still bothers me that the acting dean told me I needed to do more mainstream work and I suppose [now] we might call that gender harassment, but we sure didn't call it that back then, we thought it was bad advice'. Belinda, in Australia, explained what happened when she moved from a long-established field to what she called 'leading edge things':

> When I've tried to get money to do research about [topic] and I've wanted to do it as exploratory research and therefore use qualitative methods, I've just found I can't even get to base one. I can't even in some instances fill in the forms because of the way the forms are constructed... [Because the area is so new] we don't know what the issues are. So what I'm trying to do is to try to understand what the issues are and that sort of research does not get money.

What is the mainstream in education? Apparently, it is not any area of scholarship that relies on qualitative research, nor does it include the fields of drama, philosophy in education, sociology, health education, French education, counselling and music. Likewise, research on young people, indigenous people and on racism and sexism also fails to qualify as 'mainstream'. Delwyn, in an Australian university, provides a recent example of being positioned on the margins:

> There was the attempt to get me to write the type of thing that the senior male thought I should be writing. This was a bombshell last year. He said '[subject] is defined by certain groups of people and so find out who those groups are'. Then at the end of it he just sat and said 'if you don't your peers will come and sort you out'. Not quite those words, but that was what it was about. It was quite a direct threat and quite a specific threat.

If there is a 'mainstream', then presumably there are tributaries or margins. Establishing the credibility of 'non-mainstream' areas of research is one of the main areas where women regard themselves as 'making' the difference. The women were explicit about challenging traditional understandings of knowledge and practice of education. There were many examples in both countries of developing new methodologies for research, of extending notions of teaching in the university and of modelling new practices in classrooms. A number of the women in our study were pioneers in the establishment of qualitative research methods and in interdisciplinary studies, including women's studies. Mary, in a senior position in a Canadian university, explained her approach to changing traditional practices:

> We have certainly been trying over the last little while to be much more interdisciplinary across departments and to work with other units on campus, so that we bring the issues, questions from a variety of different perspectives. Now, my philosophy is that you have to do that in education because you can't just look at the problems in education from one discipline or from one perspective. So, in developing doctoral programmes, for example, I have tried to have only a few doctoral programmes in broad areas, and then you would have people from all of the curriculum areas interested, trying to break down the walls that departments build up.

Mary's strategy was to restructure programmes, bringing people from different discipline areas together in their work with students. Kolodny (1998) provides similar examples. Underpinning this strategy is a relational understanding of difference, in which 'other' is not an oppositional category (Young, 1990). This conception of difference emphasises specificity, variation and heterogeneity.

It allows the possibility of 'fortifying the differences' in perspective and approach that are associated with gender, class or racial and ethnic identifications (Woolf, 1957). Our research provides evidence that women in management are often successful in employing a 'non-oppositional' understanding of difference – despite the necessity to be confrontational at times.

The women frequently referred to leadership in terms of making a difference for others, using the concepts of equity, democracy, anti-sexism, anti-racism and participation. Although not all had been themselves mentored, mentoring others was seen as a key part of their work ('good-girl feminism'). Here, Judith speaks about caring for the people in her department, contrasting her leadership style with that of others in the university:

> [As an administrator] I spent more time getting to know the individuals. I think I was more honest with them about why things were being done as they were. I shared more information with them. I encouraged a lot of people to apply for scholarships for different kinds of things...I would never say to an individual, you're teaching so and so...I would negotiate with them... I always tried to read papers that people had written...And that was also very, very much appreciated.

In Australia, Helen noted that mentoring can be affirming for the mentor herself: 'I have lots of opportunities to do good things for people. And I get a lot of people who come and thank me and write me letters saying how much I've helped them at the right time. It can be very positive!'

In other words, many of the women in this study provide examples of using their positioning as 'different' as a strength. Difference is a source of pleasure and accomplishment for these women as they have learned how to move from a situation where they were defined as 'other' to a non-oppositional mode of difference. Yet, they risk rejection for any actions that make them appear overly assertive: 'It seems that to take her place in that world a woman must have abilities which then become the seeds of her rejection' (Kerman, 1995, pp. 141–142). A further element of complexity and contradiction here is that in 'making the difference', women are contributing to a construction of women in universities as necessarily 'different' – always against the grain – and in so doing, are ironically reinforcing the reality of a 'mainstream' occupied by men. While they do make a difference to their universities in the ways described, the fact that it is women doing this work – and working hard to maintain it – reinforces its marginality to the main business of universities.

Rosalind, a senior professor in a Canadian university who was explicit in the interview about her many efforts to support equity and democracy, noted how working towards equity nevertheless contains elements of maintaining the status quo:

> You do all these things to try to change things and three years later you're still where you were, or back a step, and in many ways that's what our equity work looks like. You know, we've had enough years now that I can honestly say that we are amazingly good at maintaining representation at a fairly constant rate now. It's built into the system.

Kathleen, also in a Canadian university, reflected on the double-sided nature of change. She is delighted with how much has changed to make universities a more comfortable place for women:

> I keep comparing it to 20 years ago and I say, boy, it is so much better, you can't believe how much better it is in terms of openness, and in terms of just intellectual interest. I mean, I just find it a much more interesting place than it was when I came here.

At the same time, Kathleen recognises the contested and ongoing nature of 'all the political stuff, which is very connected to gender issues', which is often played out at the departmental level. She reflected on the fact that after two decades of struggle, one's perceptions of inequality can become finely tuned. 'At the same time, you know, I'm sure there's ways in which I've learned to do things administratively in some really traditional kinds of ways because they work, because they're not as time-consuming as other kinds of ways.' Her final comment suggests that despite being sensitised to gender struggle, as a woman in a powerful position, she does not always work for radical change. Institutional practices, already in place, are easier to use than to challenge.

Difference, power and performance

The women in this study have moved beyond the insecurity and struggle of their early days in the academy. As senior staff, they have management responsibilities in a range of areas. At the same time, they must 'manage' their own performance within the culture and the micro-politics of the university (Morley, 1999). Being a senior woman means being visible; it means performing in front of students, in committees, in faculty meetings and before deans, provosts, presidents and vice-chancellors. In the previous section, we explored the women's struggles, both in the public eye and behind the scenes, to bring about change. Luke comments on the downside to visibility for feminist academics:

> Committed to non-authoritarian and student-centred pedagogy, feminist educators have refused to acknowledge, or repressed recognition of, some of the identity politics and desires endemic to our work as public women – intellectuals constantly engaged in performativity of public speech, in struggles for authority and power and in order to get the feminist agenda on the public agenda, of being both eyed by and in the eye of power.
>
> (Luke, 1997, p. 193)

Luke elaborates on performativity, exploring the ways in which the self is crafted in the workplace, through 'linguistic communicative choices, self-signification and bodily habitus in ways that often contradict the diverse entities we embody as private women' (1997, p. 194). Many of the women we interviewed, especially in Australia, commented on how they dress; for example, Catherine said, 'If I'm going into a meeting, I power dress, I wear suits with shoulder pads and high heels, maybe make-up and contact lenses... You wouldn't be taken seriously if you didn't.' Clarissa, also in an Australian university, found that once she had been promoted to a senior position, she felt freer to wear dresses and 'enjoy the feminine, because I'm not so much under threat as a woman'. She also found, however, that apparent freedom brought censure: 'I have recently discovered that I am the focus of talk: (a) because I don't wear a bra; and (b) because I have cut my hair short. Both of these are seen as shocking.'

In Clarissa's case, the pleasure of being free to be 'herself' was tinged with concern about where the line is legitimately drawn between her private and public persona. Kathleen enjoyed the power of seniority, but was also uncertain about the possibility of overstepping an invisible mark: 'The fact [is] that I am seen as powerful and I certainly at this point feel like I can tell them that they're being schmucks and I guess I do [that] maybe more than I should.' She suggested that:

> There's also certainly a sense that women administrators and feminist administrators have too much power around here at the moment and, you know, everything is too feminist and too politically correct, so there's a lot of that too. So that I would be seen as powerful beyond what I would think of actually [laugh]. Too bad but.

The participants were also conscious that there is the potential to be seen to be co-opted into the very hierarchy that they have challenged. Morley (1999, p. 77) notes the vehemence with which junior women academics in her study expressed their distrust of senior women academics. Rosalind is now uncertain about how she is positioned in relation to issues of gender equity because she is a part of the power hierarchy:

> I would not be [name of current position] if I hadn't proven as [name of past position] that I can work on the inside…and that I can work with men. I mean, I wouldn't you know, we would have parted ways a long time ago. So I need women to say that the university stinks and that nothing's changed and everything is awful but now those kinds of comments reflect on me, so it's an interesting [situation]. So I think that structurally I'm in a different position now. I'm thought to be one of the guys by some people in a negative way.

The danger of being positioned in a different way was a concern for Clarissa, who stated:

> I now have a lot of influence and am seen as one of the key players in the university. That is exhausting and exhilarating at the same time. I think it is also dangerous. I would hate to lose my humility or to get an unrealistic sense of my own importance.

Enjoyment of being powerful was also evident ('bad-girl feminism'). Nadine, a Canadian professor, commented on the pleasure of being empowered:

> If you're not empowered to do anything you spend the whole year battling, especially if you have integrity and you think there are things that have to be done. So it's been heaven in the past two years.

Kathleen also expressed pleasure and enjoyment in the relative freedom her status offers:

> I quite enjoy it; I mean it's fun. It does give me a lot of latitude. If I want to teach I can; if I don't want to, I don't have to. I found the time to do my own research and writing.

For Mary, too, seniority brought less pressure to perform and less anxiety about performance:

> For the first few years as [current position] I worked every day on the weekend, for example, and I worked late in the evenings. I don't work every day on the weekends any more. I'm saying that it's just not worth it, and things seem to get done; maybe I'm more relaxed about it. I've been in it long enough now that I keep telling myself, all of these issues you've dealt with before. They shouldn't be so new that you have to be starting off from scratch.

Conclusion

> When participation is taken to imply assimilation, the oppressed person is caught in an irresolvable dilemma: to participate means to accept and adopt an identity one is not and to try and participate means to be reminded by oneself and others of the identity one is.
>
> (Young, 1990, p. 165)

To return to the themes raised at the beginning of this article, we can conclude that the women in this study have consciously striven to 'make' themselves senior academics and managers, 'differently' from their perceptions of the traditional male academic. As the research reveals, even as relatively powerful players, they are also conscious of the impossibility of being assimilated fully into the taken-for-granted university processes. Hence, to be a woman manager in a university is indeed to be reminded of an identity one is not, and constantly to have to define the identity one is.

Our study depends on qualitative, narrative techniques to focus on the fine details of everyday experience in the lives of senior women in faculties of education. Their tales of inclusion and exclusion, centrality and marginalisation, innovation and tradition are documented, with attention to the contradictions apparent in the stories of women who find themselves in senior positions in situations where they have few predecessors. Their perspectives support the view that, while we have much to gain from studying women's participation in the management of universities, their contribution cannot be simply characterised as a 'women's way' of leading (Blackmore, 1999, p. 56). The study has provided a perspective on a cohort of women that has engaged in similar struggles in universities across two countries during the 1970s, 1980s and 1990s. Their overwhelming concerns reflect the ideals of this period: those of the improvement of educational opportunity for disadvantaged groups, and the creation of more diverse and inclusive practices within the institution.

In both countries, these senior women saw themselves as being forces for change, with greater or lesser success. Many had feminist commitments (although they might define feminism in individual ways) and wanted to make the academy a better place for both women and men. Many believed they had something unique to offer as women in leadership roles. Some had instituted specific practices towards that end, for example, making special efforts to mentor and support junior faculty. Both optimism and disappointment framed their accounts. Paradoxically, they were simultaneously central and marginal within their institutions. They might be well placed to innovate and improve aspects of academic work or university practice, but at the same time, they were frequently themselves isolated and acutely conscious of their 'difference' from men senior colleagues and sometimes from other women colleagues as well. There were also some country-based variations; for example, women in Canadian universities were not as affected by major structural changes as those in Australia. The evaluation and promotion systems worked differently in each country, although in both situations the extent to which research activities were scrutinised had increased markedly in recent years. We have chosen not to emphasise country differences, however, because in the respects with which we are concerned in this article, the responses in each country were very similar. In both cases, women with management responsibilities were working in uncharted territory and experiencing tensions in the process of trying to make a difference.

Further tension is created by the relationship that women have with universities at this time in history. As Kenway and Langmead point out, feminist academics are located in a particularly difficult position in the 'new university', where knowledge is transformed into a commodity in order to yield economic returns to the university and to serve the 'owners of large scale industrial and administrative complexes' (1998, p. 30). In support of this view, some accounts, such as Leonard's study of women in management in the further education sector in the UK, provide a perspective on the incorporation of women into 'a new masculinist managerialism' (Leonard, 1998, p. 78). In such a culture, decisions based on market forces, performance indicators and efficiency criteria supplant those based on collegiality or equity (Davies and Holloway, 1995). Blackmore, too, discusses the complex location of women in leadership, and especially feminists, in these 'new hard times', in which, for many, 'the contradictions are too great, the emotional labour and physical work too demanding' (1999, p. 2).

Feminist knowledge production and political work would seem to be at odds with the direction of these changes. Yet, the informal demands on women's emotional labour are likely to increase as women 'struggle to undertake feminist work in conditions which are both increasingly hostile to it and increase the need for it' (Kenway and Langmead, 1998, p. 30). Not all the women interviewed considered themselves feminists, but as we have shown, all were committed to 'making a difference', often along feminist lines. Is the university to which women are making a difference more in tune with the university of the past than that of the future? To the extent that the answer is 'yes', there is a need to develop a new understanding of the role of women in leadership. The women whose perspectives are described in this article have used a range of strategies in 'fortifying the difference', and their views provide a key to understanding what it means to be leaders and managers in these times. We would suggest that the insights gained from their experiences over the last quarter of a century are an important element in the process of developing a new feminist politics of leadership for the twenty-first century.

Acknowledgements

Sandra Acker and Johanna Wyn would like to thank the Social Sciences and Humanities Research Council of Canada and the Faculty of Education, University of Melbourne, Australia, for their financial support; graduate student Elisabeth Richards for help with the analysis of data; the anonymous reviewers for their useful comments; and the women who made this research possible by their participation.

NOTE

1   In North America, these responsibilities would usually be termed administration rather than management, at the risk of some confusion with the jobs of administrators who are not also academics. In this article, we have used the terminology more often found in Britain and Australia.

REFERENCES

Acker, S. (1999a) 'Caring as work for women educators', in E. Smyth, S. Acker, P. Bourne and A. Prentice (eds), *Challenging Professions: Historical and Contemporary Perspectives on Women's Professional Work* (Toronto, University of Toronto Press).

Acker, S. (1999b) *The Realities of Teachers' Work: Never a Dull Moment* (London, Cassell/Continuum).

Acker, S. and Feuerverger, G. (1996) 'Doing good and feeling bad: the work of women university teachers', *Cambridge Journal of Education*, 26: 401–422.

Blackmore, J. (1999) *Troubling Women: Feminism, Leadership and Educational Change* (Buckingham, Open University Press).

Carty, L. (1991) 'Black women in academia: a statement from the periphery', in H. Bannerji, L. Carty, K. Dehli, S. Heald and K. McKenna (eds), *Unsettling Relations: The University as a Site of Feminist Struggles* (Toronto, Women's Press).

Cassin, M. and Morgan, J.G. (1992) 'The professoriate and the market-driven university: transforming the control of work in the academy', in W. Carroll, L. Christiansen-Ruffman, R. Currie and D. Harrison (eds), *Fragile Truths: 25 Years of Sociology and Anthropology in Canada* (Ottawa, Carleton University Press).

David, M.E. and Woodward, D. (eds) (1998) *Negotiating the Glass Ceiling: Careers of Senior Women in the Academic World* (London, Falmer Press).

Davies, B. (1996) *Power, Knowledge, Desire* (Canberra, Department of Employment, Education, Training and Youth Affairs).

Davies, C. and Holloway, P. (1995) 'Troubling transformations: gender regimes and organizational culture in the academy', in L. Morley and V. Walsh (eds), *Feminist Academics: Creative Agents for Change* (London, Taylor & Francis).

Deem, R. and Ozga, J. (1997) 'Women managing for diversity in a postmodern world', in C. Marshall (ed.), *Feminist Critical Policy Analysis: A Perspective from Post-Secondary Education* (London, Falmer Press).

Doyle Walton, K. (ed.) (1996) *Against the Tide: Career Paths of Women Leaders in American and British Higher Education* (Bloomington, IN, Phi Delta Kappan).

Drakich, J. and Stewart, P. (1998) 'A profile of women faculty in Canada: rank, discipline and age 1957–1994', *Canadian Association of University Teachers Bulletin, Status of Women Supplement*, 45: 7–11.

Dyhouse, C. (1995) *No Distinction of Sex? Women in British Universities, 1870–1939* (London, UCL Press).

Eagleton, M. (1998) 'Reading between bodies and institutions', *Gender and Education*, 10: 343–349.

Eggins, H. (ed.) (1997) *Women as Leaders and Managers in Higher Education* (Buckingham, Open University Press).

Gallop, J. (1995) 'The teacher's breasts', in J. Gallop (ed.), *Pedagogy: The Question of Impersonation* (Bloomington, IN, Indiana University Press).

Gilligan, C. (1982) *In a Different Voice: Psychological Theory and Women* (Cambridge, MA, Harvard University Press).

Johnson, L. (1993) *The Modern Girl* (Sydney, Allen & Unwin).

Kenway, J. and Langmead, D. (1998) 'Governmentality, the "now" university and the future of knowledge work', *Australian Universities' Review*, 41(2): 28–31.

Kerman, L. (1995) 'The good witch: advice to women in management', in L. Morley and V. Walsh (eds), *Feminist Academics* (London, Taylor & Francis).

Kolodny, A. (1998) *Failing the Future: A Dean Looks at Higher Education in the Twenty-First Century* (Durham, NC, Duke University Press).

Leonard, P. (1998) 'Gendering change? Management, masculinity and the dynamics of incorporation', *Gender and Education*, 10: 71–84.

Luke, C. (1997) 'Feminist pedagogy theory in higher education: reflections on power and authority', in C. Marshall (ed.), *Feminist Critical Policy Analysis: A Perspective from Post-Secondary Education* (London, Falmer Press).

Marginson, S. (1997) *Markets in Education* (Sydney, Allen & Unwin).

Marshall, C. (1997) 'Dismantling and reconstructing policy analysis', in C. Marshall (ed.), *Feminist Critical Policy Analysis: A Perspective from Primary and Secondary Schooling* (London, Falmer Press).

Morley, L. (1999) *Organizing Feminisms: The Micropolitics of the Academy* (London, Macmillan).

Morley, L. and Walsh, V. (eds) (1995) *Feminist Academics: Creative Agents for Change* (London, Taylor & Francis).

Noddings, N. (1992) *The Challenge to Care in Schools* (New York, Teachers College Press).

Park, S. (1996) 'Research, teaching and service: why shouldn't women's work count?', *Journal of Higher Education*, 67: 47–84.

Pratt, M.B. (1984) 'Identity: skin blood heart', in E. Bulkin, M.B. Pratt and B. Smith (eds), *Yours in Struggle: Three Feminist Perspectives on Anti-Semitism and Racism* (New York, Long Haul Press).

Probert, B., Ewer, P. and Whiting, K. (1998) *Gender Pay Equity in Australian Higher Education* (South Melbourne, National Tertiary Education Union).

Sinclair, A. (1998) *Doing Leadership Differently* (Melbourne, Melbourne University Press).

Sernak, K. (1998) *School Leadership – Balancing Power with Caring* (New York, Teachers College Press).

Slaughter, S. and Leslie, L. (1997) *Academic Capitalism* (Baltimore, MD, Johns Hopkins University Press).

Strachan, J. (1999) 'Feminist educational leadership: locating the concepts in practice', *Gender and Education*, 11: 309–322.

Tamboukou, M. (1999) 'Spacing herself: women in education', *Gender and Education*, 11: 125–139.

Woolf, V. (1957) *A Room of One's Own* (New York, Harcourt, Brace & World).

Wyn, J. (1997) 'Senior women academics in education: working through restructuring in Australian universities', *Melbourne Studies in Education*, 38: 103–128.

Yeatman, A. (1995) 'The gendered management of equity-oriented change in higher education', in J. Smyth (ed.), *Academic Work* (Buckingham, Open University Press).

Young, I.M. (1990) *Justice and the Politics of Difference* (Princeton, NJ, Princeton University Press).

ELEVEN

CONSUMERISM AND GENDER IN AN ERA OF SCHOOL CHOICE: A LOOK AT US CHARTER SCHOOLS

Amy Stambach

Source: 'Consumerism and gender in an era of school choice: a look at US Charter Schools', *Gender and Education*, 13(2): 199–216, 2001.

Introduction

When it comes to understanding the trajectory of school reform, gender relations play an underacknowledged role (cf. David, 1993, 1997; David *et al.*, 1997). Yet, understanding how gender is selectively invoked and at other times ignored, and how cultural beliefs about gender subtly inform impressions upon which people reason, judge, debate and act, enables us to see how school reform, itself a complicated sociocultural process, proceeds *not* down a single course predetermined or spelled out clearly by policy, but in several directions simultaneously, often led by persons working from structurally competing and cross-cutting positions. It provides an opportunity to observe, in-the-making, cultural debates about public life,[1] and it has implications for the crafting and implementation of educational policy.

This article explores the ways multiple and changing gender dynamics within middle-class suburban families, in the Midwestern USA, exist in tension with gendered aspects of school institutional structures. I examine and compare from an anthropological perspective parental involvement in two US charter schools. By looking at events and debates surrounding parents' charter school involvement, I address several questions about the scope and quality of parental involvement in school reform. Whose familial and social values receive firmest expression in the schools' practices and policies? Can we discern gendered visions of American families and society embedded in schools' operations? What is the relationship of the charter schools to the overarching public school system? How, if at all, do people identify and talk about gender as a factor in explaining charter schools' trajectories?

In answering these questions, I have sought to balance a rich body of knowledge about charter schools derived from polling, national reports and the media (e.g. Office of Educational Research and Improvement, 1999; Charter School Discussion Groups, 2000; Education Mailing List Archive, 2000) with a body of 'ethnographic knowledge' (Ortner, 1993, p. 413) that illustrates some of the conceptual categories local persons bring to their decisions and actions involving school reform. I begin with a brief discussion of charter schools and the theoretical literature that informs my study. I then discuss my research methods and present the two schools from the perspectives of founding parents. Finally, I analyse the data and discuss their implications for understanding school reform. Throughout, I develop the argument that, although more often implicit than explicit in what people say and do, gender emerges as an explanation for understanding how parental involvement in school reform is sometimes limited by competing ideas of parents as caregivers versus their roles as administrative reformers.

Charter schools

Briefly put, charter schools are public non-sectarian schools created through a contract, or charter, between a sponsoring authority – usually a public school district – and a charter school operator – often a parent or group of parents, a teacher–parent coalition, or a private school looking to convert to a public charter institution. Some charter schools target a small population of academically at-risk students; others offer a choice to parents in areas of curriculum and teaching. Federal and state charter school legislation, passed in more than 36 states to date, authorizes parents, teachers and private and public organizations to propose and initiate charter schools (Charter Schools Website, 2000). Funding procedures vary by state, but generally, the district per-pupil expenditure follows the student to the charter school, which is usually housed in an existing district facility. Occasionally, schools are sponsored and funded by non-district organizations, such as city councils, colleges or universities. Increasingly, for-profit organizations are starting charter schools, a source of concern to some advocates of public education (see, e.g. the National Education Association's Charter School Web Site, 2000).

In scope and organization, charter schools are numerous, yet as public alternatives within the public school system they condense a range of views about parental involvement in public education. On the one hand, they represent some parents' desires to have more control over their children's education – a phenomenon sometimes popularly expressed in terms of 'parents' values' and 'children's protection,' as in: 'How can we as parents and community members protect our children from the irresponsible watering down of academic education and the undermining of our own individual parental values?' – the words of a mother writing a letter to a Midwestern US newspaper editor (her answer was: charter schools). On the other hand, charter schools reflect the logical extension of an education system that is dedicated to reaching every student individually. As such, the movement is part of a wider trend toward greater state involvement in public education. Rather than local boards and parents setting schools' policy agendas, the state is defining the parameters such that parents have less direct voice in educational programming and policy formation. This is an observation others have made of the state of US public education (Paris, 1998; Nappi, 1999) and one that I observed in studying the formation and the trajectories of these two charter schools.

Literature review

Scholarly research on charter schooling has focused primarily on schools' organizational structures. With the exception of several studies (e.g. Paris, 1998; Wells *et al.*, 1999), few attempt to use charter schools as a heuristic lens for exploring the role of schooling in US society. Several sociological studies have emphasized the administrative aspects of charter schools (e.g. SRI International, 1997; Office of Educational Research and Improvement, 1999), often looking at such issues as accountability, autonomy and strategies for educational improvement (e.g. Hassel, 1996; Millot, 1996). Several works on school selection processes in general have considered the place of social class and ethnicity in parents' school involvement (e.g. see Yancey and Saporito, 1995; Lareau and Horvat, 1999; Saporito and Lareau, 1999). Yet, few analyses of contemporary US school reform, and none to my knowledge on charter schooling, have discussed social class and ethnicity in combination with gender as factors that play into parents' roles and parent–school interactions.

This is surprising, given what we know from a body of rich sociological research on the family and school selection: namely that decision-making processes and home–school relations are culturally gendered across the social spectrum (Lareau, 1989; Reay, 1996; David, 1997). As documented in the USA, Britain, and Canada, for instance (Manicom, 1984; Reay, 1996; Luttrell, 1997), working- and middle-class fathers and mothers of different ethnic self-identity spend different amounts of time and energy investing in their children's schooling. When decisions about school selection are viewed as processes that extend across space and time, and are not regarded as merely instantaneous decisions that take the form of 'yes' or 'no,' the greater involvement of mothers becomes much more evident (David *et al.*, 1993). When the 'hidden psychological costs' (Reay, 1996, p. 594) of working-class and ethnic minority mothers are viewed in the context of parents' broader lives, middle-class norms embedded in educational policy come to the fore as beliefs that apply to parents differentially (Luttrell, 1997, pp. 91–105).

Analysis of contemporary US educational policy might more clearly link questions about the structuring of social differences through school reform to the rise of market structures and discourses of consumerism in public education.[2] Over the course of the past decade and a half, and arguably since the publication of *A Nation at Risk* in 1983, Deweyian conceptions of schooling as democratic institutions and as providing vocational opportunity for everyone regardless of background have given way to a language of schools as competitive institutions that prepare students differentially (Chubb and Moe, 1990) – a market place where parents are consumers and the product is 'the educated child' (Bennett *et al.*, 1999).

Within this time period, parents have emerged in new roles as producers *and* consumers. Increasingly, parents have been called upon to design educational programmes that serve their school district and wider community. The difficulty arises when parents' interests are regarded as particularistic and as being in conflict with the totality, and when parents are seen as intruding upon the professionalism of certified and experienced teachers. In the context of 'school choice', when parents are called upon both to produce and consume new educational programmes, parents – practically speaking, mothers – who involve themselves in organizing new programmes run the risk of being seen as stepping out of their roles as willing consumers and caregivers and, as such, acting beyond the realm of their socially prescribed authority. Such does not have to be the case, of course (see Wagner, 1990; Risman, 1998); however, it is one aspect of the story I encountered at both New Millennium and Academic Charter Schools. In the following sections, I illustrate this phenomenon, drawing on conversations, interviews and participant observations.

Background and methods

Like most suburban charter schools nationwide, the two schools I present in this article are 'choice' programmes, not at-risk alternative charter schools; that is, their charters have been designed to serve all students equally, not to assist a body of academically underperforming students or students with special needs. Both were founded in the mid-1990s, in a Midwestern state, by parents with children in public elementary schools. Together, they epitomize a shared commitment to parental involvement in public education. Yet, their curricula and instructional philosophies suggest very different understandings of education and choice. One school provides a multi-age, collaborative-learning curriculum, with team-teaching and parental involvement. The other school offers a direct instructional programme with a self-appointed parental advisory board and a fixed curriculum. Both schools are housed in buildings owned and maintained by the public district: one is divided and located in two district elementary schools; the other is housed in a partly renovated building, attached by a catwalk to an adjacent elementary school. Although their full enrolments (and in one case, lengthy waiting list) might suggest that they receive majority parental support, parents across the district, as a whole, are far from united on the value of the two charter schools.

Beginning in June 1999, and continuing for the next several months, I explored the community surrounding New Millennium and Academic Charter Schools. I visited and spoke with people in civic, government and community organizations (the Chamber of Commerce, the City Council offices, parent–teacher associations) and developed an ethnographic picture of the wider community – a community characterized by its rural roots and rapid suburban/sub-divisional expansion. Within the school, I began by contacting members of the Dover Area School District (a pseudonym),[3] the larger district within which the two charter schools are set. Working first from the administrative top, I contacted the school superintendent, who introduced the charter schools to me as some of the 'key features of our nationally recognized school district'. I met three times and spoke on the telephone with the school district community education officer, whose qualified support of the charter schools mirrored that of the superintendent. Both the superintendent and the community education officer supported the trend toward increased parental involvement in education, even though both were dubious of parents' educational expertise and know-how. In snowball methodology fashion, both offered me names of parents, teachers and board members to contact, who in turn suggested more people whom I might interview.

By February 2000, I had conducted 35 open-ended interviews, approximately 1 hour each, with 5 district administrators, 4 teachers, 2 board members and 24 parents, including 12 parents whose children attended the 'common school' (as people in this community refer to the non-charter schools in the district) and 12 parents whose children attended one of the two charter schools (8 with children enrolled at Academic Charter, 4 with children at New Millennium); 2 teachers at New Millennium, 1 at Academic Charter School and 1 in the common school. I also attended a parent-run meeting at Academic Charter School and, with research assistance of sociologist Natalie Crow Becker,[4] obtained information on a district-wide kindergarten informational meeting, at which each of the district's 4 'common' elementary schools and 2 charter schools presented their programmes to incoming families. Seven months into the research, I developed and sent a mail survey to approximately 500 families in the community, including all of the families with children in the 2 charter schools and a random sample of 250 parents with children in the common school.[5]

In my conversations with and observations of parents and educators, gendered aspects and incompatibilities between parents' and administrators' views of gender roles and leadership (as well, interestingly, among mothers themselves) quickly came to the fore. I emphasize them here within the context of white suburban models of families and schooling in order to help articulate an aspect of parental involvement in school reform that is easily overlooked: processes by which parent- (again, mainly mother-) initiated school reform programmes are gradually co-opted into, and in some aspects, phased out of, districts' larger administrative goals.

Case studies, key players

Among the most cogent and purposeful accounts of charter schooling were the stories of three parents – all mothers – involved in establishing charter schools. Two of these mothers worked together to initiate Academic Charter School; the other worked closely with the District Community Education Officer to develop and organize New Millennium. I recount aspects of my conversations with these mothers to illustrate: (a) their reasons for setting up charter schools; (b) the views they express about parents' roles as children's advocates within a pluralistic, democratic society; and (c) these mothers' eventual disengagement from the charter schools and their reasons for pulling out of school reform.

Carol Sweeney

After three years of more than full-time, unpaid work in conjunction with the charter school, Carol Sweeney had recently fully disengaged herself from the char- ter school and was contemplating sending her children to a private institution. She was working now as an office receptionist in an industrial supply company near the neighbouring city's beltline. Although the position called upon her to use her administrative and organizational skills, Sweeney exercised little of the institu- tional leadership in her new job that she had enjoyed as 'charter school parent co-founder'.

Sweeney began our conversation by noting that her reasons for leaving the charter school had to do with the administration's 'failure', as she put it, to 'fully take advantage of the ideas and resources of parents'. She maintained that, as co-founder and volunteer director of Academic Charter School, she ought to have been considered for the position of full-time, paid director, but that her request to apply for the job had been turned down due to a technicality – she did not, as she put it, 'hold a piece of paper from a School of Education', and as such had not been considered qualified to lead and supervise teachers at the charter school:

> I put a lot of work into that school. Hours and hours of time and overtime. None of it paid. And then in the end, even though I had been involved in starting the whole thing, I was told that I wasn't qualified to direct it! I mean, come on.

Sweeney had founded Academic Charter (along with Susan Moser, see later) as a way of continuing what she thought had been an academically successful pilot math programme that had been initiated in the common elementary school: namely, a method of teaching mathematics using 'direct instruction' and 'teacher-centred' teaching techniques (on which, see Tarver and Jung, 1995). In her view, the method had been successful not only for her child, but for many who had been involved: 'Why doesn't the school continue to provide this programme? It seems to make sense for so many children.'

When the school phased out the pilot programme, Sweeney and Moser approached the district with a charter school proposal. The district had already approved one charter school – New Millennium, founded by Barbara Todd (see later), and had put in place a series of policies that could be used to establish a second one. Sweeney perceived that the district was less enthusiastic about the Academic Charter School application, which proposed to continue the direct instruction programme, than it had been with New Millennium, in part because the direct instruction teaching philosophy – or at any rate, didactic aspects of it that Academic Charter School founders championed – contradicted a more institutionally supported 'child-centred' approach, such as had been incorporated into New Millennium's charter.

> We learned a lot from New Millennium. We watched how they started everything and then built upon what we learned from them. It was all smooth-sailing except that they [the district] didn't want us to start our charter school. They didn't believe in what we wanted to do, even after they saw how successful the pilot had been.

As Sweeney described it, the charter school proposal was a well-researched and policy-supported document. At 24 pages, it included analysis of district costs, results from a survey Sweeney and Moser had conducted on parents' school preferences regarding locations and report cards, discussion and bibliographic citations to research literature on the teaching curriculum and method of instruction, an outline of the proposed charter school curriculum, as well as justifications for starting the school, an accountability plan, discussion of the relationship of the charter school to district, state and national educational goals, and discussion of budget and fiscal accountability. Although soundly conceived in Sweeney's view, the charter school came under heavy criticism: 'We faced attacks from people who questioned the way we recruited people. They thought we were elitist and wealthy or that we brainwashed students into thinking they were "smarter" because they participated in our program.' Sweeney pointed to the strong support she had received from district teachers who had participated in the direct instructional programme as evidence that the teaching philosophy was not misguided but produced 'measurable, concrete academic results'; and she maintained that the school had been advertised to all parents equally and that it was simply 'an unfortunate thing' that mainly 'white suburbanites' had enrolled their children in the school.

Towards the waning months of Sweeney's leadership, the school was experiencing increased conflict with the 'common school'. Although Sweeney saw the conflict as a matter of 'teachers not wanting to hear what parents had to say', teachers and school district administrators, in my later conversations with them, maintained that Carol Sweeney, and parent leaders generally, were 'interested primarily in their own children' and 'too subjective'. Like Barbara Todd (see later), who organized and administered New Millennium, Carol Sweeney thought that teachers were in fact responsible to parents – 'accountable' was how she put it, using the managerial language of our day. In the end, Sweeney said she was left with the sense that two things stood in the way of school reform: 'teachers who were not willing to let parents lead', and 'administrators who thought parents were self-interested and not able to formulate a bigger picture' for charter school reform.

Susan Moser

Susan Moser was more reluctant than Carol Sweeney to speak about her involvement with Academic Charter, feeling, as she put it, 'still really burned by what the administration has done to the school'. Whereas Sweeney had championed the direct instructional component, Moser had promoted the adoption of the Core Knowledge curriculum, a sequenced instructional programme designed to provide same-aged children with a body of shared facts and knowledge (Hirsch, 1995; this curriculum has its critics, see, for instance, Peterson, 1995; Lowe and Miner, 1996). A particular intersection of events prompted Moser to look into the Core Knowledge curriculum:

> My kindergartener came home one afternoon, talking about insects and butterflies. He had been talking about caterpillars and moths in school and was now supposed draw these pictures of butterflies at home. Then, a couple of days later, my second grader was given an assignment about butterflies, and then my sixth grader was studying insects, including a component on butter-flies. Who was coordinating this? The principal? The curriculum coordinator?

Moser was concerned that children were not building on prior knowledge, and she questioned whether the school administration was adequately coordinating the curriculum: 'If this is what's happening with my children, what's going on across the entire district? How many kids are sitting in class year after year, learning the same thing over and over again?'

Moser saw it as her civic duty to change the system for many children.

> When it became clear that we had the chance to propose a charter school for our kids, I thought it was important to include a curriculum that would be cumulative and age-graded. That way [in keeping with E. D. Hirsch's (1988) philosophy of cultural literacy that Moser discussed earlier in our conversation], we would be educating students for citizenship and society.

Moser worked with Sweeney and a network of family friends to clarify technical aspects of the application process. When enrolment policies at Academic Charter came under scrutiny, she and Sweeney wrote to John Fiegel (not a pseudonym), Director of Community Services, US Department of Education Public Charter School Programme, asking for clarification about a weighted lottery system for admissions: the district advocated using a weighted lottery to allow for Exceptional Education Needs (EEN) diversity, a proxy for low socio-economic and minority cultural diversity in the school. Fiegel answered that Academic Charter was following admissions procedures correctly (letter dated 14 January 1998), a response that amounted to a victory for the parent leaders at Academic Charter and a setback for the school administration.

For the next several months, relations continued to deteriorate between parent leaders at Academic Charter and public school district administrators. Not only did the two disagree over how to admit families into the Academic Charter School programme, they also had different views about the role of parents in influencing classroom practice and instruction.

When it came to understanding why, in the end, the charter school appeared to be slipping from parents' control, Moser again turned to an informal network of prominently placed friends and asked them for opinions and advice.

> I asked an attorney friend and politician if there was anything parents could do [in reference to the fact that parents were being excluded from the charter school programming]. He said that people always end up going back to what they are most comfortable with.

Moser took this as a signal that parental involvement had run its course at Academic Charter. At the time of our conversation, she had withdrawn her children and was planning to send them to a private school the following year.

Barbara Todd

In June 1994, slightly more than one year before Sweeney and Moser proposed Academic Charter School, Barbara Todd contacted the public school district about establishing New Millennium Charter School. A mother of three, Todd was concerned that her youngest child might suffer developmentally were the school board to adopt a Back to Basics approach – an academically oriented, teacher-directed pedagogy, aspects of which were eventually reformulated within the curriculum at Academic Charter School. She reasoned, along the lines that Sweeney did, that if her particular child was benefiting from an open-ended instructional method at the school, weren't many?

> Aren't there other kids who benefit from a curriculum that is more open-ended than rigidly defined? Don't we have to make sure schools serve a variety of needs? Why should we move to any one approach? I can't believe the board was even talking about adopting Back to Basics when we know that kids learn in different ways.

Key administrators within the public school district supported the multi-age, collaborative learning approach that Barbara Todd proposed and worked with her to develop a charter school that would ensure the continuation of this teaching philosophy. At the time, the school board was uneasily divided between people who supported Back to Basics and those who did not. Establishing a charter school that emphasized multi-age classrooms with child-centred learning would supersede the board's possible decisions about going to a Back to Basics curriculum, at least during the term of the five-year charter contract that Todd received in May 1995.

Like Sweeney and Moser, by early 1999, Todd had pulled out of the charter school. Her reasons, she said, had to do with the 'wall' she had come up against in her involvement with some of the charter school teachers. On one level, her frustration was born from what she perceived as a lack of teachers' professionalism and their unwillingness to work beyond the terms of their contract – which was what, Todd said, 'other professionals do'. At another level, interrelated with the first, she was frustrated by the competing positions that parents and teachers sometimes vied for. Concerned that some teachers had an unrealistic view of what parents, as workers, expected from themselves, Todd described a pivotal event – a meeting between union members and parents – that, to her, epitomized some major obstacles to school reform.

> Parents work just as hard as teachers. Some of these teachers think we sit around all day and just wait for our kids to get home. We don't. Well, we had a big meeting with the union rep, because it just wasn't working. Teachers said parents weren't qualified to supervise them; parents said teachers weren't being accountable to parents for their work and time. And so we had this big meeting. And I spoke for a time and then at one point the district union representative got up and said something that made me so furious. She said that in all this time, she hasn't heard anything about kids. 'What we're really about is kids,' she said, 'and yet I haven't heard anything about kids.' And I mean, of course we're interested in our kids, but come on. Why do they dumb it down and say it's all about kids? Of course it's about kids or we wouldn't be here. But that just diffused the whole thing. We should be working from the premise that it is all about kids and then figuring out what best system we can do to make it best for everyone. I mean, this is the kind of thing teachers do. Educators just drop everything they've created and fall back on kids as though any trouble we have could be resolved by thinking that 'it's all about kids.'

Described by the superintendent as a 'just a mom, a skinny, courageous little mom – I don't know what she'd be like if she were full-sized', Barbara Todd, judging from the previously cited interview excerpt, was aware of the sometimes awkward and competing 'dance' parents and teachers were structurally engaged in, between acting as professionals – or more generally, with a disinterested air of objectivity – and claiming (as well as being culturally assigned to the role of having) care-taking responsibilities and close emotional bonds with children. Todd described parents who had taken responsibility within charter schools as taking on a more professional role at school, a role that was potentially undermined when teachers recast parents as caregivers, not objective professionals. And she recognized that parental involvement meant changes for teachers that would require time.

In the end, however, she was not convinced that the teaching profession was willing to 'let parents in', nor did she believe that teachers necessarily had a commitment to the larger good: 'They're not really willing to consider what's best for each kid and develop it for that kid. They're more interested in teaching whichever curriculum they are most familiar with and like best.'

Todd decided to get out of the charter school project in the fall of 1999, noting in our conversation that charter schooling: 'is not a reform any more... [but that] schools are smack in the middle of our community and everybody should be involved in them. Teachers and administrators need to understand that'. Her words, like those of Sweeney and Moser, conveyed regret *not* at having started the charter school, but at not having been able to continue the project or to make, as she put it, 'a lasting difference'.

Discussion: working at odds, but not necessarily in opposition

To better understand teacher–parent interactions, I take a page from the work of Sarah Lawrence Lightfoot, a sociologist of education whose analysis of public schooling, although qualified by researchers more recently (e.g. Manicom, 1984; Biklen, 1995; Brantlinger *et al.*, 1996), reflects popular cultural conceptions about societal tensions that underlie parent–teacher interrelationships. In their different orientations to the educational development of children, Lightfoot tells us, parents and teachers are locked in a structural tension.

> Parents have *particularistic* expectations for their children while teachers have universalistic expectations. When parents ask the teacher to 'be fair' with their child or to give him/her 'a chance,' they are usually asking that the teacher give special attention (i.e. consider the individual qualities, the developmental and motivational characteristics) to their child. When teachers talk about being 'fair' to everyone they mean giving equal amounts of attention, judging everyone by the same objective standards, using explicit and public criteria for making judgment.
>
> (Lightfoot, 1975, p. 34)

Lightfoot contends that this structural tension boils down to an antagonism between mothers and teachers. 'Because mothers and teachers are at the center of these discontinuities and conflicts...and because all mothers and many elementary school teachers are women, the antagonisms I have described [are] largely...between women' (Lightfoot, 1977, p. 402).

In so far as some parents in my study argued that charter school teachers are not accountable, and in so far as some teachers themselves thought parents were meddling in areas where they were not qualified, the difficulties that emerged between founding parents and charter school teachers were seen by these actors as epitomizing universalistic versus particularistic social tensions. Indeed, charter school opponents described charter school advocates as persons who were interested in individual children; and teachers, even those in charter schools, contrasted themselves with charter school parents by emphasizing teachers' obligations to the community. To some extent, although not across the board, parent–teacher antagonisms were framed as antagonisms among women. Todd was upset that teachers framed parents as 'caregivers' only interested in the emotional needs of their children, and Sweeney was offended that teachers would not listen to her, a mother, but only to administrators who held teaching certificates. Although neither mentioned men or women specifically, the cultural connotations of care giving and administration are such that gender lay at the base of their associations.

Yet, this popular characterization of mothers as particularistic and teachers as universalistic needs to be revisited in the context of 'choice programs' in education, and more generally within a framework that allows for actors to challenge institutional structures (see Manicom, 1984; Biklen, 1995). In particular, it needs to be put into a historical framework that sees public schools as rapidly changing. It also needs to be framed in terms that capture the multiple and in some cases changing gender dynamics that characterize parental relationships in the middle class. For even though structural tensions may be embedded in institutional organizations (such as between mothers and teachers in schools) and in large-scale public narratives (as when state and federally legislated charter school policies position parents as consumers and producers) structural tensions are as well susceptible to being identified, challenged and redefined. Gendered tensions such as those between teachers and parents are not beyond actors' scrutiny – particularly not in social domains like schools, where critical inquiry remains (at least a little bit, one would hope!) a collectively agreed-upon institutional characteristic.

Over the course of the past five years, and continuing to the present day in these charter schools, parent–teachers alliances have led to novel relationships. One of the most apparent of these brings us back to the recent literature on consumerism and parent involvement that I mentioned at the outset. Even if founders characterize their involvement in charter schooling as an act of civic responsibility, many also include an account of the ways their own children, and other individuals' children, benefit. Founders' own chartering narratives typically include a chapter linking 'my children's needs' to a particular 'curriculum'. Mothers who had been involved with starting new schools carefully balanced their motivations against what they recognized as a democratic public system. Even as they cited their children's school experiences as motivation for their own school involvement, they also employed an inclusive language to suggest that, although unique, their schools were in fact open to everyone. 'Schools are smack in the middle of our community', Todd, at one point, said. 'Everybody should be involved in them, and teachers and administrators need to understand that.'

One consequence of working within a system that frames its mission as 'public' is that founders have had to think about many children as a collectivist strategy. In an increasingly market-oriented system, and in a contemporary world where social justice is sometimes linked with arguments about maximizing the educational potential of many individuals, mothers' shift away from supporting 'the one best system' and toward supporting 'different systems that work best for different children' might more clearly be seen as a collectivist strategy that rests on arguments about the collective social value of individuals. Put another way, maternal involvement may indeed focus on individuals, but it may not be entirely particularistic; it could as well be a collectivist strategy for maximizing the potential of many children and, as such, an effort these mothers advance in the interest of their understanding of social justice.[6]

Although some charter school opponents view this 'reaching out' as a gesture of apparent, not genuine, democratic plurality, it is, in any event, a strategy charter school founders have had to employ – indeed, a strategy they are bound to by the conditions of district, state, and federal policy. Charter school founders have had to produce what they themselves would also want to consume. They have had to think both like public servants working in the interest of the common good, or, as Todd characteristically succinctly put it, reflecting a discourse of privatization and competition that has proliferated with the advent of choice programs: they 'have had to think like entrepreneurs looking to model a product that others would buy'.

In this latter sense that parents see themselves as entrepreneurs looking to design a better product, parents' views of schooling today reflect a shift of opinion from several years ago. Both teachers and parents, contrary to what either side may say of the other, *do* have a sense of universal and particular values, although today they are being increasingly couched in terms of collective versus individualistic preferences. If the balance remains somewhat differently distributed for the two groups, parents arguably are being asked – indeed, they are being required by policy – to think more collectively about their involvement in public schooling. The new language of collectivism is, however, a language of 'markets' and 'consumer demand' – a line of Western civic and political discourse that reflects libertarian values (in the vein of John Stuart Mill's *On Liberty*) – *not* the Deweyian discourse of egalitarianism and progressiveness that is deeply institutionalized in schools of education (see Kliebard, 1986).

As a consequence of their consumeristic framework, parents appear, from some positions, to be working at odds with a system that is democratic-egalitarian – a system that, like them, values the equal education of all, but in terms of individual *attainment* not equal opportunity. In the sense that some parents are pursuing individualistic and not egalitarian lines of democratic action, parents appear, from some angles, to be undoing the American fabric. However, parents and teachers are not exactly working in opposition; both are in fact working for (and in) 'the public' – a public that is increasingly being defined and organized according to the terms of a market system. Todd, for instance, commented, by way of showing her commitment to public education: 'Public education is a closed and outdated system. People sometimes think that because I think this I'm also supporting vouchers. But I'm not. That's not the public system. I'm anti-voucher.' In the sense that people are talking about old institutions differently, public education does indeed seem to be undergoing important transformations: the discourse of provision, if not the institutional structures of governance (see later), have changed from a decade or more ago.

'Particularistic mothers' in an age of consumerism

At the same time, however, that consumerism is reframing the terms of public school debate, and with it popular notions about 'pushy versus pluralistically oriented mothers', large-scale gendered relations continue to inform the trajectory some school reforms take – including charter schooling. The two charter schools I have examined are both entering a second contract period.[7] As mentioned, all founders within the past academic year pulled out of the charter schools. Their positions have been defined and formalized and are now filled by paid district employees.

Parents in the larger district have had mixed responses to this turn of events. Seven of the 12 I spoke with in interviews (among parents from the 'common' school) mentioned that this transition reflects the first step toward co-opting the charter schools.[8] Said one mother whose two children were enrolled in one of the district's 'common' schools:

SHELLY: The fact that there are now two directors paid by the district running the programs just shows you that the charter schools are being taken from parents' control.

AMY: What do you think of this?

SHELLY: I think it's a good thing. The schools are draining resources from the main district.

Yet, this position, although expressed by more than half of the parents with children in the 'common school' who responded to the open-ended questions in my mail survey, disregards the fact that so long as the charter schools continue to demonstrate a distinct mission, academic credibility and fiscal responsibility, schools' requests for renewing their status are difficult to deny. As one study on charter schooling in California indicates, charter schools are more likely to be judged and have their charters renewed on the basis of fiscal accountability than not on the basis of how well they have implemented their charter or taught students (UCLA, 1998). More pertinent to understanding these charter schools' trajectories here is understanding how the appointment of professionally certified administrators served to legitimize these charter schools as *public*. Said one mother, Jenny, who has had her children enrolled in Academic Charter School since its inception:

> I think it's good that they [the school board] hired directors who hold teaching credentials, I mean, from Schools of Education. I mean, these are public schools. We've always said 'charter schools are public schools' so why shouldn't we have school district leaders in them?

This view was prominent among a subgroup of charter school parents – not those who founded them, but those who enroled their children and were committed to 'choice' in public education.

As though rearticulating their critics' views that charter schools were not public institutions, and in rearticulating them, redefining, again, the diversity of meaning when people speak of 'public education', parents who sent their children to charter schools said founders' ousting was for the public good. Said another Academic Charter School parent, Jenny's neighbour and, like Jenny, involved in fund-raising for the charter school:

> I think that first groups of parents *should* have been replaced by trained directors. The parents were kind of, like, starting a school of their own. They forgot that these weren't private teaching academies but part of the public system. We're part of the public school. We should be tied into the [district] administration.

This general line of argument held that charter school founders were not in fact representing the views of the parent majority; that founding-parents had been too administratively powerful in the school and positionally weak in the eyes of teachers and district administrators. In fact, 8 out of the 12 charter school parents I interviewed – including 5 at Academic Charter – maintained that parents were incapable of administering the schools; that teachers needed professionals to evaluate their performance; and that the district-appointed administrators were in the best positions to do this.

Fascinating are the terms in which parents described the *reason* for parents' ousting: structural tensions between parents and educators, specifically between parent-mothers and male-administrators. Said one charter school parent, mother of two, about the district's decision to appoint a new charter school administrator:

BRENDA: The founder of [one of the schools] was a real nice woman, but I don't think she was all there businesswise. I think Dave [the new director of Academic Charter School] is much better. Dave is...[she paused, left her thought unfinished, then continued], you know, plus I think the male figure was very much needed in the organization too.

AMY: Why?

BRENDA: You know, it's just, um, her expertise just didn't work. There were teachers, and very good teachers, but it's still the man's world out there. So the superintendents [*sic*], and the principals, and when you had to deal with them, they were just kind of like always talking down to them and always fighting them and always giving them a hard time. And anyway, that was the impression we as parents got. And I haven't seen that. I think Dave comes in with a much more positive attitude, saying, 'I'm working with these people and they're gonna work with me, and that's...we're equals.

This charter school mother – herself not a founder, though like Jenny and Jenny's neighbour, mentioned earlier, active in fund-raising programmes for the school – articulated something the three founding mothers never directly identified: a generalized association of charter school founders as women, and as such, as perceived subordinates to district administrators. It is important to distinguish between Brenda's views of the way she thought administrators perceived charter founders on the one hand, and administrators' own characterizations, on the other, of founders as courageous people with whom they could work profession-ally. Indeed, administrators' narratives (notwithstanding the earlier comment about the 'skinny but courageous' charter school mother) emphasized the respect they held for founding parents. Time and again, the district community education officer acknowledged these parents' skills and intellect:

> Carol Sweeney and Barbara Todd are really smart in thinking through the ins and outs of policies. They put together amazing documents [the charter school proposals] and they, um, I mean, look, they set up these brand new charter schools! And they kept coming back to us with more questions and more ideas. They saw things we never did. They made these charter schools really happen.

Likewise, the district superintendent praised the founders' organizational skills and leadership abilities.

> Barbara and Carol put together impressive proposals and worked with the board and community members to bring this thing to fruition…Whether you're for or against them, they know how to work the system. They know their rights within the policies and they go up the system [even above the superintendent, to the US Department of Education] to get their answers.

Nonetheless, comments like Brenda's, about the need for a 'male figure' to lead the charter schools, suggest that founding parents, no matter how administrators described them, were painted (by at least some players) in the broader scenario as child-oriented mothers, lacking reason.

That gender should be pulled out as a card that explains founders' inadequacies is telling: telling of the tensions that persist in suburban models of parenthood. Teachers, administrators and most suburban parents themselves define good parenthood in terms of schooling: positive involvement is seen as evidence of good parenting and upbringing. Yet the over-involved mother is the cause, in this era of parental involvement, not only of a child's individual downfall, but also the curse of an entire school system that is attempting to reform. Perhaps, this is why the founder of the New Millennium Charter School protested so loudly at the union representative's insistence that charter school parents should talk more about children than they were at the meeting about programming. Creating a discussion about school reform around the focus and needs of children catches these charter school founders – because they are women – in a structural position directly pitting their identities as mothers against the educational roles of public school teachers. Not only are parents here both producers and consumers and, as such, trying to develop and market what is best for children, they are also both mothers and educators and in structural tension with their children's teachers. As culturally assigned early childhood educators, both mothers and teachers histori-cally have been treated, and popularly seen, as functional substitutes, yet they have also been seen as existing in tension in that one works for her child, the other for society. Although school reform – and parent-initiated charter schools in particular – effect a change in this culturally produced structural relation, these reforms are, as well, susceptible to falling apart if these tensions are not kept out of the picture or at least minimized.

'Choosy moms have to choose charter schools'

'Falling apart' is in fact too strong a phrase to describe what is happening at these two charter schools. Both schools are thriving and have enrolments that suggest they adequately meet the needs of a subgroup of the district's parents. However, founders' resignations and the district's hiring of professional directors greatly transforms the meaning of 'parent involvement'. At New Millennium Charter School, the new director is herself a mother and former principal. Although she has a teaching certificate and was, indeed, formerly a full-time elementary school principal, her new directorship is a part-time position, which, she says, allows her to take care of her own kindergartener. As such, this new director's positional authority as an evaluator of the charter school teachers, and the personal authority she embodies by virtue of having a child in kindergarten, allows for a synthesis of competing roles that mothers experience as educators and child advocates. (At least this director is in a position to use these to the school's advantage.)

Whether or not the charter schools will be further incorporated into the structures of the common school, this early process of development illustrates some of the ways 'local control' is in fact in play with school institutional and gendered social structures. Parents' involvement in starting charter schools shows us not only the interplay of institutional structures with human agency. More to the point, it begins to demonstrate how education – schooling – is itself not always about providing an instructional model but about negotiating within a system that figures people differentially – parents as mothers, mothers as educators, educators as certified professionals, certified professionals as in positions of authority and in some regards as structurally and symbolically 'male'. I have not even begun to address very important issues of race and class here, but have focused instead on how the administrative direction of two contrasting charter schools mirrors models of suburban families.

My point, in short, is that the language of 'choice' in schooling puts parents at the centre of school reform. 'Choosy moms have to choose charter schools', said Brenda, Academic Charter School parent, quoted earlier, mocking the Jiff peanut butter advertisement of her childhood; if they did not, they would be acting irrationally, unless, of course, the common school met their children's individual needs. This choice implies a paradox, of course, as I have been arguing all along, for in today's school restructuring climate, when parents are invited to participate, parents must not only choose what they think is best for their children but they must frame their choices in terms of what they think might also be best for other individuals. In this regard, popular perceptions that women approach the school system not as parties co-invested with teachers in the project of children's education but as child-oriented parents whose educational role is defined by popular conceptions that they rival teachers as childhood educators – requires rethinking. For, in the market scenario, where parents have choice, parents *must* be involved in their children's education. When these parents are mothers, they risk setting off a chain of associations that are subtly – but powerfully – gendered.

Acknowledgements

I am grateful to Natalie Crow Becker, Miriam David, Stacey Lee, Wendy Luttrell and anonymous reviewers for providing me with constructive feedback on this article. I am also grateful to members of the Dover Area School District Community for providing me access to their schools, and to the University of Wisconsin-Madison Faculty Fund for Financial Assistance in support of research and write-up.

NOTES

1   The anthropological study of middle-class Americans' personal involvement in public life is a growing area of policy-relevant research. For discussion of middle-class Americans' changing conceptions of the public good, see Holland *et al.* (1999). For discussion of the ways some Americans perceive themselves as *shaping* public life, see Lutz (1998).
2   As does a body of sociological work, much of it produced in, and about, schools in Britain. For examples, see Ball, 1993; Mac an Ghaill, 1994; Gewirtz *et al.*, 1995; Whitty, 1997; Woods *et al.*, 1998.
3   Unless otherwise noted, all proper names used in connection with the two charter schools and overarching school district are pseudonyms.
4   Doctoral candidate in the Department of Educational Policy Studies at the University of Wisconsin-Madison, whose own expertise on parent-teacher interactions informs this analysis.
5   The survey provided data on some of the issues that had arisen in interviews: whether parents thought charter schools were open to all students equally or that charter schools reflected an innovation in school organization and instruction; whether they felt charter schools represented the boards' response to parents' expressed interests; and whether they were interested in sending their children to charter schools in the future.
6   Especially helpful in my thinking here has been David's work on educational policy in Britain, which illustrates how considerations of opportunity and educational equity are calculated in the context of public policy debates about market forces and changing family structures (David, 1993; see also David *et al.*, 1997).
7   I am not in a position to know how representative the trajectories of these schools are of charter schooling nationally. For some indication of the national profiles of charter schools, see SRI, 1997 and Office of Educational Research and Improvement, 1999. However, the fact that both schools followed a similar organizational path, and that, in their social, political and familial patterns the communities in which these schools are located resemble other middle-class suburban communities, leads me to consider that the schools' trajectories may be more common than unique.
8   Quotations I use in this section are intended to illustrate themes, not to demonstrate majority trends.

REFERENCES

Ball, S.J. (1993) 'Education markets, choice, and social class: the market as a class strategy in the UK and the USA', *British Journal of Sociology of Education*, 14: 3–20.
Bennett, W.J., Finn, C.E., Jr and Cribbs, J.T.E., Jr (1999) *The Educated Child: A Parent's Guide from Preschool Through Eighth Grade* (New York, Free Press).
Biklen, S.K. (1995) *School Work: Gender and The Cultural Construction of Teaching* (New York, Teachers College Press).
Brantlinger, E., Majd-Jabbari, M. and Guskin, S.L. (1996) 'Self-interest and liberal educational discourse: how ideology works for middle-class mothers', *Signs*, 33: 571–597.

Charter School Discussion Groups (July 2000) www.uscharterschools.org/gen_info/gi_ discussions.html. Developed by WestEd in collaboration with the California State University Charter Schools Development Center and the US Department of Education.

Charter School Web Site (July 2000) www.uscharterschools.org. Developed by WestEd in collaboration with the California State University Charter Schools Development Center and the US Department of Education.

Chubb, J.E. and Moe, T.M. (1990) *Politics, Markets, and America's Schools* (Washington, DC, Brookings Institute).

David, M., Davies, J., Edwards, R., Reay, D. and Standing, K. (1997) 'Choice within constraints: mothers and schooling', *Gender and Education*, 9(4): 397–410.

David, M.E. (1993) *Parents, Gender, and Education Reform* (Cambridge, MA, Polity Press).

David, M.E. (1997) Diversity, choice, and gender, *Oxford Review of Education*, 23: 77–87.

David, M.E., Edwards, R., Hughes, M. and Ribbens, J. (1993) *Mothers and Education: Inside Out? Exploring Family-Education Policy and Experience* (New York, St Martin's Press).

Education Mailing List Archive (July 2000) 'CSR-List Archives'. www.askeric.org/Virtual/ Listserv_Archives/Csr-List.html.

Gewirtz, S., Ball, S.J. and Bowe, R. (1995) *Markets, Choice, and Equity in Education* (Philadelphia, PA, Open University Press).

Hassel, B. (1996) *Autonomy and Constraint in Charter Schools: The Case of Charter School*, Taubman (Cambridge, MA, Center for State and Local Government).

Hirsch, E.D., Jr (1988) *Cultural Literacy: What Every American Needs to Know* (New York, Vintage Books).

Hirsch, E.D., Jr (1995) *Core Knowledge Sequence: Content Guideline for Grades K-6* (Charlottesville, VA, Core Knowledge Foundation).

Holland, D., Lutz, C. and Nonini, D. (1999) 'Public life, public good', *American Anthropological Association: Anthropology Newsletter*, 49: 1, 4.

Kliebard, H.M. (1986) *The Struggle for the American Curriculum, 1893–1958* (London, Routledge & Kegan Paul).

Lareau, A. (1989) *Home Advantage: Social Class and Parental Intervention in Elementary Education* (New York, Falmer Press).

Lareau, A. and Mcnamara Horvat, E. (1999) 'Moments of social inclusion and exclusion: race, class, and cultural capital in family–school relationships', *Sociology of Education*, 72: 37–53.

Lightfoot, S.L. (1975) 'Families and schools: creative conflict or negative dissonance?', *Journal of Research and Development in Education*, 9: 4–44.

Lightfoot, S.L. (1977) 'Family–school interactions: the cultural image of mothers and teachers', *Signs*, 3: 395–408.

Lowe, R. and Miner, B. (eds) (1996) *Selling Our Schools: Vouchers, Markets, and The Future of Public Education* (Milwaukee, WI, Rethinking Schools).

Luttrell, W. (1997) *Schoolsmart and Motherwise: Working-Class Women's Identity and Schooling* (New York, Routledge).

Lutz, C. (1998) 'Making a life and making history: from private preoccupations to public concerns in political autobiography', paper presented at the *Annual Meetings of the American Anthropological Association*, Philadelphia, PA, 6 December.

Mac an Ghaill, M. (1994) *The Making of Men: Masculinities, Sexualities and Schooling* (Philadelphia, PA, Open University Press).

Manicom, A. (1984) 'Feminist frameworks and teacher education', *Journal of Education*, 166: 77–88.

Mill, J.S. (1975) *On Liberty*, D. Spitz (ed.) (New York, W. W. Norton & Co.).

Millot, M. (1996) *Autonomy, Accountability, and the Values of Public Education: A Comparative Assessment of Charter School Statutes Leading to Model Legislation* (Seattle, University of Washington Center on Reinventing Public Education).

Nappi, C.R. (1999) 'Charter schools represent a compromise in education', *New York Times*, letter to the editor, 18 January.

National Education Association Charter School Web Site (July 2000) Charter Schools Overview; www.nea.org/issues.charter/by Carole Sund, 3 March 2000 (Washington, DC, National Education Association).

Office of Educational Research and Improvement (1999) *The State of Charter Schools: Third Year Report* (Prepared by RPP International for the US Department of Education).

Ortner, S. (1993) 'The ethnography of the Newark: the class of "58 of Weequahic High School"', *Michigan Quarterly Review*, 32: 411–429.

Ortner, S. (1996) 'Making gender: toward a feminist, minority, postcolonial, subaltern, etc., theory of practice', in S. Ortner (ed.) *Making Gender: The Politics and Erotics of Culture* (Boston, MA, Beacon Press).

Paris, D.C. (1998) 'Standards and charters: Horace Mann meets Tinker Bell', *Educational Policy*, 2: 380–396.

Peterson, B. (1995) 'What should children learn? A teacher looks at E. D. Hirsch', in D. Levine, R. Lowe, B. Peterson and R. Tenorio (eds), *Rethinking Schools: An Agenda for Change* (New York, New Press).

Reay, D. (1996) 'Contextualising choice: social power and parental involvement', *British Educational Research Journal*, 22: 581–596.

Risman, B. (1998) *Gender Vertigo: American Families in Transition* (New Haven, CT, Yale University Press).

Saporito, S. and Lareau, A. (1999) 'School selection as a process: the multiple dimensions of race in framing educational choice', *Social Problems*, 46: 418–439.

SRI International (1997) *Evaluation of Charter School Effectiveness*, prepared for Joel Schwartz, Project Director, Evaluation of Charter School Effectiveness, Office of the Legislative Analyst (Sacramento, CA).

Tarver, S. and Jung, J.S. (1995) 'A comparison of mathematics achievement and mathematics attitudes of first and second graders instructed with either a discovery-learning mathematics curriculum or a direct instruction curriculum', *Effective School Practices*, 14: 49–57.

The US Department of Education (1983) *A Nation at Risk: The Imperative for Educational Reform* (Washington DC) (www.ed.gov/pubs/NatAtRisk/).

University of California, Los Angeles (UCLA) (1998) *Beyond the Rhetoric of Charter School Reform: A Study of Ten California School Districts*, Amy Stuart Wells, Principal Investigator (UCLA Charter School Study, UCLA: School of Education).

Wells, A., Lopez, A., Scott, J. and Jellison Holme, J. (1999) 'Charter schools as postmodern paradox: rethinking social stratification in an age of deregulated choice', *Harvard Educational Review*, 69: 172–204.

Whitty, G. (1997) 'Creating quasi-markets in education: a review of recent research on parental and school autonomy in three countries', in M. Apple (ed.), *Review of Research in Education*, 22 (Washington, DC, American Educational Research Association).

Woods, P.A., Bagley, C. and Glatter, R. (1998) *School Choice and Competition: Markets in The Public Interest* (New York, Routledge).

Yancey, W. and Saporito, S. (1995) 'Racial and economic segregation and educational outcomes: one tale – two cities', *Journal of Applied Behavioral Science*, 3: 105–225.

TWELVE

DEATH TO CRITIQUE AND DISSENT? THE POLICIES AND PRACTICES OF NEW MANAGERIALISM AND OF 'EVIDENCE-BASED PRACTICE'

Bronwyn Davies

Source: 'Death to critique and dissent? The policies and practices of new managerialism and of "evidence-based practice"', *Gender and Education*, 15(1): 91–103, 2003.

New managerialism, which is also referred to as neo-liberalism in the UK and total quality management in the USA, is a system of government of individuals invented during the Thatcher and Reagan years. It may well involve the most significant shift in the discursive construction of professional practice and professional responsibility that any of us will ever experience. It is characterised by the removal of the locus of power from the knowledge of practising professionals to auditors, policy-makers and statisticians, none of whom need know anything about the profession in question (Rose, 1999). Neo-liberalism is characterised by Thatcher's 'death of society' and the rise of 'individuals' who are in need of management, surveillance and control.

Management, surveillance and control are not new of course. Foucault (1977, 1980) analysed the panopticon as a form of government in which 'relatively few officials control large numbers of [workers] by foregrounding both hierarchy and visibility' (Schmelzer, 1993, p. 127). The new panopticon, however, that can be observed in new managerialist worksites, works quite differently. Schmelzer observes that it is invisible and operates through *multiple eyes* at every level – eyes whose gaze is finely tuned to the inflow and outflow of funding and to the multitude of mechanisms that have been generated to manipulate those flows. This *multiplied gaze* works in such a way that it seems natural and makes us blind to its effects. It enables, according to Schmelzer (1993, pp. 127–128):

> meticulous control over the network of power relations that produce and sustain the truth claims of an institution by means of an economical surveillance.

It multiplies and mystifies the visible and centered gaze of the machine into the countless instances of observation of a mechanism. Its operation is distributed to every body in a system of power relations that constitute an institution. It works pervasively and invisibly. Every *I* in that system becomes an eye that sees what the institution asks it to see, in a request so naturalized that it is often no more than a subliminal echo. Panopticism blinds to other ways of seeing and controls gazes and gazers. It most blinds a body to its own objectification, to its having become a site and a sight line. Moreover, panopticism seems to work most efficiently when bodies are set in opposition [for limited funds, for example, or for limited rewards].

So how did the panopticon work before the advent of new managerialism? In the university context, in the early 1970s, the period that can be characterised as high modernity (Archer, 2002), we had (generally) benign leaders who observed the professional work of their staff at a distance. They assumed those staff were driven neither by them, nor by rules or by surveillance, but by a desire for mutual respect shared with colleagues and students, a desire to make a contribution to knowledge in their chosen area and a desire for personal freedom. As Foucault has shown, this earlier form of panopticism encouraged members of institutions to conduct their own conduct in internalised structures of surveillance. Subjects were expected to take up as their own the necessity of conducting their own conduct – and each individual's capacity and will to do so was fundamental to the forms of government that characterised high modernity. Under those systems of management each professional person (more or less) willingly took up multiple forms of self-surveillance and correction in order to become legitimate subjects, accountable to themselves and to others. Their value in their professional lives was tied, in part, to their capacity to do so, but also to their professional expertise and knowledge. The quality of institutional life was characterised by a high level of social integration and individual commitment to being socially responsible (Archer, 2002). Of course, some individuals did not live up to the ideals encapsulated in this description, and women and members of other groups could be excluded, exploited and otherwise badly treated. I am not arguing here that the system was perfect, but trying to characterise the principles or rationalities through which it made sense of itself.

Now, as Schmelzer (1993) shows, instead of these (more or less) benign leaders who could rely on our own internalised gaze to monitor our own work, we have the multiplied gaze of the workers on each other, their gaze shaped by the policies and practices emanating from management. The multiplied gaze infiltrates and shapes the way work is understood. Little or no attention is paid to the actual effects on the work that this new panopticism might have, other than to monitor the meeting of institutional objectives. As long as objectives have been specified and strategies for their management and surveillance put in place, the nature of the work itself is of little relevance to anyone. If the auditing tools say that the work has, on average, met the objectives, it is simply assumed that the work has been appropriately and satisfactorily tailored according to the requirements of the institution (and often of the relevant funding body).

Within new managerialist systems, the individual's sense of their own value is no longer primarily derived from responsible self-conduct and competent knowledge and practice of professional knowledge. *And yet, at the same time*, new managerialism relies on habitual, internalised surveillance, through which the conduct of conduct is carried out, to press subjects into making and remaking themselves as legitimate and appropriate(d) members of the latest shift within the particular new managerialist systems that they are caught up in. The requirement of 'continuous improvement', and documented individual commitment towards and striving for it, is one of the strategies for creating this continually changing individual.

Within the terms of the new system individuals will be presented with an (often overwhelming) range of pressing choices and administrative tasks for which they are responsible. But any questioning of the system itself is silenced or trivialised. The system itself is characterised as both natural and inevitable. Resistance to it by individuals (and that includes critiques such as this) is constituted as ignorance of what the 'real' (financial) 'bottom-line' issues are, as sheer cussedness, or as a sign reminding management of individual workers' replaceability. As Hammersley (2001, p. 9) points out, '[D]emands for "transparent" accountability' (along with many other of managerialism's terms), are made into imperatives that are in turn justified as a response to severely limited financial resources. The fact that much of the resource base that was previously available to support professional work has been redirected into surveillance and auditing somehow remains invisible, or at least is generally not spoken about, or subjected to critique.

The impetus of the individual's direction and judgement, under new managerialism, is moved by a thousand minute accretions to an external (and potentially punitive) source. The individual's sense of agency and freedom through which professional energy, dedication and power were formerly generated are overlaid and in tension with an almost subliminal anxiety and fear of surveillance. That fear may, of course, be defined as the individual's fear, and therefore pathological, even though the surveillance is generally linked to the pervasive new discourse that constitutes all workers as replaceable. The fear and anxiety are useful, from a systems point of view, as they work to fuel a constantly renewed (though largely futile) resolution to remake a self who is appropriate to, and regarded as good enough within, the new system. As Schmelzer points out, that remade self is extraordinarily vulnerable and peculiarly unable to hold on to the openness of mind so valued within the professional ethics of teachers and scholars.

New managerialism relies on a complex combination of the two forms of morality that Foucault observed, the first requiring compliance and the second driven by individuals' desires to shape their own directions. It works, on the one hand, to gain compliance, relying on that form of morality driven by 'obedience to a heteronomous code which we must accept, and to which we are bound by fear and guilt' (Rose, 1999, p. 97). On the other hand, it partially disguises the coercion by placing increased emphasis on 'personal responsibility' within the new system (an emphasis that flows in part from the abdication by government and governing bodies from their former role in taking care of aspects of the social fabric). This is not a sense of responsibility that works in relation to a sense of trust of the social fabric or of one's colleagues, since trust is fundamentally undermined through the multiplied gaze of every I/eye. It is a lonely kind of responsibility and one that is driven by the almost subliminal anxiety and fear of surveillance rather than a sense of personal value within the social fabric. Nevertheless, this increased emphasis on personal responsibility may be read as invoking the second kind of morality that Foucault observed, where 'morality is an exercise in ascetics, whereby through experimentation, exercise and permanent work on oneself one can make life into its own *telos*' (Rose, 1999, p. 97). That *telos*, or direction, however, without individuals necessarily realising it, is constituted through the multiplied gaze. *And* it is directed by the (now redundant) selves generated in the period of high modernity who still feel responsible for making things work, however difficult the system might be. An example of this dynamic, in the context of university life, was told in a collective biography workshop that I conducted recently on embodiment in the workplace.[1] Members of the collective wrote remembered stories from childhood and from their workplace as data through which to explore the ways in which the embodied self is constituted in the workplace. The story went as follows:

> The Vice Chancellor sat around the table with us. He was here to listen and to answer questions from members of the School. *You can even shout at me*, he said, *I can take it.* She told him, in a calm but strong voice, that they were feeling demoralised because the practices of forcing them (but not other schools) to enrol poor students who couldn't possibly pass, *and* of withdrawing funds to reallocate to schools who achieved high retention rates, meant that they were necessarily losers. This, combined with their high teaching loads (again compared to other schools), which made working with individual students impossible, was demoralising for them as a group.
>
> *This is just what I would expect from you, Doctor X*, he replied. *You always see the negative side. I see things positively. The reallocated funds are a reward, not a punishment. And the fact is, I don't think the 2% makes enough difference to the distribution of funding. I am considering changing it to 4% next year.*
>
> Afterwards some of her colleagues told her she should have kept quiet – not got him offside: *He was really listening to us.*
>
> *You are joking*, she said, *he will remember nothing of what we said.*
>
> *Oh yes, just wait and see. I think it will make a difference. We have been heard this time.*
>
> The moral of the story: be one of the group, don't rock the boat; trust the managers to have your best interest at heart; be flexible – bend to the way things are – bend to the new constraints and you will be rewarded. By what? A quiet life, a harmonious group, an approving manager – maybe even a balanced budget – while each one of us goes home exhausted, agonising about how to make ourselves strong enough or competent enough or clever enough or healthy enough to do this job well.

Dennis (1995), writing in the North American context, puts his finger on a central problem of new managerialism. He says that through an emphasis on measurable outcomes, on goals defined by management at the highest levels and on the systems through which such goals are achieved, new managerialism is always dangerously at risk of cutting its populace adrift from moral and political debate:

> Make no mistake about it. When Deming[2] says that quality-reality is determined by top management and cannot be delegated, he privileges the executive production of meaning as a morally unimpeachable event. In this aspect, TQM is a philosophy of due obedience whose effects, if implemented, would be devastating to the practice of critical thought and the expression of responsible dissent.

Given all of these negatives (the reduction in critical thought and responsible dissent, the pervasive subliminal fear and anxiety, the sense of personal pressure and responsibility combined with a devalued sense of self, the shift of value away from personal and professional considerations towards the single consideration of the economy), it is relevant to ask why so many of us have willingly worked towards the instalment and maintenance of new managerialist systems. Individuals involved in implementing (or simply caught within) new managerialist systems are often seduced by its rhetoric of efficiency and accountability, and by its morally ascendant promise of a desired comeuppance for those perceived to be faulty or inadequate in conducting their own conduct. The perceived flaws in individuals, particularly during the 1970s, where professional responsibility was paramount, and where some individuals did not live up to others' expectations of them, have thus been used, in part, to create the downfall of the old system (Biggs, 2002). There was a strong and widespread belief generated at that time that education systems needed changing. Feminists, for example, were drawn to the possibility of breaking up old networks of power that held them on the margins and in low-status positions. The idea of a new system that could bring about change, breaking up old hegemonies and mandating equity, was seductive and appealing.

Those working to implement new managerialism set up systems in which *everyone* (subtext: specifically, those who did not satisfactorily conduct their own conduct under previous systems) will have to work harder to be 'good enough', to meet the exacting standards required of them. What they do not anticipate is that the constant threat of external punitive surveillance potentially erodes the professional judgement of everyone (including those who have, until now, successfully conducted their own conduct). The personal dynamic that is set up is potentially exhausting and debilitating, since it is likely that no one can experience themselves as 'good enough' when the basis of assessment is externalised, constantly escalating, subject to change and often at odds with the professional knowledge on which previous good practice was based. Both those who engage in establishing new managerialist systems, and those working within them, can exhaust themselves in their struggle to create a satisfying professional life within parameters that mean that the satisfaction of work well done may always be negated by those engaging in overt or covert surveillance over them.[3]

The persuasive power of new managerialist systems would appear to be staggering. Given the general difficulty, often written about, of engineering social change, the implementation of new managerialist systems is, in a sense, a freakish phenomenon that can be compared to 're-education' in communist China. Indeed, the similarities and differences in strategy would make for a fascinating historical study.

One of its cleverest and perhaps the most devious strategies of new managerialism has been the inclusion of equity discourses in the objectives that institutions were impelled to include. Many feminists were drawn into managerialism – and so into the new *episteme* – in which their professional life was reconstituted in the terms of auditors and economists because of their desire for change. It seemed to offer an alternative to the old hierarchies of power and control. What new managerialism has achieved, however, is a far cry from the radical re-visioning of universities that they had imagined in which the locus of power would shift and disrupt the apparent naturalness and inevitability of male hierarchies, and in which women's ways of being would become respected and valued, their histories told and their literature read and valued. As Johanna Wyn wrote to me, in an elaborate and insightful analysis when I was undertaking research for a paper on women in academe (Davies, 2000):

> The changes over the last few years are both detrimental and positive to different women, but almost completely detrimental to the feminist goals of

academic women. I am currently a visitor in a department which has a female head of department. The Dean is a woman and the President is also a woman. Now is a time when individual women may well reach the highest ranks of the profession.

But this does not mean that the university has become a more egalitarian, intellectual, supportive workplace. On the contrary. Putting it simply (and simplistically), the changes to universities, especially in Australia, but also to some extent in Canada, have been largely in response to the need to find alternative sources of funding, as public funding has gradually been withdrawn. In response to this, many universities have instituted the 'new management' and their processes. This has resulted in attempts to get more for less from staff – workloads have gone up, pressures to generate funds have been dramatically increased, and thinking has changed – managers see their role as curtailing academic staff flexibility and freedom in order to get the kind of performance managers want.

Some women fit into this context very well. But, for many women (and some men too), the costs are too great. For one thing, staff are put into a competitive relationship for ever-reduced resources. For another, market forces are being brought to bear, so some kinds of teaching – and knowledge – are given priority. E.g., Educational Administration (sometimes reinvented as 'leadership') is favoured in the faculty in which I usually work. Feminist courses have been deleted from the books as of last year. There is a rush to use information technology, which can be very flexible, but fits best with modulated, unitised, prepackaged kinds of teaching. It is possible, but not usual, to have critical, challenging and student-centred discussion through the technology.

The need to keep up rates of publication (in specific journals only), research project funding (especially prestigious ARC [Australian Research Council] funding, but also consultancies), and teaching to larger groups of students have pushed up the hours of academic work. The eagerness to take on consultancies means that academics are not using their freedom to determine research agendas – they are driven by the funding bodies.

Finally, there is a rush to get funding from rich students and from consultancies in third world countries. This may mean working overseas for long periods of time, or making many, many trips.

These changes are favouring a much tougher, more 'macho' kind of academic, and encourage a climate where due process, equity, and respect for academic freedom are overwhelmed by the need to respond quickly to opportunities, reinvent, repackage and position oneself and one's institution in the marketplace.

Ironically, the reduction of freedom, the loss of a moral base in favour of an economic base, the celebration of the new macho individual, are presented within new managerialism as fundamental to the new morally ascendant position – the only position any reasonable person could have. That morally ascendant view has, as its fundamental tenet, survival of the imposed systems. Dissent, just like dissent amongst soldiers in times of war, cannot be tolerated. Dennis (1995) observes that the war metaphor is commonly used to spell out how new managerialism works. He quotes James H. Saylor's (1992, p. xvi) TQM Field Manual where he offers a rationale for the constant use of the war metaphor:

The war theme is used to convey the seriousness of the economic situation in the US today. We are engaged in total economic war. Our very survival as an economic force is at stake. Already there have been many casualties. Many organizations and people have been wounded, and some have been destroyed...[TQM] is the process that can turn defeat into victory...in the economic war.

'Gender equity' is thus, arguably, not an outcome of the new system, as promised, but a strategy to win and maintain consent from potential dissidents within the new system. It is in part because of its apparently virtuous and morally ascendant language that otherwise critical professionals may be blind to the necessity for critique of the new managerialist discursive framework through which they are about to be, or are being, constituted. They may also be drawn into the sticky net of managerialism's agenda if they find themselves in policy-making positions where they can place their political demands, such as equal educational opportunity or gender reform, on the agenda. Clare Burton (1993), for example, argued that corporate plans have been very useful places for inserting equal employment opportunity policies and practices and achieving them as mandatory for educational institutions. She strongly advocated using the language of corporate managerialism (another name for new managerialism) to feminist advantage, though she also warned, in the words of Ferguson, that 'feminism is not compatible with bureaucracy, and like all forms of opposition, it is endangered by too-close contact with bureaucratic linguistic and institutional forms' (Ferguson, 1984, p. 180). These words have turned out to be truer than she might have guessed. In general the situation of women in universities has worsened, though as Wyn points out, some individual women have prospered.

So how do managerialist agendas play out in schools, and in particular how might the new push towards evidence-based practice be understood in this context?

A critique of the concept of 'evidence-based practice'

Hammersley (2001) provides a critique of evidence-based practice, also analysing it as a new managerialist strategy. He points out that managerialism is based on an assumption that professional practice 'should take the form of specifying goals explicitly, selecting strategies for achieving them on the basis of objective evidence about their effectiveness, and then measuring outcomes in order to assess their degree of success (thereby providing the knowledge required for improving future performance)' (2001, p. 5). These are not, when it comes to teaching, individually set goals, but the goals of the institution, or even of the state. While individual teachers may be responsible for providing the 'objective evidence', and may be held individually accountable if their evidence does not provide the institution with what it needs to make an acceptable account of itself to government, the definition of what is 'effective', of what counts as 'success', will not be something they have any control over. When Davies et al. (2000, p. 2) observe that 'in contrast to the preceding culture of largely judgement-based professional practice, there has risen the important notion of evidence-based practice as a means of ensuring that what is being done is worthwhile and that it is being done in the best possible way', we can be sure that it is not the teachers who are being asked to judge what is worthwhile, nor what might be regarded as the 'best possible way'. Of course, 'consultations' with representative teachers may have taken place, but those consultations will have been undertaken in such a way that the representatives will have acquired the new discourse and so become party to its dissemination (the only alternative being to be marginalised or replaced). Neither the teachers, nor their representatives, will have had freedom to dispute or resile from the institution's or state's criteria of effectivity and success, since both their own livelihood and the funding of their institution may well be tied in whole or in part to their satisfactory fulfilment. As Grundy points out:

> Leaders will be expected to exercise control so that the objectives of the organisations, clearly defined and articulated, will be achieved. There will be a division of labour between the leader who plans (or who receives and interprets plans imposed from elsewhere) and the practitioners who implement the plans. The language of administrative planning will be 'end-directed', with criteria for the achievement of the objectives being articulated along with the plans. It will be the leader who is responsible for the training of the practitioners, and such training will be oriented towards the development of skills. It will also be the responsibility of the leader to motivate and enthuse practitioners to embrace the specified objectives and work for their achievement.
>
> (1993, p. 168)

To this end, the language of managerialism cleverly cannibalises the liberal humanist terms in vogue during the period of high modernity that seem, on the face of it, indisputably virtuous and desirable. Take 'literacy', for example. Who can dispute the desirability of every child achieving a minimum standard of literacy and thus achieving not only the potential to be active citizens of democracy but also the potential to survive in the new information technology driven global world? The means of achieving this may actually be at the expense of the teaching strategies through which critical literacy or any other critical/analytic skills are taught. They may also draw massive resources away from teaching itself and into the bureaucracy that stages and evaluates the testing and other strategies through which the 'new' objectives are to be achieved. Individual resistance to the strategies through which these new/old ideals are implemented are likely to be read as inflexible, or conservative, or worse, as motivated by individual incompetence or laziness. Resistance may well position you as one of those whom the systems are supposedly designed to catch out.[4]

The proponents of evidence-based practice propose an unproblematic relationship between research and practice, and also amongst policy, research and practice. At first glance the idea of evidence-based practice appears to be so obviously desirable (like universal literacy, or continuous improvement) that it might be regarded as a truism. Who could argue against the idea that professional practice should be based on evidence? Its opposite, teaching without evidence, or against the evidence, sounds absurd. Read in this way, a move towards evidence-based practice seems impossible to disagree with. But another reading can be produced if we understand evidence-based practice as a product of new managerialism and as no more than a means of implementing managerialist agendas.

To get beyond the obviousness of the first reading it is useful to focus on the 'based' of evidence-based and ask, *which evidence should be the base, and who selects it?* In what ways, we might then ask, are the choices and decisions teachers make in the classroom and playground to be founded in (based on) the evidence, not only that someone else provides, but that someone else (another someone, located in the bureaucracy) selects. Are those who produce the evidence and those who select it members of the profession of teaching? How have they chosen what counts as evidence, and how have they selected the particular evidence that is to be acted on? And, finally, how are the links to the everyday practice of teaching to be accomplished? How is the teacher to alter her/his practices of teaching in light of this 'evidence'? Such questions immediately alert us to a possible hidden agenda – to a plan to change what it is that teachers produce through the adoption of a language and a system that guarantees its sense of inevitability. The question we might then go on to ask is: are the practices of teaching so susceptible to this kind of subterfuge?

The right to be taught is now being framed through new managerialist strategies, in terms of measured outcomes, and *yet at the same time* relies on the very professional base of knowing one's subject that new managerialism potentially undermines. Instructions from bureaucrats to produce specific outcomes (instructions backed by 'evidence') *can only* (logically speaking) be interpreted/practised in terms of the teachers' already (per)formed, and (per)forming, profession-in-practice. But that profession-in-practice is what made sense in high modernity when there was a personal and professional commitment to the pursuit of knowledge inside mutually respectful relations amongst colleagues and between teachers and students. So the profession-in-practice – or professional knowledge – is *both* relied on *and* undermined by new managerialist strategies such as the implementation of evidence-based practice.

So how are we to make sense of what it is that evidence-based practice sets out to achieve and its methods for doing so? There are two major considerations that I will elaborate here that are relevant to this questioning of an ideal, or real, connection between evidence and practice. These relate to the interpretation and use of experimental evidence by the advocates of evidence-based practice and to the necessity for an underlying philosophy of the profession of teaching.

Interpreting statistical/experimental evidence

As Hammersley (2001) points out, the proponents of evidence-based practice, for example, Blunkett (2000), argue that statistically based, experimental research is to be preferred by evidence-based practitioners since it is less biased by the interests of the researcher. This trust in the objectivity of experimental research is embarrassingly naïve. Experimental researchers, even those gazing down a microscope, are as capable of finding what they expect to find, or want to find, as anyone else. Martin (1991) showed, for example, how generations of scientists gazing down microscopes at the moment of meeting between sperm and egg in human conception failed to see the active part that the egg played. The metaphor informing and shaping their gaze, evident in the texts of their reports, revealed the sperm as an active, competitive knight in shining armour, and the egg as passive, receptive damsel. This elaborate metaphor not only shaped the descriptive language that scientists used to report their observations, but it shaped what it is they understood themselves to be seeing. Microscopes and the scientific method were no protection against discourse's ability to articulate and make real the thing it describes. As Butler says, 'Discourse is not merely spoken words, but a notion of signification which concerns not merely how it is that certain signifiers come to mean what they mean, but how certain discursive forms articulate objects and subjects in their intelligibility' (Butler, 1995, p. 138).

It is well known amongst statisticians that statistics can be used to 'prove' almost anything that the researcher wishes to prove. The sleights of hand that are used to arrive at one or another 'research finding' may or may not be in the conscious purview of the researcher. And they may or may not be visible in the reporting. In the academic world, dispute over interpretations is a legitimate aspect of intellectual work. Experiments do not remove the subjectivity of researchers; they simply work to conceal it. 'Findings' are not guaranteed – they are more like working propositions that make sense within particular frameworks of assumptions and of practice.

Yet it is in order to give an appearance of an *unchallengeable* link between evidence and practice that the advocates of evidence-based practice rely on experimental research. They engage the authority of 'hard science' to give weight to their propositions. Although the words 'evidence-based practice' might be read as if there is an immediate connection between the individual practitioner and the selection, reading and interpretation of evidence, teachers are not allocated time (let alone given appropriate library resources) to read the research being produced relevant to their practice (Davies *et al.*, 1996). Nor are they trained to interpret research evidence and to work out the relations between research and practice. There is thus an invisible sleight of hand embedded in the term itself which makes invisible the managers and policy-makers who will select what is relevant, and who will dictate how it is to be audited and deemed to have been put into practice.

An apparent (invisible) assumption is made by the advocates of evidence-based practice that bureaucrats and policy-makers do have the skills (and resources) to read all the possible available research, select what is relevant to particular schools and classrooms and teachers and to the particular problems they encounter, and then to assess whether or not the teachers have understood the implications of the selected research and acted accordingly. Since this is such an absurd assumption, we can guess immediately that this is not how evidence-based practice will work. Through an understanding of how new managerialism works, we can guess that the objectives will come first and that the 'experimental research evidence' will be generated to justify them. As long as the objectives have been met (according to the auditors), then questions about the appropriateness of the evidence for good teaching or the capacity of the teachers to act on it can be left unasked and unanswered. Critique, in this model, becomes irrelevant.

Since the *desire* to meet the objectives has already been generated through the systems of surveillance and management and the subliminal fear and anxiety they can generate, then there is no need to worry about how teachers managed to make the links between evidence and practice. Withdrawal of funds from schools and programmes is one of a battery of manipulative strategies to ensure that the appropriate fear and guilt, through the operation of the multiplied gaze, is generated to ensure the meeting of the objectives.

Am I being too cynical, you might ask? Is it possible that the processes of evidence-based practice might lead to better teaching?

My own work with teachers would suggest that it takes years of concerted effort for teachers to learn to read research and to generate new teaching practices based on that research. I have worked collaboratively with individual teachers, often over several years, guiding them in becoming reflexive researchers who can read *both* the assumptions and theoretical frameworks that inform research findings, *and* the details of their own practices. Only after such intensive work, driven by the teachers' own desire to develop their own capacity for critique and analysis, would I be willing to claim with any confidence that a productive link between research and practice can be established (see, for example, Davies *et al.*, 1996; Davies and Hunt, 2000; Laws and Davies, 2000). If, in contrast, teachers are presented with 'research findings' and policy objectives as a guide to practice, along with a range of surveillance strategies to monitor their performance, there can be no assumption of a straightforward link between research and practice. Nor can we assume there should be – that the experimental research that is deemed to be relevant would, if acted on, lead to better teaching.

Evidence-based practice's preference for experimental evidence reveals *either* a naivety about research, *or* a hidden, managerialist agenda that has little to do with research findings and their implications for practice.

The underlying philosophy of the profession of teaching

The idea that professionals can be shaped by 'evidence' legitimated by managers and funding bodies and by coercive policies that mandate action on the basis of that evidence belies the complexity of professional work. As Derrida points out in *Who's Afraid of Philosophy?* (2002, p. 69), the relations of power and the lines of force acting on teaching are heterogeneous and marked by agonistic struggles:

> The structures of a pedagogical institution, its forms, norms, visible or invisible constraints, settings, the entire apparatus...that, appearing to surround it, determines that institution right to the center of its content, and no doubt from the center, one carefully conceals the forces and interests that, without the slightest neutrality, dominate and master – impose themselves upon – the process of teaching from within a heterogeneous and divided agonistic field racked (sic) with constant struggle.

The teachers who work in pedagogical institutions are multiply inscribed, subjected to discursive lines of force pushing and pulling in contradictory directions. Multiple discourses operate in a palimpsest of overlapping meanings that do not totally occlude each other. Teachers work in and through the dynamic tensions of these multiple discourses and relations of power to produce that complex set of processes that we call teaching.

Any new discourse (such as that encoded as 'evidence-based' and related to policy imperatives) necessarily jostles alongside these other discourses that make up the discursive field of teaching (see Honan (2001) for teachers' reflections on how they accommodate and resist new curricula). Many teachers tenaciously hold on to the philosophies that inform their teaching: their teaching is, in effect, the construction of that philosophy. We might even go so far as to say that their teaching cannot exist without that (implicit or explicit) philosophy. When teaching has been deserted by such philosophical bases, we find, according to Derrida, the perfect seeding ground for new managerialism: the ultimate manifestations of *phallogocentric hegemony.*[5] He describes such places as 'places that have apparently been deserted by philosophy and that are therefore occupied, preoccupied, by empiricism, technocracy, moralism or religion (indeed, all of them at the same time)' (2002, pp. 73–74). This occupation and abandonment comes from a belief, he says, that 'one can no longer defend the old machine (a machine one has even contributed to dismantling)' (2002, p. 74). Derrida's analysis, while based on university teaching, is compatible with the observations that I have made about the implementation of new managerialism in schools (Davies *et al.*, 1996). But the abandonment of the philosophies that are accomplished by particular teaching practices and that are developed out of philosophical commitments are, even when one has been critical of them, not so easy to abandon, even if teachers wish to do so. New managerialism's requirements must be managed, and held in tension with what teachers know and accomplish in their everyday practices. Teachers literally cannot become automatons who parrot the new practices dictated by the phallogocentric practices driven by new managerialism's passion for empiricism, technocracy and moralism, since the teaching enterprise requires much more of them than that. The specific requirements of 'evidence-based practice' can only exist as one of the heterogeneous forces acting on teachers. Their philosophies of teaching, even if apparently erased, will nonetheless be visible in the palimpsest of meaning making and practices that make up classroom practice.

The importance of critique and debate is fundamental to the kind of teaching that might be called professional. This is particularly true as successive world leaderships move to the right and occupy a space devoid of any considerations other than the plays of power and economy. And while it is true that teaching exists as a palimpsest of competing and agonistic discourses, and that one discourse is unlikely to completely dominate teachers' thinking, the potential conflict between ethical reflections and managerialism's agenda is a dangerous one, if only because of managerialism's power to eclipse other discourses (Dennis, 1995) and to both normalise its practices and to silence dissent.

A first and necessary step in counteracting the force of any discourse is to recognise its constitutive power, its capacity to become hegemonic, 'to "saturate" our very consciousness, so that the...world we see and interact with, and the commonsense interpretations we put on it, become the world *tout court*, the only world' (Apple, 1979, p. 5). By denaturalising new managerialism, by making its assumptions and mechanisms visible, we open up the possibility of new cultural narratives or collective stories with transformative potential (Richardson, 1990, pp. 25–26). Thatcher announced the death of society and set about generating the elaborate mechanisms through which to control the potentially wild individuals who exist without the social fabric that once accorded them (at least some of them) identity and value. If and when we dismantle new managerialism and recuperate the resources that are currently ploughed into surveillance and control, we will have to find creative ways to recuperate the social and our places in it. This cannot mean a return to some idyllic dreamed of past, since the faults of the past were what we have been caught up in moving beyond. We must turn our collective minds to active contemplation of just what a post-new managerialist society might look like. Just what are the collective stories we might tell ourselves about this period of our history and about why and how it is another world that we want to live in?

Acknowledgements

I would like to thank Eva Bendix Petersen, Sue Gannon and Eileen Honan for their comments on an earlier draft, and Johanna Wyn for the discussions I have had with her and for permission to use her analysis of the situation of women in universities.

NOTES

1   The participants in this workshop on Embodiment in the Workplace were Jenny Browne, Sue Gannon, Eileen Honan and Margaret Somerville.
2   Author of *The New Economics for Industry, Government and Education.*

3   It is possible, however, that some workers see the new systems in terms of a game with explicit rules that they can play and win at. They may thus be unconcerned about the lack of value accorded to their professional knowledge. It is *possible* that some men will be more likely than most women to engage with it in this way. There is also a possibility that some people will enjoy being watched, as emerged in an evaluation recently of people in home detention monitored by surveillance cameras, or as has emerged in the *Big Brother* real life television.

4   Even the collective resistance still being staged by some unions has been corporatised and managed through such strategies as enterprise bargaining. Through enterprise bargaining, unions are persuaded to agree to managerialist strategies (after a little negotiation on the detail) in return for having salary rises that often do not even match the rate of inflation.

5   'Hegemony acts to "saturate" our very consciousness, so that the educational, economic and social world we see and interact with, and the commonsense interpretations we put on it, become the world *tout court*, the only world. Hence hegemony refers not to congeries of meaning that reside at the abstract level somewhere at the "roof of our brain". Rather it refers to an organised assemblage of meanings and practices, the central, effective and dominant systems of meanings, values and actions which are lived' (Apple, 1979, p. 5).

REFERENCES

Apple, M. (1979) *Ideology and Curriculum* (London, Routledge & Kegan Paul).

Archer, M. (2002) 'The disappearance of institutional subsidiarity', paper presented to the *15th World Congress of Sociology*, 'The social world in the twenty-first century: ambivalent legacies and rising challenges', Brisbane.

Biggs, J. (2002) 'The University of Newcastle: prelude to Dawkins', in J. Biggs and R. Davis (eds), *The Subversion of Australian Universities* (Wollongong, Fund for Intellectual Dissent).

Blunkett, D. (2000) 'Influence or irrelevance: can social science improve government?', *Research Intelligence*, 71: 12–21.

Burton, C. (1993) 'Equal employment opportunity and corporate planning', in J. Blackmore and J. Kenway (eds), *Gender Matters in Educational Administration and Policy* (London, Falmer Press).

Butler, J. (1995) 'For a careful reading', in S. Benhabib, J. Butler, D. Cornell and N. Fraser (eds), *Feminist Contentions. A Philosophical Exchange*, pp. 127–143 (New York, Routledge).

Davies, B. (1996) *Power/Knowledge/Desire: Changing School Organisation and Management Practices* (Canberra, Department of Employment, Education and Youth Affairs).

Davies, B. (2000) 'Troubling gender, troubling academe', *University Structures, Knowledge Production and Gender Construction Conference* (University of Copenhagen, March).

Davies, B. and Hunt, R. (2000) 'Classroom competencies and marginal positionings', in B. Davies (ed.), *A Body of Writing 1989–1999* (Walnut Creek, AltaMira Press).

Davies, H.T.O., Nutley, S.M. and Smith, P.C. (eds) (2000) *What Works? Evidence-based Policy and Practice in the Public Services* (Bristol, Policy Press).

Dennis, D. (1995) 'Brave new reductionism: TQM as ethnocentrism', *Education Policy Analysis Archives*, 3(9).

Derrida, J. (2002) 'Who's afraid of philosophy?' (trans. Jan Plug) (Stanford, CA, Stanford University Press).

Ferguson, K. (1984) *The Feminist Case against Bureaucracy* (Philadelphia, PA, Temple University Press).

Foucault, M. (1977) *Discipline and Punish: The Birth of the Prison* (New York, Vintage).

Foucault, M. (1980) *Power/Knowledge: Selected Interviews and Other Writings: 1972–1977* (New York, Pantheon).

Grundy, S. (1993) 'Educational leadership as emancipatory praxis', in J. Blackmore and J. Kenway (eds), *Gender Matters in Educational Administration and Policy* (London, Falmer Press).

Hammersley, M. (2001) 'Some questions about evidence-based practice in education', *Annual Conference of the British Educational Research Association*, Leeds, September.

Honan, E. (2001) '(Im)Plausibilities: a rhizo-textual analysis of the Queensland English Syllabus', PhD thesis, James Cook University, Townsville.

Laws, C. and Davies, B. (2000) 'Poststructuralist theory in practice: working with "behaviourally disturbed" children', in B. Davies (ed.), *A Body of Writing 1989–1999* (Walnut Creek, AltaMira Press).

Martin, E. (1991) 'The egg and the sperm', *Signs*, 16: 485–501.

Richardson, L. (1990) *Writing Strategies. Reaching Diverse Audiences* (Newbury Park, CA, Sage).

Rose, N. (1999) *Powers of Freedom* (Cambridge, Cambridge University Press).

Schmelzer, M. (1993) 'Panopticism and postmodern pedagogy', in J. Caputo and M. Yount (eds), *Foucault and the Critique of Institutions* (University Park, PA, Pennsylvania State University Press).

PART IV

HISTORY

VIEWPOINT: A LOST DIMENSION? THE POLITICAL EDUCATION OF WOMEN IN THE SUFFRAGETTE MOVEMENT IN EDWARDIAN BRITAIN

June Purvis

Source: 'Viewpoint: a lost dimension? The political education of women in the suffragette movement in Edwardian Britain', *Gender and Education*, 6(3): 319–327, 1994.

There is always the danger that any present-day attempt to define education in the past will encompass in its scope only those educational forms, structures and activities that have relevance for the late twentieth century. Indeed, we can see this scenario being acted out in the pages of this journal where 'education' is predominantly interpreted as what goes on in formal educational institutions that are relevant to the 1990s, namely schools, further education, universities and adult education. Yet such a focus has little relevance for the educational experiences of the majority of women in the past. In Victorian England and Wales in 1851, for example, only approximately 5710 female students were recorded in the major adult education movement of the nineteenth century, namely the mechanics' institute movement.[1] Similarly, the number of women who struggled to enter that bastion of male privilege in Victorian society, the university was small.[2] In 1897, for example, one listing claimed that the number of women in attendance at the women's colleges was 784.[3]

For a much larger number of women in the past, their 'education' was acquired through informal self-education or through settings other than those that were termed 'educational'. Some of the key political movements in nineteenth-century Britain, for example, offered women access to lectures or to formal classes, and even indeed the chance to learn how to speak in public. Owenism, for example, in the 1830s and 1840s, as Barbara Taylor has brilliantly revealed, had an extensive education programme in which women could participate. Thus branches were exhorted in 1840 not only to distribute Owenite tracts but to 'let the lecture rooms be made as attractive as possible...Commence, where possible, private classes, lyceums, reading rooms and other means of instruction and innocent recreation'.[4] Similarly, the organised women's movement in the nineteenth century, which gathered momentum from the 1860s, although not developing such extensive lecturing and class provision as that organised by the Owenites, was nevertheless an important educational influence in the lives of many women. Yet, this aspect of the feminist movement is rarely given coverage in the pages of an 'education' journal, such as *Gender and Education*. My aim in this article is to illustrate how this dimension has been lost by focusing on the political education of women in the suffragette movement in Edwardian Britain, and specifically within the most militant of the societies that campaigned for the vote for women on equal terms with men, namely the Women's Social and Political Union (WSPU).

The WSPU was founded on 10 October 1903 by Mrs Emmeline Pankhurst and her eldest daughter, Christabel. At that time, both women were members of the Independent Labour Party (ILP) and had campaigned for many years for the ILP to adopt a women's suffrage policy. Success came at the ILP annual conference in Liverpool in April 1902 when Mrs Pankhurst's resolution 'That in order to improve the economic and social condition of women it is necessary to take immediate steps to secure the granting of the suffrage to women on the same terms on which it is or may be granted to men' was carried unanimously.[5] However, aware of the many disappointments she had encountered after 'a long experience in men's movements'.[6] Mrs Pankhurst decided that the resolution needed an extra push from the women in order to make it effective policy. Thus she decided to form a women-only political grouping that would demand the 'immediate enfranchisement' of her sex.[7] Accordingly, on 10 October in the following year, she called to her house at 62 Nelson Street, Manchester, a number of working women, mainly wives of ILP members, to form the new organisation. As she later recalled in her autobiography, published in 1914:

> We voted to call our new society the Women's Social and Political Union, partly to emphasise its democracy, and partly to define its object as political rather than propagandist. We resolved to limit our membership exclusively to women, to keep ourselves absolutely free from any party affiliation, and to be satisfied with nothing but action on our question. Deeds, not words, was to be our permanent motto.[8]

From this time until August 1914 when, on the eve of a world war, Mrs Pankhurst called an end to all 'deeds', the WSPU offered a political education to many thousands of women who joined its ranks. It is impossible to state the size of its membership since accurate records were not held by the central office at Clement's Inn in London, nor in the many local groupings. Nevertheless, statistics about the number of local branches, about the circulation of *Votes for Women*, the first official newspaper of the WSPU, and about the size of various WSPU demonstrations and rallies reveal the extent of its popularity. During the period March 1908–28 February 1909, for example, the number of paid organisers had increased from 14 to 30, and the number of paid London office staff from 18 to 45, including the staff of *Votes for Women*, and of the WSPU's own publishing house, the Women's Press.[9] The circulation of *Votes for Women* was estimated to be 50,000 and it was undoubtedly read by many more.[10] By 1909 too, 19 rooms were occupied by the WSPU at Clement's Inn, in comparison with 15 a year earlier; and 11 regional offices had been established in 8 provincial districts.[11] Large gatherings were often attracted to WSPU demonstrations and rallies. In 1908, for example, 20,000 attended a WSPU rally on Clapham Common on 15 July, 150,000 came to Heaton Park, Manchester on 19 July, and 100,000 came to hear WSPU women speak from 10 different platforms on Woodhouse Moor, Leeds, on 26 July.[12] When the WSPU member Emily Davison died as a result of terrible injuries inflicted on her when she ran on to the race-course at Epsom, the first stage of her funeral, in London, on 14 June 1913 attracted a crowd of over 50,000.[13] Her coffin was draped in the purple, white and green colours of the WSPU and was escorted by more than 2000 suffragists, representing all sections of the suffrage movement.[14] The suffragists, each with a black band on her left arm, were divided into subsections, each of which was subdivided into three. The first of these subsections wore white, the second black and the third purple. As *The Sunday Times* commented on 15 June 1913, 'it was the most remarkable funeral procession London has ever seen'; furthermore, it was predominantly an all-women procession with scarcely a man in sight, apart from a few bandsmen, a few clergymen and half a dozen silk-hatted gentlemen. Even those who lived in London's 'pleasure district' came to see the cortège as it passed through: 'There were painted women, sisters of the world's sorrow and vice, who stood on tiptoe to see the coffin of one of their sex who died for them…Their tribute was wonderful.'[15]

It is important to stress that the political role which Emily Davison and other WSPU activists epitomised, ran very much against the grain of women's 'expected' place in late Victorian and early Edwardian society. Thus the ideal end state for all women, irrespective of their social class background, was marriage and full-time wifehood and motherhood. In particular, the bourgeois family form of a wage-earning husband and a financially dependent wife and children was considered the essential building block of 'civilised' society. Such an ideal, of course, was rarely reality in working-class households. Working-class mothers with dependent children usually undertook poorly paid work at home, such as sewing, in order to contribute to the family income. Single working-class women usually had little choice but to earn a livelihood, perhaps as a domestic servant or in the more lucrative world of factory work. 'Necessitous' middle-class women too, as well as those 'new women' seeking a career in the male dominated professions, might earn a living in the public world outside the home. But the sphere of politics was considered a male space, an arena that women did not enter. What the WSPU taught their members was how to invade this space, how to 'trespass' in male territory. Although an older women's suffrage society, namely the National Union of Women's Suffrage Societies (NUWSS), was already in existence when the WSPU was founded, its leader, Millicent Garret Fawcett, believed in 'constitutional' rather than the so-called 'militant' methods.[16] Consequently, the NUWSS adopted law-abiding means of campaigning, such as presenting petitions to parliament.

The range of so-called 'militant' actions in which the WSPU engaged may be divided into two main phases. The first phase is what Christabel Pankhurst termed 'mild' or 'symbolic'[17] militancy, and involved various forms of peaceful action such as heckling politicians, carrying petitions to the House of Commons, speaking at rallies and participation in demonstrations. Any of these activities could result in rough handling by the public and police, and even imprisonment. The first WSPU act that resulted in imprisonment took place on 15 October 1905 when Christabel and Annie Kenney, two working-class women from Oldham, heckled speakers at a Liberal party meeting at the Free Trade Hall, Manchester. They dared to unfurl a banner on which had been painted with black furniture stain 'Will you give votes for women?' and to ask the question 'Will the Liberal government give women the vote?' The women were hastily dragged from their seats by stewards and taken outside where Christabel, a law student at Manchester University at that time, knowingly pouted her lips in order to commit the technical offence of spitting at a police officer. Charged with disorderly conduct, punishable by imprisonment or a fine, both had already decided that they would choose imprisonment since they knew it would bring publicity to the women's cause – which it did.[18] Newspapers carried the story in full.

Other suffragettes soon followed their example, finding the courage to speak out, sharing their experiences with each other and planning their interventions beforehand. Marie Brackenbury, a WSPU member, recollected in 1930 just how important these tactics were in giving women a voice in a previously defined male public sphere:

> The heckling of Cabinet Ministers by women was found to be such a powerful weapon, both in it's [sic] effect on the Government and on the public, that it became one of our most efficient, organised, activities. Speakers at meetings were so accustomed to the interruptions of *men* that they merely gave them a more or less satisfactory reply, and no disturbance followed; but a woman's voice, however quiet, seemed to act like a match to gunpowder. An explosion inevitably followed and scenes of great violence occurred. The woman heckler found herself surrounded by shouting stewards pulling her every way, after striking her and throwing her down the steps that led to the Hall.[19]

For Marie and others like her, heckling involved throwing off the constraints of 'womanly' or even 'ladylike' behaviour; indeed, hecklers could be referred to as 'cats mewing' and as 'wild women'.[20] Since rough handling was almost a certainty, many women made sure their clothing offered some protection. Grace Roe, for example, would never heckle without wearing 'suitable underwear, as for a hockey match'.[21] Heckling was often the first stage in learning to be a political activist, and if any suffragette desired to extend her talent in this field and learn how to give short speeches at public meetings, help was offered by the Speakers' Classes, as they were called. These classes had the aim of giving 'platform experience' to WSPU members.[22] Members might also supplement such classes by engaging in writing indignant letters to the local newspapers, whenever suffrage was attacked or suffrage news distorted, or by sending in regular weekly articles – activities that might be co-ordinated by the local WSPU branch secretary. Viscountess Rhondda, for example, regularly wrote two or three articles weekly in praise of militancy, lifting 'chunks' of text from the leading article in *Votes for Women*.[23] The WSPU, she claimed, not only forced her to learn to speak in public, 'it also made me take to writing'.[24]

From 1905 until the official cessation of militant activity in 1914, about 1000 women and 40 men were sent to prison.[25] Many, although not all, of these imprisonments were especially associated with the second fiercer phase of militancy from 1910 when, tired with the repeated refusals of the government of the day to grant women the vote, the WSPU engaged in a range of attacks against property although never against human life. Thus activists might break windows (usually with stones or toffee hammers) in fashionable shops in London's West End and in government offices, vandalise art treasures, set fire to empty houses and to pillar boxes, and pour acid on golf courses. From July 1909, WSPU prisoners used the hunger strike (and later also the thirst strike) as a protest against the government's policy of not granting them political prisoner status and thus the right to be placed in the First Division in prison, rather than in the less privileged Second and Third Divisions. The government responded to the hunger strike by introducing, in October of the same year, forcible feeding. Then in April 1913, the Prisoners' Temporary Discharge for Ill Health Act, more commonly known as 'The Cat and Mouse Act', was passed. Under this Act, a hunger striker or 'mouse' could be released into the community on a special licence for a specified period of time until she was well enough to be re-arrested by the authorities or 'Cat' and serve her full sentence. By this time, of course, only the most dedicated of WSPU members were active militants. A number of members had left, when militancy became violent, and the rate of new recruiting slowed down; indeed, Rosen estimates that only 2380 new members joined the WSPU during 1912–13.[26] That minority of members who remained 'militant' rather than 'feminist' members of the WSPU in this second phase of militancy probably numbered about 1000.[27] And they had to learn another political role, that of the guerrilla activist.

Many of these guerrilla militants acted on their own initiative, taking orders from the leadership of the WSPU if and when they pleased.[28] A typical example was Mary Richardson who, as a 'mouse' on release, entered the National Gallery on 10 March 1914 and used a small chopper with a long narrow blade to slash the famous painting by Velazquez, *Rokeby Venus*. Her act was in protest against the government's re-arrest in Glasgow, the day before, of Mrs Pankhurst who many WSPU members feared would the as her health was deteriorating under the cruel conditions imposed by the Cat and Mouse Act. 'Mrs. Pankhurst seeks to procure justice for womanhood', proclaimed Mary Richardson, 'and for this she is being slowly murdered by a Government of Iscariot politicians'.[29] Mary's life as a guerrilla activist was one of daring and courage, learning how and when to time her forays and how to conceal from the general public the nature of her activities. On one occasion, in Bristol, she successfully evaded the strenuous efforts of the authorities to let any suffragettes near the King who was making a visit to the city. One unsuspecting man standing by her, waiting in the crowd for the King to appear, boasted 'In Bristol we know how to handle wild women'.[30] Mary nodded at him and kept on smiling until she saw the cavalry escorting the King's carriage appear. Split-second timing was critical:

> I was forced to look sharply and decide quickly behind which horse I would make my dash in order to gain the step of the open carriage. Out I shot then; and, by some miracle, I got to the carriage, leapt on to the step and deposited my petition on the King's knee, keeping my hand on it for a moment as I gasped out, 'A petition, Your Majesty!'[31]

On another occasion, Mary Richardson and another suffragette were sent to Birmingham to commit arson. Their home-made time bomb, contained in an everyday marmalade pot, was carefully deposited in the wardrobe in their bedroom. In the middle of the night, they crept surreptitiously out of their lodgings, with the bomb spluttering and hissing, and deposited it in the ticket office of the local railway station – where it exploded at about 3 o'clock in the morning.[32] The next morning, at breakfast, they feigned 'mild agitation' when their landlord read his newspapers and complained of 'Those blasted women again!'.[33] As Mary observed, 'I doubt if there is anything much more difficult than to play the part of a normal, quiet individual when one is thoroughly involved in the most abnormal activities'.[34]

Those WSPU members who felt unable to engage in such acts of daring or heckling, public speaking or writing to the press, could contribute to 'the cause' in a multitude of other ways, for example, secretarial support, distributing leaflets, running WSPU shops, selling *Votes for Women* or *The Suffragette*, chalking the pavements to advertise meetings and organising fund-raising events. Cicely Hale, for example, who was unsuccessful as a speaker on a soap box at a street corner, became a part-time paid assistant (at 10 shillings weekly) for Mary Home in the Information Department at the WSPU headquarters in London. Her job entailed such tasks as scanning the daily, weekly and evening papers to select data relative to the movement, supplying pithy material for speakers, verifying quotations, and looking up facts in the British Museum. 'If anyone wanted to know anything', she recollected, 'they asked us to find it for them'.[35] As these testimonies illustrate, the WSPU was a complex organisation with a formal structure at the London headquarters (and at the other smaller provincial centres) and webs of informal networks amongst its members, some of whom were close friends with women in other feminist groupings, such as the Women's Freedom League and the Actresses' Franchise League.[36] The WSPU had not only paid officers in London, but also paid regional organizers – and a host of voluntary workers. One American visitor to England found its organisation impressive, even though the discipline was 'severe':

> I had to admire the almost perfect organization through which those women conducted their business. Their offices [in London]...were frequently raided and every single woman of any importance arrested. But every woman had her understudy – perhaps two or three of them. The day after a raid the understudies were in the building, each at her proper desk, carrying on methodologically. Every letter that came in or went out of the office must have been done into many duplicates, for the new officials knew to the last detail what their first day's work was to be. The discipline of the Party was severe.[37]

The effectiveness of the political education that the WSPU offered was directly related to its efficiency and sound financial management. The latter was especially due to Emmeline Pethick-Lawrence, one of the leaders of the WSPU and its treasurer, until ousted by Mrs Pankhurst and Christabel in 1912. Money, claimed Annie Kenney, was 'scrupulously valued' by Mrs Pethick-Lawrence.[38] Furthermore, Emmeline and her husband, Fred, were brilliant at organising donations and even subscribed £6610 in identifiable donations themselves between 1906 and 1912.[39] Mrs Pethick-Lawrence was assisted in her job as treasurer by Mrs Sanders who made sure that every penny entered in the cash books of the paid organisers was accounted for; if the books did not balance, the money had to come out of the organiser's own pocket.[40] Many years later, Annie Kenney still marvelled at the efficiency of it all as she remembered how WSPU members were always encouraged to think of cheaper alternatives before any planned expenditure:

> I always admired, and still admire, the careful and methodical way in which the money was spent...Where hard work would tell, no money was spent on advertising. If a chair would be suitable as a platform, why pay a few shillings for a trolley? If the weather was fine, why hire a hall? If the pavements were dry, why not chalk advertisements of the meeting instead of paying printers' bills? If a tram would take us, why hire a taxi?[41]

As this example and other illustrative material cited in this article demonstrate, women in the WSPU learnt not only about 'becoming a feminist' but also about working collectively in the name of the women's cause. Eliding differences between women,[42] so commonly emphasised in some feminist writing of today, they learnt through their political education about the bonds that unite all women, about the power of sisterhood. Indeed, as Vicinus aptly notes, the greatest gift the WSPU offered its activists was 'self-discovery' through the experience of sharing friendship, sacrifice and even danger.[43] As Emmeline Pethick-Lawrence observed, the women's movement meant to women 'the discovery of their own identity, that source within of purpose power and will, the *real* person' that often remains throughout a lifetime hidden under the mask of appearances.[44] It meant also to women, she continued, 'the discovery of the wealth of spiritual sympathy, loyalty and affection' that could be formed in friendship and companionship with one another.[45] For Mrs Pethick-Lawrence, as for so many of her comrades, the WSPU was 'our education' in the identification of the self with the women's movement.[46] Such thoughts were echoed time and time again by suffragettes who saw their involvement in feminist politics as the educational experience of a lifetime. As one former WSPU member, reflecting on her militant days, recollected in 1933:

> Certainly it was during those years of fused enthusiasm rather than during the ordinary years of school and college, that, reading, studying, thinking, puzzling, I got the best of what education I have had. And...I suspect that that is true of many another militant of my generation.[47]

In 1918, 15 years after the foundation of the WSPU, the Representation of the People Act was passed. This Act allowed women over 30 years of age to vote if they were householders, the wives of householders, occupiers of property with an annual rent of £5 or more, or graduates of British universities.[48] The long battle for voting rights on equal terms with men was not won until 1928 when all adults, over the age of 21, were enfranchised irrespective of sex, property ownership or any other qualification. The political education of women within the WSPU had been a decisive factor in helping to win this right. Its significance within the history of women's education has been a long forgotten and neglected dimension.

NOTES

1 Purvis, J. (1989) *Hard Lessons, The Lives and Education of Working-class Women in Nineteenth-century England*, p. 107 (Oxford, Polity Press).
2 Purvis, J. (1991) *A History of Women's Education in England*, p. 120 (Milton Keynes, Open University Press).
3 Quoted in Vicinus, M. (1985) *Independent Women, Work and Community for Single Women 1850–1920*, p. 127 (London, Virago).
4 Taylor, B. (1983) *Eve and the New Jerusalem, Socialism and Feminism in the Nineteenth Century*, pp. 230–231 (London, Virago). Some Owenite women, such as Emma Martin and Frances Morrison, also became lecturers, see pp. 75–82 and 130–135.
5 *The Manchester Guardian*, 2 April 1902.
6 Pankhurst, E. (1909) 'The Deputation of June 29', *Votes for Women*, 25 June, p. 848.
7 Pankhurst, E. (1914) *My Own Story*, p. 38 (London, Eveleigh Nash).
8 Ibid., p. 38.
9 Rosen, A. (1974) *Rise Up, Women! The Militant Campaign of the Women's Social and Political Union 1903–1914*, p. 114 (London, Routledge & Kegan Paul). Other accounts of the WSPU include Fulford, R. (1957) *Votes for Women, The Story of a Struggle* (London, Faber & Faber), Mitchell, D. (1967) *The Fighting Pankhursts, A Study in Tenacity* (London, Jonathan Cape), Rover, C. (1967) *Women's Suffrage and Party Politics in Britain 1866–1914* (London, Routledge & Kegan Paul), Raeburn, Antonia

(1973) *The Militant Suffragettes* (London, Michael Joseph), Morgan, D. (1975) *Suffragists and Liberals, The Politics of Woman Suffrage in England* (Oxford, Basil Blackwell), Pugh, M. (1980) *Women's Suffrage in Britain 1867–1928* (London, The Historical Association), Garner, L. (1984) *Stepping Stones to Women's Liberty, Feminist Ideas in the Women's Suffrage Movement 1900–1918* (London, Heinemann Educational), Harrison, B. (1987) *Prudent Revolutionaries, Portraits of British Feminists between the Wars* (Oxford, Oxford University Press), Tickner, L. (1987) *The Spectacle of Women, Imagery of the Suffrage Campaign 1907–14* (London, Chatto & Windus), Kent, K. Susan (1987) *Sex and Suffrage in Britain 1860–1914* (Princeton, NJ, Princeton University Press), Marcus, J. (ed.) (1987) *Suffrage and the Pankhursts* (London, Routledge & Kegan Paul), Atkinson, D. (1988) *Suffragettes* (London, Museum of London), Atkinson, D. (1988) *Votes for Women* (Cambridge, Cambridge University Press), Leneman, L. (1991) *A Guid Cause, The Women's Suffrage Movement in Scotland* (Aberdeen, Aberdeen University Press), Holton, S. Sandra (1992) 'The suffragist and the "average" woman', *Women's History Review*, 1(1): 9–24, Bolt, C. (1933) *The Women's Movements in the United States and Britain from the 1790s to the 1920s* (Hemel Hempstead, Harvester) and King, E. (1993) *The Hidden History of Glasgow's Women* (Edinburgh and London, Mainstream Publishing).

10 Pethick-LE, F. (n.d. 1943?) *Fate Has Been Kind*, p. 86 (London, Hutchinson & Co.).

11 Rosen, A. (1974) *Rise Up, Women!, The Militant Campaign of the Women's Social and Political Union 1903–1914*, p. 114 (London, Routledge & Kegan Paul).

12 Ibid., p. 109.

13 Sleight, J. (1988) *One-Way Ticket to Epsom*, p. 86 (Morpeth, Bridge Studios).

14 The following information is taken from the story 'Dead suffragist Miss Davison's funeral', *The Sunday Times*, 15 June 1913.

15 'Grand triumphal funeral march', *Daily Herald*, 16 June 1913.

16 The dividing line between 'constitutional' and 'militant' is not always neat – see Holton, Sandra Stanley (1986) *Feminism' and Democracy, Women's Suffrage and Reform Politics in Britain 1900–1918*, p. 4 (Cambridge, Cambridge University Press). In addition, also see Strachey, R. (1931) *Millicent Garrett Fawcett* (London, John Murray), Hume, Leslie, P. (1982) *The National Union of Women's Suffrage Societies, 1897–1914* (New York and London, Garland Publishing), Oakley, Ann (1983) 'Millicent Garrett Fawcett: duty and determination', in D. Spender (ed.) *Feminist Theorists, Three Centuries of Women's Intellectual Traditions* (London, The Women's Press), Harrison, B. (1987) *Prudent Revolutionaries*, Chapter 1, 'Two models of feminist leadership: Millicent Fawcett and Emmeline Pankhurst', Rubinstein, D. (1991) *A Different World for Women, The Life of Millicent Garrett Fawcett* (Hemel Hempstead, Harvester), Caine, B. (1992) *Victorian Feminists* (Oxford, Oxford University Press), Ch. 6 'Millicent Garrett Fawcett'.

17 Pankhurst, C. (1959) *Unshackled, The Story of How We Won the Vote*, p. 226 (London, Hutchinson).

18 Ibid., pp. 49–52.

19 Brackenbury, M. (1930) *The Militant Suffragettes' Campaign, 1905–1914*, Suffragette Fellowship Collection, Museum of London, Vol. II, Group D, 57. 116/32.

20 Pankhurst, E. (1914) *My Own Story*, pp. 67, 72 (London, Eveleigh Nash).

21 'Obituary by Jill Craigie of Grace Roe', *The Guardian*, 31 August 1979.

22 *Votes for Women*, January 1908, p. 60.

23 Rhondda, The Viscountess (1933) *This Was My World*, p. 131 (London, Macmillan & Co.). For an interesting account of the way in which former militant suffrage feminists constructed their autobiographies in the 1920s and 1930s see Kean, H. (1994) 'Searching for the past in present defeat: the construction of historical and political identity in British feminism in the 1920s and 1930s', *Women's History Review* 3(1): 57–80. See also T. Davis, M. Durham, C. Hall, M. Langan and D. Sutton (1982) "The public face of feminism": early twentieth-century writings on women's suffrage', in Centre for Contemporary Cultural Studies (ed.) *Making Histories, Studies in History-Writing and Politics* (London, Hutchinson).

24 Ibid., p. 130.

25 It is impossible to give exact figures here. These figures are based on the male and female names in *Roll of Honour Suffragette Prisoners 1905–1914* (n.d.) (Keighley, The Rydal

Press), and do not include the 49 people listed with a surname and no Christian name or initial. Although most of these prisoners were WSPU members, some were members of other suffrage groups, such as the Women's Freedom League, or indeed of both.

26 Rosen, A. (1974) *Rise Up, Women!, The Militant Campaign of the Women's Social and Political Union 1903–1914*, p. 211 (London, Routledge & Kegan Paul).

27 Purvis, J. (1994) ' "Deeds, not words": the daily lives of militant suffragettes in Edwardian Britain', *Women's Studies International Forum*, 17(4): 1–11 makes the point that the vast majority of WSPU did not engage in militant activity and may be termed 'feminists' as opposed to that minority who were 'militants'.

28 See Stanley, L. and Morley, A. (1988) *The Life and Death of Emily Wilding Davison* (London, The Women's Press) for a discussion of this.

29 *The Times*, 11 March 1914.

30 Richardson, R. Mary (1953) *Laugh a Defiance*, p. 115 (London, Weidenfeld & Nicholson).

31 Ibid., p. 116.

32 Ibid., pp. 142–144.

33 Ibid., p. 146.

34 Ibid., p. 139.

35 Hale, Cicely, B. (1973) *A Good Long Time (The autobiography of an octogenarian)*, p. 49 (London, Regency Press).

36 For further discussion of this see Stanley, Liz With Morley, Ann (1988) *The Life and Death of Emily Wilding Davison* (London, The Women's Press). For an account that covers the Actresses' Franchise League see Holledge, Julie (1981) *Innocent Flowers, Women in the Edwardian Theatre* (London, Virago Press) and Gardner, Viv and Rutherford, Susan (eds) (1992) *The New Woman and her Sisters, Feminism and Theatre 1850–1914* (Hemel Hempstead, Harvester Wheatsheaf).

37 Dorr, R. Childe (1924) *A Woman of Fifty*, p. 261 (New York and London, Funk & Wagnalls).

38 Kenney, A. (1924) *Memories of a Militant*, p. 82 (London, Edward Arnold).

39 Harrison, B. (1987) *Prudent Revolutionaries*, p. 248 (Oxford, Oxford University Press).

40 Kenney, Annie (1924) *Memories of a Militant*, p. 82 (London, Edward Arnold).

41 Ibid., p. 83.

42 Corbett, J.M. (1992) *Representing Femininity, Middle-class Subjectivity in Victorian and Edwardian Women's Autobiographies*, p. 158 (New York and Oxford, Oxford University Press).

43 Vicinus, M. (1985) *Independent Women, Work and Community for Single Women 1850–1920*, p. 258 (London, Virago).

44 Pethick-Lawrence, E. (1938) *My Part in a Changing World*, p. 215 (London, Victor Gollancz).

45 Ibid., p. 215.

46 Ibid., p. 215.

47 Rhondda, The Viscountess (1933) *This Was My World*, p. 130 (London, Macmillan & Co).

48 Rosen, A. (1974) *Rise Up, Women!, The Militant Campaign of the Women's Social and Political Union 1903–1914*, p. 266 (London, Routledge & Kegan Paul).

FOURTEEN

TO 'BLAISE THE TRAIL FOR WOMEN TO FOLLOW ALONG': SEX, GENDER AND THE POLITICS OF EDUCATION ON THE LONDON SCHOOL BOARD, 1870–1904

Jane Martin

Source: 'To "blaise the trail for women to follow along": sex, gender and the politics of education on the London School Board, 1870–1904', *Gender and Education*, 12(2): 165–181, 2000.

Introduction

In October 1876, Florence Fenwick Miller (1854–1935) received a letter from the Reverend Stewart Headlam on behalf of the Bethnal Green Commonwealth Club, inviting her to become a candidate for the Hackney division of the London School Board. Educated, socially aware and a member of the first women's movement in Britain, Florence accepted the offer because she was interested in the education of the working classes and wished to speak on behalf of elementary school girls and women teachers. She was also motivated by what she described as the 'scandalous shortage' of women with the drive and ambition to pursue interesting careers in the public arena. Florence had strong connections with pioneer doctors Elizabeth Garrett Anderson and Sophia Jex-Blake, was well known to the leaders of the major suffrage societies and had reached the point of enjoying an established reputation among the intellectual elite of the London Dialectical Society. At 22 years old, she became the youngest woman ever elected to the largest and most powerful organ of local government then in existence.

Opportunities for women in local government increased greatly in the last third of the nineteenth century. Although civic policies and administration were complicated by a tangle of authorities and agencies, the Municipal Franchise Act of 1869 was the first of a number of measures that were to affect women's democratic participation. This piece of legislation restored the local vote to women ratepayers (a right they had lost under the 1835 Municipal Corporations Act). The following year the passing of the Elementary Education Act made women eligible for nomination and election to the thousands of locally elected school boards set up in and after 1870. The extension of Victorian state activity engendered new forms of public service and women were active in their localities as elected and appointed officials responsible for the administration of most education and welfare services. Thane has noted the unique quality of the British situation by highlighting the fact that no other major state in Europe or America offered women 'a comparable institutional role at such an early date' (1993, p. 351). Nonetheless, female involvement in the development of the state system of elementary education has been neglected in the traditional historiography of mass schooling. Besides debates about female invisibility, this is because the activities of the central state apparatus have been accentuated and 'these histories have been written from the records of the official central state run by male bureaucrats and politicians' (Koven, 1993, pp. 94–95). Consequently, there has been little work on the often lengthy public careers of local activists. However, recent work by Hollis (1989), Hughes (1992), Martin (1991, 1995, 1999) and Turnbull (1983) aims to understand and rediscover the position of women in the process of local educational policy-making. Therefore, women's participation in the politics of schooling is beginning to be released from historical obscurity.

This article considers the issue of female involvement by focusing on the work of the 29 women elected to serve on the London School Board.[1] It is based largely on a quite new source of manuscript material (the unpublished autobiographical fragment written by Florence Fenwick Miller) among papers in the Contemporary Medical Archives Centre at the Wellcome Institute for the History of Medicine.[2] The object is to place Florence as a central character in the analysis. The availability of her memoir has thrown up issues pertinent to current debates about the history of English feminism and produced new interpretations of the friendship networks that made up the metropolitan women's movement. However, there is no attempt to categorise these women as feminists. As elected women, they all publicised the work of women in local government but this did not mean they were all motivated by interest in sex equality issues. The term 'feminism' was not widely used until the First World War (Caine, 1997, p. 8), and it will become clear that sexual politics needs to be considered alongside party politics. Different class interests were also important and this article seeks to emphasise the diversities amongst activist women considered in relation to thought and actions. These themes will be located within a discussion of the role of women as educational policy-makers.

The article is divided into three parts. The first part looks at the issue of women's representation. In so doing it will focus on the selection process, as well as the background and the political beginnings of these female politicians. The main focus is the recollections of Florence Fenwick Miller and a biographical method is used to make visible the links between private life and public practice. Part two considers the political culture of the institution itself. The London School Board was the world's largest educational authority and the presence of women immediately complicated and partly contradicted the general connection of authority with masculinity. Hence, the third part uses a historical methodology to explore women's careers as educational policy-makers. Overall, the article throws up the following questions. Did the involvement of women change the political culture; and what impact did they have on the education policy agenda?

Political candidature

Up to a point, the school boards were democratic institutions. They were the first elected bodies to admit women on the same terms as men, but most people lacked the necessary resources and motivation to contest the elections. However, political conviction combined with the tradition of female philanthropy and, especially in the towns, school board politics provided an important field of endeavour for the women's movement (Turnbull, 1983; Hollis, 1989; Martin, 1993, 1999). This was because the new franchise allowed women with the necessary property qualifications to vote, while multiple voting and the possibility of giving all your votes to one candidate favoured the representation of electoral minorities. Created under the terms of the 1870 Education Act, factors of size and formation placed the London School Board in a unique position. Whereas other school boards were restricted to between 5 and 13 members, the first London Board had 49 members, rising to 55 by the mid-1880s. In addition, the metropolis was divided into 10 vast wards (except the inner square mile of the City itself), which each returned a number of candidates. As might be expected, the School Board for London was a flagship institution and played a vital role in setting the educational standards for other school boards to follow. London was the centre and symbol of imperial and national power and the letters MSBL (Member of the School Board for London), served to convey a certain sense of prestige and social status among one's peers.

The conditions for public life will be investigated in terms of political background, socio-economic status, education, marital status and family commitments. Florence Fenwick Miller has supplied a vivid record, which, while it may not be wholly representative, is illuminating. Florence was the eldest child of John Miller, a captain in the British merchant marine, and Eleanor Fenwick, the daughter of a civil engineer. She grew up in London in the 1850s and 1860s, in comfortable middle-class surroundings (the family had an income of between £600 and £700 per annum). First educated at a dame school, her mother then gave her lessons at home before she entered a Young Ladies' Seminary at the age of six; a year later, she was sent away to complete her education at boarding school. In her late teens Florence was attracted to medical training and it is noteworthy that her father supported her decision, whereas her more socially conservative mother was left feeling 'she had three sons and no daughter' (Fenwick Miller, ch. 4, unpaginated). One of the first seven women students at Edinburgh University in 1871, she enroled at the Ladies' Medical College, London, in the autumn, finished with honours and gained a portion of clinical instruction at the British Lying-In Hospital. In the 1870s, she ran a practice for women and children from her parents' home in Victoria Park. In 1879 she married Frederick Ford (honorary secretary of the London Dialectical Society). He was not very successful in business and Florence had to rely on daily or weekly journalism to support herself economically. By the 1880s she was writing steadily for a variety of publications including the *Modern Review, Lady's Pictorial, Fraser's* and *The Governess*; as well as being the author of several teaching texts. Marriage was quickly followed by motherhood (the couple had two daughters, Irene, born 15 April 1880, and Helen, born 1 July 1881), yet Fenwick Miller managed also to occupy significant public positions. Possibly her ego helped. We learn that her 'success as a public speaker was from the first quite exceptional' and that despite maternal opposition she found the electoral contest 'most exhilarating' (Fenwick Miller, GC/228/15; GC/228/27). She also gained advantage from her participation in the suffrage campaigns and membership of a social-cum-intellectual circle who carried on public debate from a position of centrality in the capital city. Was this kind of experience a familiar pattern for women's public activity in the past?

For the most part the 29 women considered here were well connected and better educated than others of their sex and class. A certain sort of familial background was an advantage when embarking on a public career and they formed part of a social and intellectual stratum of London society whose families were largely drawn from the traditional genteel professions, as well as wealthy businessmen (Martin, 1993). The one exception was the service of Mary Bridges Adams (nee Daltry), the daughter of an engine fitter, who represented Greenwich from 1897 to 1904. The pupil-teacher system enabled Mary to establish herself as an independent person and in the 1870s she held posts as a teacher and head teacher in Newcastle and Birmingham. The first women members, Emily Davies and Elizabeth Garrett, were associated with the first women's network in Britain, established in the late 1850s and named the Langham Place group after its cultural centre in London. This forum served as a conduit for political patronage and in the division of Marylebone, Elizabeth Garrett was succeeded by her younger sister, Alice Cowell; who served alongside the educationalist Jane Chessar. All but written out of history, Jane Chessar had close connections with the Langham Place social network but was forced to retire from public life on the grounds of ill health. Alice Westlake was selected in her place. She also belonged to the Langham Place group, canvassed for Elizabeth Garrett in 1870 and went on to hold elected office until 1888 when her place was filled by Emma Maitland. Emma was unsuccessful at the polls in 1891 and this marked the end of Marylebone's record of continuous female representation. However, the biggest breakthrough in terms of female representation came in 1879 when 9 of the 50 successful candidates were female.[3] It is instructive to look more closely at the selection process in 1879, which suggests that there were clear divisions among activists over the question of tactics.

Florence Fenwick Miller left a detailed account of a campaign meeting attended by herself, Elizabeth Garrett Anderson, Elizabeth Surr, Helen Taylor and Alice Westlake (among others). What is especially interesting is that Florence describes a clash over tactics and among personalities, a story that runs counter to earlier representations of past and present women members acting as support networks (Turnbull, 1983; Hollis, 1993; Martin, 1993). In any event, Alice Westlake and Elizabeth Garrett Anderson both counselled against women standing, explaining how difficult and costly an election was. It is possible that they acted out of concern at the more strident political behaviour of the other elected women and certainly there were manoeuvrings over the selection of a female candidate for Hackney, where Florence was the serving woman member. In an attempt to split her vote, Sir Charles Reed (Board chair and divisional colleague) proposed that the local Liberal Party adopt Jane Chessar as their official candidate and when nothing came of it, Alice Westlake asked the middle-aged and highly conventional Rosamond Davenport Hill if she would contest Hackney. A clear example of recruitment by patronage, the criteria of political recruitment were hardly auspicious for anyone who did not play by the rules. As Norris and Lovenduski make clear, in political recruitment the key question 'is whether the applicant is "one of us": party loyalty and personal character are seen as more important than policy expertise or formal qualifications' (Norris and Lovenduski, 1995, p. 238).

In addition to the women's network, party organisations steadily increased their grip on school board elections. In London they were contested by two loosely organised groupings of individuals running as the Progressive and Moderate parties. The Progressives included all shades of liberal opinion, later fortified by the socialist groups. The Moderates were allied with the Anglican clergy and the Conservative Party. Only four Moderate women served on the London School Board – Eugenie Dibdin, Frances Hastings, Susan Lawrence and Mrs Wright. The rest were Progressives. Then, as now, it seems likely that the political bias reflected powerful social conventions. For instance, evidence drawn from the British Candidate Study in the 1992 election established that few Tory women came forward as applicants for political recruitment, despite the predominance of older women as party activists (Norris and Lovenduski, 1995, p. 248). The women who served in the 1880s and 1890s had strong party political connections. This pattern clearly fits in with the recruitment of Mary Bridges Adams, who was first selected as a candidate in 1894. In demand locally as a public speaker, she was sponsored by the Royal Arsenal Cooperative Society (RACS), 60 trade organisations and the London Nonconformist Council; 3 years later she was returned as member for Greenwich by a Progressive Election Committee that included the RACS, the Woolwich Trades Council and the local Radical Clubs (*School Board Chronicle*, 17 November 1894; 29 November 1897). Her election was a triumph for the organised labour movement and an extraordinary woman. But what was the specific organisational setting to which she had gained access? The next section looks at the institutional practices and cultures of the London School Board in order to consider the gendered division of labour and the efficacy of female interventions.

The political culture of the London School Board

Feminist critics of contemporary British politics argue that the distribution of political power reflects a certain bias in the way society is organised that makes it easier for some individuals and groups than others to see their objectives come to fruition (Lovenduski and Norris, 1996). In this context, it is useful to draw on the concept of gender balance that is being developed for the Gender and New Urban Governance Project (Lovenduski, 1996). To simplify, this typology draws out the sex and/or gender biases of contemporary politics by distinguishing between positional, policy and organisational balances. First, positional balance 'refers to the numbers of men and women in organisations as a whole and, within those organisations, to their presence in decision-making positions' (Lovenduski, 1996, p. 5). Second, policy gender balance points up the extent to which public policies impact on women and men in somewhat different ways, as well as the question of who plays the majority role in the policy-making process. Finally, organisational bias alerts us to the biases integral to the rules, values, norms, structures and policies of a specific organisation.

Taking each in turn, male bias was evident in quantitative terms. This is so even though the lowest level of female representation, just over 4 per cent in 1870 and 1873, contrasts favourably with the absence at that time of women from the House of Commons. Nonetheless, women were contained at the lowest levels of power and responsibility. The three most powerful posts were chair and vice-chair of the Board and chair of the School Management Committee, which were always held by men. Helen Taylor was the only woman to become chair of a permanent standing committee. Elected for the first time in 1876, she created a stir by adopting a more open and generalised popular appeal to the working-class electorate, which centred on questions of active participation and control. Opinions towards her were mixed. Emily Davies found her tactless and overbearing. Male opponents

Table 14.1 Party allegiance among school board women (sample = 27)

Member	Service on board	Attitude to party
A. Besant	1888–1891	Loyalist
M. Bridges Adams	1897–1904	Independent
J. Chessar	1873–1876	Independent
A. Cowell	1873–1876	Independent
E. Davies	1870–1873	Independent
R. Davenport-Hill	1879–1897	Loyalist
E. Dibdin	1897–1900	Loyalist
M. Dilke	1888–1891	Loyalist
C. Elder	1897–1900	Loyalist
M. Eve	1891–1904	Loyalist
E. Garrett	1870–1873	Independent
F. Hastings	1882–1885	Independent
R. Homan	1891–1904	Loyalist
M. Lawrence	1900–1904	Loyalist
S. Lawrence	1900–1904	Loyalist
E. Maitland	1888–1891, 1894–1902	Loyalist
E. McKee	1897–1904	Loyalist
H. Miall-Smith	1900–1904	Loyalist
F. Fenwick Miller	1876–1885	Independent
V.H. Morten	1897–1902	Independent
H. Muller	1879–1885	Independent
M. Richardson	1879–1885	Loyalist
E. Simcox	1879–1882	Loyalist
E. Surr	1876–1882	Independent
H. Taylor	1876–1885	Independent
A. Webster	1876–1888	Loyalist
A. Westlake	1879–1882, 1885–1888	Independent

nicknamed her the acid maiden. Yet in June 1883, members set a precedent by pro-moting Helen to a position of authority as chair of the Educational Endowments Committee – even though recruitment by patronage is based on criteria of accept-ability and she did not play by the male rules. It may be that the great majority of the men were afraid of the rivalry of women and that this was a way of containing her within a context they could deal with. Helen resented a rigid allegiance to party and for six years was part of a women's caucus consisting of herself, Florence Fenwick Miller and Elizabeth Surr. Eager to promote a non-party approach, Florence thought the relationship between the Board Chair:

> and the Chairmen of Committees in some sort resembled the Premier and his Cabinet, and looked to Members who wished to be 'in the swim' to vote very much to order as is done in the House of Commons.
>
> ('An Uncommon Girlhood', GC/228/28)

On the 1876 Board, these three women politicians sought to challenge institutional norms and certainly behaved differently to Alice Westlake *and* their male counter-parts. But was gender the major fault line in school board politics? To examine gender differences in political behaviour, the 27 women who served for one full term or more are considered in terms of their attitude to party.

I would argue that 12 women members attempted to adopt an independent approach to politics, albeit with different goals. Thus, Jane Chessar, Alice Cowell, Emily Davies and Elizabeth Garrett are labelled Independent, as the party machines were not in control on the 1870 and 1873 Boards. By the late 1870s, Henrietta Muller and Augusta Webster stood on Independent platforms, while Florence Fenwick Miller, Elizabeth Surr and Helen Taylor did not want to play by the rules:

> Anything was justifiable, so long as it was safe, that would tend to the success of a man's Party... We three women Members, Elizabeth Surr, Helen Taylor and myself were a thorn in the side of the Party management of affairs. We were genuinely independent on which ground we had all been elected. We would deliberate and consider every question on its merits... and if we saw anything that ought to be blamed... exposed it regardless of the question of personality and Party ties.
>
> ('An Uncommon Girlhood', GC/228/34)

Mary Bridges Adams and Honnor Morten were elected for their radical views, which set them apart from the Progressives, and Frances Hastings did not always adhere to the Moderate party line. By contrast, the four longest serving female representatives, Rosamond Davenport Hill (18 years), Margaret Eve (13 years), Ruth Homan (13 years) and Alice Westlake (12 years) were Progressive party loyalists. These successful women gave high priority to their role as party representatives and won promotion to middle-ranking appointments. At 50, Ruth Homan became vice-chair of the Industrial Schools Committee and Margaret Eve was appointed vice-chair of the Evening Continuation Schools Committee in 1900 (*School Board Chronicle*, 22 October 1900; 16 February 1901). In terms of the gender balance, there was a distinct male positional bias on the London School Board. This certainly had an impact on the political culture of the institution and it is this aspect that will be considered next; policy gender balance will be examined later in the section exploring women's careers as educational policy-makers.

From the start, three parties were involved in the management of London's board schools – the Board itself (working through a School Management Committee), individual members and local school managers. The Board held open meetings every Wednesday, beginning at 3 pm and usually continuing until 6.30 pm, although it was often much later. Their main purpose was to hear the recommendations set out in reports from the various committees that conducted the work of the Board; these were accepted, amended or referred back. Members had a right to propose alternate motions of policy, and debate them, before an open vote was taken, with each individual answering 'yes' or 'no' at the division. Overall, new members found an elaborately ritualised and formalised politics that followed 'the precedent of the customs of the House of Commons' (Florence Fenwick Miller, 'An Uncommon Girlhood', GC/228/28). The accent on parliamentary tradition meant that the male organisational bias was very apparent, and female members undoubtedly felt uncomfortable and out of place at times. For instance, Florence Fenwick Miller testified to a rather bizarre difficulty she encountered on her second attendance at the Board. She recalled that the boardroom porter approached her and said, 'The lady members of the Board always wear bonnets, Ma'am' (Florence Fenwick Miller, 'An Uncommon Girlhood', GC/228/28). Florence disliked wearing a hat and had left her bonnet in the ladies' dressing room:

> He said no more; but when I came to reflect, I felt certain he would not have spoken on his own initiative; Sir Charles Reed must have ordered him to say what he did. This droll insistence on women's heads being covered no doubt

owes its origin to St Paul's observation on the point. As that Eastern person had made a woman's wearing a covering on her head a symbol of her inferiority to her brother man.

('An Uncommon Girlhood', GC/228/28)

At other times, a culture of male fraternity was reinforced by the exclusion of women members from the annual Lord Mayor's Banquet. Previously, Jane Chessar, Alice Cowell, Emily Davies, Elizabeth Garrett and Alice Westlake had acquiesced with male wishes by declining their invitation to attend what they were told would be an exclusively male event. On this occasion Florence Fenwick Miller, Elizabeth Surr and Helen Taylor accepted. According to Florence:

It was then represented to us that our demand for equal rights could be met by our being invited on the distinct understanding that we would all three have a previous engagement that we regretted would prevent us from having the pleasure of accepting. But still we were stubborn and attended.

('An Uncommon Girlhood', GC/228/34)

Although the presence of woman members immediately complicated struggles over power and advantage in public life, male and female territories and responsibilities reflected traditional notions of the sexual division of labour. Women dominated the membership of the Cookery, Laundry and Needlework Sub-Committee and this was the only sub-committee never to have a male chair. By contrast, female members rarely served on the Finance Committee or the Works Committee responsible for the purchase of school sites and school furniture, the erection and enlargement of school buildings and the general care of Board properties. Emma Maitland asserted that she wanted to bring a female perspective to all areas of the Board's work, but the great majority were more likely to subscribe to conventional ideas about women's skills and interests. Once again, the service of Mary Bridges Adams is a notable exception. In 1897, she joined the traditional male territory of the Works Committee. Three years later she brought her professional expertise to the service of the Teaching Staff Sub-Committee.

Irrespective of the social and political pressures on women members, they also had to adapt to the demands of public office. Many members regarded the School Board as the main business of their lives and an indication of the workload can be gauged by reference to the weekly timetables of Florence Fenwick Miller in the 1870s and Emma Maitland in the 1890s. Thus, Florence spent two or three days a week at the Board offices on the Embankment, while Emma found that Mondays, Thursdays and Fridays were taken up with central Board work, as were alternate Wednesdays. Financial worries pressed hard on Florence. She frequently went without food on Board days and thought it a 'wild extravagance' to lunch out, on top of the 2s spent on fares and 9d on a cup of tea at the Board's tearoom. She spent hours on committee work, especially the powerful School Management Committee:

I remember once a long discussion over the request of a headmistress to be allowed a larger quantity of soap, because her school was in such a poor neighbourhood and the children came so dirty. At last I exclaimed: 'It would pay me better to supply this soap myself for the winter than to spend any more time over it', to which the Chairman answered wearily: 'But we all feel like that, you know!'

('An Uncommon Girlhood', GC/228/34)

Both women devoted the rest of the week to constituency work, which included the supervision of local schools, to which they nominated teachers, ancillary staff and resources. As Emma explained to Frederick Dolman during an interview for the *Young Woman* in 1896, she also played a part in developing schools for children with disabilities; taking advantage of a continental visit to investigate German and Austrian methods for teaching deaf and dumb children (The Young Woman, January 1896).

The next section explores the implications of the female presence. Of course, it was clearly an advance for women to be elected to positions of this kind of political responsibility, but did they bring important perspectives and priorities to educational policy-making? The focus here concerns the impact of women's contribution to the politics of education. In particular, what were their policy priorities and what did they set out to achieve?

Women's careers as educational policy-makers

The evidence presented here shows a male gender bias along the different dimensions of positional balance and organisational balance. But does this mean women had little impact on the policy-making process? This article considers what Hunt (1991, p. 11) defines as the 'middle level of decision making which intervenes between government policy and actual school practice', taking the chance to focus upon the way female representatives sought to influence the decision-making process. Women's claims to political power were based on the distinctive character of the female contribution. In particular, they were contingent upon a gendered and classed construction of 'special needs'. Girls were regarded as having different requirements to boys (either physical, emotional or intellectual) and women candidates found it advantageous to campaign as being ready to champion the interests of girls and women teachers. Moreover, just as researchers today are finding evidence of a 'widespread popular conception that women politicians are more compassionate' than men, this was true in the period between 1870 and 1904 (Norris, 1996, p. 93). Then and now, these assumptions were based on deep-rooted social stereotypes, but gender was not the only factor shaping political attitudes and in fact, 12 of the 27 women who served for a minimum of one term were loyal to parties dominated by men. Here, the varied influence and policy priorities of women members will be considered in relation to some of the 'women's questions' mentioned earlier. The elementary schoolgirls' curriculum and the interests of women teachers make it possible to assess whether they made a distinctive stand on the interests of girls and women. The final example of school attendance will be used to assess the policy gender bias in the politics of schooling.

The schoolgirls' curriculum

Ostensibly co-educational, in London the new board schools frequently had different entrances for the sexes, as well as separate playgrounds and separate departments for older children (Turnbull, 1987). Concern about value for money led central government to impose payment by results in 1862, and although each pupil earned the school the same amount for successful examination performance (Weiner,

1994, p. 35), failing to teach girls needlework became one of the few offences for which an elementary school could lose its government grant (Davin, 1996). In 1878, theoretical domestic economy was made a compulsory specific (optional) subject for girls; four years later the Government gave grants for the teaching of cookery. By the 1890s, this sex-differentiated curriculum had expanded to include laundry work and housewifery. Despite the addition of handicraft (workshop instruction, woodwork or manual work), Turnbull (1987, p. 86) concludes that working-class boys 'did not receive practical instruction equivalent to the girls' needlework, cookery, laundry work and so on'. Thus, it has been argued that the purpose of mass schooling was to impose an ideal family form of a male breadwinner and an economically dependent, full-time wife and mother:

> This was an ideal that came broadly to be shared by the bourgeoisie and men and women of the working classes alike, each for their own particular economic, political, cultural and social reasons. That it was unattainable for most outside the ranks of skilled and unionised labour was seen as unproblematic; it integrated the goals of the powerful men of the working classes with those of the dominant social and economic groups and served as an aspirational ideal to the unskilled, unorganised work-force.
>
> (Gomersall, 1994, p. 238)

So the intentions in educating boys and girls were different. Excluded from national politics on the grounds of their sex, it is important to explicate women's involvement in school gender training.

Female reformers served as elected members of school boards and as co-opted members of the Technical Instruction Committees set up following the Technical Instruction Act of 1889, and some tried to win friends and influential allies under the auspices of the domestic subjects movement (see Turnbull, 1994; Bird, 1998). Women spoke with different voices and the question of school gender training clearly exposes the tensions in the period 1870–1904 (see Dyhouse, 1981; Hollis, 1987; Bird, 1991; Martin, 1995). A minority wanted girls and women to have access to the same educational provision as boys and men but the female curriculum was generally discussed as if biology was destiny. Yet, any discussion of the purpose of education was complicated by enduring social and educational distinctions. Thus, Clara Collet, Labour Correspondent to the Board of Trade, submitted a memorandum to the Bryce Commission, investigating secondary education in the 1890s, which endorsed the principle of class-based educational provision. She argued strongly in favour of divided aims and touched on the theme of education versus instruction. This meant an emphasis on the cultivation of mental culture for middle-class girls, whereas 'any system of education for working girls should have as its object their training for the responsibilities of married life' (*British Parliamentary Papers*, Secondary Education, 1895 session, p. 380). To what extent her attitude was representative of women on the London School Board will be considered later in this article.

An analysis of the voting record of women Board members in the 1870s and early 1880s shows that Rosamond Davenport Hill and Alice Westlake were ready to concede the place of domestic economy in the curriculum. By contrast, Jane Chessar, Alice Cowell, Emily Davies, Elizabeth Garrett, Frances Hastings, Florence Fenwick Miller, Henrietta Muller, Elizabeth Surr and Helen Taylor all tried to limit this kind of training. After 1882, changes in government policy and the influence of Social Darwinistic thinking put female opponents on the defensive and they had difficulty in making their presence felt. However, the 1879 Board provides an interesting example of an oppositional alliance that crossed class and gender groupings. It included the two working men elected in the 1870s, the ex-Chartist and cabinet-maker Benjamin Lucraft and the trade unionist George Potter; as well as Florence Fenwick Miller, Henrietta Muller, Elizabeth Surr and Helen Taylor. These six stand out as the most persistent opponents of single-sex classes in cookery, arguing that the teaching was inappropriate to the realities of working-class life since the cooking was done on gas cookers that were quite beyond the reach of working-class housewives. George observed, 'the girls must be intended for service. Such knowledge would not be of much use to them in an artisan's home' (*School Board Chronicle*, 30 March 1878).

Cookery was a grant-aided subject when the Moderate, Frances Hastings, was first elected in 1882; three years later, she seconded Helen's unsuccessful motion to reduce the number of cookery classes (*School Board Chronicle*, 12 March 1885). She also attacked the time girls spent sewing. In her contribution to the debate on needlework, for instance, Frances argued that much of the practical instruction was unnecessary. She wanted the girls to receive 'a foundation of general knowledge' instead (*The Governess*, 17 November 1883, p. 138). Writing to Helen Taylor in March 1886, Elizabeth Surr expressed regret over her defeat at the polls:

> I am sorry Miss Hastings is off, and that she was not re-elected; but although she is upright and well-meaning she was decidedly harsh in her dealings with the poor so that they would not care to vote for her; and she is too honest to be supported by any of the parties.
>
> (E. Surr to H. Taylor, March 1886)

In terms of their impact on policy-making, the Independent women were always struggling against the odds but managed to score some victories. Thus, for example, Henrietta Muller 'sought and obtained a reduction in the number of stitches to the inch required in the schools' (*The Times*, 17 January 1906). Neither she nor Florence could see the necessity of this fine needlework and the teachers reported that it was damaging the girls' eyesight. By contrast, the more socially conservative party women supported and influenced these developments. In the late 1870s, Alice Westlake told female head teachers to reduce their workload by substituting cookery for classes in 'drawing and grammar' (*School Board Chronicle*, 3 March 1877). Her colleague Rosamond Davenport Hill also wanted to consolidate the teaching of practical subjects related directly to domestic work. By the early 1880s, Hill was promoted to the position of chair of the Cookery Sub-Committee and subsequently gave evidence to the Cross Commission investigating the effects and working of the Elementary Education Act (1870). When questioned as to whether any of the girls become cooks or domestic servants, she replied:

> We hope they do. I heard a little time ago that a girl had taken a place, and that her employer was quite delighted with her because she could cook the dinner while the family attended chapel on a Sunday morning.
>
> (*Royal Commission on Elementary Education (Cross) 1887*, evidence of Miss R. Davenport Hill, p. 712)

At the turn of the century, Ruth Homan used her position on the School Management Committee to debate the question of whether cookery should be taught to boys. Assisted by Emma Maitland, she mobilised support for a pilot scheme at the Bow Creek School in Poplar where she was manager. For a year the boys attended the cookery centre attached to the school and a copy of the Cookery Superintendent's report was sent to the Education Department, ironically referred to as the Board's 'upper house' by Florence Fenwick Miller. Significantly, the report notes the vocational aspects of the teaching, with its emphasis on naval fare and promises of employment at the seamen's home, and Ruth achieved a pyrrhic victory when the 1902 Elementary Education Code allowed for the instruction of boys in 'seaport towns' (*School Board Chronicle*, 3 March 1900; Bird, 1998, p. 127).

Women teachers

This discussion will focus on three issues that were crucial to the career development of London's women teachers: pay, promotion and opposition to married women's employment. Once again, the Independent women pursued a distinct policy agenda; the rest supported the party line. Florence Fenwick Miller has left a narrative account of the decision-making process, showing a trend towards policy formation by the School Management Committee. This was true of promotions to headships:

> The Scheme was to appoint the headmaster of a boys' school Head Teacher also of the girls in the same block of buildings. It was necessary by the laws of the Board that every Head Teachers' name should be submitted, on his or her appointment, to the full Board for confirmation but in the case of the appointment of the men over the girls' schools I found that it was being made a practice to simply pass the Master's appointment through the School Management Committee and not to send it up to the full Board for confirmation at all.
>
> ('An Uncommon Girlhood', GC/228/34)

Florence saw this as discriminatory. It certainly confirms Copelman's (1996, p. 50) suspicion that those in positions of power and authority were more concerned to establish a career ladder for men than for women. In 1876, the average salary of the head master of a boys' school was £305 while the average salary of an assistant was only £104. Florence argued that if this situation was allowed to continue, the practice would effectively deny women teachers opportunities for advancement beyond the post of assistant. So, she successfully moved that: 'No male teacher should in future be appointed to be the Head Master of a girls' school, without the special sanction of the Board being previously obtained' ('An Uncommon Girlhood', GC/228/34).

In February 1878, there was an attempt to ban the employment of married women elementary school teachers with 'rapidly increasing families'. This time Elizabeth Surr led the successful opposition, saying she 'feared this suggestion emanated from gentlemen who wished to introduce the thin end of the wedge for the ultimate exclusion of all female teachers from Board schools' (*School Board Chronicle*, 9 February 1878). The following year, she and Florence were frustrated in their attempt to overturn a proposal that the Board receive three months' notice of maternity leave from married women teachers. Elizabeth thought it 'indelicate'; the vice-chair retorted she could have 'opposed the proposal in committee instead of doing so openly and publicly before the Board and the press' (*School Board*

Chronicle, 15 November 1879). Gradually the regulations defining the position of married women teachers grew more stringent. By the 1880s, for example, those who took confinement leave had to arrange for their own replacement and pay them out of their own salary. Florence Fenwick Miller, Henrietta Muller, Elizabeth Surr and Helen Taylor opposed the changes; Rosamond Davenport Hill, Mary Richardson and Alice Westlake did not. Far from it. Alice Westlake led the attack on the employment of married women teachers when working in the School Management Committee and speaking in debate. In the winter of 1881, for instance, she seconded a committee resolution to bar married women teachers with children under 2 (*School Board Chronicle*, 26 November 1881; *The Governess*, June 1882, p. 122). The *School Board Chronicle* offered a blow-by-blow account of debate within the School Board. Press reports show the adversarial nature of School Board politics, as well as the concentration on aspects of women's personal lives. In one debate, Florence launched a personal attack on the character of her childless colleague Alice Westlake:

> ... she had been waiting in expectation that the lady who was largely responsible for this resolution would justify it. The resolution had been brought forward three times at the instance of that lady. She (Mrs Miller) was thankful that this Board was not composed entirely of married ladies without children... The true womanly instinct and feeling and sympathy for children did not arise in a woman until she had had children of her own in her arms... it was not for the Board to say that every teacher who married should become a household drudge instead of continuing to engage in intellectual work.
>
> (*School Board Chronicle*, 26 November 1881)

The personal animosity is evident and exceptional because Florence was one of only two women Board members who married whilst serving (the other was Elizabeth Garrett); and the only woman who gave birth during her period in office. There were nine women on the 1879 Board and they each articulate different dimensions of women's experience. Unlike Florence, Rosamond Davenport Hill, Frances Hastings, Henrietta Muller, Mary Richardson, Edith Simcox and Helen Taylor were single, Alice Westlake was married but childless, whilst Elizabeth Surr was married with two grown-up daughters and two small sons. Evidently, there was no correlation between personal biography and attitude to the employment of married woman. Attitude to party was a far more reliable guide. Even though they won the battle, Independents did not think they had won the war. Concern was expressed that the authority might yet attempt to dismiss married women and Florence and Helen helped launch the Metropolitan Board Mistresses' Association to support and protect women teachers (*The Governess*, June 1882, p. 122).

School attendance

The final example is used to show the extent to which specific policies impact on girls and boys in somewhat different ways, as well as to examine the question of who plays the majority role in the policy-making process. The significance of the women's role has been analysed in earlier work (Martin, 1991, 1999); here new source material is used to highlight the issue of legislative styles.

Local authorities prioritised the issue because the size of government grants, and until 1883, teachers' salaries, depended directly on average attendance levels.

However, many of the urban poor saw mass schooling as an intrusion into family life that reduced the household's earning capacity and imposed an extra burden in the shape of school fees. Then, as now, pupil absenteeism was a persistent problem. It also had a gender dimension. Girls' average attendance was consistently lower than the boys'; it was also more irregular because they often had to care for younger siblings. However, there was a tendency for girl absentees to be treated sympathetically, whereas boys were more likely to be defined as truants and dealt with severely. The ultimate sanction was committal to one of two types of corrective institutions. The first was a single-sex residential truant or industrial school. The second was a co-educational day industrial school provided for under the 1876 Education Act. Although the London School Board did not establish a day industrial school until 1895, it founded three residential schools in the 1870s, two more in the 1890s and a sixth in 1903. Five out of the six were for boys.

Further analysis shows that many women members prioritised this area of the Board's work. For example, on the 1876 Board, Helen Taylor promoted the establishment of babies' rooms as a way of encouraging the attendance of girls who were frequently kept home to 'mind baby'; in 1881 she and Elizabeth Surr persuaded the Board to press for government legislation to provide for the establishment of nursery schools and they were part of a deputation to the Education Department on the subject (*School Board Chronicle*, 14 April 1877; 24 February 1881). Henrietta Muller shared their anxiety over female attendance, and in August 1881 she unsuccessfully sought to encourage the girls by enabling them to qualify for a book prize on the strength of one, as opposed to two, complete attendance cards (*School Board Chronicle*, 4 August 1881). Social and cultural values were reflected in a tendency for the punitive aspects of Board policy to impact more heavily on boys. Thus, Home Office regulations refused to allow corporal punishment to be inflicted on industrial schoolgirls and Ruth Homan led the opposition to Athelstan Riley's campaign to change the rules in the mid-1890s. First elected in the Moderate election victory of 1891, he ardently supported the attempt to make religious instruction more denominational and Ruth Homan presumed the 'Rileyite floggers' wanted to 'thrash theology' into the girls. In a letter to the press she concluded, 'We know what the natural impulse of every manly, chivalrous Briton would be – and that is to birch the floggers' (Fawcett Library news cuttings, 'School Boards', London 1896–97). She also fought moves to reinstate the ritual of flogging boys as a punishment for being sent back to industrial school and in 1898 she joined forces with Honnor Morten in an attempt to ban the use of corporal punishment in the Board's reformatory institutions. There were eight women members of the 1897 Board, and aside from Emma Maitland, there was general agreement with Ruth that the punishments were too harsh. However, her proposal was successfully watered down by two male Progressives who thought the powers were necessary but recommended that the practice be carried out in private. Although Ruth Homan did not accomplish her objective, she did achieve recognition in the shape of promotion to vice-chair of the Industrial Schools Committee.

Twenty years earlier, Elizabeth Surr gained a high public profile through her membership of the School Board's Special Committee on Incorrigible Truants, which later became the Industrial Schools Committee. With the support of Florence Fenwick Miller and Helen Taylor she was largely responsible for drawing public attention to overexpenditure on the *Shaftesbury* training ship, as well as exposing the cruelties practised by the superintendents of the Board's first truant school and a voluntary industrial school for boys owned by the chair of the

Industrial Schools Committee, Thomas Scrutton. The debate over the *Shaftesbury* provides the clearest expression of gender issues because it sought to breach the male bastion of finance and public exposure (Dyhouse, 1987).

In 1878 the Board decided to refit a vessel for use as an industrial training ship with the aim of encouraging boys to develop a taste for life at sea, with lessons in seamanship and extra-curricular activities like gun, rifle and cutlass drill (London County Council *Report with regard to Industrial Schools*, 1870–1904, p. 53). However, the cost of the refit soon exceeded the original estimate and there were mutterings of discontent from the women's caucus on the 1876 Board, supported by Benjamin Lucraft. In October 1878 members authorised the expenditure of a further £6000, the Industrial Schools Committee having exhausted the £28,000 already voted. Three months later they voted a further £2000, despite the note of caution sounded by Elizabeth Surr and Helen Taylor. Not unreasonably, the two women recommended that they wait to see the findings of a Special Committee appointed to inquire into levels of expenditure on the *Shaftesbury*. In the face of growing public concern, Alice Westlake gave high priority to sustaining the com-mittee chair and defending party policy. An example of her role as a party loyalist is to be found in her behaviour as a standard-bearer of the party line at the next election. In a letter to the editor of *The Times*, Alice cast doubt on the veracity of Elizabeth Surr's information about Thomas Scrutton's expenditure on the refit. These two were the only female members of the Industrial Schools Committee and the day after, Elizabeth protested her colleague's intrusion into a difference between herself and the chair:

> I regret it lest the public might imagine that women on the School Board cannot work harmoniously together; therefore I deem it worth stating that nothing has disturbed the harmony with which two of my colleagues and myself have laboured, and that my behaviour to Mrs Westlake has always been courteous.
>
> (*The Times*, 26 November 1879)

Alice Westlake was a more conventional activist in the public sphere than Elizabeth, Florence or Helen. The more radical women were prepared to challenge institutional procedures in defence of a principle they believed in, and it was Florence Fenwick Miller who moved a vote of censure:

> It was not by my own design or desire that I took the leading place in this public duty. One of our Members, Mr Lovell, said to Mrs Surr that the women Members ought not to have taken the lead in censuring the Industrial Schools Committee on which she immediately compared him to Abimelech in the Bible. But she and I *had* to lead, simply because the men would not undertake the task of censure which appeared to us necessary.
>
> ('An Uncommon Girlhood', GC/228/34)

Ultimately, the strength of party discipline kept other members under control and the guilty parties clung on to their positions of authority on the Committee and the Board (*School Board Chronicle*, 22 March 1879). Significantly, Florence recalled that several who voted against her motion to dissolve the Committee only did so because Mr Scrutton was a prominent Liberal. Writing in the *Women's Penny Paper* a decade later, Henrietta Muller recalled Florence's power as a speaker in debate: 'I have seen men grow visibly pale, as she dissected – or rather vivisected – their halting arguments with her pitiless logic, leaving nothing but shreds behind' (*Women's Penny Paper*, 23 February 1889).

Conclusion

For a 34-year period women members of the London School Board drew upon and developed the ideology of domesticity to create empowering public identities. It has been argued (Yeo, 1998, p. 12) that British women 'stretched various family roles precisely to ratify their public activism'. Thus, Mary Bridges Adams mobilised her identity as a mother in electoral addresses, while Helen Taylor told the Metropolitan Board Mistresses' Association that she cared for the children 'from the point of view of a maiden aunt' (*The Governess*, June 1882, p. 122). On the same occasion Florence Fenwick Miller subverted the dominant ideas about femininity as domestic married motherhood to promote the work of married women teachers:

> I believed that mothers would be very likely to be the most efficient teachers, partly because the sympathy of young women is often dormant until they have children of their own, when they understand and sympathise better with all the little ones; and partly I urged, because the woman who is married and has made up her mind to continue her work is more settled in it, and less distracted by her personal emotions, than one who is still single.
>
> ('An Uncommon Girlhood', GC/228/34)

This quotation shows how elected women used the rhetoric of familial femininity to justify their political actions and to set forth an ideal for imitation in public life. They must have felt satisfaction at feeling a sense of power but the evidence suggests that there were tensions between those who gave high priority to their role as party representatives and those who challenged the direction of the policy agenda. Certainly, some female politicians preferred the quieter work in private committees while others liked speaking in debate and some gave greater priority to constituency matters. For instance, Eugenie Dibdin kept a low profile on the Board but Hugh Philpott (1904, p. 24), a contemporary chronicler of London education, was fulsome in his praise of her role as chair of the managers of the Drury Lane industrial school. Her daughter taught the girls to swim and she proved 'a most devoted and sympathetic friend, who knows every one' of the children 'by name and takes quite a motherly interest in them all'. But whatever activities they perceived as appropriate and whatever their political behaviour, the presence of women in local educational policy-making contested the idea that a woman's place is in the home and the case studies suggest that they secured a number of significant policy decisions.

Overall, school board politics provided some middle-class females with a position of authority and a position of fulfilment. These women were a powerful force in their local communities and the preceding discussion highlights a distinct and vocal minority who acted in a less institutionalised way. More competitive than the average woman, the youthful Florence Fenwick Miller found the environment of power scintillating. Her objective was 'to blaise the trail for women to follow along' and like the other women policy-makers, her presence made more than just a symbolic difference to the politics of education.

NOTES

1   The 29 women were Annie Besant, Mary Bridges Adams, Jane Chessar, Alice Cowell, Rosamond Davenport Hill, Emily Davies, Eugenie Dibdin, Margaret Dilke, Constance Elder, Margaret Eve, Elizabeth Garrett, Edith Glover, Frances Hastings, Ruth Homan, Susan Lawrence, Maude Lawrence, Emma Maitland, Ellen McKee, Hilda Miall-Smith, Florence Fenwick Miller, Honnor Morten, Henrietta Muller, Mary Richardson, Edith Simcox, Elizabeth Surr, Helen Taylor, Julia Augusta Webster, Alice Westlake and F.L. Wright.
2   With grateful acknowledgements to Carol Dyhouse for this reference. Archival references have been used, as the pagination of the original manuscript is inconsistent.
3   The nine women were Rosamond Davenport Hill, Florence Fenwick Miller, Henrietta Muller, Mary Richardson, Edith Simcox, Elizabeth Surr, Helen Taylor, Augusta Webster and Alice Westlake.

ARCHIVAL SOURCES

Fawcett Library, London
Newscuttings, 'School Boards', London 1896–97

London Metropolitan Archives
London County Council *Report on Industrial Schools*, 1870–1904
School Board Chronicle, 1870–1903
School Board for London, *Minutes*, 1870–1904

London School of Economics
Mill/Taylor Special Collection

Wellcome Trust Contemporary Medical Archives Centre, London
'An Uncommon Girlhood' by Mrs Florence Fenwick Miller

REFERENCES

Bird, E. (1991) 'To cook or to conjugate: gender and class in the adult curriculum 1865–1900 in Bristol, United Kingdom', *Gender and Education*, 3: 183–197.
Bird, E. (1998) ' "High class cookery": gender, status and domestic subjects, 1890–1930', *Gender and Education*, 10: 117–131.
Caine, B. (1997) *English Feminism 1780–1980* (Oxford, Oxford University Press).
Copelman, D.M. (1996) *London's Women Teachers: Gender, Class and Feminism, 1870–1930* (London, Routledge).
Davin, A. (1996) *Growing Up Poor. Home, School and Street in London, 1870–1914* (London, Rivers Oram Press).
Dolman, F. (January 1896) 'The lady members of the London School Board', *The Young Woman*, pp. 129–132 (London, Horace Marshall & Son).
Dyhouse, C. (1981) *Girls Growing Up in Late Victorian and Edwardian England* (London, Routledge & Kegan Paul).
Dyhouse, C. (1987) 'Miss Buss and Miss Beale: gender and authority in the history of education', in F. Hunt (ed.), *Lessons for Life. The Schooling of Girls and Women 1850–1950* (Oxford, Basil Blackwell).
Gomersall, M. (1994) 'Education for domesticity? A nineteenth-century perspective on girls' schooling and domesticity', *Gender and Education*, 6: 235–247.
Hollis, P. (1989) *Ladies Elect: Women in English Local Government, 1865–1914* (Oxford, Clarendon Press).
Hughes, M. (1992) ' "The Shrieking Sisterhood": women as educational policy-makers', *Gender and Education*, 4: 255–272.

Hunt, F. (1991) *Gender and Policy in English Education 1902–1944* (London, Harvester Wheatsheaf).

Koven, S. (1993) 'Borderlands: women, voluntary action, and child welfare in Britain, 1840–1914', in S. Koven and S. Michel (eds), *Mothers of a New World: Maternalist Politics and the Origins of Welfare States* (London, Routledge).

London County Council, *Report with regard to Industrial Schools*, 1870–1904.

Lovenduski, J. (1996) 'Sex, gender and British politics', in J. Lovenduski and P. Norris (eds), *Women in Politics* (Oxford, Oxford University Press).

Lovenduski, J. and Norris, P. (eds) (1996) *Women in Politics* (Oxford, Oxford University Press).

Martin, J. (1991) ' "Hard-headed and large-hearted": women and the industrial schools 1870–1885', *History of Education*, 20: 187–201.

Martin, J. (1993) 'Entering the public arena: the female members of the London School Board, 1870–1904', *History of Education*, 22: 225–240.

Martin, J. (1995) 'Fighting down the idea that the only place for women was home?', *History of Education*, 24: 277–292.

Martin, J. (1999) *Women and the Politics of Schooling in Victorian and Edwardian England* (Leicester, Leicester University Press).

Norris, P. (1996) 'Women Politicians: transforming Westminster?', in J. Lovenduski and P. Norris (eds), *Women in Politics* (Oxford, Oxford University Press).

Norris, P. and Lovenduski, J. (1995) *Political Recruitment: Gender, Race and Class in the British Parliament* (Oxford, Oxford University Press).

Philpott, H.B. (1904) *London at School* (London, T. Fisher Unwin).

Report of the Royal Commission on the Elementary Education Acts (1888) (Cross Report) (Report of the Commissioners with Minutes of Evidence, London, HMSO).

Royal Commission on Secondary Education (1895) (Bryce Commission) (Report of the Commissioners with Minutes of Evidence, London, HMSO).

Thane, P. (1993) 'Women in the British Labour Party and the construction of state welfare', in S. Koven and S. Michel (eds), *Mothers of a New World. Maternalist Politics and the Origins of Welfare States* (London, Routledge).

Turnbull, A. (1983) ' "So extremely like Parliament": the work of the women members of the London School Board, 1870–1904', in The London Feminist History Group (eds), *The Sexual Dynamics of History* (London, Pluto Press).

Turnbull, A. (1987) 'Learning her womanly work: the elementary school curriculum 1870–1914', in F. Hunt (ed.), *Lessons for Life: The Schooling of Girls and Women 1850–1950* (Oxford, Basil Blackwell).

Turnbull, A. (1994) 'An isolated missionary: the domestic subjects teacher in England, 1870–1914', *Women's History Review*, 3: 81–100.

Weiner, G. (1994) *Feminisms in Education* (Buckingham, Open University Press).

Yeo, E.J. (1998) (ed.) *Radical Femininity: Women's Self-representation in the Public Sphere* (Manchester, Manchester University Press).

PART V

SEXUALITY

FIFTEEN

TEACHERS AND ISSUES OF SEXUAL ORIENTATION

Gillian Squirrell

Source: 'Teachers and issues of sexual orientation',
Gender and Education, 1(1): 17–34, 1989.

Opening the debate

Although there has been a lot of press, parliamentary and public debate about the role of homosexuals in education, there still appears to be very little academic interest in this area of equal opportunities. There may be a number of reasons for this. Plummer, in *The Making of the Modern Homosexual*, writes of the stigma associated with any form of homosexual research:

> Since homosexuality in this culture remains largely taboo and subject to hostility and attack,... it is still possible for research into homosexuality to invite condemnation from colleagues, community and family. Anybody embarking upon such research should thus give serious consideration to being discreditable or discredited... Anybody entering this field may become 'guilty through contamination'.
>
> (Plummer, 1981, p. 227)

This perhaps explains some of the disinclination to work in this area. It may seem 'safer' to confine political perspective and interest to areas of gender and ethnicity, where perhaps there is less possible stigma and more respectability.

The year 1988 has seen the successful passages through Parliament of the much publicised Clause 28 of the Local Government Amendment Act. Although the Act purports to deal only with local authorities, preventing them from promoting homosexuality through the funding and licensing of local groups or through the purchase, production and promotion of educational and other materials, the effect has been much broader. Clause 28 has created a climate of nervousness in regard to the employment of known gay or lesbian staff. A nervousness is also found within the school context: in Avon, for example, a play with a homosexual scene was cancelled (*The Times*, 27.10.88). Terry Furlong at this year's National Association of English Teachers' Conference warned of a self-censorship in education, borne from fear (*The Times Educational Supplement*, 15.4.88). And the fear is not limited to schools. Publishers are also wary. For example, Manchester University Press halted the production of a research publication on homosexuality that was commissioned prior to Section 28 and stopped in response to the 1988 Act.

Simply, one could state that the reasons for the prejudices surrounding homosexuality lie in its supposed powers to corrupt, in both the physical and ideological senses (Newton and Risch, 1981). This year, through the agencies of press and parliamentary debate, perceived physical and ideological corruption have achieved great prominence, becoming extremely potent when coupled with the care and development of young people. Those fears, centring on physical corruption, arise from the belief that lesbians and gay men are predatory by nature, and that homosexuality can be identified with paedophilia (Galloway, 1983, p. 23). Such views are frequently expressed in the tabloid press and little is done to counter this misinformation. Indeed, through their actions the medical and legal professions have often added to the popular stereotypes. A powerful example is that of the precedent ruling of the Employment Appeal Tribunal (ETA) in April 1980 against John Saunders. The ETA upheld that it was reasonable to dismiss someone for homosexuality if they had contact with children. Hitherto, homosexuality has not been seen as an issue for dismissal. This ruling was taken against psychiatric advice that 'homosexuals were of no greater risk than heterosexuals' (McFadyen, 1980, p. 7).

Work by the NCCL has shown how strongly these prejudices and ignorances have gripped local authorities. One Yorkshire councillor wrote to the NCCL Survey Team: '... to suggest that homosexuals should be allowed to work with vulnerable children is appalling. I wonder would H. Samuels employ a kleptomaniac' (Ferris, 1977, p. 18). The potency of such prejudice shows itself in the findings of the Commission on Discrimination: 'those most likely to suffer dismissal from work are gay men who are employed in working with children' (Daly, 1981).

The second area in which homosexuality is supposedly vested with power is that of ideological corruption. It is this which has lain behind a number of recent political moves, such as Section 28. It was also the reason behind the Campaign for Normal Family Life which sought to quash Haringey Council's attempts to 'indoctrinate them [children] into homosexuality from the age of three upwards'. It therefore comes as no surprise that Rhodes Boyson, when speaking of the amendment to the 1986 Local Government Act, should state, 'any school which taught that homosexual and heterosexual relations were equally acceptable was embracing the death of society' (ACE, 1986, p. 12).

The press, not to be excluded, has engaged in the creation of a controversy over a children's picturebook *Jenny Lives with Martin and Eric* (Bosche, 1983), a rather unreadable text which describes a weekend in the life of Jenny, her father and his lover – a weekend filled with mundane activities of potato peeling and doing the washing. Billed as a 'REAL fairy story' by *The Sun*, the book was portrayed as a tool to pervert 6–8-year-olds' sexual development. Between the Scylla of press-hyped abuse and the Charybdis of parliamentary discussion, it is hardly surprising that homosexuality appears to be a fraught and uncongenial area for research.

A third area meriting discussion is that of heterosexism, which can be defined as a belief in the universality of heterosexuality (Egerton *et al.*, 1986). This may mean that rather than acting from homophobia or fear of guilt by association, educational researchers and teacher trainers simply fail to mention homosexuality because they are quite unaware of its existence. This is hardly surprising given the fact that gays and lesbians in real life are not an identifiable group according to stereotyped images (Warren, 1984). The existing sociological literature on gays and lesbians carries sections on 'passing' (Warren, 1974; Weinberg and Williams, 1974; Harry and DeVall, 1978), a phrase covering the various strategies used deliberately to hide sexual orientation, to protect employment and prevent victimisation (McFadyen, 1980). The continued need for such strategies and the prevalence of crude stereotypes only encourages heterosexism.

Issues of gender

The issue of invisibility takes on further dimensions when considering lesbians. Within the tradition of homosexual research little attention is devoted to women. Faraday suggests that this is: 'a reflection of the neglect or denial of women in the broader field of sociology...' She continues:

> Suggested reasons for the interest paid to gay men tend to centre on their greater visibility through their involvement in public and impersonal sex, and the consequent problems this poses for them. The fact that their greater visibility makes them easier to recruit for research purposes...that research funding bodies tend to be more interested in the 'problem' of gay men...
>
> (1981, p. 114)

The invisibility of lesbians is also evident in parliamentary discussions about homosexuality. In a recent House of Lords debate, Lord Halsbury makes it clear that he feels that homosexuality is a male issue:

> I was referring to male homosexuals. I do not think that lesbians were [sic] a problem. They do not molest little girls. They do not indulge in disgusting and unnatural practices like buggery. They are not wildly promiscuous and do not spread venereal disease. It is part of the softening propaganda that lesbians and gays are nearly always referred to in that order. The relatively harmless lesbian leads on to the viscious gay.

Within the gay community a recent, self-appointed spokesman on sexuality and education has sought to offer his explanations (Stafford, 1988a,b); however, he too ignores the position of lesbian teachers and pupils, seeing them as their gay male counterpart. The following data would suggest this position to be untenable.

Insights from the literature to date

From what has been said so far it will be obvious that there has been little research on which I can draw. This has meant that in writing this paper there have been very few 'orthodox' sources to call upon. The existing literature offers three main foci: curriculum development largely within English, PSE and RE (Patrick, 1983; Slayton and Vogel, 1986); growing up gay and the role of school (Heron, 1983; Trenchard and Warren, 1984; Warren, 1984; Plummer, 1986); and some work on gay and lesbian teachers (Leicester City NUT, 1987; London Gay Teachers Group, 1987). The materials produced on gay and lesbian teachers have often been written by teachers themselves and directed towards a minority audience. They have tended to be 'campaign' documents; since they are largely autobiographical, they perhaps lack breadth, and since they are often about gay males they tend to emphasise 'coming out'. Considering the preceding section on gender this may not be surprising. However, one can speculate about the implications of recommendations for 'coming out'. 'Coming out' may be difficult for those teachers isolated from other gay and lesbian teachers. It may also be more difficult for lesbian teachers who would have to confront both the phallocentric and patriarchal environment of school. Minson, in a short article on John Warburton, explores the political consequences of coming out for both lesbians and gay males. Such a move:

> ...fails to tap the material roots of homosexual oppression, which lie in capitalist and, or patriarchal, economic and political structures. Hence, while it may secure some legal concessions under a liberal regime, it fails to challenge the domination of a heterosexist ideology and power structure which will only tolerate homosexuality on the grounds that it retain its deviant status.
>
> (1981, p. 19)

Furthermore, Minson suggests that coming out makes homosexuality the defining characteristics of the person which thus consolidates the assumptions made by those hostile to homosexuality, for example, it gives an employer a justification for giving a 'known' homosexual the sack.

The teachers

In order to find out about the effects of a differing sexual orientation on the daily lives of teachers in staffrooms and classrooms, contact with the teachers themselves obviously had to be made. But there was some difficulty in gaining access. Advertisements were placed in some educational newspapers – but there were few responses. The reasons for this are clearly articulated in this anonymous letter:

> Dear Sir/Madam,
> I was interested to read your ad in the TES. I wish you success with your endeavours and I hope that you will treat the subject sympathetically as you stated in your ad.
> However I wonder how representative your sample will be. Through no fault of your own, I feel that those who will reply to your ad may not be typical – whatever typical is.
> Basically what I'm trying to point out is that we do not all teach in Brent. The majority of us are professionally 'in the closet' and fully intend to remain that way. The risk of doing otherwise is too great.
> In this part of Scotland, there are many of us and most of those whom I know are in promoted positions. Here we cannot be sacked for being gay. Under Section 99, we could only be sacked for conviction of a sexual nature...Being open is impossible because any whiff of being gay would be the end of promotion prospects. There is no way that a known gay would be promoted. You could never prove, of course, that this was the reason for not being promoted. Yet it would be the case.

If any rumour of being gay was spread among the parents, life in school would be unbearable. Transfer would be ineffective as the grapevine works faster than that. So we keep a low profile. We may be suspected of being gay but there is a world of difference between suspect and know. Thus it is unlikely that a large section of gay teachers would be inclined to respond to your ad. I would like to help you but I cannot take the risk. Thus this will not be signed and the address no more specific than the postmark!

Since the advertisements yielded a low response, I employed the most commonly used method in this type of research, that of 'word of mouth', leaving the power in the respondents' hands to vet and recommend the research. It was a slow process which led to collecting the life stories of some 30 teachers over the past academic year. Interestingly enough I found it easier to gather male than female teachers, although finally there were equal numbers of men and women.

The interviewees represented a spread of ages, lengths of teaching experience, teaching subject and ages taught. All were teaching outside London.

The interviews themselves lasted anything from one to four hours. I had a prepared series of question areas which covered training and teaching careers, career decisions, personal biographies, the overlaps of sexuality and the school, relationships with colleagues and pupils, and the role of the unions, LEA, governors and school hierarchies in supporting gay and lesbian teachers and pupils.

The interviews covered all of these areas, although interest and personal need sometimes dictated the emphasis given to certain issues. Given assurances of confidentiality and the fact that I usually arrived having been introduced by someone else, I was only once refused permission to tape-record the interview.

The interviews

The interview data offer a number of insights into teachers' daily experiences of school – relations with colleagues and pupils, thoughts about promotions, their teaching materials and issues of gender. It offers understandings of the ways in which these teachers perceive their homosexuality and how consciousness of this impinges on their daily teaching. This was stated in a speech at last year's NUT conference: 'People like me have to lie and be deliberately vague about every aspect of their private lives' (*The Guardian*, 5.4.88). The teacher spoke of having to give 'whispered' accounts of her weekends. Presumably she had to whisper through fear of causing offence to some colleagues and soliciting abuse or hostility from others. A number of the interviewees spoke of their own self-censorship, a few of the reasons for which are given later. However, before rehearsing some of these reasons, if it significant to consider the experiences of Johnson and Whitman (1985) who, writing of their heterosexism awareness courses, comment that:

It is significant that the sessions emphasising the problems experienced by lesbian and gay students and staff were better received than those that encouraged heterosexual staff to see their own sexuality as political and to acknowledge the privilege which it gives them.

(1985, p. 17)

Perhaps this is a danger to consider while reading the following pages?

Teachers suggested a number of possible consequences, both professional and personal, of allowing their sexuality to become common knowledge. The most obvious consequence was a loss of job security. A recent and well-known case of a sexuality related dismissal is that of Austin Allen in Bradford. Dismissed and reinstated twice, his sexuality became common knowledge following local and national media coverage. Such public accounts, sensational headlines ('Lesbian love lesson Miss quits', *Sun*, 3.7.87; 'Gay staff face selective job ban', *The Times Educational Supplement*, 23.11.84) and a flourishing mythology in gay and lesbian fiction (Black, 1984; Ireland, 1984; Forrest, 1987) do little to offer a sense of employment security. Many of the interviewees were able to recount tales of dismissals and victimisation. However apocryphal this oral tradition, there was felt to be little foundation for belief in those equal opportunities policies which covered sexual orientation: 'they can still get you out if they want to...it would be nearly impossible for a teacher not to do anything wrong'. It would appear that teachers in further education are also not immune: 'A lesbian lecturer who mentioned Section 28 during her work (a lecture on art and politics)...has learnt that the college concerned has promised she will never work there again' (*Pink Paper*, 19.5.88).

At a time of job scarcity, the prevalence of fixed-term contracts and Section 28, a recent and as yet untested piece of legislation, many teachers may well not wish to endanger their professional and economic security.

Closely allied with fears for job security are risks to promotion prospects and good references: 'Head teachers are reputed to get on the phone to one another. Heaven knows what wouldn't have been said. I can't prove it [as a reason for not getting a job] but I wouldn't be at all surprised'. Although a successful head of department, another teacher was warned that he may go no further:

> He [the deputy head] has coded conversations with me on the necessity for a conventional family life to achieve deputy headships and headships. He jokingly suggested that a single man shouldn't get a headship otherwise... They're coded ways of spelling out truths to me – there will be difficulties in getting those kind of jobs.

Another said:

> Three people in the English department asked if I was gay – quite jocularly. I denied it. I was on probation and felt very much on probation. I knew that I didn't want to stay there so I was worried that I might not get a good reference.

Others spoke of the fear of being discredited if their sexuality were known about, again comments spanned primary to tertiary sectors:

> If it got round the sixth form and to colleagues, it might not undermine my role as advisor to the sixths, but there would certainly be a general prejudice against the value of the rest of my judgement.
> Once labelled you get in a box and don't get taken seriously.

The same woman also said that she felt if she criticised the WEA decision not to allow her to run a day workshop on sexuality, then her future employability with them might suffer: 'Homosexuality puts into question all your other work. It makes it invalid and you don't get taken seriously. A deviant, a nut-case'.

The fears for reputation and competence proved to be well grounded for one primary school deputy speaking of his career: 'I've been in teaching for 17 years, 15 are logged up as very successful. Now the last two are known as a disaster. If people say it long enough then it'll stick'. He was in fact the victim of the most recent manifestation of homophobia, that of the AIDS hysteria. Having been revealed as a homosexual during a protracted period of absence from school, he found that on his return he was the brunt of colleagues' fears about AIDS and that he was precluded from effectively discharging his duties as a deputy head. The head refused to work with him and tried to retain a supply teacher for his class once he was back in school, offering him only withdrawal teaching in the cloakrooms. The technician was told not to produce the materials that he had ordered. In the following academic year he was moved to the classroom farthest from the head's office, so that on the rounds of the school the head would never meet him. His pupils were victimised, not being involved in some whole-school treats and being overlooked by the head when it came to school trips and sports events. The man further suffered at a personal level: four teachers would regularly leave the staffroom when he entered and he was forced to take lunch on his own. Possibly most damaging to his position with parents and pupils was that, prior to his return to school, the supply teacher covering his class refused to do so until the room had been 'scrubbed out'.

His experiences are not unique. The London Gay Teachers Group produced the pamphlet, *AIDS Hysteria*, in an attempt to disseminate information and debunk prejudice:

> This media coverage is helping to justify the discrimination and harassment of lesbians and gays. In the education system as in other areas people are refusing to work with or provide services for women or men who are openly lesbian or gays. For example, in one London school two openly gay teachers have been ostracised with colleagues refusing to use the same toilets or even coffee mugs. Teachers who are, or are suspected of being gay are suffering increased harassment from both pupils and colleagues.
>
> (London Gay Teachers Group, 1985, p. 1)

Promotion, job insecurity and victimisation are some of the tangible consequences these teachers suffered as a result of any openness about their sexuality. Not surprisingly, the interviewees decided to obscure their sexual orientation as much as possible in the staffroom and classroom.

Relationships with colleagues

A number of the teachers refrained from telling colleagues about their personal lives which, given the highly interactive nature of staffrooms, was felt to produce unnecessary stress: 'It's a strain being anti-social when you're a social person. And they eek it out of you anyway: with questions: Where do you live? Do you live on your own?' There were a number of accounts of misinformation or the giving of partial information and indeed simple lying:

> When they get too close I just steer the conversation away.
> I haven't told too many barefaced lies. I'm just economic with the truth.
> I hold back, just keep acquaintances superficial.
> I concentrate on being neutral, on not letting certain conversations develop.

There was felt to be a certain unpleasantness in this: 'It takes something out of the working day not being able to be yourself'. Worse perhaps was the feeling that one woman teacher described of being totally misunderstood: 'I feel that I'm only able to talk about my dog or rows with my parents – no wonder they think that I'm so young. They think I've not had a relationship with anybody since I arrived here'. The real significance of feeling unable to 'tell the truth' arose when this woman teacher decided to leave the school, in order to move away with her lover. Colleagues questioned and countered her decision: 'I don't want them necessarily to know... but I don't want them to think that I'm mad. They're incredulous that I'm leaving. People don't unless they go for a scale point or...'. Presumably she was going to say 'get married'. The feeling of being unable to talk was expressed by a number of teachers. One man said he was not sure if he would have wanted to talk to any of his workmates even if he had been heterosexual, but 'the possibility is not there if you are gay'.

This seems to have been especially significant at times when relationships were undergoing periods of change, when heterosexual colleagues might perhaps have expected some understanding. The impossibility of talking about lesbian or gay private lives in the staffroom led one lesbian teacher into the unenviable position of having to overhear colleagues talking about her new relationship with a colleague's ex-wife: ' "She's left him for another woman..." I could have died a thousand deaths – I felt sure that they knew it was me'. A necessary part of evading questions was lying. One male teacher remarked, 'You become tremendously good at lying'. There was the subterfuge of the invented girlfriend miles away: 'I'd always say that I was going to Liverpool to see my girlfriend. I knew that a girl I had been friendly with at college had gone there'.

There must have been stress in maintaining such an invention, just as there would be in the duplicity of transposing the sex of a partner or referring to one's lover as 'friends':

> That summer M. and I went to Peru and Bolivia. It was a big trip. I had to say I went with 'some friends'. 'Oh you must bring in the photographs'. Can you imagine the slide show!
> You can't say 'we'. It's hopeless. It's, 'I did this', 'I did that' or 'some friends'.

A number spoke of simply trying to become invisible when it came to staff events:

> I became very adept at refusing invitations. That way I wouldn't have to have people back.
> There is a strong staff association I never get involved with that. Those things are always geared around couples.
> (Heterosexual of course)

Lying to 'put people off the scent' could also involve clothing:

> I always wear a skirt it makes me feel safe.
> I was dressing so that I thought I looked the part, so that people wouldn't know what a mess I was in.
> I don't dress any differently, but I can get away with it, the young trendy English teacher.

I was dressing straight and constantly consciousness of suppressing a crucial part of my lifestyle, of myself, me...Wearing what I want to wear has brought together two identities...I tried to keep them separate – this sounds silly, by having a different costume for each.

A further useful device was that of quite simply not debunking colleagues' assumptions of the universality of heterosexuality: 'But they'd say I couldn't be a lesbian because I've got two children.' 'They think that I'm alright because I was married and I've got a child. I just share a house with a man.'

Closer relationships with colleagues

Every teacher mentioned one or more ways of disguising their sexuality and lifestyle to the majority of their colleagues. There were, however, instances where the interviewees mentioned closer relationships with colleagues and the presence of other gay and lesbian teachers on the school's staff. However, the very fact that a teacher may suspect that a colleague was gay or lesbian did not naturally lead to a closer relationship. There was a fear of not being totally sure of another's sexuality and fears that self-disclosure might lead to others finding out. Additionally there were a number of factors that preclude a sharing of experience just as there might be between any colleagues – status and length of teaching at the school and the subject taught:

> The other gay teacher was suggesting that we have some discussions on gay life – a gay studies. I had very little to do with it I don't know if it went on. I had just started out in teaching I was keen to get myself established I didn't want to become involved in his plans for what sounded like a 'gay studies'.

Such a programme would have made his sexuality obvious to the rest of his colleagues and would he felt, have set him apart from the task of teaching his subject. In cases where gay and lesbian teachers did come together in the school it was usually in response to an external need, to work on an equal opportunities policy for school or union rather than simply for mutual support. There were instances where homosexual and heterosexual colleagues became close when working on issues of anti-gay prejudice:

> 'Stereotypes' – it was a package for the fifth years. It requires kids to ask questions. We didn't duck it. I don't think that I could have done it without Kate. It's difficult to initiate something like that, I went in a committed supporter of it knowing that I wasn't standing on my own...If I had been head of department I rather doubt that it would have been done. The head of department would have to answer for it – to parents, governors.

In talking to a gay teacher and his heterosexual union representative about their initiatives on gay and lesbian rights in school, they shared an awareness of their differing positions of safety. The gay teacher made the following observation:

> At the end of it, it's just another union issue. He [the rep] can walk off and he's still safe being heterosexual. He can always count on that even if he is seen as a troublemaker. I'm left out on my own.

Having spent so much time thinking about the strategies for hiding it is important to note that a number of teachers said that with the passing of time and familiarity with a school that there were fewer problems than may have occurred at the outset of their careers. It was felt that if colleagues had once speculated they no longer did so, and that the possibilities of being confronted had diminished. One commented, 'the only thing left is to say it'. That, however, was something he could never do, or polite ignorance would vanish. In plumping for polite non-comment the problem remained – 'I don't like feeling negated'.

Issues of gender in relationships with colleagues

Faraday (1981) stresses that lesbians should not be seen simply as the counterpart of the male homosexual, 'it is essential that notions of the lesbian are reconceptualised within the context of her oppressed social position as a woman and not as "female homosexual"' (Faraday, 1981, p. 112).

It is clear from the data that there were a significant number of differences between the experiences of the lesbians and the gay males who made up this sample group. A most obvious one was promotion, thereby supporting Faraday in her claim that lesbians share a common situation with other women. Certainly all women would be debarred from the 'old boy' network, the importance of which is well documented. The situation for a lesbian feminist may be worsened by the fact that she refuses to play the usual female role of bolstering male teachers or being compliant. This rejection of the male's role and power might put lesbians beyond the pale: 'How can I trust the hierarchy to support me when I share with that hierarchy no common language or experience? If men are not the center of my world, then why am I coming to them for help?' (Anon., 1984, p. 3).

For lesbian feminists there may be further complications, in that they may fear that discovery of their sexuality may discredit their political beliefs. A black lesbian teacher wrote that many staff: 'believe that any woman who asserts herself, is too aggressive and therefore must be a lesbian. The fact that a woman is a lesbian explains her views on any subject' (Hope, 1987, p. 17). This may discourage a high political profile; thus one teacher wrote:

> In any school based meeting around anti-sexist or anti-racist issues I worry in case opening my mouth will discredit the very cause I am supporting. Of course she's bound to speak up and of course I do.
>
> (Anon., 1984, p. 3)

The conflation of feminism with lesbianism and the resulting fears of the ideological castration of boys is something that has gripped both the imagination of the media and a number of employers (Hemmings, 1980; Taylor, 1986). This is something which does not arise with male gay teachers.

Within the staffroom as a whole there are a number of other differences between gay and lesbian teachers. It is possible that lesbians have to suffer more sexual harassment than their gay colleagues, both on the grounds of their sexual orientation and in their role as women (Taylor, 1986). A number of gay teachers also described the use of female colleagues as 'cover' or camouflage. They were also invested with the role of confidant, 'It helped that she was a woman', and are described as making more congenial lunch-time companions than some male members of staff.

It is likely that lesbian teachers cannot make use of male teachers in quite the same way. They might also face more chance of rejection than their gay male colleagues from women teachers who do not want to be thought 'one of those'. A lesbian teacher wrote of the problems she faced in a woman teachers' support group which she had helped set up:

> and then I found it difficult to use this group for support in my specific harassment as a lesbian – in case it frightened off women who had already found it difficult to come to an 'only-women' meeting.
>
> (Anon., 1984, p. 3; see also McDaniel, 1985)

The effects of heterosexism and homophobia amongst colleagues and hierarchy

In talking about the reasons and the ways to obscure their sexuality the interviewees also spoke of some of the personal effects of being hidden. A number mentioned the guilt that they felt when they did not 'bear witness', when they ignored the homophobic jokes or conversation:

> Every time that I don't do it it makes it harder for everyone else.
> Sometimes I just don't have the energy to take them on and I get up and walk out of the staffroom. Then I feel really bad about not having bothered.

In keeping their private lives hidden there was a stress between their private and public selves, which could affect personal relationships:

> I said that I did not have a relationship, called her my lodger. The more I pretended that I did not have a relationship the more I felt that I had to live up to that.
> When I started teaching I was in the beginnings of a relationship with another man. The strain of starting teaching and keeping the teacher part of me and the gay man separate soon took its toll and I fell back on the tactic of throwing myself totally into my work. In fact after a year I went even further and tried to make a go of a relationship with a woman rather than come to terms with myself.
> I always answered the phone if it could be somebody from school. I didn't like being seen around with my boyfriend in case people 'sussed' it out. This led to arguments, 'Was I ashamed of him?'
>
> (Leicester NUT, 1987, p. 92)

In trying to orchestrate their personal and professional lives and the lack of time, fears of colleagues' heterosexual and homophobia led some teachers into a tortured relationship with their sexuality. One man described his distancing strategies as: 'living a twilight existence. Just going out to clubs in the evening and keeping it at that, at a distance'. Another went 'cottaging' (impersonal sex in public toilets): 'then I used to try and pretend it was a binge, that it wasn't me. Then I'd throw myself back into work'.

These conflicts might eventually be suppressed by a denial of sexuality. One teacher described the behaviour of two of his gay acquaintances as: 'Giving up an earlier gay existence and throwing everything into career and promotions or isolating oneself and living in a state of fear that something might eventually be said.' Others spoke of the pressure to have heterosexual relationships. Three found that in embarking on such relationships there was a tremendous release in having a personal life that could be openly acknowledged:

> It was curiously liberating having a boyfriend for a bit, normal again, telling my dearest friend at school all about dear Graham.
>   At school there was an extraordinary feeling of exhilaration and relief. I felt I could shout, 'It's okay, I'm like the rest of you'.

The possibility of being found out influenced some teachers' decisions to adopt an insurance policy:

> being in the union certainly was…a factor involved in doing the union stuff was that they would find it difficult not to back up one of their officials. I deliberately set out to make myself more secure.
>   So I joined the governing body as a teacher-governor. I wouldn't do it if I didn't think that I had something to contribute.

However, some decided to leave teaching rather than run risks. One former deputy commented:

> I was getting more and more involved in things and I thought it wouldn't be long before someone found out. I wanted to leave on my own terms, not be pushed out. I couldn't stand the conflicts for much longer.

Others may decide denial to be their best policy if they were challenged: 'I'd deny it, lie through my teeth. Anything rather than let it be known. I'd hush it up'. One is forced to consider what personal cost might lie in living with this self-knowledge.

Relationships in the classroom

The interview data suggest that there are a number of similarities in the ways that these teachers behaved to colleagues and pupils. Towards both there was felt to be a need for great discretion, arising from the anticipated consequences of homophobia and heterosexism – fears for job security and fears of hostility. This discretion was in marked contrast with much that has been recently suggested in parliament and in the press. In one exceptional case, a middle school teacher spoke of a child in her class undergoing a custody case between the father and lesbian mother:

> It would be the most awful thing for him because it would have to be a secret otherwise I would be worried that the other children would find out. Having a terrible secret and a mum the same wouldn't be any good for him.

A similar concern for the role of the teacher was exhibited by a further-education art teacher who, in speaking of his subject, described the confidences and closeness it might engender:

> It's the kind of subject that they have to build up a lot of confidence in you and relax. They open up a lot to me. They'll come and chat a lot. They work individually and some will stay late or work at lunch times. I'll talk loosely about myself. I draw the line at what I tell them. Sometimes I'll chip into their conversation.

This contrasts with what he later said of his relations with staff: 'At the lunch table I will hold out for what I believe in. I'll show them the light'.

The London Gay Teenage Group Survey suggested that homosexuality was rarely if ever mentioned as part of the curriculum and where it was it was likely to be negative. The teachers' comments suggested this to be the case. They expressed real difficulties in dealing with abuse and prejudicial comments in class. 'Possibly I feel a little more awkward because I'm more involved'. 'If I hadn't been gay then I would have been able to say something'.

Some teachers also suggested that there were some dilemmas in dealing with the issues as they arose as part of the curriculum:

> The thing I find it really impossible to talk about is homosexuality. I feel really bad about that – a failure...When it comes up in Shakespeare's sonnets or Forster I'm unable to think of anything sensible to say – it's a psychological thing – no matter how good my intentions. I feel in a false position about that taking an aloof pseudo-liberal stance...I suppose on most subjects I hold strong opinions but I can stand it if they disagree, but if they attacked homosexuality it would strike at the roots of my character and set up a lot of conflicts for me.
>
> One of the topics I was always careful to include was homosexuality and invariably this was the set of lessons which more than any other I grew to dread and which made me doubt my ability as a teacher...It seemed to breed a whole range of explosive emotions from bewilderment, through distaste to sheer naked hatred...'cut their balls off' 'send them to the gas chamber' and always the opportunity was taken for a cheap gibe a joke a good laugh...Certainly, a dogmatic stance on sexual morality would have been easier for me than the questioning, exploring attitudes I tried to foster...
>
> (Leicester NUT, 1987, p. 56)

As with their colleagues, teachers had to deal with some of the pupils' personal comments and questions; there were a number of strategies which did not involve 'telling the truth':

> Boyfriends? (I say) I've had hundreds.
> When they say things I just wink and they keep guessing.
> I ask them (irrespective of their sex) if they're going to make me an offer. That usually gets them so embarrassed that we just get back to the lesson.

The younger teachers are especially prey to the pupils' questioning: 'Pupils feel that they can ask a lot more, can go further with a younger teacher than an older. It is more of a challenge to their discipline'. As with colleagues, pupils' assumptions are used against them: 'Because I'm young they assume that I'm having affairs with all the young female members of staff'.

The issue of gender in the classroom

Gender figures in relationships with pupils just as it does with colleagues. Delamont (1983) describes the ways in which pupils categorise staff according to their potential or actual marital status. She argues that the spinster teacher is more likely to be stigmatised by pupils and held to a certain role in class. One woman who left teaching altogether commented: 'I am glad that I left when I did I wouldn't have wanted to be the archetypal spinster teacher. As a woman, as you get older, I think you get more vulnerable to pupils' comments and questions'. Following social norms, pupils appear more likely to evaluate their female teachers' attractiveness and sexuality than that of their male teachers. A lesbian teacher wrote: 'In most kids eyes, being a lesbian means being unattractive, desperate and unable to get a man' (Hope, 1987, p. 16).

Given such a negative perception, it may lead lesbian feminists to moderate their politics for fear of bringing them into discredit. Roanna Hibbert, writing about her experience as a visitor to school, offers useful reflections on this:

> Would an announcement of my non-heterosexuality have done something to reinforce the feminism which I was trying to bring to their attention?...But I could easily have sent the boys off chasing lesbians. I can imagine my chair scraper in School One, consumed by heterosexual aggression, rising and shouting to the rest of the room that he was having to listen to a fucking dyke. How would the gum-chewing girls have responded to that? Would their femaleness have been reinforced? Or would they have felt threatened?
>
> (1987, p. 24)

Possibly too the fear of the popular conflation of feminism with lesbian and thus the possibility of being found out would militate against some lesbians talking about feminism. It is possible that these fears decrease with experience in the classroom. One feminist of 13 years' experience said: 'I don't let any instances of sexism go passed'. Part of this may be that boys heckle younger teachers and especially female teachers more. Again the fear of discovery might well prevent the lesbian teacher from taking a stronger line with sexual harassment and instances of sexism.

The effects of the classroom

A number of teachers spoke of the sense of failure they felt in not being able to provide positive role models for pupils.

> I'm very concerned at the prejudice that the kids feel from the popular media, etc. If they were aware that you're gay, if you could be open then you could be a positive role model so they might reconsider other misconceptions, question other things. But you're inhibited from doing this.

There were also feelings of dishonesty at having to lie to pupils: 'With the sixth form that you get to know well, there is always an unnecessary sort of distance.' One young teacher at the outset of his career wrote of the dilemmas he was facing. He wanted to teach, he did not want to lie nor to be a martyr nor have to face abuse from his pupils such as, 'backs to the wall, boys'. He wrote:

> ...nevertheless at the outset I decided that I was not going to deny my gayness if challenged. I found myself in a paradoxical situation. On the one hand I revolted against leading a double life, cultivating a public persona to hide my true one. On the other hand I knew that my survival might necessitate some compromise in that direction.

In thinking about the possible repercussions of colleagues' homophobia, some teachers noted the effects that it had on their daily activities:

> I had to cover a games lesson It was awful having to got in the girls' changing room.
>   No one thinks about the problems that I have going into the boys' toilets to stop them from smoking.

It is impossible to calculate the effect on teachers of hearing prejudicial comments and being able to do little about it.

> I get frustrated and angry. It's not simply anti-gay comments. It's not their fault. The silliness that they are fed with from the press and their parents. I say that people have a right to live life. I make a statement against prejudice of any sort. It is sometimes possible to get an exchange. Kids have got more conscious of it [homosexuality]. The last 6–7 years...there's been a lot on the television. You only have to find gay in a poem and they fall about laughing.

Conclusion

It is hoped that the inclusion of this paper in an academic journal will be more that a tokenistic acknowledgement of the existence of this difficult area within educational research and educational practice. In particular, I want to encourage dialogue. It is hoped that in looking at a number of teachers so regularly ignored and thus negated in educational writing, some of the roots of prejudice and fear surrounding them will have come to light. It is clear from the teachers interviewed for my research that, far from engaging in widespread ideological corruption of the young, awareness of colleagues' and pupils' heterosexism and homophobia act as powerful inhibitors to discussing the issue of sexual orientation and to challenging bigotry.

There were clearly a number of differences in the experiences of lesbian and gay teachers. Lesbians were liable to harassment for both their sexuality and their gender. Within this small sample they were less likely to have achieved promotion and so had to do without that protection which authority sometimes invests. A number of lesbian feminists commented that they felt inhibited from discussing their political perspectives, both for fear of discrediting their politics and from a more personal fear of making themselves more obvious.

Age was also significant. Younger gay and lesbian teachers appeared to have a more difficult time, partly as a function of age and experience and partly because pupils were more likely to speculate about their sexuality and sexual partners.

The anticipated heterosexism and homophobia of colleagues and pupils led to many of the teachers adopting disguises or at the very least omitting to tell all but very few colleagues that they were not heterosexual. It is not possible to calculate the effects of such near daily depredations against the self.

It is to be remembered that this has been written from the responses of a small number of gay and lesbian teachers. The data are clearly very powerful and the area a fruitful one for further study and discussion. All but fleeting reference has been made to a number of important areas: curriculum development, role shift and forced conformity, the role of heterosexual colleagues, the role of government and censorship, control of sex education and the pervasiveness of heterosexism and homophobia in education. In addition to further research, it is clear that there is an urgent need for an awareness of heterosexism and homophobia to be incorporated into initial and in-service training.

Acknowledgement

For Helen and also for Neil, who have shared living this with me.

REFERENCES

Ace (1986) *Advisory Centre for Education Bulletin*, July/August, 12, p. 1.
Anon. (1984) 'Miss is a lesbian', *Teaching London Kids*, 23: 2–4.
Baker, M. (1984) *Gays and Education*, unpublished PGCE dissertation.
Black, J. (1985) *Extra Credit* (Boston, MA, Alyson Publications).
Bosche, S. (1983) *Jenny Lives with Martin and Eric* (London, Gay Men's Press).
Daly, M. (1981) *What About the Gay Workers?* (London, CHE).
Delamont, S. (1983) *Interaction in the Classroom* (London, Methuen).
DES (1987) *Circular 11/87, Sex Education in Schools* (London, DES).
Egerton, J. *et al.* (1986) *Danger Heterosexism at Work* (London, GLC).
Faraday, A. (1981) 'Liberating lesbian research', in K. Plummer (ed.), *The Making of the Modern Homosexual* (London, Hutchinson).
Ferris, D. (1977) *Social Work Survey* (London, NCCL).
Forrest, K. (1987) *Murder in the Nightwood Bar* (London, Pandora Press).
Galloway, B. (ed.) (1983) *Prejudice and Pride* (London, Routledge & Kegan Paul).
Harry, J. and DeVall, W. (1978) *The Social Organization of Gay* (New York, Praeger).
Hedge, A. (1985) *Gay Students at School* (Advisory Council for Education).
Hemmings, S. (1980) 'Horrific practices', in Gay Left Collective (eds), *Homosexuality: Power and Politics* (London, Allison & Busby).
Heron, A. (1983) *One Teenager in Ten* (Boston, MA, Alyson Publications).
Hibbert, R. (1987) 'Teacher training', in G. Hanscombe and M. Humphries (eds), *Heterosexuality* (London, Gay Men's Press).
HMSO (1986) *Education Act (2) 1986* (London, HMSO).
HMSO (1986b) *Health Education 5–16* (London, HMSO).
Hooker, E. (1962) 'The homosexual community', *Personality Research*, pp. 40–59.
Hooker, E. (1965) 'Male homosexuals and their worlds', in J. Marmor (ed.), *Sexual Inversion* (New York, Basic Books).
Hope (1987) 'My experience as a black lesbian teacher, in challenging heterosexism', GEN, 10/11: 16–17.
Ireland, T. (1984) *Who Lies Inside* (London, Gay Men's Press).
Johnson, P. and Whitman, L. (1985) 'Heterosexism awareness', GEN, 5: 16–17.
Leicester City NUT Association (1987) *Outlaws in the Classroom* (Leicester, NUT Association).
London Gay Teachers' Group (1985) AIDS *Hysteria*.
London Gay Teachers' Group (1987) *School's Out*, 2nd edn (London, Gay Teachers' Group).

McDaniel, J. (1985) 'Is there room for me in the closet?', in M. Culley and C. Portuges (eds), *Gendered Subjects* (Boston, MA, Routledge & Kegan Paul).

McFadyen, T. (ed.) (1980) *Gays at Work* (London, Gay Rights at Work Committee).

Minson, J. (1981) 'The assertion of homosexuality', *m/f*, 5(6): 19–39.

Newton, D.E. and Risch, S.J. (1981) 'Homosexuality in education: a review of the issues', *High School Journal*, 21: 191–202.

Patrick, P. (1983) 'Trying hard to hear you', *Teaching London*, 23.

Plummer, K. (1981) *The Making of the Modern Homosexual* (London, Hutchinson).

Plummer, K. (1986) *Growing up Gay in England*, mimeograph.

Pollard, N. (1978) *Homosexuality and the Teaching Profession* (London, NCCL).

Slayton, P. and Vogel, B. (1986) 'People with faces', *English in Education*, 20: 5–13.

Stafford, J.M. (1988a) 'In defence of gay lessons', *Journal of Moral Education*, 17: 11–20.

Stafford, J.M. (1988b) *Homosexuality and Education* (Manchester, by the author).

Taylor, N. (ed.) (1986) *All in a Day's Work* (London, Lesbian Employment Rights).

Trenchard, L. and Warren, H. (1984) *Something to Tell You* (London, Gay Teenagers Project).

Warren, C. (1974) *Identity and Community in the Gay World* (Canada, Wiley).

Warren, C. (1984) *Talking about School* (London, Gay Teenagers Project).

Weinberg, M. and Williams, C. (1974) *Homosexuals: Their Problems and Adaptions* (New York, Oxford University Press).

SIXTEEN

WALKING THROUGH WALLS: THE SEXUAL HARASSMENT OF HIGH SCHOOL GIRLS

June Larkin

Source: 'Walking through walls: the sexual harassment of high school girls', *Gender and Education*, 6(3): 263–280, 1994.

In the following excerpt from her book *Cat's Eye*, Margaret Atwood captures the stark reality of everyday life for many high school girls.

> Stunned broad, dog, bag, and bitch are words that apply to girls as well as worse words. I don't hold these words against them. I know they are another version of pickled ox eyes and snot eating, they're prove it words boys need to exchange to show they are strong and not to be taken in ...
>
> I don't think any of these words apply to me. They apply to other girls, girls who walk along the halls in ignorance of them, swinging their hair, swaying their hips as if they're seductive, talking too loudly and carelessly to one another, fooling nobody; or else acting pastel, blank, daisy-fresh. And all the time these clouds of silent words surround them, stunned broad, dog, bag, and bitch, pointing at them, reducing them, cutting them down to size so they can be handled. The trick with these silent words is to walk in the spaces between them, turn your head sideways, evade. Like walking through walls.
>
> (Atwood, 1988, pp. 244, 245)

For most females, crude language and other forms of sexually harassing behaviour are part of the fabric of our daily lives. To date, however, our focus on sexual harassment has been limited primarily to the experiences of adult women in academic and work place settings. Educational researchers in Britain and the USA are beginning to explore the problem of sexual harassment in schools (see e.g. Jones, 1985; Halson, 1988; Herbert, 1989; Stein, 1993) but there has been little discussion about the way this behaviour interferes with young women's attempts to get an education. Equal opportunity initiatives are of limited use if, for example, female students are urged into mathematics and science fields but we neglect to consider the hostile climate they encounter there. In this study, I explore young women's experiences of sexual harassment in Canadian schools and I examine the deleterious effects of this behaviour on their education. Building on the testimonies of young women I suggest how educators can make high school a more equitable place for female students.

Why focus on schools?

I recognise, of course, that young women's experiences of sexual harassment are not limited to schools; these students were also harassed on the streets, in public places, and in their part-time jobs. But the harassment they experienced at school set a precedent for the type of behaviour they expected to encounter elsewhere. After all, school was the nucleus of their adolescent lives: the place where they came to increase their life opportunities. As one student put it, 'If you get treated badly here, you know you can expect to get the same thing in public'. Being harassed at school teaches young women to accept this behaviour as an inevitable component of their everyday life.

Sexual harassment and other forms of violence against women are the logical products of a society in which females are generally devalued, reviled and mistreated. If unchecked, these misogynist attitudes seep into our schools and breed a new generation of male abusers. Young men soon learn that acting out their contempt for women is a way of confirming their own manhood (Frye, 1983). When the sexual harassment that young women experience at school is tolerated, educators contribute to the reproduction of a patriarchal society in which men frequently use violence to express their sexual domination over women. Halson (1988) has written that:

> Schools help to reproduce, rather than to change the existing imbalance of power between men and women in different ways, not least by failing to recognize the extent to which young women are subjected to sexual harassment, by failing to note the significant impact which these experiences have on their lives and personalities [and] by failing to intervene. In these circumstances young women can cope as best they can in the full and certain knowledge that many of the boys and men with whom they come into contact behave with disrespect, contempt and violence towards them and this is considered normal.
>
> (p. 141)

One reason that sexual harassment has received so little attention in schools is the difficulty in disentangling harassing incidents from what have come to be accepted as typical male–female interactions. However, educators are beginning to consider how males' diminishment of young women contributes to the decline in self-esteem and career aspirations that female students experience over their high school years (American Association of University Women, 1990). In her work with adolescent girls, Carrie Herbert (1989) has suggested that:

> sexual harassment may be one reason girls become disenchanted with school...unwanted sexual attention or confusing sexual attention which [is] defined as flattery but [makes] them embarrassed or angry may be one of the reasons for girls' lack of achievement. It has been documented that between

the ages of thirteen and sixteen some girls in school lose confidence, become more passive, publicly contribute less in class and generally lose their eagerness to participate...

(p. 37)

Clearly, in our efforts to provide equitable education for female students, we have neglected to consider a primary factor that impedes their academic success. As some educators are suggesting, sexual harassment may be 'the key to unlocking the whole debate on inequality of education for girls' (Brunswick Secondary Education Committee, 1982, p. 12) because it is one of the most powerful forces acting against young women.

The study

The students who participated in this study were from four Canadian high schools located in urban, rural and small-town settings and represented a variety of racial, cultural and economic populations. In each school, the administration had expressed an interest in educating students about sexual harassment and other forms of violence against women and were supportive of those female students who volunteered to participate in the project. The study was designed to provide the students with a variety of ways to express themselves and included three components: journal writing, group discussions and individual interviews.

Considering the backlash experienced by adult women who have dared to label certain forms of males' behaviour as sexual harassment (see e.g. McIntyre, 1986; Ramazanoglu, 1987), I believed that a journal might be a safe place for young women to express and reflect upon what they were choosing to record as sexual harassment. I also believed that the process of keeping a journal, coupled with reflection on their comments during group discussions, would prepare the students for their individual interviews. While interviews are considered by many to be the essence of qualitative research (Roberts, 1981; Bogdan and Biklen, 1982) they are limited somewhat by the short period in which the interview is conducted. In this study, the students had four months to think about their experiences of and perspectives on sexual harassment as they recorded incidents and thoughts in their personal journals. They also met on at least four occasions to share and discuss their journal entries with other female students. I believed that their interview comments would therefore be reflective, as opposed to spontaneous, responses to the questions I posed. More importantly, I hoped they would develop a way of thinking about sexual harassment that was embedded in their personal experiences because young women's voices were absent from the current discussions on this issue.

Approximately, 60 students participated in the study in at least one way. Most attended the group sessions; some also kept journals and/or agreed to be interviewed. Although the students varied in age, I only interviewed students who were 16 years of age or older because I wanted to assure the students that the information they shared with me would be confidential. I could not offer this assurance to students under 16 years of age because I would be legally obligated to report any incident of abuse they might disclose during our interview. In total, I interviewed 25 students.

I had assumed, as I developed the study, that many young women would have a limited understanding of the range of sexually harassing behaviour. This assumption was based on the work of other feminist researchers (see e.g. Kelly, 1988) who had found that women tended to consider the more common forms of sexually harassing behaviour as 'normal' or 'typical' males behaviour and not as sexual harassment. My first task, then, was to give young women the opportunity to identify the harassing behaviour that permeated their school lives.

Naming the problem

Prior to their involvement in the study, most of these young women had adopted the popular and contradictory notions of sexual harassment as an extreme form of violence (i.e. 'rape') or a trivial and harmless act (i.e. 'no big deal'). Many students had considered the more common forms of sexually harassing behaviour to be just 'typical' male behaviour, or as Jessica put it, 'just guys being guys'.

Through their discussions with other young women in the group setting the students realised how often they were sexually harassed and how their experiences of sexual harassment were similar to those of other female students. Alison explained that:

> before when I thought about sexual harassment, I used to think it was rape. I wasn't sure...My friend was telling me about sexual harassment because she heard about the meetings before I did...and I told her I thought it was rape and she said no. And she told me about the meetings and I said well I'll go because that's happened to me a lot.

For many students, the testimony of other young women led them to recall certain behaviour that, until that point, they had not identified as harassment. These testimonies, however, did not come easily. As facilitator of the group, my aim was to encourage young women to discuss and interpret sexually harassing behaviour from their own experience; I did not define it for them. Initially, my invitation for students to share their experiences of sexual harassment was met with silence. Dora explained in her interview that she had been 'scared to open up' because, until she attended the meetings, she didn't know 'how much it happens to everyone else and you think people are going to make fun of you'.

Eventually, a young woman would relay an incident that she thought might be sexual harassment. Her story was often followed by the comment 'that happened to me too' and from that point on the stories flowed. During the course of the discussions most students altered their definition of sexual harassment to include non-physical acts. Like many students, Jennifer had always thought that sexual harassment was 'molesting'. In her words: 'I never thought of it as being vocal'. When I asked the students in their interviews how they would previously have labelled the more frequent forms of verbal harassment, they used terms that included: 'bugging', 'teasing', 'flirting' and 'annoyances'. Helen simply stated that she had considered such behaviour 'just a fact of life'.

The students identified three factors that contributed to their normalisation of males' harassing behaviour at school: (1) the frequency of the behaviour; (2) the way it was interpreted by others, particularly the male harassers; and (3) the fact that the topic of sexual harassment was seldom, if ever, discussed at school.

In terms of frequency, the young women had come to accept as natural those forms of harassment they had experienced on a regular basis. Some indicated that this behaviour was part of the backdrop of their everyday life. Fatima explained it this way:

> You don't even think about it really...because it happens all the time...it's a part of life...it's like you're walking down the street, someone whistles at you...it's as if it's natural to do that and if somebody doesn't do that then something's wrong.... It's like, say it rains every day and then it doesn't rain, it's like 'Wow, it didn't rain'. It's like whistles.... It's there all the time, [you] don't even pay attention to it...it's a part of life.

The second factor that limited young women's ability to identify sexual harassment was the way the behaviour was minimised by others, particularly the male harassers. Many of the young women found that their feelings when harassed contrasted sharply with the perpetrators' assertions that this behaviour was simply 'a joke'. However, with no external validation that they had been violated, the young women would begin to question their own visceral responses and attempt to take on the perceptions of others. As Ruth explained: 'Before, you know it would bug me but I didn't show it...everybody was laughing so I had to laugh...I didn't know about sexual harassment.'

The third reason that the young women considered the harassing behaviour of males as normal was school officials' failure to address the problem of sexual harassment. It followed, then, that many students had no way of naming the abusive behaviour to which they were routinely exposed. The problem was compounded when teachers failed to respond to harassing incidents. For example, one student who complained about male students who continually lifted up her skirt in class was told to return to her seat and stop interrupting the lesson. After that, she stopped wearing skirts to school: 'I only wear trousers, I tell you.' Another young woman had to endure a male student putting his book down her trousers and making suggestive comments while the teacher looked on. In her words, 'What can you do when the person in authority doesn't do a thing about it?'

I want to clarify here that it is not my intention to blame teachers for the sexual harassment that goes on in their schools (unless, of course, they are perpetrators) but to emphasise that they need to acknowledge and confront it, for although these students had been unable to label certain acts as sexual harassment, many claimed this behaviour had always had an impact on them. As Tanya put it: 'It drove me crazy.'

Hearing the stories of other young women in group discussions allowed the students to broaden the parameters of *what* constituted sexual harassment and *who* could be sexually harassed. In recognising, like Clare, that 'everybody had something in common', the young women began to see sexual harassment as a general problem they all shared. In the process of connecting their personal meanings to the term 'sexual harassment', they began to identify as harassment behaviour they had previously been unable to separate from their ordinary interactions with males. According to Tanya: 'This has just totally opened my eyes. I feel like I have been walking around blind while all this stuff was happening around me and I was looking the other way'.

Now clearly, for Tanya, 'all this stuff' is not a new phenomenon. It is only recently, however, that she has been able to label it and so she and many other students 'tend to notice it more'. These young women had not been 'walking around blind', but without the power of a name they had no way to make the behaviour visible. Now they were able to speak out about the behaviour they had experienced as distressing. They were becoming fluent in the language of their own lives.

The experiences

All the young women had experienced some form of verbal, physical and/or visual sexual harassment in their high schools. Although the perpetrators of the abuse were generally male students, harassment by male teachers was not uncommon. I always asked the students to specify the gender of the harasser, so they understood that I did not assume that harassment was behaviour that only male teachers or students could exhibit. Despite this, no student reported being harassed by a female teacher and female students' harassment by female students consisted primarily of graffiti written on bathroom walls. Ironically, when one student told me about a young woman she observed harassing male students she expressed concern about the safety of the young woman, not her male targets. It appears that young women's expression of sexually harassing behaviour can provide males with a rationale for abusing them.

> I know one female...who does it with males.... She'll go up and grab their rear end. She'll say things to them like 'Hi sexy', or she'll ask them 'What are you doing tonight?'...A few of the guys have actually come over to her, after she says that. And I'm afraid for her because if she keeps that up she could get in trouble with the guy.... He might try something...it might turn out to be something bad.

Overall, verbal abuse was the most frequent form of harassment reported, although some students also relayed incidents of physical and visual harassment. While the accounts recorded here reflect the wide range of harassing behaviour the young women encountered, I make no claims to have tapped the totality of each students' experience. Comments such as 'I'm just starting to remember all these things' and 'So many things come to mind now that I'm talking' made by students during their interviews suggest that a quantitative assessment of their incidents would have been unreliable. One student, for example, found it difficult to recount specific incidents because they were so frequent. In her words: 'You just get used to it.'

In the following section I present the sexual harassment experiences of 25 high school girls. Although the young women often experienced the various forms of verbal, physical and visual harassment simultaneously, I have categorised their accounts according to the type of harassment that was most salient in the overall incident. What follows, then, is the raw material of their everyday school lives.

The forms of harassment

1 *Verbal Harassment*   Verbal harassment was the most common form of harassing behaviour the young women encountered at school. 'Put-downs' by male students and teachers appeared to be integral parts of their everyday school life. The frequent levelling of words like 'bitch', 'witch', 'fucking broad', 'douche', 'dog', 'bimbo', 'baby' and 'chick' against these students or in relation to women in general often occurred in the context of allegations that women were inferior to or less capable than men: 'In English class we were talking about women's equality; 50–50 in politics. The guys said that the 'chicks' would talk too much; we don't shut up.'

Through expressions such as 'A woman who makes $40,000 a year is a rich bitch', female students were warned that even the successful woman (in the conventional sense) is not immune to males' verbal degradation. Similarly, comments such as 'Women don't play basketball. It's a man's sport' were used to remind young women of their perceived weaknesses.

Many remarks directed at the students by both male teachers and male students included the traditional cliché about women belonging 'barefoot and pregnant in the kitchen':

> Last year in my English class, I had three guys...sitting there saying 'Oh, you should be at home, you're a woman. I'm sure there's laundry to do and you should be at home barefoot and pregnant'. They're going on like this and they wrote that in my yearbook.... And then yesterday I was sitting outside my science room waiting for my teacher to come, and two guys walked by me and one of them says, 'Don't you know you should be at home in the kitchen?' And the other one turns and says, 'Yeah, I'm sure there's tons of laundry to be done'.

Lyla experienced a similar situation with a male teacher. Such comments made by teachers in class settings are particularly damaging because negative messages about women are conveyed to large numbers of male *and* female students. 'This one teacher, he is very sexist. He makes comments about girls all the time, about the way they dress, or what they shouldn't do, what they should do. [He says] women should be barefoot, pregnant and everything.' Considering the force of the women's movement over the past two decades, it is astonishing that such comments are expressed at all. However, when they are spoken by a teacher who has the power to assess and evaluate you, they can be profoundly abusive and damaging.

A small number of male teachers appeared to use their classes as a forum for the expression of their general contempt for women:

> It was in my science class, and we had this teacher who was totally against women and everything about them.... He called his own wife a bitch, things that were unbelievable. In that class we learned everything he felt about women and towards women...like I learned nothing about science that year.

Undoubtedly, being verbally demeaned is distressing for any young woman, but minority women students also had to deal with the racist slurs and stereotypes that were salient features of the harassment they endured. The underlying message in the comments frequently made to these students was that their race or colour would make them more pleasing or unique sexual partners than white girls:

> ...there was one guy in my first class...he'll go, 'When are you going to sleep with me?'...He'll go 'I hear black women are good in bed'.
> ...they were bugging me and they were grabbing my shoulders. They were like touching my hips...and he's going, 'When are we going to get together because I've never made love to a Chinese woman before, I wonder how it feels'.

Unfortunately, while there appears to be minimal support for any young woman who is the target of sexual harassment at school, minority students are particularly isolated because they are less likely than white girls to be defended by other students:

> I think for the guys it's kinda like a power trip…They get to tease some girl, especially a minority girl…and nobody's going to say anything. First of all, if it's a girl a lot of guys won't say anything, and a lot of girls won't say anything. You get the minority in there, and *definitely* nobody's going to say anything.

Male students' objectification of women's bodies was another routine type of sexual harassment. According to Mary, it was a common practice for 'guys to talk about your body parts in the halls at school'. The statement, 'Look at the tits on that one' is one example of the objectifying remarks made by male students in Beth's class. Terms such as 'nice ass', 'nice tits' and 'sexy legs' were used to evaluate individual female students or to refer to women generally.

According to some students, the telling of crude jokes about women occurred 'all the time: during classes, out of school, at lunch-time'. Helen complained that even during her class presentation on the topic of Violence against Women, '[the guys] were making jokes about women'. Although male teachers seldom initiated sexual joking, they sometimes participated in the behaviour by 'laughing along with the guys' or supporting the male students' comments.

Sexual joking, of course, is not always female-focused. These students indicated, however, that sexual joking was generally at the expense of women and that, ironically, similar comments about men evoked strong protests: 'The jokes are always about the girls and never about the guys and when you say a guy joke he'll go mental. He'll turn around and say, "How can you say that?" ' Verbal harassment in the form of allegations about young women's sexual activity and provocativeness frequently placed young women in the position of defending their reputations. Amelia explained that this task was made more difficult by male students' practice of 'telling stories about the stuff they've supposedly done with girls'. Such accounts, whether fabricated or real, empowered young men at the same time as they disempowered young women because of the double standard that exists in relation to male–female sexual activity. A common way, then, for the young women to be diminished was through remarks about their assumed participation, or interest, in sexual activity:

> Like one of the guys…he likes to flirt a lot with the girls…. In one of my classes he turned around and said, 'I know you want it bad…you play with your hair and this and that. I know you want it bad so why don't you come to my house?'

The underlying message in many of the comments directed towards the young women was that they were primarily sexual beings and that the male student or teacher had little regard for their feelings.

According to Dora and other students, the rating of young women in school hallways was a standard practice. Typical comments included, 'I like the way she walks, I give her 10 out of 10'; 'Her body's not bad, I give her a 7'; 'What a dog, that one's a real 2'. Although all the young women were vulnerable to this form of males' scrutiny and evaluation, black students were generally given lower ratings than white students. Fatima observed male students playing the following game:

> [the guys] each had a number and whoever passed by them would be the one they would say they would have sex with.... If it was a pretty girl they'd say, 'Right on, you've got her!' If a black girl walks by they'd go, 'Oh, my God...she's got such a big ass'.... They'd put her down majorly.

Comments about one's clothing and personal appearance are not always sexual harassment. Generally, those incidents the young women perceived as harassing were the ones they experienced as depersonalising, demeaning and/or threatening. However, because women's value in our society is tied to males' evaluation of their personal appearance, some students felt flattered at the same time as they felt threatened by males' comments about their body or their dress. This conflict seemed to stem from their concern that what they perceived as a compliment might in fact be a precursor to a demeaning or threatening act. Alison provided the following example:

> I was wearing a short mini skirt and I was walking down the hall and there were two guys down at the end of the hall and they started whistling. One guy yelled out, 'Hey you in the black skirt'. They kept bugging me and bugging me. I finally turned around and said, 'What do you want?' They said, 'You got legs that just don't quit'. It made me feel good but it made me feel scared...I was afraid they would keep this up. And they did...the one guy said to my friend, 'Tell her I want to sleep with her'. And I said to my friend, 'I'm not sleeping with him'.... The next day my friend told me 'Because you won't sleep with him, he wants you to give him a blow-job'.

Two students recounted situations in which they had been threatened by male students. Beth experienced the following incident in one of her classes:

> I was talking to a guy...who sits behind me.... He said a sentence and ended up calling me 'a bonehead'. I then said, 'You're the one who's a boner'. He said, 'You better shut-up before I stick my dick up your ass so hard you won't be able to breathe'.

The second incident involved a threatening phone-call made to the vice-principal at Dora's school:

> This guy called up the school.... He called my house first and said, 'I went to school with her a year ago'...and my mother goes, 'Well, she's not home, she's in school'.... Then he called the school...and he talked to the vice-principal and said, 'Tell her that I'm going to rape her...I'm going to kill her'.... After that the vice-principal thought that I would be better off and have better protection [if] someone [was] with me all the time. So I was in all my classes and I had this undercover cop sitting at the back of my shoulder.

In general, for these young women, verbal harassment appeared to be inherent in their everyday school lives. Although, I have highlighted here the incidents in which verbal abuse was the most pronounced form of harassment, in many cases it acted as a backdrop to the physically harassing behaviour to which the young women were frequently exposed.

2 *Physical harassment* Grabbing, touching and rubbing were the forms of physical harassment most frequently mentioned by the students. According to Clare, 'guys grabbing you in the butt...anywhere they can' was an 'everyday ritual'. Even as she headed to one of our sessions on sexual harassment, Amelia said she 'got [her] ass grabbed'. Frequently, according to Tara, 'I will be standing at my locker and someone will come up and start rubbing against me' or the 'guys will walk out and they'll try to touch your chest'.

For some young men, grabbing and other physical actions were the primary (if not the only) way they related to the young women:

> Either he ignores me completely and doesn't talk to me or he comes up and grabs me, like he hugs me and stuff...I would rather have him ignore me than grab me 'cause he always does it in front of his friends and he always says, 'Oh, she is going to be my wife'...And like since this semester he grabbed me three times [otherwise] he ignored me completely.

The young women also spoke about being followed around the school by male students. Uncertainty about the *reasons* they were being followed rendered many of these incidents particularly disturbing:

> I've been followed around the school by a guy...he just kept following me so I go: 'What are you following me for?' [He said] 'Just to see what classes you have'...It got me thinking, 'What does this guy want from me?'

In some cases, the young women were eventually trapped or physically restrained by male students who had been following them around.

> I was walking down the ramp near the gym and he wouldn't let me go. He covered me this way, covered me that way and I said, 'OK, let me go now'. [When] he finally let me go, he said, 'Be that way'.

The young women also experienced or observed pushing, pinching, kicking and/or slapping by male students. Mary recounted a particularly disturbing incident in which 'a guy held a girl up to a locker and made her stay there while he kicked her'. For a three week period, Beatrice was subjected to a series of kicks and pushes by a male student:

> The pushing and kicking happened with a guy at school...for about three weeks when he saw me he couldn't come up and say, 'Hi', he had to push me, or if I was walking he had to kick me. If I was by my locker he would just come up and kick me in the ass...When it got really serious was when I was walking down the hallway in the school and he came behind me and choked me. I turned around and I said, 'What the fuck are you doing man?'

The final category of physical harassment the young women noted was sexual assault. Because the point at which physical acts such as rubbing and touching become sexual assault is not clear, distinguishing between sexual harassment and sexual assault can be difficult. Sexual assault differs from sexual harassment in that the former always involves physical contact. However, in many cases sexual assault is an extreme expression of the various forms of harassing behaviour. While the intensity of the behaviour may account for its being labelled as sexual assault, the context in which the behaviour occurs is also a factor. Consider the impact of the following behaviour on a female student alone in a classroom with a teacher she has grown to know and trust:

> One thing happened with a teacher. Like me and my friends we have dinner with him and his wife. We go out, we talk, like I can talk to him...And then one time...he goes, 'Hmmmm, you're looking nice today'. Like you know, he looked me up and down. He goes, 'Why don't you come here?' So I [went] there. He showed me some papers and stuff and he started putting his hands on my bum, squeezing my bum. I go, 'Heyy, what are you doing?' He goes, 'You got a nice bum...you got a nice ass'...I was sitting on the desk and he was right behind me. So he went to grab me and he put his hand on my breast and I'm, 'Heyyy...Oh my God, what are you doing?' Like my God, I trusted him and he does this.

Overall, the physical sexual harassment experienced by these young women intensified the impact of the verbally harassing behaviour they routinely encountered. In the same way, these acts were a way of reminding young women that the visual displays of harassment they encountered were also serious business.

3 *Visual harassment* Leering was the form of visual harassment reported most often by students. A leer is a form of invasive watching, a look that continues for a length of time and is experienced by the recipient as intimidating or intrusive. As Hilary Searles-Iversen (1990) puts it: 'A leer is a wrong kind of interested look'. It was a feeling of apprehensiveness that the young women seemed to use as a criterion for differentiating between a leer and a look:

FUNE: So if someone said, 'Well, gee, you can't even look at somebody anymore', what would you say?
CHEN: You can look at them, it all depends on how you look at them...the way you and I are looking, like just eye to eye contact. The way somebody will look at you dreamy like, you wonder what is going through their mind...Or when someone [is] just staring at you, like your body...you feel like he or she is going to attack you or something. So it all depends on how you look at them.

In some cases, as Beatrice indicated, the young women were unaware of males' ogling. However, young men's public sharing of these incidents acted as a reminder to female students that they were never beyond the daunting and judging males' gaze.

> Some guys were sitting there and they were just talking and I overheard them. One guy was saying that his friend Joe was having a laugh in gym class. They have swimming right now and he wears goggles and goes right under water and watches the girls' pussies.

A few young women also talked about 'perverted teachers' who had eyes that would always 'drift down' when they spoke to students:

> I felt like he was perverted...I just really didn't clue in in that class...He would come up and talk to me and he would look down at my chest...I wouldn't spend time with him or talk to him [even] if I had a problem.

Sexual gesturing was another common form of visual harassment. According to Alison:

> [It] happens a lot at school. Guys if you say something to them and they don't like what you're doing they'll grab themselves and pretend they're jerking off.

Beatrice recounted the following story:

> I was in the middle of a soccer game, and someone called me from the stands. I looked over and this guy in the stands grabbed his crotch with his hands and moved it in the up and down motion.

Many of the young women were teased with pornography and other demeaning material: 'I bet you wished you had a set like these'. Beth's reaction to the disturbing graffiti she uncovered in her art classroom clearly demonstrates the connection between sexual harassment and other forms of violence against women.

> I was looking for coloured paper when I came across a stack of boards piled in the corner with graffiti written all over them. I expected to read 'So and so, true love' or the names of people's favourite bands. [Instead] I saw a picture of a naked woman (no arms, head, calves, or knees) with her legs wide open showing her vagina, anal opening and breasts. I was shocked to see such explicit graffiti in my favourite class. To me that picture says mutilating is OK, sexual assault is OK, rape is OK, and that is what I'm scared of the most.

The testimonies of these young women paint a depressing picture of high school life for female students. The cost to these young women of their constant efforts to avoid, ignore, or respond to the sexually harassing incidents was high. The self-protective strategies they developed trying to avoid harassing behaviour must be seen as positive expressions of their strength and resistance. Although these tactics often had negative implications for their personal and academic development, in most cases, the young women had few alternatives. They were struggling to deal with a problem that had yet to be acknowledged as an impediment to their education. While these students were constantly the targets of demeaning and abusive behaviour, they were seldom passive victims.

Not passive victims

The young women adopted a number of strategies in an effort to reduce their exposure to harassing behaviour, but these strategies often seriously hindered their attempts to get an education and made school an unwelcoming, even menacing place. Often, they avoided areas of the school where they were likely to be subjected to verbal and physical harassment. Hallways in particular were identified as harassment zones that were to be bypassed if at all possible. Zoë was so nervous about a group of male students who constantly demeaned young women in public that her 'stomach would turn' when she walked through the hallways. When they were unable to avoid a likely sexual harassment area in the school, many female students would travel in pairs 'for protection'. Tara told me: 'I won't walk down the hall by myself. Not if there's a bunch of guys there. I have to have at least one person with me or else I will take a longer route.'

Some students monitored the clothing they wore to school for fear of being sexually harassed. Jessica would stand in front of her closet anticipating the comments she would receive if she wore various outfits. In fact, some young women began to lose control of their self-definition as they adjusted their appearance in attempts to avoid harassing comments from male students. Alison, for example, changed her whole image in response to allegations that she was a slut:

> I used to listen to heavy metal, my hair used to be long. I used to have the jackets, the trousers, everything... When I went to another school it was alright the way I dressed because everybody did it... Now all those clothes are in the garbage because they wouldn't leave me alone. They kept calling me a slut.

Another way the students avoided sexual harassment was by limiting their associations with male students. Although Joan associated only with male students who didn't 'talk about girls' she wished that she could have more male friends. Unfortunately, she didn't think that could happen unless the boys changed the way they communicated with the girls.

Helen found that female students tended to restrict their participation in school activities – 'sports for instance' – for fear of being sexually harassed. For this reason, she felt that many young women 'don't perform to their full level'. If female students didn't have to be concerned about harassment, she believed,

> they wouldn't have to restrain themselves, they could go loose and wild and they would be surprised what they could do 'cause they have had all the restraints on them. But if they had all the restraints taken off and they knew that they were off then I think that would have a big bearing on their performance in class and in sports.

In their efforts to avoid harassing behaviour in the classroom, many students limited their participation in class discussions and their enrolment or attendance in various courses. Zoë, for example, monitored the behaviour of male students in her classes for the first month of school to see how they responded to female students. During this period she did not participate orally in class: 'Like the first month or so I'd be quiet, you know, real quiet. If they're quiet and they don't do anything [to the girls] then I can talk afterwards'. Some young women were reluctant to get up and do presentations in class because the male students were often disruptive. Clare became embarrassed and 'goofed up her lines' when a group of male students chanted 'Airhead, airhead' as she spoke to the class. She explained that this type of behaviour happened 'with [such] great regularity' that the anxiety most students experience during class presentations was magnified for female students.

The harassment young women experienced in the non-traditional courses seemed to have a more profound impact on young women's academic and career choices. As they ventured beyond the boundaries traditionally defined for women, sexual harassment was a reminder of their infringement on male terrain. Students like Lyla feared it would only get worse:

> A lot of girls who take science, they're really interested in the medical field... A lot of them afterwards don't even want to take science anymore. Like they figure if this is what I'm meeting in school, what kind of opposition am I going to meet when I go to university or college... As long as they pass

they don't give a shit anymore what kind of marks they get. As long as they pass they don't have to take the teacher again, they don't have to take science again.

Lyla believed that more young women would enrol in science classes if they didn't have to worry about sexual harassment.

Some students withdrew from courses rather than endure the harassing behaviour of teachers. Jennifer dropped a course because she resented the demeaning comments the teacher continually made about women:

We have one really bad teacher here…a lot of girls dropped his course last year…He's a pig. That's the only thing I can think of to call him. He does not think a female can do anything.

Unfortunately, a few students who were subjected to extreme forms of sexual harassment felt they had no option but to leave the school. In speaking of a close friend, Izabela explained:

She didn't want to leave, she likes this school, but there was nothing else she could do. The school wasn't going to do anything and she wasn't going to be subjected to this kind of harassment for another year…you never know where it might lead to.

Beth followed up her account of a particularly disturbing incident of sexual harassment with the comment: 'I hate school…Maybe an all girls' school would be better for me'. I heard later that she had left the school.

As evident in the stories of these young women, life for many female students is often a grim battle against a hostile and threatening school environment. The perilous situation of female students is shocking when one considers that the term 'equal opportunity' has become so entrenched within the discourse of education that the commitment to equitable education is lauded as a primary objective of most school boards. And yet, as one hears the testimonies of these young women it is clear that something is amiss. The road to equality carved for female students is fraught with cracks and barriers, so that young women move with trepidation if they dare to move at all. Despite the efforts of many caring educators dedicated to the philosophy of equitable education for female students, schools remain places where young women's opportunities are limited. This situation exists, in part, because the focus on equal *access* (e.g. to science courses, sports, equipment, computers, etc.) has thwarted the development of equal opportunity initiatives that address the root causes of women's inequality. As Gaskell *et al.* (1989) put it, 'Equal opportunity means much more than equal access on a formal basis. The problem lies much deeper' (p. 22).

As we attempt to deal with this issue it is useful to consider the young women's comments. For although they were frequently the targets of sexually harassing acts, most claimed that many male students and most male teachers *did not* harass them. This belies the popular notion that such behaviour is an intrinsic expression of masculinity or an unfortunate consequence of the myriad and inescapable social forces that operate to construct male abusers. The fact that all males do not engage in harassing behaviour despite the similarities in their physiological make-up and their similar exposure to the beliefs and institutions that ostensibly account for the expression of such demeaning behaviour, suggests that some males make a conscious choice to harass females. I suspect, as Mary Beth told me, that 'some guys do this *because they can*'. This is what educators can change.

Towards a more equitable education for young women

As a way of supporting those educators who want to provide a more equitable education for female students I offer suggestions generated from the information provided by the young women whose stories have been recorded here. These suggestions are based on the assumption that young women's inequitable position in education is not a product of their own deficiencies; rather, the emphasis is on the creation of a learning environment in which female students are acknowledged as equals. The foci of the following recommendations extend from the more specific problem of sexual harassment to the larger issue of equal opportunity in education.

1 *Policy*   The development and implementation of a sexual harassment policy that covers students is a strong, public statement that school boards acknowledge and they will not tolerate the sexually harassing behaviour to which many students are subjected. Aside from moral principles, a primary reason that students need to be accounted for in policies of sexual harassment is the increased likelihood that school boards may face legal liability if they fail to deal with the harassing behaviour to which students are being subjected. In the USA, a recent ruling by the Minnesota Human Rights Department has sent a strong message to all school districts that the issue of sexual harassment must be taken seriously (Boyd, 1991). In this case, a female high school student presented evidence that school authorities had not dealt effectively with her complaints about the demeaning graffiti, lewd comments and humiliating and degrading acts that she endured at school. As a result,

> The state...found probable cause that Chaska High and School District 112 had not responded appropriately to Olson's complaints about sexual harassment. In fact, the department said, school officials had created 'an offensive atmosphere that promotes sexual harassment in general.
>
> (Boyd, 1991, p. 12)

However, it would be naïve to assume that the mere implementation of a policy will resolve the problem of sexual harassment. Although a policy is a statement of institutional support and offers redress to those who are sexually harassed, educators' ultimate goal should be to change the attitudes that perpetuate sexually harassing behaviour. As these students put it, 'Education is the key to prevention'.

2 *Education*   Because sexual harassment is part of the hidden curriculum in the school life of many female students, educators must ensure that this problem is made visible. The recent decision by the Minnesota Human Rights Department has prompted some school boards to strengthen their sexual harassment policies by providing education about the topic for all members of the school community. In the Chaska school district, for example,

> all district employees [have] attended seminars on sexual harassment and students in grade four through twelve [have] studied the issue. Students are helping rewrite pupil handbooks to include a definition of sexual harassment,

and high school students serve as members of a new Human Worth and Dignity task force.

(Boyd, 1991, p. 12)

Based on the information provided by young women who participated in this study, and considering their comments about the activities I conducted with them in group settings, I developed an educational kit on sexual harassment to be used in high schools. Activities such as those included in the kit could be conducted with students, teachers and administrators so that *all* members of the school community are sensitised to this problem.

In planning educational sessions, it is helpful to consider the suggestions offered by the young women. For example, separating young women from young men in the initial stages of the educational process may be advisable as a way of providing female students, in particular, with a safe environment in which to express their opinions and share their experiences. In addition, the display of posters and the availability of brochures on sexual harassment are visible reminders that the school considers sexual harassment a problem and is committed to eliminating it.

However, the transformation to a harassment-free educational environment is unlikely to be rapid. By challenging the attitudes that produce sexual harassment, we are attempting to eliminate one of the tools used by men to reinforce their power over women. In essence, what we are advocating is radical social change.

In the interim, to support young women as they attempt to move along the difficult road to equality, it is important that we offer them refuge from the forces that operate against them. Male students' appropriation of so much of the physical space within the school places female students in a vulnerable position as they try to weave their way through a threatening school environment. Young women need a place within the school where they can relax their endless vigilance; they need a place to call their own.

3 *A separate place*   One of the most significant outcomes of this research was the solidarity that developed among young women as they met to share their experiences of harassment. As Janice Raymond points out in her book, *A Passion for Friends*, the development of strong bonds between women provides them with: 'a common world that becomes a reference point for location in a larger world. The sharing of common views, attractions, and energies gives women a common connection to the world so that they do not lose their bearing' (p. 8).

Through the creation of separate spaces for young women, educators can provide places where female students can dare to assert themselves and where the strength of their collective voice can rise above the drone of debilitating messages that permeate their lives. In such places young women can exist,

> somewhat sheltered from the prevailing winds of patriarchal culture and try to stand up straight for once. One needs a place to practice an erect posture, one cannot just will it to happen. To retrain one's body one needs physical freedom from what are in the last analysis physical forces misshaping it to the contours of the subordinate.
>
> (Frye, 1983, p. 38, emphasis in original)

Separate spaces for young women in educational settings can take a variety of forms. These include more all-girls' schools, the creation of single-sex classes in mixed-sex schools, young women's clubs, and designated rooms for female students within co-educational environments.

By providing spaces where young women can come together, educators can provide antidotes to the destructive messages that underlie the harassing behaviour female students endure both within and beyond the high school setting. In such places young women may come to realise that their experiences of sexual harassment and other forms of discrimination are part of a general problem they all share. Then, collectively, they can begin to resist the chilling winds of tradition that bring 'a message of exclusion – stay out' and 'a message of subordination – stay under' (Gilligan, 1990, p. 27). In doing so, they can begin to claim their rightful place in education.

Educators truly committed to the provision of equitable education for female students need to broaden the limited focus of traditional equal opportunity initiatives by considering also the hostile climate in which young women are educated and the need for young women to be empowered. As a final suggestion, I propose that educators adopt an expanded model of equal opportunity that incorporates four foci: (1) Access; (2) Inclusion; (3) Climate; and (4) Empowerment. This I have labelled as the AICE (pronounced 'ace') model of equal opportunity.

4 *The AICE model of equal opportunity*   By concentrating primarily on the issue of access, educators have been unable to address the range of factors that limit young women's educational opportunities. This is not to detract from the importance of encouraging female students to enter non-traditional fields; rather, it is to suggest that this strategy alone will not remove all barriers that young women encounter as they pursue their education. As part of a Ministry-funded project on sexual harassment (1992), Pat Staton and I surveyed Ontario School Boards about the formal and informal strategies they had implemented or were developing in their efforts to create a gender-equitable educational environment for female high school students. We found that few boards had addressed issues of inclusion, climate and empowerment. In an effort to assist educators in the development of a more balanced and effective equal opportunity programme, we suggested the development of strategies from each of the four key areas outlined in the AICE model:

> Access – encouraging equal opportunity in instruction, particularly in fields related to non-traditional jobs. Enabling young women to choose from a range of careers.
>
> Inclusion – looking at gender bias in teaching and learning materials in terms both of inclusive language and content.
>
> Climate – creating an educational environment that is safe and supports equity. Dealing with violence against women. Looking at 'What goes on the walls [and] what goes on in the halls'.
>
> Empowerment – creating a space within the school where young women can develop a sense of solidarity. Providing an antidote to counter the negative messages young women receive both within and beyond the school setting.
>
> (Staton and Larkin, 1992, p. 28)

By meeting the criteria of the AICE model of equal opportunity, educators will be addressing factors such as sexual harassment that seriously limit the educational experiences of young women. In doing so, their commitments to the provision of an equitable education for young women will be validated.

Conclusion

Sexual harassment acts like a wall that blocks young women's movement towards equality. By ignoring this obstacle, we have placed female students in a confusing situation. As they are being inundated with messages that their opportunities are unlimited, many are feeling increasingly more confined as they restrict their behaviour in an effort to avoid sexual harassment. In short, equal opportunity has increased young women's access to education but sexual harassment ensures that they remain unequal.

The movement for equitable education for female students cannot be separated from the larger political struggle against male dominance and one of its primary weapons: sexual harassment. Certainly, educators cannot be charged with the sole responsibility of transforming a patriarchal society but they can begin to confront the power imbalances that maintain it. Developing policies and educational programmes on sexual harassment, providing safe spaces for female students, and expanding the traditional focus of equal opportunity initiatives are all positive steps.

Unless we are prepared to deal with the factors that work against young women 'philosophical statements about providing a gender equitable environment will have neither force nor meaning' (Staton and Larkin, 1992, p. 37). As Lyla put it, when educators confront the problem of sexual harassment, 'that's when equality will begin. That's when we will really start being equal'.

Acknowledgements

This research was supported by a grant from the Social Sciences and Humanities Research Council of Canada. The author wishes to thank Paula Caplan for her helpful comments and suggestions.

REFERENCES

American Association of University Women (1990) *Shortchanging Girls: Shortchanging America* (Greenberg Lake, The Analyses Group Incorporated).

Atwood, M. (1988) *Cat's Eye* (Toronto, Seal Books).

Bogdan, R. and Biklen, S. (1982). *Qualitative research for Education* (Toronto, Allyn & Bacon).

Boyd, C. (29 December 1991) 'How one teen fought sex harassment in school', *St. Paul Pioneer Press*, p. 12.

Brunswick Secondary Education Committee (1982) *Equal Opportunities Project 1982 Report* (Melbourne, Transition Education Advisory Committee).

Frye, M. (1983) *The Politics of Reality: Essays in Feminist Theory* (Freedom, CA, The Crossing Press).

Gaskell, J., Mclaren, A. and Novogrodsky, M. (1989) *Claiming an Education: feminism and Canadian schools* (Toronto, Our Schools/Our Selves Education Foundation).

Gilligan, C. (1990) 'Teaching Shakespeare's sister: notes from the underground of female adolescence', in C. Gilligan, N. Lyons and I. Hanmer (eds), *Making Connections: The Relational Worlds of Adolescent Girls at Emma Willard School*, pp. 6–29 (Cambridge, MA, Harvard University Press).

Halson, J. (1988) 'The sexual harassment of young women', in L. Holly (ed.), *Girls and Sexuality: Teaching and Learning*, pp. 130–142 (Milton Keynes and Philadelphia, PA, Open University Press).

Herbert, C. (1989) *Talking of Silence: The Sexual Harassment of Schoolgirls* (London, Falmer Press).

Iversen, H. (1990) Personal communication.

Jones, C. (1985) 'Sexual tyranny: male violence in a mixed secondary school', in G. Weiner (ed.), *Just a Bunch of Girls* (Milton Keynes, Open University Press).

Kelly, L. (1988) *Surviving Sexual Violence* (Minnesota, MI, University of Minnesota Press).

Mcintyre, S. (1986) 'Gender bias within the law school: memo to faculty' (Kingston, Queen's University).

Ramazanoglu, C. (1987) 'Sex and violence in academic life or you can keep a good woman down', in J. Hanmer and M. Maynard (eds), *Women, Violence and Social Control*, pp. 61–74 (London, Macmillan).

Raymond, J. (1986) *A Passion for Friends* (Boston, MA, Beacon Press).

Roberts, H. (1981) *Doing Feminist Research* (London, Routledge & Kegan Paul).

Staton, P. and Larkin, J. (1992) *Sexual Harassment: The Intimidation Factor*, A report to the Ontario Ministry of Education (Toronto, Green Dragon Press).

Stein, N. (1993) 'Secrets in public: sexual harassment in public (and private) schools', *Working Paper; 256* (Wellesley, MA, Center for Research on Women).

SEVENTEEN

BOYZ' OWN STORIES: MASCULINITIES AND SEXUALITIES IN SCHOOLS

Debbie Epstein

Source: 'Boyz' own stories: masculinities and sexualities in schools',
Gender and Education, 9(1): 105–115, 1997.

STEVE: I mean, *do* heterosexual men and women actually debate with, y'know, why am I straight?...I don't believe so.
CLIVE: But everything that we see affirms their sexuality: books, TV, when you're out at work, people you meet on the bus, buying a newspaper, doing your shopping. Everything confirms, reinforces their sexuality...
RANEE: I mean, it's considered normal.
STEVE: And yet, in my experience, I have a suspicion, y'know, basically heterosexual people are not very secure in what they are and that that is part of the hostility and the whole debate around homosexuality versus heterosexuality.

(Group discussion by KOLA, Birmingham
Black Lesbian and Gay Group)[1]

Introduction

Steve's opinion that 'heterosexual people are not very secure in what they are' is one that I met frequently during the course of the Sexuality in Education Research Project which began in October 1991. When examining the level of hysteria generated in the mass media (especially the tabloid press) around issues of sexuality, particularly in relation to education, it is hard to avoid agreeing with Steve's conclusion: that there is a level of uncertainty, of feeling threatened, which contributes to the moral panic. In this paper, I am particularly interested in the importance that homophobia (and its performance, see Nayak and Kehily, 1997) plays in the production of conventional, heterosexual masculinities. Their argument, that the (performance of) homophobia both polices and constructs heterosexual masculinities in schools, has implications for the school lives of those boys/young men who resist conventional masculine identities as well as for girls/young women. Moreover, homophobia and (hetero)sexism are themselves imbricated with racialised meanings. The normative heterosexual family is, by implication if not definition, white and middle class; heterosexuality, masculinities and femininities are all played out in relation to this particular 'imagined community' (Said, 1978) of this fantasy happy family.

This paper examines these dynamics of English[2] schools in the period 1979–93. It does so primarily through the memories of lesbian and gay teachers, students and parents in England as expressed in a series of interviews carried out during 1992 and 1993,[3] although data from school observation in the same period are also used where they are relevant. For the most part, our respondents spoke about their experience in secondary schools, and our concurrent school and youth group ethnography also took place with secondary age young people. For this reason, the main focus of the paper is on the ways in which normative, often macho and misogynistic, versions of masculinity are constructed and played out within secondary school environments. However, where there is evidence from the primary sector through the narratives of our interviewees, those are used as well.

In discourse, schools are constituted as public arenas, in contrast to the supposed private space of sexuality. Nevertheless, schools are places where young people and their teachers do a great deal of cultural work on the construction of their identities in a whole range of ways, importantly, around issues of sexuality. I will suggest that these struggles are intimately connected with struggles around gender (in this instance, primarily masculinity), and, following Butler (1990), that it is impossible to develop a full understanding of gender relations without examining them in the context of compulsory heterosexuality, or, as she puts in, through the lens of the heterosexual matrix. In other words, sexism in schools needs to be understood through the lens of heterosexism. The early parts of the paper will examine this from the perspective of gay students; the latter parts will look through the lens of gay teachers.

Doing a thing on weddings

I have suggested earlier that sexism in schools needs to be understood through the lens of heterosexism. Many examples of the use of sexuality as a form of control and of resistance constitute both heterosexism *and* a reinforcement to particular versions of masculinity and femininity. For example, the instruction not to be a 'Nancy-boy' is not simply about not being gay, but clearly also about not being a 'real man' (of a particular type). Similarly, instructions to girls/young women to behave in more 'ladylike' fashion are not only about particular versions of femininity but also about behaving in ways which signify heterosexuality. Equally, even successful resistance by girls/young women to particular types of male teacher behaviour can become a way of reinscribing heterosexuality. For example, one of our interviewees described how girls in her class had adopted the wearing of high stiletto heels in order to stamp 'accidentally' on the foot of a male teacher who was sexually harassing them. This had the desired effect of stopping him from touching them, but at the cost of wearing a particular signifier of heterosexual femininity (for fuller discussion see Epstein, 1996a).

Both heterosexuality and conventional gender relations are also often (re)produced through the taught curriculum itself. For example, one of our interviewees,

Ayo,[4] told me a story about how, while in the infant school, his teacher organised some 'mock weddings'. He did not remember the particular context of this event, but knew that he had been about 6 years old when it took place. It seems likely to me from his age that this was at the time of the marriage of Charles and Diana, a time when infant and junior teachers up and down the country were undertaking projects about 'weddings' and 'marriage':

AYO: We were doing a thing on weddings.

DE: So, what, you were about 6 or 7?

AYO: Yeah, and they decided that we should all play at getting married.

DE: *They* decided? The teachers?

AYO: Yeah. As a fun thing to do, I suppose...And we, some, I think two other 'couples' or, you know, speech marks, they progressed up an imaginary aisle and had confetti and things thrown at them and this girl who I was supposed to get married to didn't want to, and she started screaming the place down, and I was really rattled.

DE: Yeah. Do you know why she didn't want to?

AYO: No, it was just she didn't want to. And she started blubbering all over the place, and I remember this was just a lesson.

DE: Did she just not want to get married? Did she not want to do the getting married bit, or did she not want to do the getting married bit to you?

AYO: I definitely think it was to me. And I was told it was to me. Some of the other kids were saying, 'Look, she didn't want to do that', and it made a really deep impression. I thought, oh, she doesn't like me...but after the break period, the teacher got, I think had done things, or whatever, made things happen, and it was all done very quickly and rushed. You know, let's get this over with so everyone's satisfied, so we rushed through this pretend ceremony and stuff, and that was it.

DE: Did the kids sort of enjoy that? Did they think it was sort of...

AYO: Yeah, they thought it was a giggle...And you know there were actual dresses and stuff, brides' dresses and little doll things that they got dressed up in and we were dressed in our ordinary clothes I think. We didn't do any black history.

Here, we see the mutual reinforcement of compulsory heterosexuality and of conventional gender relations inescapably intertwined. The playing out of the heterosexual marriage ceremony in its traditional (white, British) form with 'an imaginary aisle and...confetti and things thrown at them' assumes the desirability of marriage and institutionally heterosexist forms of relating, and reinforces the fantasies of imaginary futures which children (and particularly girls) often express. Moreover, the dressing of the girls in 'brides' dresses' while the boys remained in their ordinary clothes represents a further reinforcement of particular ways of being boys and girls, of particular masculinities and femininities: girls wear pretty, frilly clothes and the teachers expect them to gain something from dressing up in 'brides' dresses and little dolls' things'; boys, on the other hand, are more careless about their appearance and would not enjoy or gain anything from dressing up in 'bridegrooms' clothes. What we see here is the explicit production of macho versions of masculinity and what Bob Connell has called 'exaggerated femininities' (Connell, 1989).

Valerie Walkerdine has argued (Walkerdine, 1996, in press) that popular culture in its various manifestations (in particular, advertising and pop songs and their videos, but also television programming) can frequently be read as eroticising young girls (especially young working-class girls) and that they, in their turn, enter into these fantasies in ways which cannot be interpreted simply; these are neither examples of young girls-as-whores nor of child sexual abuse. Similarly, the pleasures of dressing up as brides are both about the fantasies of adults (in this instance teachers) and of the girls themselves. And the 'prettiness' of the 'wedding dress', the mythology of the 'blushing bride', enter into constructions of heterosexualised femininities, distinct from and other than the masculine, 'rational' of the boys wearing their everyday clothes. In this way, the co-construction of masculinity and femininity as binary, heterosexual opposites is achieved.

Ayo's apparent leap from the weddings to the statement that 'we didn't do any black history' is less random than it might at first appear. The particular form of wedding played out was, as I have already pointed out, traditionally white British, while the objections of the little girl to marrying him seem not to have been an objection to getting married as such, but a rejection of Ayo himself. Whether this hostility was, as seems likely, founded on racism is neither here nor there in terms of the way Ayo understood it. His immediate shift to black history is a clear indication that he experienced this episode as an example of racism. In this example, then, we see the intertwining of racism, sexism and heterosexism in a particularly powerful (and to Ayo painfully memorable) form.

They didn't bother me

The constant reinforcement of compulsory heterosexuality through particular sexist discourses about masculinity and femininity was a constant theme of all our interviews. Even in those few cases where respondents spoke about having no problem with being 'out' at school (and as school students), this was in the context of being able to carry off particular gendered styles which are usually coded heterosexual. For boys, this was invariably to do with exhibiting those characteristics associated with 'real manhood'. For example, Simon[5] told me that:

> I...came out at a very early age. I was rugby captain, very macho, very masculine, didn't have any problems with anybody picking on me. When you're six foot two, six foot one, six foot at a very early age, you don't tend to have many problems... So I eventually came out at school when I was 14, although I was aware of my sexuality, end of cubs, beginning of scouts, which would have been 10, 11 years of age. I'm an only child, so I had developed a very close friendship with a kid from school and negotiated puberty without too many problems at a relatively early age and so did my friend. And basically when we started secondary school at 11, sex between the two of us was more than a regular occurrence, whether it be in my house or in his house. It was only ever between the two of us, but as we went through school, there was no secret that the two of us were very attached to each other. Whether people thought we were best friends or whether they thought we were lovers was of no consequence to us. We were both in the rugby team and everybody left us alone.

Simon is very clear, here, that his ability to come out while still a school student without being, as he put it, 'picked on', rested on his size and perceived macho version of masculinity in what was, as he described it later, 'a very traditional school...very boys only, very rugby orientated, very win, win, win, very academic'.

This theme of his macho appearance and, at times, behaviour as a protection against being victimised for his gay sexuality reappeared frequently throughout the interview:

> People just left us alone. You just didn't mess with Simon and Peter, cos they would beat you up. But we never, ever had to beat anybody up whatsoever. When you were as tall and as powerful as we were, people just didn't mess, you know.

On occasions, he had recourse to homophobic abuse against boys who were not sufficiently macho:

SIMON: But thinking back to when I was 13/14/15, if people weren't strong enough to play rugby for the school, then my biggest upset is that 'oh', you're a pooftah, you Nancy boy', you know.

DE: And you would actually use those?

SIMON: And I know that I used those words, yeah. If people, if people, weren't strong enough to support the school, then I would certainly have a go at them. People who wanted to be in the school play, rather than play football, would get a lashing. And, you know, that's adolescence for you, you know, you, you would attack, perhaps rather than being attacked yourself.

DE: So, I'm interested in this business of the use of the abuse, and the use of the rugby team macho image as a protection... but also using the abuse itself as a protection for yourself. Is that fair?

SIMON: We, whether we were doing it knowingly or not, we felt that if we maintain this image, if we maintain this macho image, and we attacked others, we would be left alone, and nobody would attack us, you know. 'Look at Simon and Peter. They're not queer. Why don't we all strive to be like Simon and Peter?' you know.

From the perspective of a gay man now involved in all kinds of gay activism (e.g. the organisation of Gay Pride), Simon remembered these moments with some embarrassment (hence, perhaps, the use of the word 'upset'). What is interesting, however, is that what was being required here both of him and by him was a version of masculinity which was not only apparently heterosexual *because* it was macho, but one which is particularly unfriendly to women (see also Connell, 1995, chapter 6). The misogyny and generally offensive sexist behaviour of groups of men in rugby clubs is legendary! Furthermore, other, less macho ways of inhabiting masculinity were derided – 'People who wanted to be in the school play, rather than play football, would get a [homophobic] lashing'.

Sue Lees also draws attention to the fact that: 'to call a boy a "poof" is derogatory but this term, in denoting lack of guts, suggests femininity – weakness, softness and inferiority' (Lees, 1987, p. 180). This was confirmed time and time again in our research. Frequently, the homophobia expressed towards non-macho boys was in terms of the assertion of their similarity to girls. That this takes place in primary as well as secondary schools is confirmed in my other research (Epstein, 1995, 1997). Indeed, it is interesting to note that the behaviour of 'tomboys' within the primary context is much more acceptable than the behaviour of 'cissies'. This, I would suggest, is because for a girl to be more like a boy can be interpreted positively, while for a boy to be more like a girl is, almost invariably, seen as problematic because being a girl is, in some sense, disreputable. Insults like 'poof' and 'Nancy-boy' are used, then, to control not only the sexuality of boys but also the forms of masculinity they are likely to adopt, at least within the school context. Interestingly, Mac an Ghaill (1994, p. 93) gives an example of a boy who was enabled to occupy a non-macho version of masculinity (including the achievement of academic success) by virtue of his previous association with a 'hard' gang and his consequent reputation as a 'hard man'.

Boys frequently seem to survive by dint of appearing 'hard' and macho, especially in boys only schools. At the conference (held in April 1995) of the London Association for the Teaching of English, I attended a workshop on anti-sexist work with boys. Here the facilitator, Rav Bansal, pointed out that as soon as he started overtly anti-sexist work in his single-sex boys' school, he was labelled as gay and that, in order to retain any kind of credibility, he took care to drop remarks about having a girlfriend. Furthermore, in the tape of a lesson which he played for the workshop, we heard him clearing the air for discussion of feelings and sexism with the remark that 'we know that none of us here are gay'. As he explained, he was distinctly uncomfortable about this but felt that it was only way in which the boys in the class would even begin to entertain the ideas with which he was confronting them. In a context like this, it is hardly surprising that both teachers and students find it extraordinarily difficult to come out.[6]

Support for students

Of course, where lesbian and gay teachers feel unable to come out at school, they are often unable to provide support for those students identifying as lesbian, gay, bisexual or, indeed, unsure about their sexuality. Chris,[7] for example, spoke about her experiences in a coeducational setting:

> I had a series of [threatening] letters put into my desk at school saying...'if you don't meet me, I'm going to tell everyone in the school hall at lunch time'...There were about two letters that I received in the fifth year, and I actually showed them to my form tutor, and I told her how I was, you know, what was going on, and she said 'Oh'. I thought she was a lesbian, but obviously she wasn't, because I wanted to talk to her about it and she just turned round and said, 'Well, I think you should just work harder. I think you're worrying about nothing. I think you should just concentrate on your exams'.

In this context, Chris assumed that the threatening letters had come from one of the boys. She had no proof of this, but had also met with overt adverse reaction from some of them. Furthermore, it seemed to her a reasonable assumption that the boys would want to attack her because her coming out as a lesbian seemed like a threat to their masculinities. It is also significant that the teacher (whether a lesbian or not) felt unable to support her. One might speculate that the overwhelming weight of masculine hostility was too much to confront.

In our interviews, those who had been 'cissies' felt the hostility of other boys and lack of support from teachers at least as strongly. Michael,[8] for example, in one of our group discussions, spoke about how:

> There was absolutely nobody I could go to. There was, the teachers were just as bad as the pupils. There was no way that any of them were prepared to be supportive. Or if they were, it would be sort of, that smarmy liberal support

you can get, about, well, oh great, that's really wonderful, you're making an alternative life choice. But I mean, it's not informative. You can't sit down and talk to somebody who, about, you know, specifically issues around coming out, around having boyfriends, trouble with that, about whether you're gay or not, if that person isn't themselves...I think it's really important at that point and stage in your life to have somebody around who is gay themselves, who knows what you're talking about...

I'm just very lucky in as much as, having been alienated all the way through my school, through having come from abroad, through...never having fitted in, it didn't, it wasn't a major trauma for me and I was able to get through it. But equally, I know friends of mine who, you know, reached that stage, that fatal age of fifteen or sixteen, decided to come out, had no support at all and were completely scarred by it. Some of them still carry scars today. It took them years to get over what they went through. And it's simply not good enough to have somebody who says yes, that's fine, that's your alternative life choice and you're entitled to make it, because you don't have any social back up.

The importance of Michael's statement, here, lies in the need he expresses for support from other gay men in the process of coming out. The appeal is not so much to a crude identity politics (though there may be something of that in it) but comes from an experience of lack of support from anyone who could understand the experience of being young and gay in school from a gay perspective. In this it has some similarities with the experiences of racism of those young black people who find themselves in predominantly white schools.[9] Indeed, one of the things that Michael is saying here is that as a person of colour he had already learnt to deal with racism and this (in itself traumatic) experience enabled him to cope better when he came out as an adolescent. As one experienced gay teacher, active in the union and generally out, said, 'I wouldn't advise any kid to come out at school, even if their immediate circle is supportive'.

Michael's story is one of early identification of himself as 'different'. From nursery school on, he preferred playing in the 'Wendy house' [sic] and dressing up (as a girl) to playing more physical games with the boys. During primary school he made close friends with another non-macho boy, Alan:

...we became really good friends and I remember one day actually just completely spontaneously, um, the bell went and we were off...And we just grabbed each others' hands and ran off, together, holding hands and all the other people in the class started shouting homo, homo, yurgh, homo, and I didn't understand what it meant, um, but I just realised that, you know, they were sort of shouting something abusive, and it was obviously something to do with Alan and something to do with us holding hands, so we stopped, and, um, felt quite guilty about it actually. I didn't really understand why and then a couple of days later there was this joke going around...Um, somebody would come up to you and say, so are you a, and you know this idea of homo somehow had stuck in my head as something bad and then somebody came up to me...and said are you a *Homo sapien* [sic] and I didn't know what that meant, but I just heard the word homo and I thought, no no no, I'm not a *Homo sapien* and everyone laughed at me.

In this case, Michael's friendship with Alan was made the subject of verbal harassment in such a way that both of them felt constrained to cool the friendship.

Furthermore, the later teasing of Michael by others whose vocabulary allowed them to play on the word 'homo' was an additional punishment for his deviations from the norms of heterosexual masculinity. Michael was, then, made to feel guilty about being 'homo'(sexual) in the first instance and through the later teasing, he was put in a situation whereby the denial of being 'homo' meant that he had also to deny being human. The joke, here, was not only about his naiveté, but about the catch-22 situation in which he was placed – a situation made more significant because the denial of full humanity to particular groups has, historically, been one of the ways in which a variety of oppressions have been held in place.

Teaching from the closet

As pointed out earlier, it is often very difficult for teachers to come out. Indeed, all the teachers (and whether they were out at school or not) we interviewed during the course of our project spoke of the risks both of coming out *and* of staying in the closet. Nigel, for example, spoke about how:

> I live very close to the school I work at, not actually in the catchment area – that was a deliberate choice. But two gay friends do live in the catchment area, and, horror of horrors, some new neighbours moved in...and then it turned out that the children had been allocated a place at the school I teach in.
>
> And then, just before Christmas...the head summoned me. She said, 'I just wanted a word with you', and I went in and she said that this particular mother had been and complained. And I said, 'Why, I don't teach this child?' But she said, 'She thinks you are a danger to the children in your class and I said, 'Well, why? Because I'm not adequate?' and she said, 'Well, let it just be said that she considers you to be, to have dangerous friends, friends who could be a danger to children.

Here, the risk of being 'outed' *at school* (as against in the rest of his life) is vividly captured in the phrase 'horror of horrors'; the safety of the closet is dubious at best. This 'horror' is often avoided by dint of distancing oneself from anything to do with lesbian or gay sexuality and, for gay men, this can be most easily achieved through resort to macho styles of masculinity, as became particularly evident in another interview:

DE: You were saying that you felt like you had to definitely play a part?
HARRY: Oh yes, yes!
DE: Can you tell me a bit about the part?
HARRY: The part, I guess the part was to emulate the straight male teachers.
DE: What does that entail?
HARRY: It entailed initially hitting pupils and being physically violent, or physically intimidating and [*taking a deep breath*] trying desperately not to appear soft.
DE: Yeah? Because that was the give-away?
HARRY: That seemed to be the give-away, yeah.... I think that perhaps I was also steering clear of talking about anything that would suggest, give the children an opportunity to point the finger at me, or ask that awful question, which children in school are perfectly capable of asking.

Harry's evident distress during this part of the interview was compounded by his view that hitting children and being physically violent was both wrong in itself and constituted a truly terrible form of pedagogy. What is captured here is the strongly felt necessity to take any means available to avoid the inference that he was gay. Later in the interview he talked about an incident in which he was 'outed':

> ...I just panicked. All I could do really was play up the stereotype, as a defence. So I camped it up a bit, and died inside, and I managed to get through all the games and whatever we had to do on stage [during a teacher/student fund-raising performance] and then walked off and I nearly just walked out of school.

This narrative captures a memory of terror. Harry's impulse to resign on the spot was not carried out though he later left teaching. Here we see the opposite defence from the one he deployed in the classroom. Interestingly, Harry commented that this incident led to his 'relaxing' in the classroom, adopting a less macho teaching style and, in fact, improved his teaching. However, the choice he felt he had, between acting macho and acting camp is not a happy one.

Conclusion

Feminists interested in education have frequently written about the misogyny of schools (see especially Lees, 1986, 1987, 1993; Mahony, 1985, 1989). Sue Lees and Pat Mahony have also pointed to the homophobia of, in particular, boys. Their concerns have been primarily about what this means for girls in schools. Recent authors on masculinity have been primarily concerned about the effects of macho norms and behaviours on boys, particularly those not conforming to these norms (Connell, 1987, 1989; Mac an Ghaill, 1994; Redman and Mac an Ghaill, 1997). While I have focused here mainly on evidence from gay men, the argument of this paper is that misogyny and homophobia are not merely linked but are so closely intertwined as to be inseparable: misogyny is homophobic and homophobia is misogynist. The dual Others to normative heterosexual masculinities in schools are girls/women and non-macho boys/men. It is *against* these that many, perhaps most, boys seek to define their identities. The psychic and social defences which they build up against contamination are damaging to their Others (who have to put up with more or less constant harassment), to themselves (e.g. in relation to boys' attitudes to schoolwork and current debates around boys' 'underachievement')[10] and to the wider society (e.g. in the social cost of macho behaviours).

If, as I have shown, homophobia is constitutive of normative heterosexual masculinities in schools and is also part of the daily misogyny of boys and male teachers alike, if boys have to appear to be super-heterosexual, macho studs to survive at school, then schools will be unhappy, painful places for girls, boys who do not conform and their teachers, who have to struggle against the macho behaviours of significant numbers of boys.

There are, however, (often fragmentary and fleeting) signs of change in available discourses of masculinity. While schools continue to lag behind somewhat timorously, television and bookshops are filled with representations of alternative masculinities and sexualities, many of them positive and some even downright subversive. A case in point is the recent advertisement for Levi's jeans, which showed an extremely attractive young black woman, sexily dressed in jeans and top, hailing a New York cab. She sits in the back making up her face while the cab driver positively drools over her sexiness. One's immediate reaction to this part of the advertisement is that this is astonishingly sexist and racist. Then comes the denouement as the young woman feels her cheek and gets out a battery operated razor with which she begins to shave. 'She' is a 'he' and the expression on the cab driver's face says it all: disappointment, horror, disgust, desire. The final slogan is 'Levi's, cut for men since...' Even this plays/draws on gay *double entendre*. The subversion is of dominant discourses of both masculinity and sexuality.

Acknowledgements

An earlier version of this paper was given as part of the British Educational Research Association Symposium at the American Educational Research Association Conference in San Francisco, 1995. I would like to thank the other contributors to and participants in that symposium. I would especially like to thank Fazal Rizvi for the thoughtful comments he made in his capacity as discussant. Thanks also to Richard Johnson and Deborah Lynn Steinberg for reading earlier drafts and to the two anonymous referees and Chris Griffin for their helpful comments on the article.

Sexuality in Education Research Project which began in October 1991 was funded by the University of Birmingham, the University of Central England and East Birmingham Health Authority. I would like to thank those people who carried out observation and interviews in schools and in the Birmingham Lesbian and Gay Youth Group. They are: Alistair Chisholm, Louise Curry, Mary Kehily, Gurjit Minhas, Anoop Nayak and Shruti Tanna. We also collaborated with Peter Redman, at that time employed as a researcher with East Birmingham Health Authority. I would also like to thank members of the Politics of Sexuality Group of the University of Birmingham's Department of Cultural Studies for the discussions around questions of sexuality which have informed my thinking on these issues.

NOTES

1 See also KOLA (1994). I have given all my interviewees pseudonyms in order to ensure confidentiality, unless they have specifically requested that I use their real names.
2 England and Wales share the same education system under the Education Reform Act (apart from the teaching of Welsh in Welsh but not in English schools). Scotland and Northern Ireland have their own local systems.
3 One interviewee was Scottish and also spoke about Scottish schools in the course of his interview. However, most of his teaching had taken place in London and this was the main topic of conversation with him. Altogether, we interviewed 30 teachers, students and parents and held group discussions with several different small groups of people. Most had responded to advertisements for interviewees in the *Pink Paper* and *Gay Times* though some were found through the use of a snowballing technique. These people came from London, Birmingham and the Black Country, Brighton, Bristol, Hertfordshire and Preston. We also did classroom observation and interviews with students and teachers in four Midlands secondary schools, one all girls and three mixed and an in-depth ethnographic study of the Birmingham Lesbian and Gay Youth Group.
4 While Ayo's parents were from Nigeria, he himself was born in London and identified as black, British and gay.
5 Simon was white, English and had attended a grammar school in south London.
6 This has been written up as part of his course work for his MA (Bansal, 1995).
7 Chris was white, English. She had been to a selective and very middle-class secondary school followed by a girls' sixth form college.

8 Michael's father was white, English and his mother was Indian. He had attended several different schools, some in the UK and some in other countries, especially during his early and primary years.
9 See Epstein (1993) for further discussion of this.
10 I gave a paper on this aspect of that particular debate, at the Economic and Social Research Council funded seminar 'Gender and education: are boys now underachieving?' at the Centre for Research and Education on Gender, University of London Institute of Education, November 1996 (Epstein, 1996b).

REFERENCES

Bansal, R.S. (1995) ' "Looking over your shoulder": a study of anti-sexist discussions in an all-boys classroom', MA course work, University of London, Institute of Education.
Butler, J. (1990) *Gender Trouble: Feminism and The Subversion of Identity* (New York and London, Routledge).
Connell, R.W. (1987) *Gender and Power: Society, The Person and Sexual Politics* (Cambridge, Polity Press).
Connell, R.W. (1989) 'Cool guys, swots and wimps: the interplay of masculinity and education', *Oxford Review of Education*, 13: 291–303.
Connell, R.W. (1995) *Masculinities* (Cambridge, Polity Press).
Epstein, D. (1993) *Changing Classroom Cultures: Anti-racism, Politics and Schools* (Stoke-on-Trent, Trentham Books).
Epstein, D. (1995) ' "Girls don't do bricks". Gender and sexuality in the primary classroom', in J. Siraj-Blatchford and I. Siraj-Blatchford (eds), *Educating the Whole Child: Cross-Curricular Skills, Themes and Dimensions* (Buckingham, Open University Press).
Epstein, D. (1996a) 'Keeping them in their place: hetero/sexist harassment, gender and the enforcement of heterosexuality', in L. Adkins and J. Holland (eds), *Sexualising the Social* (Basingstoke, Macmillan).
Epstein, D. (1996b) 'Real boys don't work: boys' underachievement, masculinities and the harassment of cissies', paper presented at the ESRC-funded seminar series *Gender and Education: Are Boys Now Underachieving?* University of London Institute of Education, 15 November 1996.
Epstein, D. (1997) 'Cultures of schooling/cultures of sexuality', *Journal of Inclusive Education*, 1(1).
KOLA (1994) 'A burden of aloneness', in D. Epstein (ed.), *Challenging Lesbian and Gay Inequalities in Education* (Buckingham, Open University Press).
Lees, S. (1986) *Losing Out: Sexuality and Adolescent Girls* (London, Hutchinson).
Lees, S. (1987) 'The structure of sexual relations in school', in M. Arnot and G. Weiner (eds), *Gender and the Politics of Schooling* (London, Hutchinson/The Open University).
Lees, S. (1993) *Sugar and Spice: Sexuality and Adolescent Girls* (London, Penguin).
Mac an Ghaill, M. (1994) *The Making of Men: Masculinities, Sexualities and Schooling* (Buckingham, Open University Press).
Mahony, P. (1985) *Schools for the Boys? Co-education Reassessed* (London, Hutchinson).
Mahony, P. (1989) 'Sexual violence and mixed schools', in C. Jones and P. Mahony (eds), *Learning Our Lines: Sexuality and Social Control in Education* (London, Women's Press).
Nayak, A. and Kehily, M. (1997) 'Masculinities and schooling: why are young men so homophobic?', in D.L. Steinberg, D. Epstein and R. Johnson (eds), *Border Patrols: Policing the Boundaries of Heterosexuality* (London, Cassell).
Redman, P. and Mac an Ghaill, M. (1997) 'Educating Peter: the making of a history man', in D.L. Steinberg, D. Epstein and R. Johnson (eds), *Border Patrols: Policing the Boundaries of Heterosexuality* (London, Cassell).
Said, E. (1978) *Orientalism* (New York, Vintage).
Walkerdine, V. (1996) 'The eroticization of young girls', in J. Curran, D. Morley and V. Walkerdine (eds), *Cultural Studies and Communications* (London, Arnold).
Walkerdine, V. (in press) *Daddy's Girls* (Basingstoke, Macmillan).

ETHNICITY

EIGHTEEN

MODERN TRADITIONS? BRITISH MUSLIM WOMEN AND ACADEMIC ACHIEVEMENT

Fauzia Ahmad

Source: 'Modern traditions? British Muslim women and academic achievement',
Gender and Education, 13(2): 137–152, 2001.

Introduction

Whilst the ultimate goal is the attainment of a piece of paper, a qualification signifying a certain academic speciality, few of us leave higher education the same person that we entered. Apart from emerging a few years older (and hopefully wiser), we are 'transformed' in other ways. Our knowledge base is greater, our employment prospects improve (so we are led to believe), and our social and personal experiences are richer. We are all familiar with the stereotypical 'student image' – a grungy, but trendy, hip and 'right on' type who divides their time between lecture theatres and the Student Union bar, where politics is nothing less than radical. Yet, this is a very Eurocentric stereotype. British universities play host to a sizeable percentage of overseas students whose attendance and patronage generates a significant and indispensable source of funding. How do these students 'fit' into the very 'British' academic milieu? On a more local scale, what can we say about the motivations and experiences of British-born university students from migrant families?

Discussions about the experiences of British South Asian Muslim women and their post-school experiences are mainly limited to analyses of their labour market positions (Afshar, 1989a,b; cf. Brah and Shaw, 1992; Brah, 1993, 1996) and their location within patriarchal relations of both public and private spheres. My research has been heavily influenced by the framework for analyses offered by Brah (1996), namely, an endorsement of theoretical perspectives advocating links between 'structure, culture and agency' describing them as 'mutually inscribing formations' (p. 129). Therefore, developing an understanding of some of the ways that gender, 'race', ethnicity, class and religion can intersect and interact with internal dimensions of the 'self' at any given moment are crucial challenges to be addressed. These are issues that this research aims to explore at a later date.

The research presented in this article represents the preliminary findings of ongoing qualitative fieldwork with British Muslim women of South Asian origin,[1] exploring motivations for, and experiences of, studying in higher education. The women are predominantly from the majority Sunni Muslim sect (see later), who are either studying at universities in London, or have already graduated. Students from the older[2] university campuses in London were initially contacted either directly by the author or via Student Union representatives from various societies such as the Pakistan Society or the Islamic Society, and thereafter via a process of snowballing. Detailed semi-structured interviews lasting between $1\frac{1}{2}$ and $2\frac{1}{2}$ hours approximately were conducted with (at the time of writing) 15 students.

The interview covered areas such as family background and migration histories, educational experiences, motivations and influences, social activities, marriage and relationships, issues concerning religious and cultural identity, and future hopes and expectations. The vast majority of women interviewed were from predomi-nantly 'working-class' backgrounds and were current undergraduates (nine). Four interviewees were postgraduate students and two were graduates in employment. Interviewees were aged between 19 and 30 years. Ten described their ethnic origin as Pakistani, three were Bangladeshi and two were Indian. Background details on Student Union activities were gathered via unstructured participant observation where appropriate.

As a work-in-progress article, this study discusses and interrogates themes emerging from ongoing fieldwork. It asks how the data presented may be situated within the existing wider debates and discourses on the South Asian diaspora in Britain. Future work will also aim to situate these findings within current discourses surrounding South Asian Muslim women in the West.[3]

As a British-born, 'young' South Asian Muslim woman, my own experiences of higher education at both undergraduate and postgraduate levels have played a sig-nificant role in shaping various methodological issues and (in this instance), have facilitated the research process.[4] However, the accounts I draw on here are not intended to reflect a representative sample of British South Asian Muslim women in higher education. Rather, the hope is that previously neglected voices are given recognition for the *diversity* their experiences represent.

Therefore, one of the aims of this research is to question stereotypes that portray young South Asian women and, in this case, South Asian Muslim women in Britain, as 'victims' and recipients of oppression in patriarchal family relations, or as women with fixed religious identities. Bhopal's research on South Asian women in East London situates 'traditional women' as those possessing few or no qualifications, and 'educated women' as 'single, independent women' who were also described as 'deviant' (Bhopal, 1999, p. 129). This body of work (borrowing heavily from Walby's theories of patriarchy) implies that 'successful', South Asian women choose to 'turn their backs on their religion and culture' (Bhopal, 1997a, 1998).

Drawing on Labour Force Survey statistics on ethnicity, highest educational qualifications, marital status and economic activity, Bhopal demonstrates rapid social change through diversity in educational attainment and employment for the 25–30 age cohort of British South Asian women (1998). However, the interpreta-tion of some of these results warrants further scrutiny. For example, Bhopal asserts:

> The national LFS data supports recent research carried out on South Asian women aged 25–30 which had demonstrated that South Asian women with

high levels of education were in professional occupations, and as a result were choosing to reject 'arranged marriages', but instead to cohabit or remain single.

(1998, p. 13, para. 9.1)

Marrying ages for South Asians may well be increasing, but it is a mistake to assume that single, professional status leads to a 'rejection' of 'arranged marriages', or even that this concept is interpreted and practised uniformly within South Asian groups, regardless of religion (see later).[5] Apart from masking the diversity and fluidity of South Asian cultures, religions, communities and relationships, the extreme binaries presented earlier fail to situate experiences within micro- and macro-frameworks.

Although my research is ongoing and is based on a small sample of Muslim women, those interviewed were far more culturally and religiously aware *as a result of and despite* their educational experiences. This would seem to be supported by other studies documenting the importance of religious identifications in the ways that young British South Asian Muslim women articulate their experiences (see, e.g. Knott and Khokher, 1993; Butler, 1999; Dwyer, 1999). 'Agency' then, for those I interviewed, was a process of negotiation and renegotiation, through which social, cultural and religious identifications (amongst others) were expressed. Aspects of social life and the 'self' that were 'colloquialised' as either 'traditional'[6] or 'modern/Westernised' were often overlapping, suggesting their inadequacy and rigidity as descriptive concepts. Bobby Sayyid (1997), for instance, notes some interesting inconsistencies with such terms when discussing 'Islamophobia' and the West.

Muslim women are no less influenced by academic and social learning processes than other university students though their experiences in this respect are far too detailed to allow me to elaborate here. But the fact that they are *present* in higher education institutions is significant. How far do decisions to study reflect family practices, both here and in the country of origin? What perceptions do British Muslim women have of their 'positioning' within British society, their local community and their families? What benefits do they perceive and expect from participation in higher education personally and socially? Do any contradictions exist for British South Asian Muslim women in their pursuit of upward social mobility through the British higher education system? If so, how are such contradictions rationalised?

In conducting my research interviews, I have sought to consider how past and present life experiences shape individual perceptions alongside structural factors such as class (both in country of origin and in the UK), gender, ethnicity and racism. This research article, therefore, is concerned with exploring motivating factors that underlie participation in higher education for British South Asian young Muslim women. I begin with some brief background information about South Asians and Muslims in Britain before making reference to some recent statistics on ethnic minorities in higher education. I then go on to consider the growing 'visibility' of South Asian Muslim young women in institutions of higher education, before examining their motivations from two angles: their perceptions of parental influences and opinions, and their own reasons for pursuing higher qualifications.

Background

According to Britain's last Census in 1991, estimates of the size of the ethnic minority population in Britain ran at approximately 3 million, representing 5.5 per cent of the total population. South Asians made up close to half this figure (figures quoted in Anwar, 1998).

However, the lack of a religious self-identification question in Britain's last Census in 1991 means that estimates on the numbers of Muslims currently residing in Britain vary from between half a million to 2 million.[7] Surveys such as the Fourth PSI (Policy Studies Institute) Survey (Modood et al., 1997) and various Labour Force Surveys (discussed by Lewis, 1994) offer similar estimates. South Asians are believed to comprise approximately 80 per cent of Britain's Muslim population. Numbers suggested by Anwar (1998) would place them at about 850,000, though this figure is not conclusive. Those originating from the Mediterranean, Africa and the Middle East are thought to constitute the remaining 20 per cent (Peach, 1994, cited in Lewis, 1994).

Estimating the proportions of South Asians that can be described as second or third generation is also complex as the time of migration for different South Asian groups varies considerably. One estimate suggests that the proportion of British-born South Asians is about 60 per cent (Anwar, 1998). Most of those in my sample were 'second generation', with parents who had migrated to Britain in the 1960s.

Research on the first generations of migrants to Britain from South Asia were mainly ethnographic accounts, describing family and household structures and links with the country of origin. The insularity of these communities was often a key defining feature of earlier accounts (Saifullah Khan, 1977). Many new arrivals in the 1960s and 1970s expected their sojourn in the UK to be a temporary one. However, as families reunited, grew and adapted to life in Britain as communities, the prospect of 'return' decreased (for detailed accounts, see Shaw, 1988, 1994; Ballard, 1994; Brah, 1996; Anwar, 1998).

Some of these early works documented the roles first generation migrant women played in the reconstruction of cultural traditions, their contributions towards the household economy, labour movements and emerging political dialogues. These accounts provide a strong counterbalance to stereotyped images of the secluded and 'passive Asian woman' (Saifullah Khan, 1977; Wilson, 1978; Bhachu, 1988; Werbner, 1988; Brah, 1996). It is, perhaps, reasonable to assume that the women my research focuses on are, metaphorically speaking, the 'daughters' (and also, possibly, the 'granddaughters') of the women featured in some of these earlier, classic studies.[8]

The integration and achievements of second and third generation diasporic South Asians have become a focus of much research and theoretical debate. Comparative work on the educational achievements of Sikh children in the USA and Britain has shown some interesting links between current socio-economic status, whether the family's background in the country of origin is urban or rural and the timing of migration (Gibson and Bhachu, 1988). In later work, Bhachu (1991, 1996) also found that education, increased labour market participation and financial independence have profound effects on the consumption patterns of younger Sikh women. Similar correlations have been noted by others, such as Brah (1993) in her exemplary study of young Muslim women and the labour market. These themes should be borne in mind when considering the data described in the following discussion.

Ethnic minority students in higher education

Studies in the early to mid-1980s, such as the Third PSI Survey in 1982 (amongst others, such as Vellins, 1982; Ballard and Vellins, 1985), indicated that ethnic minority students in the 16–24 age group were more likely than their white counterparts to be engaged in post-compulsory education (Craft and Craft, 1983; Brown, 1984). More recent empirical research tracing the participation of ethnic minorities in further and higher education has confirmed an increase in their student numbers. However, more detailed analyses have shown that these participation rates exhibit much diversity.

A striking degree of polarisation between British South Asians with higher qualifications and those with few, or none, exists, though the reasons behind this are as yet unclear (Jones, 1996; Modood et al., 1997). For instance, the Fourth PSI Survey in 1994 showed that South Asians as a group had the highest rates of participation in post-compulsory education for the 16–24 age group.[9] Indian and African–Asian men were the most likely to possess degrees whilst Pakistani and Bangladeshi men were the least likely. Participation rates for Pakistani and Bangladeshi women were more optimistic. In comparison to Indian and African–Asian women, although Pakistani and Bangladeshi women were amongst those possessing the least number of qualifications *overall*, the authors found that 'the Bangladeshis and, especially, Pakistani women were well represented at degree level' (Modood et al., 1997, p. 74). This finding may have been reflective of a biased sample group, as postulated by the survey authors, but may also be due to 'migration and generation effects' (Modood et al., 1997, p. 74).

Clearly, more research into the reasons why such diversity exists in participation rates is required. Parental education levels and occupation, the type of school attended, the opportunities offered, the expectations and levels of encouragement for further study from teachers, are 'class-related' effects which do have *some* bearing on study patterns.

Singh (1990), in his review of ethnic minorities in higher education, suggests that their overall high participation rates are reflections of the value ethnic minorities place in academic qualifications, and their high aspirations. The desire to pursue qualifications at colleges of further education after poor school experiences may also be seen as a strategy to postpone perceived or expected unemployment after leaving school. Other research has shown that ethnic minority women, on the whole, were subject to a 'double disadvantage' (Taylor, 1993, p. 433) when applying to universities: as women within an ethnic group, and as members of an ethnic minority. Furthermore, much of the research cited earlier points towards discrepancies in the acceptance rates of ethnic minorities to varying *types* of higher education institution (see also Modood and Shiner, 1994).

Such conclusions are both frustrating and disturbing for those working in the areas of racial equality in the UK, but especially for ethnic minority students who aspire towards educational qualifications for pragmatic reasons. These are often related to a realistic assessment of the indirect and institutionalised racism they can expect to face, but also reflect personal aspirations and ambitions as demonstrated in numerous studies, including this one. The reported 'drive for qualifications' amongst all ethnic minority groups, therefore, is a testament to their determination, resilience and tenacity to succeed.

A survey of religious diversity within Britain's universities has shown that Muslims represent one of the largest non-Christian groups on campus, with distinct needs and concerns (Gilliat-Ray, 1999). However, higher education institutions, like the Census surveys, do not currently collect data on students' religious affiliations, making correlations between participation rates and religion difficult.

Large-scale quantitative analyses such as those mentioned earlier are certainly invaluable for highlighting discrimination within higher education. What they cannot do, however, is offer detailed explanations for why such diversity, particularly between and within ethnic groups, exists. Perhaps more localised, qualitative research that reflects specific regional manifestations of social and personal circumstances may help us to understand the relationships between and within ethnicity, class, gender and, in this case, higher education. Actual accounts of *experiences* in higher education are, at present, scarce in the academic literature. Effective monitoring and increased access of ethnic minority students to universities will be of limited positive effect if *discriminations*, direct and indirect, are operating within the lecture theatre or within the Student Union.

'New women'? British Muslims in higher education

The quantitative studies described earlier have drawn some worrying conclusions about the significant underachievement of some South Asian groups and the over-representation of others within tertiary education. However, within those under-represented groups, evidence points towards the relative academic success of Pakistani and Bangladeshi women. It is fair to assume that a significant number of these will have come from Muslim backgrounds. However, existing research focusing on British Muslim young women has not yet acknowledged their academic achievements at graduate level as significant enough to warrant detailed study.

Many research studies focus, instead, on Muslim schoolgirls. There is much to be learnt from these generational accounts, but there is also an issue, I believe, surrounding the 'overuse' of Muslim schoolgirls in social research. With relatively little life experience, they are placed in the awkward position of speaking as either 'representatives' for their community, or as 'experts' on their culture, especially when 'arranged marriages' are discussed (cf. Wade and Souter, 1992). Few white British girls are expected to be 'experts' on white British culture in quite the same way. For adolescents whose priorities should be 'growing up', this is a very heavy burden to carry.

Research on British Muslim women students and graduates is scanty at best, though they have been included in various other analyses of South Asian Muslim women (e.g. Afshar, 1989a,b; Brah and Shaw, 1992; Brah, 1993; West and Pilgrim, 1995). Muslim women have become increasingly visible on university campuses, especially when 'controversial' Muslim student groups hit the headlines. However, accounts of their experiences of student life may have remained submerged for *at least* three possible reasons:

- their presence in numbers was previously too small to warrant any meaningful investigation;
- the research focus from the 1970s onwards was on anti-racism and multiculturalism in primary and secondary schools and ethnic minority students' achievement there (see Tomlinson, 1983, 1986, 1991; Parekh, 1988; Verma and Mallick, 1988, e.g.); and
- they 'chose' to remain 'invisible', thus possibly suggesting that Muslim minority interests held little significance for these students. This could be envisaged if, for instance, the South Asian Muslim presence was composed of mainly 'middle-class' or overseas students, whose participation or 'integration' into British life was either found to be relatively unproblematic, or was of a temporary nature.

Muslim students as a group became 'visible' when events surrounding the publication of the controversial book *The Satanic Verses* in the late 1980s and later, the Gulf War, brought Muslims into the media spotlight, but did so in a disparaging way. Most non-Muslims found the passion and zeal which Muslims in Britain espoused towards their religion at these particular periods to be perplexing and, more seriously, threatening (Modood, 1990; Ahmed and Donnan, 1994; Werbner, 1994). 'Islamic re-assertion' (Modood, 1990, p. 271) in the wake of these two affairs, but also now in response to growing 'Islamophobia' in the West, has been particularly prevalent amongst Muslim youth and students.

The Muslim women I interviewed have not been immune to the processes of religious identification that intensified in this period. Contrary to the visual image of hijab-wearing women which such religious revivalism may lead us to expect, most of the Muslim students I interviewed have chosen not to adopt the hijab. This may be reflective of a sampling bias. A few women regarded themselves of Muslim descent only and so any 'practice' of Islam in their lives (though not necessarily their families') was absent. At the time of writing, only two students were from a Shia background, one belonged to the Ahmediya sect, and the rest were Sunni Muslims.[10]

For the majority of those interviewed, however, 'Muslimness' was a deeply embedded sense of both consciousness and unconsciousness, governing and prevailing upon their thoughts, behaviours and choices. Higher education was *not* viewed by these women or their families as being incongruous to the 'Muslim way of being'. In fact, contrary to other research that implies that arranged marriages for daughters are axiomatic soon after the age of compulsory schooling is reached (e.g. Wade and Souter, 1992; Khanum, 1995), most women in this research reported that their parents viewed higher education and careers as an absolute necessity.

Women themselves were equally unanimous in this opinion, and were also of the belief that apart from social mobility and status, they accrued other personal benefits (similar findings have been reported by Basit, 1995, 1996a,b; for Sikh women, see Gibson and Bhachu, 1988; Bhachu, 1991).

Motivations for higher education

South Asian families have placed a particular importance on the acquisition of academic qualifications (see earlier). Muslim families are often regarded as placing strict cultural or 'patriarchal constraints' ('purdah') on the movements of women. Yet, as Brah quite rightly points out:

> this social concept and its manifestations varies from one historical period to another, from one country to another, and from one social group to another. Even within the same social group its patterns of observance can differ considerably along class, caste and other dimensions.
>
> (1993, p. 448, and 1996, p. 137)

Apart from illustrating the heterogeneity of Muslim expression, Muslim parents in this research have played an instrumental role in encouraging their daughters to succeed both academically and professionally.

Through a process of 'active competition' operating within family and social networks, a daughter's education can bring 'prestigious capital', rather than economic capital (explained in greater detail later). Alongside material wealth, educational achievement has now assumed the rank of a 'commodity', or as an indicator of status and social mobility. This pursuit of 'educational prestige' is not simply a middle-class strategy.

Some structurally based assumptions situate undergraduates as coming from middle-class homes, with graduate parents, or, in the case of South Asians, of exhibiting an urban/rural divide assumed to be indicative of the social class position in the country of origin. My research sample of British Muslim women studying in London has highlighted the broad appeal of higher education to many migrant families, regardless of class and parental education. Most students in this study described their family backgrounds as predominantly 'working class'. Many had relatives in the UK or in the country of origin, or elsewhere, who were also studying for, or had obtained, degree qualifications.

When interviewed, many of the young women students, regardless of current graduate or postgraduate status, were able to identify a number of motivating factors that were important both to them and to their families. These are described next.

Parental encouragement

Parental encouragement for daughters to study at degree level was based on qualitatively *different* perceptions of the future roles and needs of sons and daughters. Sons were viewed as future breadwinners, whose status was dependent upon them securing a stable job. A great deal of honour was invested with sons, but in a qualitatively *different* way. Students in this research with brothers or male relatives talked about parental expectations for sons resting in financially lucrative professions. Many sons were strongly encouraged to pursue vocationally oriented degree subjects, such as law, medicine, dentistry, engineering and computer science for instance. Daughters were not *always* expected to participate in full-time employment after university, though most in this study have been encouraged to do so. Research conducted by Bhachu (1991) on British Sikh women and educational achievement also suggests similar trends.

Education for daughters was an 'investment', symbolising that their 'value', both within the family and to those outside it, went beyond patriarchal ideologies of women as 'homemakers'. As undergraduates and postgraduates, daughters' 'traditional' domestic roles within the home were modified to accommodate their need to study if academic success was to be attained. As I shall go on to describe, this 'extension and modification' of roles for daughters also has implications for their future marriage prospects.

Students discussed how, from an early age, their parents had forewarned them of an uncertain future based on the grim realities of racial discrimination in the labour market, and their own experiences in this respect. Education and qualifications were seen as a possible 'back-up' that assured a certain degree of security against the worst-case scenarios.

These concerns were further compounded by parental fears of failing to procure or locate 'suitable' husbands for their daughters, particularly if the extended family or a large social network was absent. Financial independence in this instance, especially in the event of the loss of either one or both parents, was imperative. 'Suitable' husbands were generally viewed as men who were more than 'graduates', in stable employment. They were likely to appreciate a potential wife's mental acumen and support her in domestic affairs, or in a career, if she chose to pursue one. Therefore, sons and sons-in-law were expected to possess less 'patriarchal' qualities in addition to being socially and academically compatible. In the event of the marriage breaking down, or if financial circumstances took a turn for the worse, an educated daughter's earnings or her earning potential, could act as a 'safety net'. The possible *relationships* between degree status and marriage will be returned to later in the article.

Faced with these two possibilities – racism in the labour market and insecurity in matrimony – daughters were encouraged to gain qualifications to enable them to 'stand on their own two feet'. A degree, thus, was perceived and portrayed as a sort of 'insurance policy'.

According to many of the young women interviewed, parental encouragement was also expressed as a family 'expectation', or a family 'ethos'. This was found regardless of parental education levels or class and is supported by other research (e.g. Afshar, 1989a; Brah and Shaw, 1992; Brah, 1993; Basit, 1996a,b). I was told:

> Well it was always taken that we would all go to university and stuff...I can't even conceive not wanting to go into higher education. I would've been a completely different person, that's what I've been brought up with, to educate ourselves, that's one of my dad's things, to educate yourselves, get yourselves out of the mess.
>
> (Arifa)

Educational achievement was thus positioned alongside 'tradition'.[11] For some respondents, not to strive for higher qualifications was inconceivable, though none spoke of extreme parental pressure. Daughters learnt about 'ambition' from an early age, and were active agents in the processes of manufacturing, manipulating and exploiting this 'family ethos'.

By encouraging their daughters into higher education, parents are not only able to rest assured by their daughter's future economic potential as individuals, they are able to attain and maintain social status and prestige within their social circles. Educated daughters signal certain levels of 'liberalism' for the family concerned. A daughter's education confers a certain level of social 'education' to the rest of the family. Parents are thus able to describe themselves as 'modern' and socially astute. They are able to distance themselves from the stereotype of the patriarchal and 'non-educated' family, often believed to confuse 'tradition' with religion by observing 'strict' purdah[12] and restricting the education and movement of women. In addition, educated daughters can be expected to attract suitors of a similar status or above, *if* the 'arranged marriage' route is chosen.

As mentioned earlier, parents have been cited as playing a major role in encouraging and motivating their daughters into higher education. It has been shown that both pragmatic and social (status) concerns feature significantly (see also Basit, 1996a). However, what is the exact nature of parental influence? Do mothers play a greater role than fathers in influencing daughters on the issue of education? During the course of my research, students talked about either one or both of their parents encouraging their daughters to study and achieve. Mothers with a variety of educational levels wished to see their daughters achieve a position of choice and independence in their lifestyles, where they would not be solely dependent upon (and perhaps subordinate to) a future husband and in-laws.

However, not all mothers placed such importance on education for their daughters, though they did not object to their daughters' wishes. In these instances, mothers tended to have had few educational opportunities or inclinations themselves. What is of interest here is that *fathers* were often far more determined to see their daughters achieve academically, and this was especially apparent in families where there were no sons. For example, Amber explained her father's view of her success:

> my dad does like the fact that we've [her and one of her sisters] got a degree, he's really proud of us. Once I had a heart-to-heart discussion with him and he said, 'I'm so proud of you, it doesn't matter what you do, you've got a degree'. It's an amazing thing for my parents.

This is in stark contrast to research that situates Muslim fathers and families as exercising extreme patriarchal restraints on the education of their daughters (cf. Wade and Souter, 1994; Khanum, 1995).

Concerns and contradictions

Within this spirit of encouragement, parents were also able to instil a sense of foreboding to their daughters regarding the possible 'adverse' effects exposure to Western secular education may have. The young women were well aware that their parents were anxious of *how* they could change and of the possible 'Anglicising' effects university life may have on them.

For instance, Rehana met with opposition, not from her parents but from her extended family in the shape of her father's brothers. She was the first female in her family both in Britain and in her parents' country of origin to enter higher education. Her entry though, was compounded by her choice to live in student accommodation for her first year. Her uncles were initially suspicious of her intentions to study, fearing that her motivations stemmed from a certain 'looseness' of morality, especially as female members of the family observed purdah (though this was practised in a fairly relaxed manner).

She argued her case successfully, with much support from other female members of her extended family, notably, her aunts. Two years on, Rehana is still wearing her headscarf and is just as committed as before (if not more so) to her culture and religion, believing firmly that her university experiences have helped her to rationalise her cultural and religious affiliations. The following extract helps to illustrate this point:

> Well, it's [higher education] definitely heightened my sense of culture; I mean it's brought me closer to my family and my traditions. I suppose that's because of the life I've had in higher education; not higher education in *itself*, not the actual 'doing the degree business', its the 'life' that I've had that's actually brought me closer; the experiences have brought me closer. The actual education has, it's 'broadened your horizons', so to speak [!] it broadens your outlook, what you want to do, what you want to be, you haven't been sheltered from your parents' home to go straight to your husband's home, you've had a break in between, you've gone on, you've been in education. I mean, they sort of tell you to think about what you're gonna be, they start talking about careers, and it starts to sort of open up your mind, and yeah, it either strengthens, or changes your views, which in my case, have been strengthened and have reaffirmed my beliefs, in not necessarily religion, but more in a cultural sense.

[F: How do you think you express that?]

> Personally, I'm more confident to talk about my family without feeling that 'it's not right', or my religion, by thinking maybe that I might offend someone,

but you don't really. I mean it's good to talk and get it out of your system, and to show people that you are firmly placed in your belief and that you're not having any doubts, because a lot of people think that 'oh God, aren't Muslim girls supposed to do this and aren't Muslim girls supposed to do that?' And in a sense going into higher education encourages those people into thinking, 'hang on a sec, she's a Muslim, what's she doing here?' But then they realise, when other people see us, they realise that it's not all like that; a lot of Muslim girls do go into higher education, they do see a lot of things and they do have fun, which is really amazing for them! They don't think we have fun, especially the guys!

Rehana's 'safe passage' through the higher education system may assist younger family members seeking higher qualifications. Her experiences have helped, in part, to 'demystify' preconceived assumptions about university life, and signal the attainability of a degree. Her sentiment about university experiences was echoed by other young Muslim women in this study. They talked about how their experiences had benefited them in deeply personal ways. They gained confidence, not only in their abilities, but also in their cultural, religious and personal identities. I plan to be able to elaborate on these aspects at a later date.

Some women expressed concerns that degree status might limit future marriage prospects, because of increasing age. There were also concerns that women may become 'too educated' to find husbands who were either of a similar stature, or who would welcome a wife with an equal, or higher, qualification level. Amber used the example of her friend to illustrate this potential difficulty:

You get more educated, you're gonna have trouble, because I have a friend who's a barrister – who's she gonna marry? Do you know what I mean? She stopped [looking] about 3 years ago, because 'Mr Other Barrister' is gonna want to marry someone who's a bit lower. He's still gonna want his dinner cooked at the end of the day.

Muslim daughters (and their parents) are thus faced with a set of conflicting interests, a double-bind situation. Too little education and the family could be viewed by the rest of the community as 'backward' and 'old fashioned'; too much education and daughters could risk 'pricing themselves outside the marriage market' and 'going past their sell-by date' (Amber).

Self-motivations

Other siblings, especially those who had already 'paved the way', were influential sources of motivation, as were other family members both in the parental country of origin and in the UK. For younger siblings then, the need to 'follow suit' was sensed. Where no other family members possessed qualifications, daughters were 'self-motivated' out of a desire to 'do something' or were keen to prove themselves to their family. Rehana, whose situation was briefly described earlier, is a case in point. Determination to succeed in their academic aspirations was particularly evident amongst those who had entered higher education through examination resits or alternative routes such as Access courses.

Concerns over racial discrimination in the labour market affecting employment prospects for ethnic minorities also inculcated a sense of 'needing to be better' than the indigenous majority, an observation also noted by the research cited earlier.

Like other studies on the employment patterns of ethnic minority young people, education was seen as necessary in the creation of opportunities and in 'striving for a better quality of life' (Amber). This assertion contrasts profoundly with work done in West Yorkshire, where young women held little faith in the potential value of education for themselves as a means of upward social mobility (Afshar, 1989b). This difference may be reflective of regional and class locations.

Many of the interviewed women spoke about higher education as 'something they knew they had to do'. As Safia put it, 'We all knew right from the year dot that university was the place to go'. It was an 'ingrained' response that was not necessarily based upon pragmatic, job-related considerations, but was instead sprouting from an individual desire to achieve at a certain level for purely personal development. Amber explained:

> My education was for pure enjoyment I have to say...I thought, I'm just going to do my degree in whatever I wanted to do it in. I was really interested in history and still am, so I pursued that.

The personal sense of satisfaction and achievement degree study had given these students was also important. The opportunity to learn and engage with academic material that was of interest to *them*, coupled with the prospect of future economic independence, and to lead lives that were, for some, qualitatively different from their parents', was immensely attractive. As many women I spoke to had parents with few academic qualifications, the personal wish to fulfil *their parents'* unrealised ambitions was another source of motivation.

Whilst the young women I interviewed were keen to honour their parents' wishes and achieve academic success, they perceived a number of distinct advantages for themselves. Pursuit of higher education, the subjects studied and choices of institution were found to be the effects of a far more complex social assessment process by students and their parents, than a pragmatic decision alone. (Of course, choice of institution and degree subject was, for some, a matter of what was offered, rather than first preference.) Prestigious career choices such as medicine, dentistry and law continue to be pursued and highly regarded within South Asian communities. At the same time though, female Muslim students are 'branching out', studying topics such as English language and literature, history, economics, international politics, media studies, fashion and (even) anthropology and sociology. Personal interest is obviously the main reason behind such diversity of choice, but it also suggests that students in *this sample* are meeting 'middle-class aspirations' through studying more arts-based subjects. They are also signalling their own individuality, by not bowing to pressure (however subtle) to study the sciences or law.

Choice of educational institution, for some students, is also subject to subtle social 'pretentiousness', where the 'old' universities are preferred as opposed to the former polytechnics. The students in my sample (from the 'old' universities) were acutely aware of these distinctions, and the implications their choices could have for their own 'positioning' within their parents' social circles. By accommodating these particular social expectations with their personal interests, students were therefore able to define a certain 'elite' status for themselves and their parents.

Another major motivating factor for many was the opportunity to leave home for a legitimate reason, even though for some, the parental home was also in London. Whilst remaining aware that 'living away from home' was going to leave room for suspicion and gossip amidst some quarters of the community, the opportunity to leave home was, nevertheless, an important consideration. It is perhaps interesting to note that the desire to live away from home whilst at university does not necessarily signify an intention to abandon or sever cultural or religious links and practices.

Therefore, this research cannot support evidence from other studies that suggest that high levels of education are associated with a renouncement of 'traditional' values and practices, such as 'arranged marriages' (Bhopal, 1997a,b, 1998). Rather, it signifies the wish to experience 'student life' and gain some level of independence during termtime at least, away from the parental gaze. Many of the women I spoke to described occasions such as 'Ramadan' and 'Eid' as being times where religion could be shared in a supportive environment within university accommodation. Recent research points towards the increased awareness some universities are displaying in meeting the needs of students of minority faiths (Gilliat-Ray, 1999). 'Leaving home' then, is significant for some parents; it symbolises trust in their daughter's own sense of 'izzat',[13] or honour, whilst away from the parental home.

Other studies have cited the pursuit of higher education by young Asian women as a strategy to postpone arranged marriages. There is some evidence within the present study to suggest that marriages *may* be postponed in this way, though this has not been the sole motivating factor to enter higher education. Moreover, 'arranged marriages' and the 'arranged marriage system' as it manifests itself in the UK today, is a process that has undergone many transformations. Space does not permit me to digress any further; suffice it to say that materialism and commercialism have also played a part in affecting the length of time parents spend searching for suitable partners for their offspring.[14]

British South Asian Muslim women as achievers

This research puts in perspective the growing number of studies that document young Muslim schoolgirls' and their parents' attitudes towards higher education and professional careers. The Muslim undergraduates and postgraduates represented in this study may serve to indicate that the aspirations of schoolgirls are achievable ones.

Throughout this article, I have sought to assert that for British South Asian Muslim women, degree status confers certain social and personal advantages. Parents, and in particular fathers, have been keen to maximise their daughters' and their own social prestige by encouraging them to succeed academically. The advantages associated with this *'commodification'* of higher education are not always the same for daughters and parents. There are, however, a number of shared goals, suggesting that the pursuit of higher education, status, social mobility, and a career are not viewed as being inimical to cultural or religious ideals.

Provided certain boundaries are not crossed in relation to behaviour, these benefits are seen, in many ways, as being a feature of the cultural and religious identities of the students involved in this study. The insights gained by examining the motivations and influences of British South Asian Muslim women suggest that internal and external factors are operating in complex combinations. The accounts presented here point towards a need for the further reassessment of categories such as 'Muslim woman', already advocated by Brah (1993, 1996). Given the supportive and encouraging role some Muslim parents play in assisting in their daughters' achievements, the category 'Muslim family' also needs redefinition.

From the preliminary research presented here, it is evident that Muslim female students play an active role in the construction and reconstruction of their social and personal identities, within and despite patriarchal structures in both public and private domains. Although generalisations cannot be posited at this stage, it is hoped that future discussion of educational experiences should yield more information on the nature and the various manifestations of this 'agency' and the 'diasporic identities' (Brah, 1996, p. 176) behind them.

Acknowledgements

This paper represents a draft of work-in progress conducted for a PhD at the University of Bristol, Department of Sociology. An earlier version of this paper entitled, 'Expressions of ethnicity: Asian Muslim women in higher education', was presented at the 15th European Conference on Modern South Asian Studies, Charles University, Prague in September 1998. Any themes discussed in this paper remain provisional. A huge debt of thanks goes towards those women who agreed to take part in this study. Their names have been changed to protect anonymity. Particular notes of gratitude are owed to Anna Laerke at the School of Oriental and African Studies, to my supervisors Jackie West and Harriet Bradley for helpful comments. Additional thanks go to the two anonymous reviewers for comments on an earlier draft of this paper.

NOTES

1   The sample was composed of British-born women whose families originated from the Indian subcontinent, namely, India, Pakistan and Bangladesh.
2   It is anticipated that current work in progress will explore similar issues with students from the newer universities (former polytechnics).
3   Further discussion of Muslim subjectivity positions and some thoughts on the processes involved in carrying out research within one's own gender, ethnic and religious group are dwelt upon in Ahmad (1999).
4   See note 3.
5   I return to this point later in this article and in future work. Other work currently in progress (with T. Modood) on South Asian women and employment, with a larger, non-religious specific sample, is also beginning to exhibit similar trends.
6   See note 11.
7   For a more detailed discussion of the problems surrounding the collection of ethnic identity data in the 1991 British Census, see the edited volume by Ceri Peach (1996), which includes chapters on the Indians (Robinson), the Pakistanis (Ballard) and the Bangladeshis (Eade, Vamplew and Peach). At the time of writing, considerable debate about the inclusion of a voluntary religious identification question in the 2001 Census was occurring, with strong lobbying from Muslim groups such as the Muslim Council of Britain. Of course, a small number of Pakistanis are Christian and Patricia Jeffery's (1976) account of the Pakistani Christians in Bristol remains a classic text.
8   I am grateful to an anonymous reviewer for drawing my attention to this point.
9   Space does not permit any further discussion of these statistics, but the interested reader is advised to consult the Fourth PSI Survey (Modood et al., 1997) and also Modood and Acland (1998).
10 It remains too early to determine whether there are any experiences that remain specific to female students from the minority Shia or Ahmediya sects. There is particular controversy surrounding the categorisation of members of the Ahmediya sect as 'Muslim' (especially in Pakistan where they are not regarded as such), but for the purposes of this

research, the interviewee in question volunteered herself for interview as 'Muslim'. Apart from raising definitional questions about the inclusion and exclusion of individuals from certain groups, the heterogeneity of 'Muslim expressions' also requires further consideration. Similar dilemmas are discussed in more detail elsewhere (Ahmad, 1999).

11 The terms 'tradition' and 'traditional' appear to be employed in a variety of distinct ways. For instance, when discussing the current subject matter, that is South Asian and South Asian cultural practices, 'tradition' and 'traditional' are commonly associated with oppressive patriarchal relations of power. Discussions with young Muslim women revealed that certain contradictions exist both in their definitions of the terms 'tradition' and 'traditional' and within the sociological literature. For my respondents, 'traditional' can mean 'unwesternised', 'backward' or 'uneducated', but it can also signify a historical link with cultural practices that have positive connotations. This may be better exemplified by reference to the re-creation of certain 'traditions' during a 'traditional' marriage, for example, many of which, such as the 'mehndi' (henna) night, the clothes and jewellery, etc., are greeted with enthusiasm. 'Traditional' can also refer to modes of behaviour, such as displaying respect towards elders. Consider also the usage of this term when describing a 'traditional English pub', or 'traditional family values'. My point here is to draw attention to the multiplicity of meanings these terms can have.

12 Of course, 'strict purdah' does not necessarily lead to a restriction of movement or of educational or work-related opportunities for women. It was originally intended as a means of religious identification and to liberate and protect Muslim women in their daily activities.

13 To briefly discuss the concepts of 'izzat' and 'gender' at this juncture will not do justice to the centrality of these terms and the multiple meanings they can hold when considering the present sample group. These are, instead, discussed in more detail elsewhere (Ahmad, 1999).

14 Perhaps 'assisted marriage' is a more appropriate term. Large numbers of matrimonial agencies exist in the UK which cater for South Asians as a group or which specialise for particular religious groups. These are, for the most part, commercial enterprises. The increase in marrying ages for both sexes is due to a variety of factors, of which studying full-time is one. Securing stable employment and property are other contributory causes.

REFERENCES

Afshar, H. (1989a) 'Gender roles and the "moral economy of kin" among Pakistani women in West Yorkshire', *New Community*, 15: 211–225.

Afshar, H. (1989b) 'Education: hopes, expectations and achievements of Muslim women in West Yorkshire', *Gender and Education*, 1: 261–272.

Ahmad, F. (1999) 'Still "in progress"? – methodological dilemmas, tensions and contradictions in theorising South Asian Muslim women', paper presented at the *British Association for South Asian Studies Conference*, London School of Economics, September.

Ahmed, A.S. and Donnan, H. (1994) 'Islam in the age of postmodernity', in A.S. Ahmed and H. Donnan (eds), *Islam, Globalization and Postmodernity* (London, Routledge).

Anwar, M. (1998) *Between Cultures, Continuity and Change in the Lives of Young Asians* (London, Routledge).

Ballard, R. (ed.) (1994) *Desh Pardesh, the South Asian Presence in Britain* (London, Hurst & Company).

Ballard, R. (1996) 'The Pakistanis: stability and introspection', in C. Peach (ed.), *Ethnicity in the 1991 Census. Vol. 2, The Ethnic Minority Populations of Great Britain* (London, HMSO).

Ballard, R. and Vellins, S. (1985) 'South Asian entrants to British universities: a comparative note', *New Community*, 12: 260–265.

Basit, T.N. (1995) ' "I want to go to college": British Muslim girls and the academic dimension of schooling', *Muslim Education Quarterly*, 12: 36–54.

Basit, T.N. (1996a) ' "Obviously I'll have an arranged marriage": Muslim marriage in the British context', *Muslim Education Quarterly*, 13: 4–19.

Basit, T.N. (1996b) ' "I'd hate to be just a housewife": career aspirations of British Muslim girls', *British Journal of Guidance and Counselling*, 24: 227–242.

Bhachu, P. (1988) 'Apni Marzi Kardi: home and work: Sikh women in Britain', in S. Westwood and P. Bhachu (eds), *Enterprising Women, Ethnicity, Economy and Gender Relations* (London, Routledge).

Bhachu, P. (1991) 'Ethnicity constructed and reconstructed: the role of Sikh women in cultural elaboration and educational decision-making in Britain', *Gender and Education*, 3: 45–60.

Bhachu, P. (1996) 'The multiple landscapes of transnational Asian women in the diaspora', in V. Amit-Talai and C. Knowles (eds), *Re-situating Identities: The politics of Race, Ethnicity and Culture* (Ontario, Broadview Press).

Bhopal, K. (1997a) 'South Asian women within households: dowries, degradation and despair', *Women's Studies International Forum*, 20: 483–492.

Bhopal, K. (1997b) *Gender, 'Race' and Patriarchy: A Study of South Asian Women* (Aldershot, Ashgate).

Bhopal, K. (1998) 'How gender and ethnicity intersect: the significance of education, employment and marital status', *Sociological Research Online*, 3: 1–16.

Bhopal, K. (1999) 'South Asian women and arranged marriages in East London', in R. Barot, H. Bradley and S. Fenton (eds), *Ethnicity, Gender and Social Change* (Basingstoke, MacMillan).

Brah, A. (1993) ' "Race" and "culture" in the gendering of labour markets: South Asian young Muslim women and the labour market', *New Community*, 29: 441–458.

Brah, A. (1996) *Cartographies of Diaspora, Contesting Identities* (London, Routledge).

Brah, A. and Shaw, S. (1992) *Working Choices: South Asian Young Muslim Women and The Labour Market*, Research Paper No. 91 (London, Department of Employment).

Brown, C. (1984) *Black and White Britain. The Third PSI Survey* (London, Policy Studies Institute).

Butler, C. (1999) 'Cultural diversity and religious conformity: dimensions of social change among second-generation Muslim women', in R. Barot, H. Bradley and S. Fenton (eds), *Ethnicity, Gender and Social Change* (Basingstoke, Macmillan).

Craft, A. and Craft, M. (1983) 'The participation of ethnic minorities in further and higher education', *Educational Research*, 25: 10–19.

Dwyer, C. (1999) 'Veiled meanings: British Muslim women and the negotiation of differences', *Gender, Place and Culture*, 6: 5–26.

Eade, J., Vamplew, T. and Peach, C. (1996) 'The Bangladeshis: the encapsulated community', in C. Peach (ed.), *Ethnicity in the 1991 Census. Vol. 2, The Ethnic Minority Populations of Great Britain* (London, HMSO).

Gibson, M.A. and Bhachu, P. (1988) 'Ethnicity and school performance: a comparative study of South Asian pupils in Britain and America', *Ethnic and Racial Studies*, 11: 239–262.

Gilliat-Ray, S. (1999) *Higher Education and Student Religious Identity* (Exeter, Department of Sociology, University of Exeter and the Interfaith Network for the UK).

Jeffery, P. (1976) *Migrants and Refugees: Muslim and Christian Families in Bristol* (Cambridge, Cambridge University Press).

Jones, T. (1996) *Britain's Ethnic Minorities* (London, Policy Studies Institute).

Khanum, S. (1995) 'Education and the Muslim girl', in M. Blair, J. Holland and S. Sheldon (eds), *Identity and Diversity: Gender and The Experience of Education* (Clevedon, Multilingual Matters).

Knott, K. and Khokher, S. (1993) 'Religious and ethnic identity among young Muslim women in Bradford', *New Community*, 19: 593–610.

Lewis, P. (1994) *Islamic Britain: Religion, Politics and Identity Among British Muslims* (London, I. B. Tauris & Co.).

Modood, T. (1990) 'British Asian Muslims and the Rushdie affair', in J. Donald and A. Rattansi (eds), *'Race', Culture and Difference* (London, Sage).

Modood, T. and Acland, T. (eds) (1998) *Race and Higher Education* (London, Policy Studies Institute).

Modood, T. and Shiner, M. (1994) *Ethnic Minorities and Higher Education – Why are There Differential Rates of Entry?* (London, Policy Studies Institute).

Modood, T., Berthoud, R., Lakey, J., Nazroo, J., Smith, P., Virdee, S. and Beishon, S. (1997) *Ethnic Minorities in Britain, Diversity and Disadvantage* (London, Policy Studies Institute).

Parekh, B. (1988) 'The Swann Report and ethnic minority attainment', in G.K. Verma and P. Pumphrey (eds), *Educational Attainments, Issues and Outcomes in Multicultural Education* (London, Falmer Press).

Peach, C. and Glebe, G. (1995) 'Muslim minorities in Western Europe', *Ethnic and Racial Studies*, 18: 26–45.

Robinson, V. (1996) 'The Indians: onward and upward', in C. Peach (ed.), *Ethnicity in the 1991 Census. Vol. 2, The Ethnic Minority Populations of Great Britain* (London, HMSO).

Saifullah Khan, V. (1977) 'The Pakistanis: Mirpuri villagers at home and in Bradford', in J.L. Watson (ed.), *Between Two Cultures: Migrants and Minorities in Britain* (Oxford, Blackwell).

Sayyid, B.S. (1997) *A Fundamental Fear: Eurocentrism and The Emergence of Islamism* (London, Zed Books).

Shaw, A. (1994) 'The Pakistani community in Oxford', in R. Ballard (ed.), *Desh Pardesh: the South Asian Presence in Britain* (London, Hurst & Company).

Singh, R. (1990) 'Ethnic minority experience in higher education', *Higher Education Quarterly*, 44: 344–359.

Taylor, P. (1993) 'Minority ethnic groups and gender in access to higher education', *New Community*, 19: 425–440.

Tomlinson, S. (1983) *Ethnic Minorities in British Schools: A Review of The Literature, 1960–82* (London, Policy Studies Institute).

Tomlinson, S. (1986) 'Ethnicity and educational achievement', in S. Modgil, G.K. Verma, K. Mallick and C. Modgil (eds), *Multicultural Education: The Interminable Debate* (London, Falmer Press).

Tomlinson, S. (1991) 'Ethnicity and educational attainment in England: an overview', *Anthropology and Education Quarterly*, 22: 121–139.

Vellins, S. (1982) 'South Asian students in British universities: a statistical note', *New Community*, 10: 206–212.

Verma, G.K. and Mallick, K. (1988) 'Self-esteem and educational achievement in British young South Asians', in G.K. Verma and P. Pumphrey (eds), *Educational Attainments, Issues and Outcomes in Multicultural Education* (London, Falmer Press).

Wade, B. and Souter, P. (1992) *Continuing to Think: The British Asian Girl* (Clevedon, Multilingual Matters).

Werbner, P. (1988) 'Taking and giving: working women and female bonds in a Pakistani immigrant neighbourhood', in S. Westwood and P. Bhachu (eds), *Enterprising Women: Ethnicity, Economy and Gender Relations* (London, Routledge).

Werbner, P. (1994) 'Diaspora and millennium: British Pakistani global-local fabulations of the Gulf War', in A. Ahmed and H. Donnan (eds), *Islam, Globalization and Postmodernity* (London, Routledge).

West, J. and Pilgrim, S. (1995) 'South Asian women in employment: the impact of migration, ethnic origin and the local economy', *New Community*, 21: 357–378.

Wilson, A. (1978) *Finding a Voice – Asian Women in Britain* (London, Virago).

NINETEEN

THEORISING INNER-CITY MASCULINITIES: 'RACE', CLASS, GENDER AND EDUCATION

Louise Archer and Hiromi Yamashita

Source: 'Theorising inner-city masculinities: "race", class, gender and education', *Gender and Education*, 15(2): 115–132, 2003.

Introduction

Working-class, inner-city and certain minority ethnic young men have been positioned as high-profile 'problems' within current social and educational policy discourses. Alarm has been expressed at these boys' generally low levels of academic attainment (Arnot *et al.*, 1998; Department for Education and Employment [DfEE], 1998), their high levels of exclusion from mainstream education (Marland, 1995) and their low participation rates in post-compulsory and higher education (National Committee of Inquiry into Higher Education [NCIHE], 1997; Lloyd, 1999; McGivney, 1999). Within popular discourses too, these young men are frequently portrayed in 'folk devil' terms, being associated with inner-city social problems such as crime, deviance and unemployment, the causes of which have been linked to the boys' problematic subcultures and/or class/ethnic cultures and their 'anti-education' masculine identities.

Concerns about inner-city, working-class boys are located within wider contemporary moral panics about boys' educational 'underachievement' and fears that masculinity is 'in crisis'. Popular media and political discourses have linked the causes of this 'crisis' in masculinity to the decline of the manufacturing industry, challenges to rationality and to the rise of feminism and the 'overachievement' of girls (Newton, 1998). A substantial feminist critique has developed in relation to the boys' underachievement debate, challenging dominant discourses for being narrow and masculinist in style and for ignoring diversity between boys from different ethnic and social backgrounds (e.g. Epstein *et al.*, 1998). Feminist critiques of popular explanations for boys' underachievement, such as 'laddishness', have also drawn attention to the complexity inherent within constructions of masculinity (Francis, 1999). For example, Francis argues that 'laddishness' – whilst popularly constructed as a working-class phenomenon, has been appropriated by, and popularised for, middle-class men. Notions of 'laddishness' have been predominantly discussed within a white context, and suggestions have been made that 'further research could usefully explore the ways in which this behaviour is adopted by different groups of boys and men' (Jackson, 2002, p. 38).

It is thus recognised that critical approaches to theorising issues of masculinity and schooling need to engage with complex identities and inequalities across 'race', ethnicity, gender and class. As Ball *et al.* (2000) stress, issues of identity and inequality are central to understanding young people's relationships to education since identities can provide important sites of resistance to participation in education. Theoretically tackling such issues is, however, highly complex. There are difficulties surrounding the conceptualisation of social class (e.g. Walkerdine *et al.*, 1999), 'race', ethnicity, culture (e.g. May and Modood, 2001) and gender (e.g. Francis and Skelton, 2001). Classed identities are 'cross-cut' by 'race' and gender (Anthias and Yuval-Davis, 1992) and analysis needs to account for the 'messy', shifting and subjectively experienced classed, racialised masculine and feminine identities whilst also locating lived identity issues to 'positionings within the broader material structures' (Mahony and Zmroczek, 1997, p. 2).

This article addresses the question of how to theorise diverse working-class young men's identities within the 'multicultural-scape' (Hesse, 2000), through an exploration of the ways in which boys at one inner-city school talked about themselves and their identities in relation to the process of leaving compulsory education.

Racialised masculinities

Critics have argued that the past decade has evidenced a subtle eradication of 'race' from the education policy agenda. This has been achieved through the normalisation of particular, middle-class, white values within policy discourse (Gewirtz, 2001) and the collapse of 'race' into 'social exclusion' (Lewis, 2000). The 'problematisation' of black masculinity has been exacerbated within New Labour policy rhetoric through assumptions that 'race' is only a minority ethnic group issue (Phoenix, 2000) and that the source of social problems can be located within the attitudes and behaviour of minority ethnic families and communities (Lewis, 2000). Thus, within policy discourses, 'race' has been both ignored, marginalised and positioned as the source of social problems (Hesse, 2000, p. 15), with the consequence that the 'normal' child or young person is constructed as white, middle class and male (Walkerdine, 1988, cited in Phoenix, 2000).

The hyper-visibility of minority ethnic young men within public and policy discourses as objects of 'problem/concern' is contrasted with their invisibility in academic literature (Alexander, 2000, p. 132). As previously suggested, 'Working class masculinity is...often conceptualised synonymously with white working class men' (Archer *et al.*, 2001, p. 433) and, consequently, 'Black masculinity is not something we consciously talk much about in academic study' (Mirza, 1999, p. 137). Dominant discourses around 'race' and masculinity have been further affected by a tendency to stereotype and homogenise Other cultures (Glissant, 1989, cited in Hesse, 2000, p. 22). As Alexander (2000, p. 135) has argued, this has resulted in the re/production of popular discourses that deny black agency and reproduce stereotypical constructions of deviant young black male identities. Thus, minority ethnic young men have been contradictorily positioned as both 'invisible' (in policy and theory) and 'hyper-visible' (in public discourses and racist stereotypes).

This article will draw upon a theorisation of masculinity as both embodied, structurally positioned *and* 'performed' (Butler, 1990, cited in Phoenix, 2000) in order to understand the texts of inner-city young men. In other words, masculinities are understood as discursively constructed and positioned, being constantly reworked, and thus always in process of 'becoming' (Hall, 1992). Within our analyses we have attempted to unpick themes of commonality and difference within the young men's accounts, identifying various ways of 'doing masculinity' and exploring struggles between competing versions of masculinity. Consideration is given to the ways in which young men's accounts are constructed within power relations and inequalities of 'race', class and gender (Edley and Wetherell, 1995, p. 17).

We attempt to foreground the young men's agency within this process, highlighting how boys may reflexively contribute to their own positionings (Phoenix, 2000) and how their constructions may disrupt/destabilise dominant (narrow) accounts of working-class urban masculinities (Hesse, 2000). The article explores how specific notions (of gender, race, territory, sexuality) are articulated, negotiated and transgressed by young men within discussions about their post-16 'choices'. We aim to produce nuanced analyses, as opposed to sensationalising or pathologising accounts, of the shifting complexity of the young men's identities (Hesse, 2000, p. 23) in order to critically contribute to discussions about inner-city youth and educational policies.

Research study and respondents

This article draws upon data from a small-scale, qualitative pilot study funded by the British Academy ('The role of identities and inequalities on the aspirations of inner city school leavers'). Interviews and small focus groups were conducted with 20 pupils (boys and girls) from Year 11 (15/16 years old) and 10 teachers at an inner-city London mixed comprehensive school ('City Park' School) during the summer term of 2001.[1] Pupils were contacted again over the summer/autumn to follow up on their General Certificate of Secondary Education (GCSE) results and their post-school routes. For the purposes of this article, however, we primarily report and discuss data collected from the boys who took part.

Semi-structured interviews and group discussions were used to explore pupils' views about education and their post-16 aspirations. Questions focused on eliciting pupils' constructions of both im/possible and un/desirable options and routes, their views on post-compulsory and higher education, and factors which would encourage, or discourage, them from remaining in education. An account of findings specifically in relation to the young people's perceived 'horizons of choice' can be found in Archer and Yamashita (2003). The length of the interviews or group discussions varied from half an hour to just under one hour and a half. Pupil respondents were informed that the purpose of the research was to ask about their plans and aspirations for when they leave school.

City Park school is located in a deprived, multi-ethnic inner London borough ('Harkton'), described by teachers as a 'very depressed' area with high rates of unemployment. The school's intake reflects the multi-ethnic locality, with about 68 different languages spoken by its pupils. The school had been placed on 'special measures' at the time of the research, and this contributed to high levels of stress and concern among staff and pupils. The pressures on space and resources within the school were evidenced by the constant interruptions experienced in all interviews and the difficulties encountered trying to find a space in which to conduct interviews. It was difficult to recruit respondents to interviews and group discussions because we were often targeting persistent truants with sporadic rates of attendance. The authors spent considerable time each day waiting to see which pupils would turn up, and fixed interview times were impossible to adhere to. The assistance of the Head of Year was invaluable in this respect; she spent considerable time identifying and recruiting all interviewees, in addition to her heavy everyday workload. But despite difficulties in recruiting volunteers, the young people we spoke with seemed pleasant and forthcoming, enjoying the opportunity to talk about themselves and give their views.

In this article, we concentrate in particular on data from 11 boys: three African boys; three Caribbean boys; two Bengali boys; one white boy; one Sikh boy; and one Cypriot boy. Pupils were all identified by teachers for the study on the grounds of being from 'working-class' backgrounds and 'unlikely to progress further in education'. Pupils were mostly predicted a range of attainment at GCSE between grades D and F. All the boys were in Year 11 at the time of the research (aged 15/16 years old).

Interviews and discussions were tape-recorded and were conducted by one of the two authors (LA, HY), who are white British (LA) and Japanese (HY) women from middle-class and working-class backgrounds respectively. As researchers, we are, of course, neither objective nor 'outside' of the research process. Our gendered, racialised and classed identities/positions interact with the identities of the respondents, providing a specific context within which the boys produced, constructed and negotiated masculine identities (see Archer, 2002). But in line with Bhavnani (1993), we hoped to use our different positions to help understand 'the ways in which the gender, "race" and social class positions of respondents intersect with those of the researcher' (Phoenix, 1994, p. 49). We thus used our different identity positions as question points within the interviews, and we used discussions between ourselves (as differently positioned researchers), during the analysis, to inform our subsequent interpretations of the data.

Territoriality and embodied identities

LA: Right. What makes the difference to get in [to college/job]?
ERKAN: You have to go there smartly dressed, and don't be rude.
LEE: I didn't go to interview smartly dressed you know, I just put on baggy trousers, my skating clothes and I just went there. They looked at me as if to say 'what you dressing like that for'.
ERKAN: They don't say it, but they want you to be smartly dressed, like talk politely and stuff.
LEE: That ain't never gonna happen to me, I can't speak [inaudible].
LA: Is that for everything, is that like jobs and college?
LEE: Yeah most places, they want you to speak all smart and stuff like that but that's not your true self and you're not gonna be like that all the time are you.
ERKAN: If you work in a place, you can't swear, but you have to be like 'can I help you?'
LEE: I can't do that.

(Lee: white, English boy; Erkan: Turkish/British boy)

The boys constructed embodied identities, expressed – for example – through their speech, style and clothing. Accent and language appeared as important defining features of Harkton masculinities (the multiracialised aspects of which are explored later in the article), and a number of boys constructed a key difference between both researchers and themselves; namely, that we would not be able to understand the 'made-up' slang that characterised Harkton boys' speech. These identifying aspects of speech and appearance were clearly classed, being described as the opposite of middle-class 'polite' talk (see Hey, 1997) and 'smart' dress. As Lee and Erkan's extract also suggests, their embodied working-class identities are imbued with inequalities, placing them at a disadvantage in the post-16 education and labour markets, where access to further education or employment will depend upon having the necessary ability and resources to engage in pretence. But these 'rough' (Walkerdine *et al.*, 2001) working-class masculinities were also valued as authentic (Wetherell and Potter, 1992), 'real' ('your true self') and were valued and defended: for example, Erkan and Lee resisted abandoning aspects of their identities in order to become more socially mobile.

A common theme across the boys' transcripts was the construction of specifically 'local' masculine identities and the identification of themselves as 'Harkton boys'. Through these identities the boys expressed a sense of territory and ownership of/ belonging to the local area. Themes of 'style', clothes and accent/speech were integral to the construction of these 'local' identities and the boys' constructions of 'Harkton masculinities' were closely tied to discourses of visibility and locality:

> Yeah, outside of Harkton a boy will come up to me if I'm in Homes or Gunnerton. They'll come up to me if I go and see my cousin and say, 'I can tell you are a Harkton boy from the way you dress'. I'll go, 'Yeah' because they are trying to start, 'Do you wanna fight?' They just wanna cause trouble. I just laugh in their face and say, 'Touch and then you'll see trouble' and then they just go, 'Yeah yeah yeah yeah' and they just leave me and I just walk on, they don't touch me. Outside Harkton, all my gold and everything I always hide because I'm outside Harkton. I only keep my gold out when I am in Harkton but if I'm outside Harkton with my boys then I keep my gold out because it is hard for someone to come through my boys and take something off me. That's how it is.
> (Solomon: black British/Nigerian boy)

As Westwood (1990) has noted, working-class urban masculinities are closely associated with notions of place/locality, safety and danger. Connolly and Neill (2001) also demonstrate how the field of social relations within the local area will influence and shape the ways in which young people think and behave. Their work with Catholic children in Northern Ireland showed how the youngsters derived status from particular relations within the locality that structured and reinforced their habitus.

Connolly and Neill (2001) highlight gender differences between boys' and girls' constructions of the local area, with boys emphasising fighting and violence, reflecting a greater sense of 'territory' (and the need to defend this territory). They related these constructions to gendered notions of strength and physicality, demonstrating how the boys performed masculinities, gaining status and capital through their knowledge, and talk, of violence.

The boys in our study demarcated surrounding geographical areas into 'safe' and 'unsafe' locales (Westwood, 1990; Watt and Stenson, 1998), but descriptions of Harkton itself contained fusions of both safety (the known, familiar) and danger. For example, an image of Harkton as characterised by crime, violence, poverty, drugs and danger (against which the young men need to 'survive') was a common script among the young men.

Even though the young people were critical of the local area and emphasised the crime and danger in Harkton, most said they would be reluctant to move away.

The need to 'keep close' (Pugsley, 1998) was mostly framed in terms of family relations and the safety of familiarity – knowing people and being known.

INTERVIEWER: So you know this area well, are you going to live close by?
SOLOMON: Yeah, because I mostly know everyone in Harkton and is better than go to other area because trouble starts, you get people bullying you all the time and you don't know things about the other area. In your area you got your people there for you.

Similarly to other studies (e.g. Archer *et al.*, 2002), the necessity to 'stay local' also strongly influenced the boys' post-16 choices, circumscribing, for example, which further education colleges they would consider attending and where they might consider seeking employment. Thus, for Solomon, the idea that he might move away to pursue either work or study was 'unthinkable' (Cohen, 1988).

Thus, for the young men, the local area was also strongly interlinked with their identities, which one young man, Richard, framed in terms of a maturity/loss of innocence that would prevent him from fitting in elsewhere.

> the reason I don't want to get out is I'm already in it. I wake up in the morning hearing all these stuff, these violence, thing like that. I see crack-heads running past my door, *smiling*. I see everything and I'm used to it now. If I come out of this I'm not going to be used to no quiet area ... I'm not playing marbles with no one.
>
> (Richard: black British/Caribbean boy)

Multiracialised, 'entangled' masculinities

In contrast to the rather simplistic treatment of 'race' and gender issues within much education policy, we would argue that the boys in our study constructed multicultural, multiracialised masculinities, drawing on a range of locally grounded, diasporic discourses. These masculinities were racialised, but not in simple or homogeneous ways – they were 'culturally entangled'. ' "Cultural entanglements" are defined as "commonplace forms of *creolization, hybridity, syncretism,* [that] represent a profound challenge to the idea that national and social forms are logically coherent, unitary or tidy" (Hesse, 2000, p. 2, emphasis in original)'.[2]

In other words, in constructing identities, we suggest that the boys' talk combined globalised and localised discourses that cross-cut ethnic and national groupings. Their identity constructions combine traces of various social, historical, geographical and cultural elements, and indicate the shifting nature of masculinities, which are created and recreated across time and context. These themes will be further explored later in the article in relation to African and Caribbean boys, but as the following extracts from Lee will illustrate, majority ethnic (white) masculinity was also culturally entangled. For example, Lee's extract suggests a shifting cultural plain, embodied through accent and modes of speech:

> Yeah, like me and him will say stuff that ain't proper English, and slang that we make up, people say it – can't help it, you're influenced by other people saying it. When I was little I used to speak properly. No actually I used to speak cockney, hard core cockney.
>
> (Lee)

Although he clearly identified himself within the research as 'white' and 'English', we would suggest that Lee is also ambiguously ethnically positioned through his 'entangled' speech, in which his working-class white London ('cockney') roots are suffused by the (Caribbean-influenced) Black British local 'accent' and slang used by his peers. He linked this change in his own accent to (we would interpret, classed, gendered and racialised)[3] changes in the wider London context: 'London used to be a place where smart people used to come, nowadays it's where bad boys come and something like that'.

Lee's positioning of himself through his style and speech could be understood as typical of the 'white wannabes' in Sewell's (Sewell, 1997, 1998) research and the young white men in Les Back's (Back, 1996) research who were attracted to 'acting black' and black male styles. Both Back and Sewell understood the young white men in their studies as wanting to emulate 'hard' black masculinities, which they associated with 'hardness' and sexual prowess. These black masculinities were, however, ambivalently positioned, being both feared and admired by the white boys ('it is admiration of a phallocentric black masculinity that most disturbs the psyche of white youths' [Sewell, 1998, p. 121]). These kinds of identification are problematic because, as Back suggests, they reflect their location within structural inequalities of racism (and heterosexism):

> For white young men, the imaging of black masculinity in heterosexual codes of 'hardness' and 'hypersexuality' is one of the core elements which attracts them to black masculine style. However, the image of black sexuality as potent and 'bad' is alarmingly similar to racist notions of dangerous/violent 'black muggers'.
>
> (Back, 1994, pp. 178–179, cited in Sewell, 1998, p. 121)

We would, however, suggest that Lee's accounts do not fit entirely neatly into this explanation due to his apparently anti-racist identification, in which he places his friendships with black boys as a key, defining identity. Harkton was generally talked about as typified by inter-ethnic friendships and a lack of racism, but Lee also asserted that his friendships with black boys positioned him differently to whites in different neighbouring areas such as 'Upham':

> Yeah and another thing, certain things that happen to white people around here as well, like racial issues. Upham and Harkton. Harkton not as much racialism, but Upham – I walked into Upham and I'll be attacked by this gang called NF, sometimes I go round Upham see my cousins, I nearly got attacked by a whole gang of these white racist people, because I've got only black friends, and I've only got a couple of white friends and they know that, and they try and attack me and because of that. There's another gang called MRB there, and they tried to attack me because I was white. I was trying to figure out what's going on here?
>
> (Lee)

This is not to deny that many white boys are attracted to a phallocentric black masculine identity, nor is it to deny the racist basis of such discourses (indeed, these issues will be returned to later within a more detailed discussion of popular 'bad boy' masculinities). Rather, we would suggest that Lee's talk points towards more nuanced and complex cultural identifications than solely a 'white wannabe' masculinity.

Lee did, at one level, identify himself unambiguously as white and English, reflecting the power and hegemony of these normalised identities. In comparison, the minority ethnic group boys negotiated between a greater range of possible ethnic, racial and national identities. For example, Erkan could not decide what his ethnicity was, debating between 'European' (although he was unclear as to whether Turkey was part of Europe), 'Turkish' and 'English'. The young black men also negotiated between 'black', 'British', 'Caribbean' and 'African' identities. These negotiations were not value-free, but were laden with meanings and formed part of the micro-, discursive power struggles between the men over the symbols of masculinity (Gilroy, 1993). For example, there was no single, agreed, black diasporic identity. Distinctions were drawn between 'authentic'/ 'cool' Caribbean masculinities and Other/ridiculed African masculinities. Boys of African heritage were more likely to identify their ethnicity as 'black' (as opposed to 'Caribbean' boys) and used popular Caribbean styles of talk and dress. However, they were often ridiculed by Caribbean boys; for example, Warren was called a 'refugee' by the other black boys, despite being born and brought up in England. They also teased him relentlessly in interviews about Africa and African identity, which they positioned as less desirable, less 'cool' but also more pompous than Caribbean identities. In a recent Channel 4 programme examining relations within the black British diaspora, Darcus Howe related such cleavages between African and Caribbean groups in Britain to historical patterns of immigration and the slave trade, which were instrumental in the formation of modern class differences between some African and Caribbean nations. There is not space here to adequately explore issues surrounding constructions of specific Caribbean and African diasporic identities; however, we would suggest that these interpretations draw attention to how diasporic identities have social and geographic 'histories' that continue to influence modern manifestations and constructions beyond the immediate time/space boundaries. Thus, class, migration and ethnicity are integrally connected concepts.

In addition to constructing differences between themselves, a key, common theme to emerge from the boys' transcripts was that dominant and attractive/ popular ('hegemonic') discourses of masculinity were drawn from black Caribbean sources, mixed with US black 'rap' elements and grounded within a local London context. These identities were 'personified' in the myth of the 'rude boy' or 'bad boy'. The following section focuses in greater detail upon the key themes of this identity construction ('Reputation', 'Slackness', Heterosexuality, Hyper-visibility) and examines how these were negotiated and taken up by boys in particular ways.

Rude boys, MCs: sex, drugs'n'rap

The boys all drew on particular aspects of the 'rude' or 'bad boy' masculinity at times within the interviews. As detailed in Francis (1999) and Epstein *et al.* (1998), popular public, educational and political discourses have put forward the notion of male 'laddishness' (and its associated 'bad' or 'naughty' behaviour) as a possible explanation for boys' underachievement at school (and resistance to participation in education more generally). We would suggest, however, that 'bad boy' identities are far more complex constructions, being specifically located, classed and racialised masculinities. For example, within the transcripts, whilst some broad notion of 'laddishness' can be identified, there are important variations and enactments between the boys. We did not identify boys as falling into different masculinity 'types' (cf. Sewell, 1997), nor did we perceive any of the young men as constructing *only* 'bad boy' masculine identities. Rather, we suggest that boys negotiated between, and took up positions across, a range of competing identity discourses. Some boys, like Richard, invested more heavily and consistently in the performance of 'bad boy' identity discourses, but we would still stress his flexible and shifting performance of this type of masculine identity. Furthermore, as we shall suggest in the following analyses, whilst these constructions of 'bad boy' masculinities often occupy positions that might be interpreted as antithetical to educational ideals, they are not straightforwardly 'anti-education'. Rather, as the examples will illustrate, for many of the boys education and school were only peripheral concerns within their identity constructions. The boys' most powerful identifications appeared to be referenced externally to the education system, within popular culture, music, the local area and gendered, classed and racialised relationships. The implications of these analyses will be returned to in the concluding section of the article.

In the following analyses we draw out the main components of this cluster of discourses which constitute this particular 'bad boy' masculinity ideal. Extracts from an impromptu rap (performed during one of the sessions by a group of black African and Caribbean boys) are also used to illustrate the ways in which the boys enacted and asserted these popular masculinities. The use of popular music as a site for the examination of multicultural and cultural entanglements is not new (e.g. Gilroy, 1991; Hebdige, 1996). For example, Hebdige has pointed to the role of entangled black musical styles, such as reggae, in creating 'a diasporan identity among the black urban dispossessed' (Hebdige, 1996, p. 138). Gilroy (1991) has also written of the importance of processes such as 'sampling', 'remixing' and 'constant repetition' (versioning) within black diasporan music and how they can operate as counter-hegemonic discourses.

The boys' rap drew on the musical styles of hip-hop, ragga and UK Garage – epitomised by anti-establishment sentiments (violence, criminality), 'gangster' identities, drug-taking, heterosexual prowess, 'flashy' symbols of material success, public hypervisibility (particularly to the police), lyrical/rap ability and competition, to which the boys added their own anti-education sentiments. The boys enacted masculinities through their rap performance, splicing familiar, well-worn lyrics, themes and lines with their own experiences, mixing the mythical/fantastical, phallocentric urban black male fantasy with both the exaggerated and the everyday of their own lives.

Central to this version of masculinity were notions of 'slackness', which Denise Noble (Noble, 2000), drawing on the work of Cooper (1993), theorises as deriving from working-class Caribbean cultures:

> Slackness represents 'backward', 'rude' folk/ghetto culture, vying for recognition and value within official Jamaican national identity.
>
> (Noble, 2000, p. 151)

> Slackness is potentially a politics of subversion...Slackness is a metaphorical revolt against law and order...It is the antithesis of Culture.
>
> (Cooper, 1993, cited in Noble, 2000, p. 154)

Noble argues that slackness and resistance to Eurocentric ideals and respectability among Caribbean women and men are enacted 'in ways that are gender specific (but not gender exclusive)' (p. 152). Noble explains how a central theme within the Slackness/Culture dichotomy involves contested values around *sex/sexuality*, and negotiation between the oppositional values of 'Reputation' versus 'Respectability'. Thus, a key element of 'slackness', and the boys' performance of 'bad boy' masculinities, is the assertion of *hyper-heterosexuality*, as demonstrated in the rap extract that follows:

> Sexy ladies come wind down low
> You're tuned into my lyrical flow
> East London ladies – wablow
> Leyton, Chingford, Plaistow
> Harkton, Stratford, Walthamstow
> East Ham, West Ham girls that know
> That I'm livin' the vida loca
> Y'joker
> Fuck that, I'm a sexy smoker
> I'm a weed promoter

The boys' lyrics contained various references to 'sexy ladies' and being 'sexy'. At other points in the rap they also boasted about real or imagined (hetero) sexual relations and incidents. They took up and 'customised' popular discourses of heterosexually successful masculinity, grounding these within the regional London context in order to assert their 'local power' (Archer *et al.*, 2001) as powerful, desirable/desired men. Sewell (1997) also found that 15-year-old black British boys located themselves within 'a phallocentric framework'. Sewell details how the boys he termed 'the Rebels' drew particularly upon machismo styles of 'hard' rap (misogynistic lyrics), boasting about heterosexual prowess, 'bopping' (a stylised walk), style and 'doing daring'. These notions of phallocentric masculinity echo themes within Caribbean ragga music: 'In Slackness/Ragga there is stress upon individual performance and skill, sexual prowess and anti-establishment sentiments which we would expect to find circulating within a value system based upon reputation' (Noble, 2000, p. 153).

We suggest, however, that the boys' assertions of phallocentric masculinities are not only forms of cultural resistance, but can be understood as ways of asserting powerful masculinities in relation to women and Other men. It has been suggested by various writers that hegemonic masculinity is organised around the discursive subordination of Others, particularly women and gay men (e.g. Connell, 1989; Edley and Wetherell, 1995; Gough and Edwards, 1998) and that the construction of binary difference between male (subject) and female (other) is a powerful and persistent feature of popular masculinity (Paechter, 1998). 'Compulsory heterosexuality' (Rich, 1976) is also a central feature of popular/'hegemonic' versions of masculinity. For example, Haywood and Mac an Ghaill (1996) have highlighted different ways in which heterosexuality can be foregrounded and normalised within performances of working-class masculinities, through 'fashion' (consumption of popular styles of clothing, night clubs, pubs, cars) or through overt misogyny, perversity, violence, sexual innuendoes and so on. Reynolds (1997, p. 321) has also found that 'symbolic sexual performances' are common among English primary school boys as young as 9–10 years old, who engage in sexual storytelling and the objectification of girls/women as part of the performance of young, popular masculinities.

We would therefore suggest that the boys' assertion of '*bad boy*', 'hyper-heterosexual' masculinities should not be reduced to explanations based solely on either 'culture' or 'patriarchy', because the two are intricately intertwined. These identities are also grounded within inequalities because it can be argued that a discourse of phallocentric black masculinity lies at the heart of dominant, oppressive myths around black masculinity (Gilroy and Lawrence, 1988; Gillborn, 1990; Sewell, 1997).

Such interplays of 'race' and gender, and their close grounding within local contexts, disrupt the notion of a singular 'hegemonic' or 'popular' (heterosexual) masculinity. As Whitehead (1999) argues, the notion of a single hegemonic masculinity is 'unable to explain the variant identity meanings attached to the concept of masculinity at this particular moment in the social history of Euro/American/ Australasian countries' (p. 58). Instead, we would agree that hegemony is never absolute (Gramsci, 1971) and masculinity is a 'contested territory' (Edley and Wetherell, 1995, p. 17) incurring struggles over the symbols of masculinity (Gilroy, 1993). Indeed, it has been argued that the assertion of patriarchal masculinities, through heterosexuality and the control of women, can form an important part of the assertion of racialised masculinities in relation to 'other' men (Alexander, 1996; Archer, 2001).

Hyper-visibility

As noted in the introductory section of the article, the boys constructed masculinities that were characterised and accentuated through particular styles of dress, speech and appearance. These themes also featured in their constructions of 'bad boy' identities, but they were exaggerated and combined with the performance of a distinctive, emblematic style of walking ('bopping' (Sewell, 1997)), that reflected the *'hyper-visibility'* of these masculinities. As illustrated by the extract that follows, the boys talked about this hyper-visibility and display of 'attitude' as differentiating them from other 'normal' people, and consequently attracting disapproval from agencies such as teachers and the police.

INTERVIEWER: What kind of things do you think I don't understand because I'm not you and I'm not living here?

STEVEN: Well you don't have to fight as much as we have to fight. We get bullied quite a lot, not only by the pupils but by the teachers, everyone. And the police like to stop us more often.

RICHARD: Black youths.

WARREN: And we have this attitude in the way we walk etc. This boy Lloyd has a walk where the police have to pull him up and tell him to walk like a normal person! [RICHARD: some of them will have their trouser rolled up.] Yeah he wears his up to his knees, he doesn't really wear trousers, he wears shorts and walks around.

STEVEN: That's right, he draws attention to himself.

RICHARD: He's made it, he draws attention to himself...the police know him off by heart, don't they?

In addition to making themselves visible in public through styles of walk, within their raps the boys used exaggerated self-praise, 'verbal virtuosity and sexual boasting' (Noble, 2000, p. 153) to draw attention to themselves, making frequent references to how 'sharp' and fast their lyrics were and how other boys cannot keep up with them (are 'floored').

Lyrics going to fly just like a Concorde
Lyrics so sharp just like a sword
Lyrics that ride just like a Ford
Listen to me you'll never get bored
Try and catch mine there's a big reward
Couple man try but then they get floored

(Boys' Rap)

Majors and Billson (1992) propose the notion of 'cool pose' to describe this form of urban black male assertion of the self through 'expressive and conspicuous styles of demeanour, speech, gesture, clothing, hairstyle, walk, stance and hand-shake' (Majors, 1990, p. 111, in Frosh *et al.*, 2002, p. 69). Majors and Billson theorise the enactment of Cool Pose as a way of responding to racism, such that young men invert their public hyper-visibility within white society into a source of identity status and reputation.

However, this explanation can be criticised for 'over-rationalising' black male expressive styles and reducing them to only a compensation for racism (Mirza, 1999). Additionally, as the earlier discussion group extract suggested, boys may take up different positions in relation to the assertion of hyper-visible masculinities across different contexts. For example, Richard and Steven constructed differences between themselves and Lloyd in terms of the extent to which they enacted the walk in public, where it would (potentially) draw attention from the police. Whilst the style in one sense could be interpreted as directed towards a public (white) audience, the boys also clearly enacted it as part of a process of 'doing boy' (Frosh *et al.*, 2002) within friendship groups, where it was a source of humour and bonding. For example, some of the boys 'played' during one of the discussion groups by showing off the walk to the researcher (HY). The extract cited earlier also contains a clear reference to the exclusively male arena within which the boys performed to one another ('couple man try...'). The boys thus engaged in 'doing friendship' by manipulating the symbols of hyper-visibility through the theme of competition. 'Winning' and 'being the best' are traditionally masculine themes. Within the boys' 'rap' discussion group, the tape-recording activity was transformed into a competition by Richard, in which the boys literally performed (masculinities) to the female researcher (HY) and the other boys in the group.

I'm gonna split lyrics on these boys cos right about now these boys – these boys ain't come with – Ah, y'know let's have a little combo yeah? Let's have a little compo yeah? Me an' Lloyd against you three yeah? Not jus' joke ting like – come. Are you up for this black?

(Richard)

Unsurprisingly, as the initiator, Richard, came out 'top' of this competition, and this translated into his greater discursive power within the discussion group.

However, whilst the performance of 'hyper-visible' and hyper-sexual masculinities provided status and was integral to the boys' friendship activities, these performances are inescapably located within structures of inequality and power, because '[h]yper-visibility...constitutes a mirage disguising a more profound "invisibility"' (Alexander, 2000, p. 133).[4] In other words, issues surrounding black masculinity can be silenced because it is assumed that male hyper-visibility reflects a position of power and dominance. Furthermore, particular hyper-visible masculine styles may obscure alternative black masculine identities, contributing to the dominance of negative stereotypical views of black masculinity. As Claire Alexander writes:

> the focus on black men, and particularly black youth, has obscured the processes by which specific configurations of black male identities, such as those centred on violence and criminality... have been placed in the public domain, at the expense and suppression of alternative formulations... which distort and obscure a wider, more complex, understanding.
>
> (Alexander, 2000, pp. 132–133)

Certainly, the boys in our study did not only position themselves in relation to 'bad boy' masculinities, although these did form a central discourse around which the young men negotiated different identity positions. These negotiations are explored in the following section.

Leaving 'bad boy' masculinities/identities in process

> [I] hang around with the people who start trouble and I'm right now trying to keep away but it's hard to just stop hanging around with them. It is easy to hang around with them but it's hard to leave them. At the end of the day if you don't leave them boys you'll get in trouble.
>
> (Solomon)

The boys did not construct 'fixed' or consistent masculinities; they shifted between alternative identity positions. In particular, the young men talked about trying to 'leave' some identities. This theme of escape and/or transgression has been explored within feminist theorising around (white) working-class women's identities. For example, Lawler (1999), Reay (1997) and Skeggs (1997) all discuss the tension between 'leaving' and 'holding on to' gendered, classed identities for working-class women who participate in higher and further education. The boys in our study also constructed their continued participation in education (and the possibility of post-compulsory participation) as creating a tension between holding on to, or leaving, 'bad boy' identities. Like the women whom Lawler interviewed, the boys were also reluctant to leave these identities because they were felt to be 'real' and authentic, representing aspects of the boys' 'true selves'. However, the source of this tension between 'leaving' and 'holding on' to these identities differed to that of the women in Lawler or Skeggs's research. As Solomon suggests, 'bad boy' masculinities can be attractive ('its easy...') and young men may be reluctant to give them up because they are a source of enjoyment, friendship, fun and power/status.

Despite the emotional pull and hegemonic benefits of these 'popular' masculinities, they were also associated with inertia, educational failure and deficit. As Solomon put it, if he 'leaves' his friends then he will be 'going up', but if he does not, 'I'm just going to be where I am right now'. Steven similarly talked about the need to get 'higher' than his current position. Javed also hinted at the ambiguity involved in negotiating a 'bad boy' identity (he talked about mucking around in class, skipping school to smoke and getting into trouble) whilst also maintaining that 'dossers' (boys who do not try or succeed) are 'low' people. Various other studies have shown that 'bad boy' masculinities are constructed as antithetical to the 'good student' identity, educational attainment, schoolwork and effort: for example,

Sewell (1997) and Frosh *et al.* (2000) found that popular masculinities centred on showing resistance to schoolwork. Similarly, boys in our study suggested that being seen to work in class would result in being labelled 'a pussy' (Lee, Erkan and Javed), hence the importance of adopting a strategy of not being seen to make an effort (Mac an Ghaill, 1994; Frosh *et al.*, 2002). The association of schoolwork/ education with effeminacy has been widely noted: As in Willis's seminal (Willis, 1977) study, 'hard' manual-working masculinity was contrasted with 'soft' middle-class/feminised education, where education was constructed as boring and unrelated to the world of manual labour. Education and reading are thus positioned as effeminate and soft, for those who cannot cope with 'real' physical work (Mac an Ghaill, 1996).

However, whilst the boys in our study resisted educational identities, they also expressed doubts as to the effects of their resistance. In particular, several boys said they now regretted their previous actions when they skipped school in favour of 'hanging around with the bad boys and getting money' (Solomon). Solomon also added, 'I think everything is money but it is not. I realise that now but still it is too late'. These concerns echo the views of the black young men in Alexander's (1996) study, who, after leaving school, expressed regret at having prioritised playing around with friends over studying. As the boys we spoke with neared the end of their compulsory schooling, they too seemed aware of the limited benefits of popular 'bad boy' masculinities in relation to academic success and future job prospects. As we have written elsewhere:

> a number of the young men suggested that their identities as young men from this particular inner city borough ('Harkton') rendered post-compulsory participation risky, precarious and unlikely. They constructed identities which were inscribed by 'the past' and 'reputation', so that past educational 'failure' prevented, or hindered, future participation.
>
> (Archer and Yamashita, 2003)

The boys' enactments and assertions of 'bad boy' popular masculine identities revealed a tension between the exercise of 'local' discursive power as compared to the 'broader' social and economic status that might be gained within the job/ education markets through further educational participation and accreditation/ engagement with institutional structures (rather than resistance to them). In other words, whilst the boys engaged with patriarchal/hegemonic masculinities (to varying degrees), these identities were circumscribed by structural inequalities, ensuring that the boys did not benefit unreservedly from patriarchal privileges. Whilst these popular masculinities were complicit in maintaining the boys in positions of disadvantage (e.g. militating against studying, promoting conflict and drug-taking), the local dividend from them was clear – hence their attractiveness and why the boys were not trying 'too hard' to leave them.

As stated earlier, it is important to highlight that 'bad boy' masculinities were not the only identity discourses drawn on by the boys. The boys also negotiated alternative masculine identities in relation to family and kinship structures. The boys talked about competing identity demands, such as the wish to be a 'good son' and to make their parent(s) proud, through which they resisted particular versions or aspects of popular masculinities and/or they combined 'private' family-oriented masculinities (seemingly unproblematically) with 'public' demonstrations of 'cool' masculinity.

However, the boys' constructions of 'bad boy' masculinities did obscure, and render illegitimate, particular alternative versions of black masculinity, notably middle-class/professional black identities. This was exemplified within teacher interviews, when one of the black Caribbean male teachers recounted engaging in a struggle of representation with the boys over the symbols of Jamaican masculinity through his wearing of a suit. John described how he attempts to persuade the boys to recognise that 'wearing a suit' and being 'a professional' could be compatible with black Jamaican masculinity. And yet, on the whole, the boys continued to define the boundaries of 'authentic' black masculinity through the symbols of 'streetwear' clothing, although this effectively closed off possible avenues for social mobility and could thus be seen as reinforcing the reproduction of classed inequalities. The talk of boys such as Richard (later) drew heavily upon a notion of 'professional' (managerial) identity as incompatible with black masculinity, because black men are structurally oppressed by the 'white man'.

RICHARD: All right Steven, do you think you is going to be a manager? How many black managers do you know?
STEVEN: [pause] Not much.
RICHARD: How many black headmasters do you know?
STEVEN: But – but.
RICHARD: I'm not asking that. How much do you know?
STEVEN: Me? None.
RICHARD: Yes, so who is giving you the jobs then?
STEVEN: A white man, innit.
RICHARD: Yes, so you think he'd give you a job yeah of being a schoolteacher when he could make you sweep the floors instead?

Thus, classed resistance formed part of the boys' negotiations around racialised masculinities.

Conclusion

In this article we have attempted to engage with questions concerning how to theorise inner-city schoolboys' racialised, classed masculinities. We have drawn attention to the centrality of locality and territory within the boys' identity constructions and we have highlighted how masculinities may be embodied through speech, dress and 'style'.

A notion of masculinities as 'culturally entangled' has also been utilised in order to understand the complex racial and diasporic influences that are enmeshed, and exercised, within the boys' identity constructions. This notion of 'entangled' identities disrupts popular common-sense theorisations of ethnic/racial and gender identities as 'neat', culturally homogeneous and clearly bounded (Glissant, 1989).

We have argued that the boys drew on, and negotiated between, a number of different discourses of masculinity, but we also drew attention to the power and attractiveness of 'bad boy' discourses, which exacted strong emotional attachments and loyalties. The notion of 'bad boy' masculinity was central to many of the boys' accounts, and yet the boys also presented themselves as, on the one hand, trying to leave these masculinities and, on the other, 'trapped' by structural inequalities of racism. As detailed by a number of other researchers, the boys' constructed popular masculinities were 'anti-schoolwork' (e.g. Francis, 1999; Frosh et al., 2002). We might speculate that the pervasiveness of resistance to school/work may derive in part because the boys invest heavily in globalised and diasporic discourses of masculinity that are grounded *outside* the education context in the local area. Thus, typically 'rational' and individualistic government education policies and strategies (Ball *et al.*, 2000) may have little impact on increasing the boys' identification with, or engagement with, formal learning since they do not address the boys' strong emotional attachment to identities grounded outside of the educational context. Furthermore, when we take into account these pupils' entrenched sense of deficit in relation to education, derived from repeated experiences of academic 'failure' (see Archer and Yamashita, 2003), it is not surprising that these young men invest more heavily in 'non-education' identities. The implications of this disidentification can translate into resistance to lifelong learning: as found with adult working-class men, who constructed participation in post-compulsory education as entailing loss, and threatening the maintenance of masculine identities. This was because participation in 'alien' (middle-class, white) educational institutions would entail moving outside of the men's familiar spheres of local power (Archer *et al.*, 2001).

We would also suggest that the boys' transcripts indicate the complexity of inequalities and the multiple ways in which identities of 'race', class and gender interact to produce resistance and engagement. These theorisations contain implications for practice as well as theory. For example, it suggests that a policy of merely increasing the number of black/male teachers to be 'role models' to young black boys (as pledged by education ministers, e.g. see Segal, 2000) is unlikely to produce dramatic results on its own, in addition to being problematic at a number of levels (see Epstein *et al.*, 1998; Raphael Reed, 1998).[5] Indeed, our own experiences as researchers within this project lead us to suggest that the boys did not identify in simplistic ways across ethnicity/race' and gender (see also Archer, 2002), and these issues should be explored further in future work.

Our analyses support arguments that policies need to move away from deficit models in which social and educational problems are located within working-class and minority ethnic cultures and families and where the problems of inner-city boys are understood in terms of their 'deviant' masculinities. Instead, we argue for further sensitive analyses to be undertaken of the complex racialised and classed aspects of urban (and other) masculinities in order to inform theories, policies and practices that can work towards challenging, rather than reproducing, multiple inequalities.

NOTES

1   Discussion groups were also conducted with an additional nine girls in Year 8, but these data are not reported here.

2   We would debate here use of the term 'hybridised' for potentially 'interpellating essentialism by the back door' (Yuval-Davis, 1997).

3   We would interpret Lee's comment as illustrating a complex interplay of gendered, racialised and classed influences: a notion of downward class mobility is suggested through his comparison between 'smart people' and 'bad boys'. But whilst the gendered context of Lee's frame of reference is explicit, we would suggest that the racialised element is 'silent', yet implicit. The notion of 'bad boys' can be commonly associated with 'rude boys' and discourses around black/Caribbean masculinity. Furthermore, the notion of an influx of different groups into particular areas of London, displacing the 'smart' (with possible dominant connotations of white/middle-class) people contains echoes of (racist) discourses around immigration, space and urban change. As

Walkerdine *et al.* (2001, pp. 34–35) note, 'the processes of residential differentiation, and crucially, the imagery of "racial segregation" have played key roles in the social reproduction of race categories and the organisation of objective and subjective space'.

4   Alexander here draws upon West's (1990) theorisation of 'invisibility' (as a powerlessness in relation to controlling dominant representations of oneself).

5   Although a separate, but related, point should also be made that the racial and gender representation of teachers in general constitutes an important issue for action.

REFERENCES

Alexander, C. (1996) *The Art of Being Black: The Creation of Black British Youth Identities* (Oxford, Oxford University Press).

Alexander, C. (2000) '(Dis)Entangling the "Asian Gang": ethnicity, identity, masculinity', in B. Hesse (ed.) (2000) *Un/Settled Multiculturalisms: Diasporas, Entanglements, Transruptions* (London, Zed Books).

Anthias, F. and Yuval-Davis, N. (1992) *Racialized Boundaries: Race, Nation, Gender, Colour and Class and The Anti-racist Struggle* (London, Routledge).

Archer, L. (2001) ' "Muslim brothers, black lads, traditional Asians": British Muslim young men's constructions of race, religion and masculinity', *Feminism & Psychology*, 11: 79–105.

Archer, L. (2002) ' "It's easier that you're a girl and that you're Asian": interactions of race and gender between researchers and participants', *Feminist Review*, 72, pp. 108–132.

Archer, L. and Yamashita, H. (2003) ' "Knowing their limits?" Identities, inequalities and inner city school leavers' post-16 aspirations', *Journal of Education Policy*.

Archer, L., Pratt, S. and Phillips, D. (2001) 'Working-class men's constructions of masculinity and negotiations of (non)participation in higher education', *Gender and Education*, 13: 431–449.

Archer, L., Hutchings, M. and Ross, A. (2002) *Higher Education and Social Class: Issues of Inclusion and Exclusion* (London, RoutledgeFalmer).

Arnot, M., Gray, J., James, M., Ruddock, J. and Duveen, G. (1998) *Recent Research on Gender and Educational Performance* (London, Office for Standards in Education).

Back, L. (1996) *New Ethnicities and Urban Culture: Racisms and Multiculture in Young Lives* (London, UCL Press).

Ball, S., Maguire, M. and Macrae, S. (2000) *Choice, Pathways and Transitions Post-16: New Youth, New Economies in The Global City* (London, RoutledgeFalmer).

Bhavnani, K.-K. (1993) 'Tracing the contours: feminist research and feminist objectivity', *Women's Studies International Forum*, 16: 95–104.

Cohen, P. (1988) 'The perversions of inheritance: studies in the making of multi-racist Britain', in P. Cohen and H.S. Bains (eds), *Multi-racist Britain* (London, Macmillan).

Connell, R. (1989) 'Cool guys, swots and wimps: the interplay of masculinity and education', *Oxford Review of Education*, 15: 291–303.

Connolly, P. and Neill, J. (2001) 'Constructions of locality and gender and their impact on the educational aspirations of working class children', paper presented at 'Addressing Issues of Social Class and Education: theory into practice', University of North London, June.

Cooper, C. (1993) *Noises in the Blood: Orality, Gender and The 'vulgar' Body of Jamaican Culture* (London, Macmillan).

Department for Education and Employment (DfEE) (1998) *Higher Education for the 21st Century: Response to The Dearing Report* (London, DfEE).

Edley, N. and Wetherell, M. (1995) *Men in Perspective: Practice, Power and Identity* (London, Prentice Hall/Harvester Wheatsheaf).

Epstein, D., Elwood, J., Hey, V. and Maw, J. (eds) (1998) *Failing Boys? Issues in Gender and Achievement* (Buckingham, Open University Press).

Francis, B. (1999) 'Lads, lasses and (New) Labour: 14–16 year old students' responses to the laddish behaviour of boys and boys' underachievement debate', *British Journal of Sociology of Education*, 20: 355–371.

Francis, B. and Skelton, C. (eds) (2001) *Investigating Gender: Contemporary Perspectives in Education* (Buckingham, Open University Press).

Frosh, S., Phoenix, A. and Pattman, R. (2002) *Young Masculinities* (Basingstoke, Palgrave).

Gewirtz, S. (2001) 'Cloning the Blairs: New Labour's programme for the re-socialization of working-class parents', *Journal of Education Policy*, 16: 365–378.

Gillborn, D. (1990) *'Race', Ethnicity and Education: Teaching and Learning in Multi-Ethnic schools* (London, Unwin Hyman).

Gilroy, G. and Lawrence, E. (1988) 'Two-tone Britain: white and black youth and the politics of anti-racism', in P. Cohen and H.S. Bains (eds), *Multi-racist Britain* (London, Macmillan).

Gilroy, P. (1991) *There Ain't No Black in the Union Fack* (reprint: Chicago, IL, University of Chicago Press).

Gilroy, P. (1993) *Small Acts* (London, Serpent's Tail).

Glissant, E. (1989) *Caribbean Discourse* (Virginia, VA, University of Virginia Press).

Gough, B. and Edwards, G. (1998) 'The beer talking: four lads, a carry out and the reproduction of masculinities', *Sociological Review*, 46: 409–435.

Gramsci, A. (1971) *Selections from the Prison Notebooks* (London, Lawrence and Wishart).

Hall, S. (1992) 'New ethnicities', in J. Donald and A. Rattansi (eds), *Race, Culture and Difference* (London, Sage).

Haywood, C. and Mac an Ghaill, M. (1996) 'Schooling masculinities', in M. Mac an Ghaill (ed.), *Understanding Masculinities* (Buckingham, Open University Press).

Hebdige, D. (1996) 'Digging for Britain: an excavation in seven parts', in: H.A. Baker, M. Diawara and R.H. Lindeborg (eds), *Black British Cultural Studies* (Chicago, IL, University of Chicago Press).

Hesse, B. (ed.) (2000) *Un/Settled Multiculturalisms: Diasporas, Entanglements, Transruptions* (London, Zed Books).

Hey, V. (1997) 'Northern accent and southern comfort: subjectivity and social class', in P. Mahony and C. Zmroczek (eds), *Class Matters: 'Working Class' Women's Perspectives on Social Class* (London, Taylor and Francis).

Jackson, C. (2002) '"Laddishness" as a self-worth protection strategy', *Gender and Education*, 14: 37–51.

Lawler, S. (1999) '"Getting out and getting away": women's narratives of class mobility', *Feminist Review*, 63: 3–23.

Lewis, G. (2000) 'Discursive histories, the pursuit of multiculturalism and social policy', in G. Lewis, S. Gewirtz and J. Clarke (eds), *Rethinking Social Policy* (Buckingham, Open University Press).

Lloyd, T. (1999) *Young Men, the Job Market and Gendered Work* (York, York Publishing Services).

Mac an Ghaill, M. (1994) 'The making of black English masculinities', in H. Brod and M. Kaufman (eds) *Theorizing Masculinities* (London, Sage Publications).

Mac an Ghaill, M. (1996) '"What about the boys?": schooling, class and crisis masculinity', *Sociological Review* 44: 381–397.

McGivney, V. (1999) *Excluded Men: Men Who are Missing from Education and Training* (Leicester, National Institute of Adult Continuing Education).

Mahony, P. and Zmroczek, C. (eds) (1997) *Class Matters: 'Working Class' Women's Perspectives on Social Class* (London, Taylor & Francis).

Majors, R. (1990) 'Cool pose: black masculinity and sports', in M. Messner and D. Sabo (eds) *Sport, Men and the Gender Order* (Illinois, IL, Human Kinetics Books).

Majors, R. and Billson, J.M. (1992) *Cool Pose: The Dilemmas of Black Manhood in America* (New York, Lexington Books).

Marland, M. (1995) 'Further improving examination results', Special Governors' Meeting report, Reproduced in *Raising Achievement in Inner City Schools* (London, Education Magazine Seminar Series).

May, S. and Modood, T. (2001) 'Editorial', *Ethnicities*, 1: 5–7.

Mirza, H.S. (1999) 'Black masculinities and schooling: a black feminist response', *British Journal of Sociology of Education*, 20: 137–147.

National Committee of Inquiry into Higher Education (1997) *Higher Education in the Learning Society (The Dearing Report)* (London, The Stationery Office).

Newton, J. (1998) 'White guys', *Feminist Studies*, 24: 574–598.

Noble, D. (2000) 'Ragga music: dis/respecting black women and dis/reputable sexualities', in B. Hesse (ed.), *Un/Settled Multiculturalisms: Diasporas, Entanglements, Transruptions* (London, Zed Books).

Paechter, C. (1998) *Educating the Other: Gender, Power and Schooling* (London, Falmer Press).

Phoenix, A. (1994) 'Practising feminist research: the intersection of gender and race in the research process', in M. Maynard and J. Purvis (eds), *Researching Women's Lives from a Feminist Perspective* (London, Taylor & Francis).

Phoenix, A. (2000) 'Constructing gendered and racialized identities: young men, masculinities and educational policy', in G. Lewis, S. Gewirtz and J. Clarke (eds), *Rethinking Social Policy* (Buckingham, Open University Press).

Pugsley, L. (1998) ' "Throwing your brains at it": higher education, markets and choice', *International Studies in Sociology of Education*, 8: 71–90.

Raphael Reed, L. (1998) ' "Zero tolerance": gender performance and school failure', in D. Epstein, J. Elwood, V. Hey and J. Maw (eds), *Failing Boys? Issues in Gender and Achievement* (Buckingham, Open University Press).

Reay, D. (1997) 'The double-bind of the "working class" feminist academic: the success of failure or the failure of success?', in P. Mahony and C. Zmroczek (eds), *Class Matters: 'Working Class' Women's Perspectives on Social Class* (London, Taylor & Francis).

Reynolds, T. (1997) 'Class matters, "race" matters, gender matters', in P. Mahony and C. Zmroczek (eds), *Class Matters: 'Working Class' Women's Perspectives on Social Class* (London, Taylor & Francis).

Rich, A. (1976) 'Women's studies – renaissance or revolution?', *Women's Studies, 3*.

Segal, L. (2000) ' "Back to the Boys?" Temptations of a good gender therapist', inaugural lecture, Weds 13 December 2000, Birkbeck College, University of London.

Sewell, T. (1997) *Black Masculinities and Schooling: How Black Boys Survive Modern Schooling* (Stoke-on-Trent, Trentham Books).

Sewell, T. (1998) 'Loose canons: exploding the myth of the "black macho" lad', in D. Epstein, J. Elwood, V. Hey and J. Maw (eds), *Failing Boys? Issues in Gender and Achievement* (Buckingham, Open University Press).

Skeggs, B. (1997) *Formations of Class and Gender: becoming respectable* (London, Sage Publications).

Walkerdine, V., Lucey, H. and Melody, J. (1999) 'Class, attainment and sexuality in late twentieth-century Britain', in P. Mahony and C. Zmroczek (eds), *Women and Social Class–International Feminist Perspectives* (London, UCL Press).

Walkerdine, V., Lucey, H. and Melody, J. (2001) *Growing Up Girl: Psychosocial Explorations of Gender and class* (Basingstoke, Palgrave).

Watt, P. and Stenson, K. (1998) ' "The street – its a bit dodgy around there": safety, danger, ethnicity and young people's use of public space', in T. Skelton and G. Valentine (eds), *Cool Places: Geographies of Youth Cultures* (London, Routledge).

West, C. (1990) 'The new cultural politics of difference', in R. Ferguson, M. Gever, T.T. Minh-ha and C. West (eds), *Out There: Marginalization and Contemporary Cultures* (US, New Museum of Contemporary Art).

Westwood, S. (1990) 'Racism, black masculinity and the politics of space', in J. Hearn and D. Morgan (eds), *Men, Masculinities and Social Theory* (London, Unwin Hyman).

Wetherell, M. and Potter, J. (1992) *Mapping the Language of Racism: Discourse and The Legitimation of Exploitation* (London, Harvester Wheatsheaf).

Whitehead, S. (1999) 'Hegemonic masculinity revisted', *Gender, Work and Organisation*, 6(1): 58–62.

Willis, P. (1977) *Learning to Labour: How working Class Kids Get Working Class Jobs* (Farnborough, Saxon House).

Yuval-Davis, N. (1997) 'Ethnicity, gender relations and multiculturalism', in P. Werbner (ed.), *Debating Cultural Hybridity* (Aldershot, Ashgate Publishing).

PART VII

SOCIAL CLASS

TWENTY

SHAUN'S STORY: TROUBLING DISCOURSES OF WHITE WORKING-CLASS MASCULINITIES

Diane Reay

Source: 'Shaun's story: troubling discourses of white working-class masculinities', *Gender and Education*, 14(3): 221–234, 2002.

Introduction

There is an extensive recent literature in the USA, Australia and the UK which examines how schooling interacts with wider social processes in the shaping of subjectivities (Wexler, 1992; Mac an Ghaill, 1994; Hey, 1997; Mcleod, 2000; Walkerdine *et al.*, 2001), while a growing body of work focuses specifically on the problem of white working-class masculinities in the schooling context (Skelton, 1997; Connolly, 1998). Less attention has been paid to the discrepancies; those instances of classed and gendered subjectivity that work against normative under-standings of the relationship between social class, gender and schooling, although there have been a few notable exceptions, for example, Stanley (1989) and Brown (1987) in the UK, Mehan *et al.* (1996) in the USA and Connell *et al.* (1982) in Australia. This article concentrates on one such discrepant case. It tells the story of a hard-working, well-behaved, poor, white, working-class boy trying to achieve academically in a 'sink' inner-city boys' comprehensive school, whilst simultane-ously trying to maintain his standing within the male peer group culture. It also raises questions about the possibilities of bringing together white working-class masculinities with educational success in inner-city working-class schooling. I argue, through Shaun's case study, that to combine the two generates heavy psychic costs,[1] involving young men not only in an enormous amount of academic labour but also an intolerable burden of psychic reparative work if they are to avoid what Bourdieu terms 'the duality of the self' (Bourdieu, 1999, p. 511).

Shaun's story resonates with many earlier stories of white working-class boys struggling to achieve academically. There are similarities with Colin Lacey's Cready, 'a working class boy from a large family, making good' (Lacey, 1968) and

Philip Brown's 'ordinary kids' (Brown, 1987). However, neither text provides sufficient information about either the boys' reputations and behaviour out of the classroom or their emotional responses to their positioning within schooling for the reader to gauge the psychological costs of their academic endeavours. In contrast, in this article I am concerned to make links between children's and young people's inner emotional worlds and external social and structural processes. To this end, Bourdieu's theoretical framework is combined with psychoanalytic theories in order to keep both internal and external processes continually in the frame.

I never expected to be engaged in recuperating white working-class masculinities, although the ways in which they have been homogenised in academic accounts and made to bear the weight of white racism and male sexism (see, e.g. Weis, 1993) has not been borne out by my experience of either teaching working-class children in the inner city or interaction with the middle classes in professional settings. Over 30 years of living in a working-class inner-city area has provided me with many examples of very different working-class masculinities to those inscribed in my memories of growing up. My own childhood and adolescent experience of white working-class masculinities was one scarred by violence, both physical and verbal abuse, plus the more symbolic, but equally damaging, violence of deeply entrenched sexism and racism within the male-dominated, coal mining community I used to be part of. However, of all the hundreds of children that I have interviewed over the past 10 years, Shaun's story resonated most powerfully, apparently independently of my female and feminist subjectivity.

I have often felt a powerful empathy and strong identification listening to, in particular, working-class girls and women; a finding of myself in them that I have written about before (Reay, 1996, 1999). I have not been able to find myself in Shaun's narrative, at least not in any obvious way, nor does he offer the fascination of an 'exotic other'; those middle classes I am still trying to make sense of. Instead, to some extent, he reflects the uncomfortable image of the familiar oppressor. His story, then, is compelling in its own right and has written itself in spite, as much as because, of me as the author. My transcriber twice on returning tapes of Shaun's interviews said that his words made her weep. I did not weep but his story did leave me with an overwhelming sense of anger at the way things are for boys like him. This article, then, is my attempt to do justice to his narrative, one that speaks to the complexities, the struggles, pains and possibilities, of white working-class masculinities at the beginning of the twenty-first century.

Shaun was part of a sample of 454 children interviewed as part of a large Economic and Social Research Council (ESRC) project on primary–secondary school transitions in two London boroughs. All the children were interviewed in focus groups, then a smaller sample of 45, including Shaun, was interviewed individually in Year 6, then three times over the course of their first year in secondary school. However, my contact with Shaun both pre-dated and post-dated the research project. He was part of a small pilot study conducted with Year 5 pupils and was also one of five children I stayed in contact with after the ESRC project finished. I have eight interviews with Shaun conducted over a four-year period from September 1997 to September 2001, four before the move to secondary school and four afterwards. As a consequence, this is primarily a tale of before and after, of anticipation and realisation, and the ways in which secondary school transfer can operate as a process of class sifting and sorting despite the egalitarian mythologising surrounding comprehensive education. This class process has changed little since Measor and Woods's (1984) and Delamont and Galton's (1986) seminal work over 15 years ago, despite enormous changes within the educational field. But the article is also more than that; it is a case study of how psychic and social processes intertwine in convoluted and contradictory ways to fashion white working-class masculinities which are far more complex, nuanced and fragile than any of the stereotypical representations in dominant discourses.

Subjectivity and schooling

Julie McLeod (2000) argues for the need to address the dynamic between subjectivity and schooling, and this article attempts to make such links through an analysis of Shaun's struggles to belong to a good place within schooling. Bourdieu writes that 'when habitus encounters a social world of which it is the product, it finds itself "as a fish in water", it does not feel the weight of the world and takes the world about it for granted' (Bourdieu and Wacquant, 1992, p. 127). Following Bourdieu, we would expect Shaun, a poor, working-class, Irish boy to feel at home in the poor, inner-city, working-class, ethnically mixed comprehensive he ends up in. However, Shaun's tale is one of ducking and diving, not swimming; of being weighted down rather than weightlessness. His words reveal both striving and struggle against the educational context he finds himself in.

Wexler (1992) writes about 'the class divided self' in his discussion of white working-class students in an urban American high school. Similarly, Shaun's tale is an example of contradiction and tension between the social order and psychological processes rather that the 'homology, redundancy and reinforcement between the two systems' that Bourdieu (1999, p. 512) asserts is normative. In contrast to the norm, Shaun's experience generates a habitus divided against itself; an experience Bourdieu (1999, p. 511) describes as 'doomed to duplication, to a double perception of self'. He is positioned in an untenable space on the boundaries of two irreconcilable ways of being and has to produce an enormous body of psychic, intellectual and interactive work in order to maintain his contradictory ways of being, his dual perception of self. There are resonances with the dilemma that the young men Edley and Wetherall (1999) interviewed found themselves in. They, too, were caught between two contradictory subject positions. However, there the similarities end. Edley and Wetherall's sample were all middle class and privately educated. Shaun, living on an inner-city, sink council estate in a lone mother family surviving on state benefits, belongs to a section of the working classes that has routinely been stigmatised within dominant discourses (Skeggs, 1997; Reay, 1998).

Shaun's narrative reveals how centrally class as well as gender is implicated in psychic processes and the fashioning of contemporary subjectivities. It provides an example of how processes behind class advantage and disadvantage work through the individual (Savage, 2000), but also of the continuing importance of material and social positioning within the educational field. Recent scholarship on masculinities has emphasised the shifting, fluid nature of identities. However, Connell cautions against too great an emphasis on fluidity, arguing that 'fluidity may be a great deal less fluid when examined in the institutional contexts of everyday life...It might indeed, be helpful to think about the "fixing" mechanisms that limit the fluidity of identities' (Connell, 2001, p. 8). Class operates as one such 'fixing mechanism', chaining Shaun to a place where his self-fashionings have limited efficacy (Bourdieu, 1999). The institutional constraints of inner-city schooling are a continual theme throughout Shaun's narrative, as when he tells me, 'we've never had a French teacher that has stayed for more that two weeks'; 'the kids that muck about all of the time, mostly they do it because they can't do the work very well. They need someone to help them but there isn't anyone', and 'I'm not so good at science cos we've had three teachers so far this year'. Sutton Boys', Shaun's third choice of secondary school, and the school he ends up in, serves an area of extreme social deprivation. Over 50% of the pupils are eligible for free school meals, and over 70% have very low or below average verbal ability on joining the school. Forty per cent of the boys speak English as an additional language. In 1995 the school was made subject to special measures on the grounds that it was failing to give its pupils an acceptable standard of education.

Bourdieu argues that 'narrative about the most "personal" difficulties, the apparently most strictly subjective tensions and contradictions, frequently articulates the deepest structures of the social world and their contradictions' (p. 511). Bourdieu's words speak to what is probably the most difficult problem for theoretical understandings of the construction of gendered subjectivities – 'the extent to which individuals are constrained by their structural contexts and how far they can build alternative identities despite their stigma' (Heward, 1996, p. 41). Shaun's text is rife with such tensions. There is a continual movement between the material and psychological consequences of poverty, which implicate both school and home, and an optimism of the will that, although at times deflated and at others fragile, Shaun manages to sustain despite the odds. And the odds are enormous, involving Shaun in the immense amount of psychic and intellectual work necessary to keep both his and his mother's hopes alive. It is the very anomalies in Shaun's situation, the discrepancies between his social practices and those normative for 'boys like him' that make his narrative so rich and vivid, full of imagery and reflection. Shaun's contradictory situation has given him access to what Bourdieu terms 'socio-analysis' (Bourdieu, 1990, p. 116). Bourdieu, in writing about lay people's access to forms of socio-analysis, argues that 'practical analysts' are those individuals situated at the point where the contradictions of social structures are most apparent, chiefly for the ways in which they 'work over' such individuals, who in order to survive such 'working over' practise a kind of self analysis. Shaun, like Bourdieu's 'practical analysts', displays an awareness both of the objective conditions that have him in their grasp and of the objective structures expressed in and by these contradictions.

Shaun's story

In 1998, when Shaun was in Year 5, he was very clear not only about the secondary school he wanted to attend but also about the schools that he considered unacceptable:

> I'm gonna go to Westbury because my mate Mark's going there and my
> girlfriend.
> Sutton Boys' is like one of the worst schools around here, only tramps go
> there.

However, by the middle of the first term of his final year in primary school, Shaun's certainties were dissolving. Confronted with the head teacher's advice that Westbury would be far too risky a choice as he lived on the edge of its catchment area, and having been warned that other popular schools in the borough were even more remote possibilities, Shaun and his mother resigned themselves to applying to Sutton Boys':

> I might not get into Westbury cos it's siblings and how far away you live and I haven't got any siblings there and I live a little way out so I might have to go on a waiting list...I might go to Sutton Boys' instead cos all my mates are going there.
>
> I could have wept at the thought of him going to Sutton but what choice did we have cos Mrs Whitticker said we didn't have any.
>
> (Maura, Shaun's mother)

By the time I next interviewed Shaun in the last term of Year 6 his narrative displayed a continual ambivalence between optimism of the soul and a negative realism:

> It's a good school for me because I know some of the teachers there. David's brother Dean goes there, my cousin Paul and this kid, John, all these kids I know from off my estate, they all go there.

and:

> It's good to go somewhere where you've got lots of older kids looking out for you and that's what I'll have at Sutton Boys'.

But in constant tension with his positive anticipations were far more negative expectations:

> I've heard it might get closed down because it's no good or something...my friend used to go but he don't go any more. He's only 15 and he don't go to school any more because all the teachers used to bully him, always pick on him so he won't go any more.

and:

> I dunno anyone who's done well there, everyone does badly there, oh yeah, I do, my cousin done well there but that was before he was excluded.

Even at this stage, Shaun's efforts to retain a degree of optimism require a great deal of psychic work. He is not going 'to get dragged down'. Instead, he is determined 'to work much harder because like it's secondary and the most important school days of your life because that's when you're coming up to your GCSEs (General Certificate of Secondary Education)'. But this positive outlook must be maintained in the face of deeply demoralising information, including knowledge of how local educational markets operate:

> My mum and I think the standards might be too low because people just bunk and everything at Sutton.
> There's a bit of a problem with Sutton Boys' having low standards because it might get closed down.

Shaun has even begun to reflect on how Sutton Boys' could be improved – 'it would be a much better school if it allowed girls to attend' – whilst arguing that this is not a realistic proposition because 'it's not a safe place for girls because of all the people that go to that school, there's Triads and everything that go to that school. And there's all the people who think they are gangsters and come with knives and stuff'. He has also started to prepare in advance for his time there:

> I know that sometimes people sit and ask for 10p in Sutton Boys', because I've been finding out quite a lot about Sutton Boys' because I am going there. So I am going to try and find out as much as I can about it, because if I don't and I go into school and people go – have you seen something or so and so? And then they are going to pull you into the toilets and beat you up. So if I find out all about it I'll know how to protect myself from the rough kids.

Both Shaun and his mother told me that they had had 'lots of serious discussions' about how Shaun could still do well at Sutton Boys' despite its poor reputation: 'Like I need to change my attitude, change the way I behave, like no fights, no cheeking in the classroom because I don't want to let my mum down, let myself down just cos no one else is getting on with it'. Maura, his mother, said, 'we've had some real heart to hearts. He's putting a brave face on it but I can see how worried he is. I've said you just have to work twice as hard to do well if you go to a school like that rather than somewhere like Westbury where the kids expect to get on with their work instead of mucking about all the time'. However, even at this stage a major tension between Shaun and his mother is the peer group, or more specifically, Shaun's friendship with a number of boys with reputations for 'messing about' and 'getting into fights'.

Before the move to secondary school, Shaun's main rationale for accepting that Sutton Boys' might be a reasonable school for him was that lots of his friends were also going there. However, at the end of his first term in the school the main change that he identifies is 'my friendship with some people'. He asserts that he can no longer be friends with David, his best friend from primary school, because whereas before:

> Whenever David was in trouble with a fight I was always there to help him. We always helped each other or if someone needed us for a fight. But here now I'm not really into fighting. Fighting ain't nothing but trouble so I try and keep out of it... Fighting is for the kids who don't want to learn and don't want to do well at school and I don't want to be like that.

This new 'non-violent' Shaun is a recent, precarious self-invention. Shaun, who has twice been suspended from his primary school for fighting, has a local reputation for being 'tough', which he sees as vital to sustain if he is to survive in Sutton Boys':

> I'm not going to get into any fights myself but like everybody said, yeah, that me and David, we've been classed as the hardest in Year 7 and we've agreed, yeah, that if kids that can't fight are getting beaten up us two are going to jump in and help them. It's just like, you can't let someone that don't know how to fight, who is little get it all the time, you can't let them get picked on or hit... so I'm not fighting I'm helping.

When I query how he is going to reconcile being tough in the playground with being hardworking and achieving in the classroom he replies, 'I am just different in the class to what I am out in the playground. I'm just different'. This duality of being is something Shaun returns to time and again in his secondary school interviews: 'You see, when I get outside I go back to being cool and bad but not when I'm in class'. Shaun constructs himself as neither a 'lad' nor an 'ear'ole' (Willis, 1977) but a self-consciously crafted concoction of the two. Yet, this double perception of the self, tough in the playground and scholarly in the classroom, as becomes evident later, is riven with contradictions and requires almost superhuman efforts to maintain.

Foucault sees self-fashioning practices as 'patterns that the individual finds in his culture and which are proposed, suggested and imposed on him by his culture, his society and his social' (Foucault, 1987, p. 122). But Shaun's practices are quite clearly not supported by the social milieu he is part of and he is, in Bourdieuian terms, resisting the imposition of cultural necessity. In the context of the secondary classroom, all his energy is expended in desperately trying to set himself apart from the rest of his peer group; 'all the other kids were spitting spit balls out of paper at the teacher and I just sat down and tried to take no notice'. But this contriving to be apart must avoid aloofness. Rather, he is attempting to carve out a space for academic success in a peer group context where, at least nominally, it is despised and where he still retains very strong desires to belong. The only other two boys 'to keep their heads down and try and get on with their work' are outsiders to the local male working-class peer group culture. One is American and in Shaun's words 'dead clever'. The other is Portuguese and has parents who are actively looking to place him in another school. Even in Martino's (1999) private mixed-sex school the scholarly displays that Shaun has begun to invest in, such as reading books and spending lots of time on homework, were pathologised among the male peer group. It is not surprising, then, that in Shaun's predominantly working-class boys' comprehensive such practices conflict with appropriate male behaviour for 'boys like us' and he has to constantly guard against being reclassified as 'a geek'. While existing research suggests that middle-class boys can continue to occupy positions of hegemonic masculinity by combining coolness with the seamless production of academic success (Mac an Ghaill, 1994; Martino, 1999), this is not a subject position available to Shaun. In contrast, Shaun has to continually negotiate peer group pressure to prove he is still really 'a lad':

> Like a kid will call you in the classroom and the others go 'Oh Shaun are you gonna take that? Are you gonna take that? Knock him out. Knock him out, he was dubbing your dad' and all that. I don't care about my dad but then they try and stir it and try and change what he said to get you to fight.

As is evident in the following excerpt, one of many Shaun recounted, the classroom context in Sutton Boys' is rarely conducive to academic learning:

> Some boys, yeah, in English yeah, some of the kids never shut up, never, ever shut up. Like, today, we were supposed to get out for lunch at ten past one, because all the bigger kids push in front of us, but because everyone was shouting and everything and I am the one that always goes – shut up. So whenever I tell them to shut up they are scared of me and they shut up, but then this boy Ryan, he always comes back and says something, so we have to stay in. He always pushes it. They all show off. Because Jay, yeah, this year, I think he's had more fights than he did out of all the time at Beckwith, so far, because like, today, yeah, that boy Ryan picked up a chair and Jay stood on

the table and flying kicked the chair into the kid's face and then punched him and he fell back on the floor. And like David is encouraging him. He was going, go on Jay, go over there and punch him in his face. And when they were fighting and everyone was going, go on Jay, go on Jay. They can't just sit down and ignore it or try and break it up.

Against this constant backdrop of classroom disruption and intermittent eruptions of violence, Shaun is endeavouring to get on with his studies despite the peer groups' disapprobation: 'When I do my work the others think "he's a fool," look he does his work. It's stupid working, he's a goody two shoes and all that.' Yet, despite the negative reaction from 'all my mates', those boys in the class whose friendship and approval he values, Shaun refuses to conform to the localised regime of normalising practices through which boys come to adopt certain practices of masculinity and display themselves as particular kinds of boys (Martino, 1999). However, this constitutes a considerable loss of face which Shaun has to recuperate in other contexts in order to be accepted. As a consequence, in contradistinction to his displays of nonconformity to prevailing peer group values in the classroom, in the playground and on the estate, he resurrects his old self, reclaiming a very different identity as 'tough' and 'a skilful footballer' which redeems, most of the time, his 'geekiness' in the classroom. However, this brings Shaun into conflict with his mother:

My mum said she don't want me mixing with the wrong people because, like the people I hang about with, like, they are all troublemakers, David, Jay and all that. My mum says she don't want me to hang around with them, but if I don't hang around with them I aint got no one to hang about with.

It is worth reiterating the tenuousness of Shaun's positioning. He is caught between two untenable positions, continually engaged in a balancing act that requires superhuman effort; on the one hand, ensuring his masculinity is kept intact and on the other hand endeavouring to maintain his academic success. Sutton Boys' is a school where success is in short supply and, as a consequence, it is resented and undermined in those who have it. By the end of the first year at secondary school the two conflicting selves that Shaun has put so much effort into reconciling are beginning to come apart:

It's getting harder because like some boys, yeah, like a couple of my friends, yeah, they go 'Oh, you are teacher's pet' and all that. Right? What? Am I teacher's pet because I do my work and tell you lot to shut up when you are talking and miss is trying to talk? And they go, 'yeah so you're still a teacher's pet'. Well, if you don't like it go away, innit.

That the effort has taken its toll is evident in Shaun's longing to be a baby again:

I want to stay younger, like I wish I was younger now. So I wouldn't have to move, just sleep in my cot and have no responsibility. But you've got to get older. You can't just stay the same age.

Shaun's ambitions are created under and against conditions of adversity. Reputation in Sutton Boys' comes not through academic achievement but is the outcome of a jockeying for position among a male peer group culture, in which boys are 'routinely reproducing versions of themselves and their peers as valued because of their hardness, appearance, or capacity to subvert schooling' (Phoenix and Frosh, 2001). As O'Donnell and Sharpe (2000) point out, schools like Sutton Boys' are engaged in a losing battle to counterbalance the collective influence of the male peer group.

How can Shaun both set himself apart from and remain part of the wider working-class male collectivity? That is the task he has set himself and the dilemma it raises lies at the very heart of class differentials in attainment within education. However, I also want to argue that we need to look outside the school and into what at first sight could be viewed as 'the unpromising spaces' of his family life on one of New Labour's socially excluded sink council estates (Social Exclusion Unit (SEU), 1998) in order to understand sustenance and support for Shaun's resolve.

I want to try to unpick what keeps Shaun going despite the unpromising conditions of his schooling and locality, the constant turnover of teaching staff and the continual negative barrage from his fellow pupils. First, Shaun's desires to do well are very clearly not rooted in any intrinsic regard for school-based knowledge. Rather, he shares with many of his peers a sense that the knowledge being offered in school is not really relevant to boys like him: 'I'd prefer to have more stuff that really prepares you for the future and you don't get that. Like some subjects I don't even know why they make us do it because it doesn't make sense for the future.' However, unlike most of them, he does have both a positive rapport and empathy with his teachers, and particularly with his female teachers. He had an especially good relationship with Claudette, his head of year. Every time I interviewed him he told me that she was brilliant. Later, when I interviewed her, the first thing she said about Shaun was 'he's just brilliant'. However, his understanding, sympathetic attitude extended to all his teachers:

> There was a time at the beginning of the term when the class was really good and then they started to go downhill and also the teachers can't really spend a lot of time with the kids because they're always having to sort out fights, sort out arguments. They can't really help because they haven't got enough time to look after the good kids.
>   I feel really sorry for my French teacher ... when Miss tell them to be quiet in French, yeah, our teacher, she always usually loses her voice. She goes, can you be quiet please? And she shouted so much she lost her voice. And I yell, oi, shut up, Miss wants everyone to be quiet. I went, Miss, shall I tell them to shut up and sit down? She goes, go on then. And I said, sit down and shut up. And everyone just sat down and shut up. And then as soon as Miss started talking they all started talking and when they don't listen to the teachers it makes me feel sorry for them.

Shaun is caught up in Bourdieu's 'paradox of the dominated'. Bourdieu, writing of the paradoxical consequences of compliance with the educational system, rejects the dichotomy between submission and resistance inherent in accounts of working-class schooling such as Paul Willis's *Learning to Labour*. Rather, he argues that 'resistance may be alienating and submission may be liberating' (Bourdieu, 1990, p. 155). Certainly, there have been tangible academic benefits in Shaun's compliance. He has received a certificate for outstanding achievement in his year and his mother recounted regular examples of letters home praising his performance and attainment in a range of subject areas. However, I want to argue that it is not just the academic rewards that motivate Shaun to veer off on his lonely path across a bleak inner-city educational landscape. Stephen Frosh and colleagues (2000) argue that many boys and young men struggle with ways of constructing masculine identities that are socially 'acceptable', particularly with, regard to the values embodied in their peer group culture, whilst striving to hold on to their felt need for intimacy and emotional contact. It is such a reconciliation between the two that Shaun is struggling to achieve. His commitment to learning and his positive identification with his teachers are rooted in his relationship with his mother; a relationship which raises another paradox because, seen through the discursive lens of healthy male development, the closeness and continuing connectivity between Shaun and his mother are viewed as pathological rather than normative. I try and grapple with this contradiction in the next section of the article.

'Mummy's boy': reworking the pathologised as privileged

Although schooling is salient in the construction of subjectivities, families are the first site in which masculinities are fashioned. It is impossible to write about Shaun's subjectivity without writing about his relationship with his family, in particular his mother. Unlike the other children that I interviewed, Shaun regularly referred to his mother and family life throughout the interviews without any prompting from me. As a consequence, while most of the interviews lasted 45 minutes to an hour, those with Shaun were always longer, one hour and 15 minutes to an hour and a half. However, in April 2000, when he turned up in the deputy head's office, he was not his usual smiling equanimous self and proceeded to talk about his mother's illness and consequent hospitalisation. We talked for 40 minutes off tape about his mother and family life before reverting to our usual pattern of discussing school-based issues. Shaun lives in a lone parent family with his mother and two sisters. The family have a third floor flat in a large council estate and are currently surviving on income support. His love, concern and strong desire to please his mother shine through all the interviews. His father, though absent for most of the three years of the research project, remains a looming terror. When I first interviewed Shaun in Year 5, his father had returned to Ireland and was the ultimate sanction in Shaun's life for bad behaviour: 'My mum says if I get into any more trouble she'll send me to my dad in Ireland and no way do I want to have to go and live with him'. However, halfway through Shaun's first year at secondary school, his father re-emerged in the locality and became a much more tangible threat, subjecting the family to harassment and minor acts of violence, at one point killing and cutting up Shaun's younger sister's pet rabbits, until Shaun's mother was finally forced to get a restraining order.

Shaun's Year 6 teacher told me:

> Someone like Shaun will come up to me, 'I just want to get away from the other boys for a little while, all of us are dragging each other down'. You know, he takes equal responsibility for it. Because of all the boys he's the one most in touch with his feminine side, believe it or not. I do think he's more in touch with his feminine side but then he lives with three women, his mum, who he idolises, his elder sister, who he idolises, and his baby sister, who he idolises, so his feminine side is very much to the fore. Also, he loves his girlfriends. I do think Shaun sees them as quite a calming effect but then he's very much in touch with that.

While Ms Keithly inscribes both Shaun's close relationship with his mother and his feminine qualities positively, that is not how they would be represented within traditional conceptions of normative masculine development. I want to push against the boundaries of conventional orthodoxies in order to understand Shaun's familial relationships as far more enhancing than mainstream psychological texts allow. In *Masculinities* (1995), Connell writes about a group of 'new' men who have attempted to reform their masculinity in a process 'that was directed at undoing the effects of Oedipal masculinization'. He goes on to argue that 'it seems likely that this project was supported by emotional currents from pre-Oedipal relationships: centrally, the primal relationship with the mother' (1995, p. 135).

Psychological theorising has traditionally focused on 'oppositional categories of masculinity or femininity, fathers or mothers, identification or rejection' (Heward, 1996, p. 37). As Heward points out, such binary categorisation does not allow for the rejection of fathers by sons except as a deviant, pathological response. The normative Oedipal model for 'healthy' male identity formation is based on identifying with the father and rejecting the mother (Edley and Wetherall, 1995). And this has been translated into populist discourses which view normal male development as 'leaving the mother and "the feminine" behind and moving on towards a real masculine identity with the father' (Elium and Elium, 1992). Yet, for boys like Shaun, mothering has a potency and positive efficacy that is actively denied in conventional accounts of normative masculine development which implicitly pathologise lone mothering. However, there are other accounts, and it is those we need to turn to, to make positive sense of Shaun's relationship with his mother. In *Anti-Oedipus* (1984), Deleuze and Guattari argue that Freud's Oedipal complex is a key structure of capitalism which represses libido and desire, internalising a patriarchal family structure at an unconscious level. They assert that conventional psychological theories collude with capitalism and its repression of sexuality by accepting the familial constellation. However, their thesis also lends itself to interpretations which position psychological orthodoxies regarding normative development as implicitly misogynistic and mother-blaming. As Jan Campbell argues, modifying the sexualised mother of Oedipal accounts with a tender mother 'is a move from cathecting her narcissistically to an interaction with her in terms of social and symbolic institutions' (Campbell, 2000, pp. 237–238). This permits a conceptual move beyond the derogation of the mother and the destructiveness of only privileging the father. Instead of denigrating the pre-Oedipal stage of connection with the mother as infantile, Deleuze and Guattari's theoretical framework opens up a space for more positive interpretations of relationships between adolescent sons and mothers in lone mother families. Such interpretations work towards addressing 'the vital need' Christine Heward identifies, for a theory of masculinities, 'in relation with fathers and mothers, identifying and rejecting features of both within a historical and social context' (1996, p. 38).

I am not arguing for a view of Shaun's relationship with his mother as uniformly positive; clearly, there are also negative aspects. Rather, I am arguing against the normative models which represent such relationships as pathological in a construction which implicitly blames the mother. Shaun's relationship with his mother, like that of all other working-class boys in lone mother families, and here class both intensifies and expands the process of pathologisation, is far too complex and multifaceted to be explained by the simplistic evoking of the Oedipal relationship. It also has a positive efficacy which merits recognition. Shaun, unlike a majority of boys his age, has not banished the feminine to the realms of 'the other' and has none of the usual adolescent male contempt for women and girls such splitting generates. Rather, he is more comfortable with the feminine both in himself as well as in others than is normative for his male peer group, although this is not to imply that there are not significant numbers of working-class boys who, like Shaun, have very close, mutually supportive relationships with their mothers. Existing research suggests that there are (Ball *et al.*, 2000). I would like to suggest that Shaun's acceptance and relative ease with the feminine in himself and others helps rather than hinders his relationship with education and remediates, whilst in no way removing, some of the class structural barriers to academic success. However, it is important to avoid conveying a sense that all is right for Shaun when patently it is not. He is left with ambivalent relationships to both femininity and masculinity. Both cause him a lot of conflict, one with authority, the other with his peer group. Rather than achieving a harmonious balance, he is caught up in a volatile state of fluctuating between acceptance and rejection of both.

Conclusion

Shaun's story troubles dominant versions of white working-class masculinities which for so long have been key repositories for all those unpleasant, uncomfortable feelings the middle classes don't want to take responsibility for – sexism, racism, homophobia, to just name a few. Shaun, who admires his mother 'more than anyone else in the world', thinks his black female teacher is just 'brilliant' and believes 'racism is the worst thing going on in the world', is just one illustration of how superficial and ill considered such discourses are. His narrative also suggests that the problem of 'failing boys' (Epstein *et al.*, 1998) cannot be solved through school-based initiatives. If part of 'normal' male development involves the expulsion of the feminine, which then becomes a target for contempt, learning, and in particular literacy-based subjects, which are encoded as feminine, will continue to be denigrated by the white working-class boys who are the main focus of concern within the 'failing boys' discourse. This is not the same as saying contempt of the 'feminine' is class- and race-specific. Rather, I would argue that it is a male trait which crosses both social class and ethnic boundaries. However, against the backdrop of contemporary economic changes and the hegemony of global capitalism, it is white working-class young men who have the strongest sense that their masculinities are under siege, and this has consequences for their defensive practices (Nayak, 2001). Until social processes of male gender socialisation move away from the imperative of privileging the masculine and allow boys to stay in touch with their feminine qualities, the problem of 'failing boys' will remain despite the best efforts of teachers and researchers.

It is not only dominant versions of white working-class masculinities that are unsettled by Shaun's story. His narrative allows us glimpses into the moral vacuum that stands for current 'common-sense' educational thinking. We can see in his account how educational processes help class processes to operate (Savage, 2000). Shaun's struggle against the educational context he finds himself in is yet one more instance of the myth of comprehensivisation and the sham of meritocracy. New Labour lashes out against 'bog standard comprehensives' (Cassidy, 2001), yet schools like Sutton Boys' do not have, and have never had, a comprehensive intake. As a previously 'failing' school which has just come out of 'special measures', both the school and its predominantly working-class, ethnic minority intake are demonised both locally and within the wider public imagination

(Lucey and Reay, 2002; Reay and Lucey, 2002). Unlike the fantasies played out in New Labour policies, this is not an issue of school effectiveness and staff performance but a matter of class and race; of social structures and material resources.

Furthermore, despite the much vaunted National Curriculum, New Labour, no less than the 'Old Tories' have no interest in what counts as 'really useful knowledge' (Johnson, 1979) for working-class students. As Jackie Brine (2001) asserts, the continued failure to critically educate and to creatively stimulate working-class students is little short of criminal, and, at the very least, morally indefensible. Even Shaun, with his strong commitment to learning, finds most of what he is taught an irrelevance. His disaffected working-class peers in Sutton, as well as contemporaries in other inner-city schools, find little to engage them in the National Curriculum (Reay, 2001). Perhaps it is worth revisiting Bernstein's counsel of 30 years ago in order to radically rethink socially equitable education for all class groupings in society:

> We must ensure that the material conditions of the schools we offer, their values, social organisation, forms of control and pedagogy, the skills and sensitivities of the teachers are refracted through an understanding of the culture the children bring to the school. After all, we do no less for the middle-class child.
>
> (Bernstein, 1973, p. 175)

Finally, Shaun's situation highlights the irrelevance of the Excellence in Cities Initiative for working-class pupils. New Labour policy, through its Excellence in Cities Initiative, might just result in a pupil like Shaun being included in a Gifted and Talented scheme, although, as a child who obtained level 4 in English, Mathematics and Science in his key stage 2, SATs (standard assessment tasks) his commitment, determination and hard work would probably not qualify him for inclusion. However, even if offered a place, taking it up would be extremely risky for Shaun, jeopardising the careful balancing act he has maintained between achievement and social acceptability. As I have tried briefly to sketch out in this conclusion, far more needs to change in inner-city schooling than extra provision for those deemed to be in 'the brightest 5–10 per cent'.

NOTE

1   Psychic work and psychic costs are apparent in the emotional labour such boys have to engage in when managing the tensions embodied in the 'duality of the self'. It became increasingly apparent over the course of the four years that I knew Shaun that he was both dealing with high levels of anxiety in relation to his 'split self' and having to mobilise an array of defence mechanisms (Klein, 1952; Winnicott, 1964) in order to protect and maintain a sense of coherent self.

REFERENCES

Ball, S.J., Maguire, M. and Macrae, S. (2000) *Choices, Pathways and Transitions Post-16* (London, RoutledgeFalmer).

Bernstein, B. (1973) *Class, Codes and Control*, vol. 1 (St Albans, Paladin).

Bourdieu, P. (1990) *In Other Words: Essays Towards a Reflexive Sociology* (Cambridge, Polity Press).

Bourdieu, P. (1999) 'The contradictions of inheritance', in P. Bourdieu et al. (1999) The Weight of the World: Social Suffering in Contemporary Societies (Cambridge, Polity Press).

Bourdieu, P. and Wacquant, L. (1992) An Invitation to Reflexive Sociology (Chicago, IL: University of Chicago Press).

Brine, J. (2001) Feet of Class, Relations of Power and Policy Research, American Educations Research Association Conference (Seattle, WA, April).

Brown, P. (1987) Schooling Ordinary Kids (London, Tavistock).

Campbell, J. (2000) Arguing with the Phallus: Feminist, Queer and Postcolonial Theory (London, Zed Books).

Cassidy, S. (2001) 'Are you a bog-standard secondary?', Times Educational Supplement, 16 February, pp. 4–5.

Connell, R.W. (1995) Masculinities (Cambridge, Polity Press).

Connell, R.W. (2001) 'Introduction and overview', Feminism & Psychology, Special Issue, Men and Masculinities: Discursive Approaches, 11: 5–9.

Connell, R.W., Ashenden, D.J., Kessler, S. and Dowsett, G.W. (1982) Making the Difference (Sydney, George Allen & Unwin).

Connolly, P. (1998) Racism, Gender Identities and Young Children: Social Relations in a Multi-ethnic, Inner-city Primary School (London, Routledge).

Delamont, S. and Galton, M. (1986) Inside the Secondary Classroom (London, Routledge).

Deleuze, G. and Guattari, F. (1984) Anti-Oedipus: Capitalism and Schizophrenia (London, Athlone Press).

Edley, N. and Wetherall, M. (1995) Men in Perspective: Practice, Power and Identity (Hemel Hempstead, Harvester Wheatsheaf).

Edley, N. and Wetherall, M. (1999) 'Imagined futures: young men's talk about fatherhood and domestic life', Journal of Social Psychology, 38: 181–194.

Elium, D. and Elium, J. (1992) Raising a Son: Parenting and the Making of a Healthy Man (Stroud, Hawthorn Press).

Epstein, D., Elwood, J., Hey, V. and Maw, J. (eds) (1998) Failing Boys? Issues in Gender and Achievement (Buckingham, Open University Press).

Foucault, M. (1987) 'The ethic of care for the self as a practice of freedom', Philosophy and Social Criticism, 12: 113–131.

Heward, C. (1996) 'Masculinities and families', in M. Mac an Ghaill (ed.), Understanding Masculinities, pp. 50–60 (Buckingham, Open University Press).

Hey, V. (1997) The Company She Keeps (Buckingham, Open University Press).

Johnson, R. (1979) 'Really useful knowledge: radical education and working-class culture 1790–1948', in J. Clarke, C. Critcher and R. Johnson (eds), Working Class Culture: Studies in History and Theory (New York, St Martin's Press).

Klein, M. (1952) Developments in Psycho-analysis (London, Hogarth Press).

Lacey, C. (1968) Hightown Grammar (Manchester, Manchester University Press).

Lucey, H. and Reay, D. (forthcoming) 'A market of waste: pyschic and structural dimensions of school-choice in the UK and children's narratives on "demonised" schools', Discourse: Studies in The Cultural Politics of Education.

Mac an Ghaill, M. (1994) The Making of Men: Masculinities, Sexualities and Schooling (Buckingham, Open University Press).

McLeod, J. (2000) 'Subjectivity and schooling in a longitudinal study of secondary students', British Journal of Sociology of Education, 21: 501–521.

Martino, W. (1999) ' "Cool boys," "party animals," "squids" and "poofters": interrogating the dynamics and politics of adolescent masculinities in school', British Journal of Sociology of Education, 20: 239–264.

Measor, L. and Woods, P. (1984) Changing Schools: Pupils' Perspectives on the Transfer to a Comprehensive (Buckingham, Open University Press).

Mehan, H., Okamoto, D. and Adams, J. (1996) Constructing School Success: Consequences of Untracking Low Achieving Students (Cambridge, Cambridge University Press).

Nayak, A. (2001) 'Ivory lives: race, ethnicity and the practice of whiteness in a northeast youth community', paper presented at the Economic and Social Research Council Research Seminar Series: Interdisciplinary Youth Research: New Approaches, Birmingham University, 18 May.

O'Donnell, M. and Sharpe, S. (2000) *Uncertain Masculinities: Youth, Ethnicity and Class in Contemporary Britain* (London, Routledge).

Phoenix, A. and Frosh, S. (2001) 'Positioned by "hegemonic" masculinities: a study of London boys' narratives of identity', *Australian Psychologist*, 36: 1–18.

Reay, D. (1996) 'Insider perspectives or stealing the words out of women's mouths: interpretation in the research process', *Feminist Review*, 53: 55–71.

Reay, D. (1998) 'Rethinking social class: qualitative perspectives on gender and social class', *Sociology*, 32: 259–275.

Reay, D. (1999) 'Children's urban landscapes: configurations of class and place', in S. Munt (ed.), *Cultural Studies and the Working Class* (London, Cassell).

Reay, D. (2001) 'Finding or losing yourself?: working class relationships to education', *Journal of Education Policy*, 16(4): 333–346.

Reay, D. and Lucey, H. (2003) 'The limits of choice: children and inner city schooling', *Sociology* (forthcoming).

Savage, M. (2000) *Class Analysis and Social Transformation* (Buckingham, Open University Press).

Skeggs, B. (1997) *Formations of Class and Gender* (London, Sage).

Skelton, C. (1997) 'Primary boys and hegemonic masculinities', *British Journal of Sociology of Education*, 18: 349–369.

Social Exclusion Unit (1998) *Bringing Britain Together: A National Strategy for Neighbourhood Renewal* (London, Social Exclusion Unit).

Stanley, J. (1989) *Marks on the Memory* (Buckingham, Open University Press).

Walkerdine, V., Lucey, H. and Melody, J. (2001) *Growing Up Girl: Gender and Class in the Twenty-first Century* (London, Macmillan).

Weis, L. (1993) 'At the intersections of silencing and voice: discursive constructions in school', *Educational Studies*, 24: 1–22.

Wexler, P. (1992) *Becoming Somebody: Towards a Social Psychology of School* (London, Falmer Press).

Willis, P. (1977) *Learning to Labour* (Lanham, MD, Lexington Books).

Winnicott, D.W. (1964) *The Child, the Family, and the Outside World* (London, Penguin).

TWENTY-ONE

UNEASY HYBRIDS: PSYCHOSOCIAL ASPECTS OF BECOMING EDUCATIONALLY SUCCESSFUL FOR WORKING-CLASS YOUNG WOMEN

Helen Lucey, June Melody and
Valerie Walkerdine

Source: 'Uneasy hybrids: psychosocial aspects of becoming educationally successful for working-class young women', *Gender and Education*, 15(3): 285–299, 2003.

That young women today can 'have it all' is an idea that had its seeds sown in the 1960s but really took root and established itself in the 1980s. It has turned out to be a particularly seductive and tenacious idea, surviving in the face of strong feminist critique and overwhelming evidence that shows the persistence of gendered inequalities. Nevertheless, from the power-dressed female executive of the 1980s, through the kick-ass and clever 'girl power' of the millennial years, modern stories of transformed contemporary femininity have, in some quarters, been unrelentingly celebratory. Discourses of endless possibility for *all* girls circulate freely, although tempered and regulated by the kind of merito-cratic principles that can explain any failure to 'achieve' and to 'have' as a personal one.

Drawing on the longitudinal study *Project 4:21 Transitions to Womanhood*, which focused on two groups of girls, both born in the 1970s and studied over a 17-year period, this article will concentrate on two of those 'success' stories of the 1990s – two working-class young women who, though coming from families where there was no history of educational achievement, nevertheless did well in school and gained enough examinations to study on undergraduate courses (for a full analysis see Walkerdine *et al.*, 2001). This process of educational success and of social mobility involves crossing borders of social class, gender and ethnicity, of negotiation between competing subjectivities as other spaces, other possibilities are opened up.

We examine the notion of hybridity, as put forward by cultural theorists in relation to new forms of ethnic subjectivities (Bhabha, 1984; Gilroy, 1993; Hall, 1993), and argue that while it is a useful concept in exploring more fully the multiple layers of experience of subjects in a context of shifting economic and social relations and adds another dimension to theories of fragmentation (Bradley, 1996), there are, however, no easy hybrids. We demonstrate how the uneasiness of hybridity in terms of social mobility through educational achievement for young women from the working classes stems partly from the difficulties of negotiating the emotions, negative as well as positive, that are aroused when aspiration and success mean becoming and being profoundly different to your family and peer group.

Even though working-class and black families have often been negatively implicated in the educational failure of their children, we do not want to abstract these young women from their families (Walkerdine and Lucey, 1989). The challenge for us is to refute those models whose explanatory power lies in pathologising any family practices not immediately recognisable as middle class and instead work towards theorisations which are able to take on board the significance of family practices in a different way.

We would argue, along with a growing body of researchers across a number of social science disciplines (Shaw, 1995; Hollway and Jefferson, 2000; Frosh et al., 2002), that to get beyond conscious, rational explanations to a greater understanding of the influences and behaviours of ourselves, both the psychic and social processes of how they have come about need to be investigated. While we would not dispute the undoubted and well-rehearsed problems with the universalism of psychoanalytic theory (Cowie, 1997; Frosh, 1997), we suggest that social and cultural analysis needs an understanding of emotional processes presented in a way which does not reduce the psychic to the social and cultural and vice versa, but recognises their interweavement (Lucey et al., 2003).

Unquestioned in contemporary social and educational policy is the notion that upward social mobility is the desired outcome of social improvement. This is an implicit assumption that runs through all variations of the discourse of 'social capital' embraced by New Labour (Coleman, 1988; Fukuyama, 1999; Putnam, 2000). However, discourses of social mobility and social capital tend to hold denials: of the losses that are fundamental to and unavoidable in change, even when those changes are desired; of the enormous amount of psychological work involved in transformation; and of the costs of that work. However, these inherent tensions are not commented on in policy debates (Thomson et al., 2003). This silence/absence in the discourse creates obstacles to exploring the ways in which the hybridisation of working-class feminine subjects through educational success, with its promise of social mobility, can provoke as many difficult feelings in families, such as anxiety and ambivalence, as it can positive ones, such as pride, excitement and love. By refusing to pay attention to them we are in danger of denying crucial aspects of our experience (Tokarczyk and Fay, 1995; Reay, 1997; Plummer, 2000). We wish to stress here that anxiety, ambivalence and the psychic mechanisms developed to defend against them are by no means the sole province of the working classes, and we have discussed their powerful articulation and effects in professional middle-class families elsewhere (Lucey and Reay, 2000, 2002; Walkerdine et al., 2001). We should not be afraid to look at the darker side of our experience, to confront the shadows cast by ambivalence. We will therefore explore some of the emotional dynamics in the working-class girls' families that have helped to sustain their success; the kinds of psychic defences that are produced to deal with difficult and contradictory feelings that educational success and failure so acutely, though often unconsciously, provoke for working-class people.

Hybridity

The concept of 'hybridity' was first developed to identify and understand new patterns of ethnic identity in a 'post-colonial' context of globalisation, shifting forms of international relations and processes of migration (Bhabha, 1984, 1990, 1996; Gilroy, 1993). Hybrid cultures are transmitted and transformed within new locations and contexts, creating new forms or developing old forms in new ways. In these changing environments we see the emergence of multiethnic, multilayered identities; what Modood calls 'hyphenated' 'identities' (Modood, 1992).

Bhabha, who developed the notion of hybridity in relation to conditions of political inequity and oppression, views it as holding positive possibilities. He stresses the constant 'negotiation of discursive doubleness' in hybridity, but is at pains to point out that by 'doubleness' he does not mean the same as binarism or duality. For Bhabha, 'the hybrid strategy or discourse opens up a space of nego-tiation where power is unequal but its articulation may be equivocal. Such negoti-ation is neither assimilation nor collaboration' (1996, p. 58) but an opportunity to take up and develop a critical stance towards hierarchy. Closely allied to the concept of hybridity are notions of 'border existences', 'liminality' (Grossberg, 1996, p. 91) and a 'third space' (Bhabha, 1990) to describe and map the existence of the hybrid.

The positive possibilities of hybridity continue to be debated. Does having to exist between competing identities mean that the hybrid subject has the best of both worlds, or that s/he is 'forced to live in the interface between the two' (Anzaldua, 1987, p. 37, quoted in Grossberg, 1996). And what of the hybrid who moves back and forth between competing identities? Can the 'border-crosser' ever find a place or condition of her own and therefore some stability?

Adkins wonders whether hybridity is a good enough concept to capture the complexities of 'current refashionings of gender' (Adkins, 2001, p. 12). In the context of changing work practices, it has been argued that there is a hybridisation and reversal of workplace gender identities (see Adkins, 1995, for a review) where men are required to adopt more 'feminine' attitudes and skills associated with the service industries. Ironically, at the same time, 'These changes involve the perform-ance of new forms of femininity, a distancing from variants traditionally perceived as normative and the adoption of qualities previously viewed as masculine' (Reay, 2001, p. 163). If we add also that women have for so long been invited to constantly remake themselves as the (changing) object of male desire, then it becomes clear that women have had to face for a long time the recognition that the unitary subject is a fraud and that constant and perpetual self-invention is neces-sary. Rather, it is men, and particularly working- and lower middle-class men, who now have to face the necessity of constant self-invention and the production of themselves in a marketable (feminised) image, perhaps for the first time.

These kinds of transformations in the economy require a new kind of feminine subject – one who is capable of understanding herself as an autonomous agent, the producer of her present and her future, an inventor and constant reinventor of the person she may be or become. Some theorists emphasise the liberating opportunities presented by these shifts; chances for us all to break free from the old constraints of gender, class and community (Giddens, 1991; Beck, 1992).

Discourses which describe young women's lives through narratives of 'wanting', 'getting' and 'having' abound, but far fewer accounts are able or willing to engage with the complex losses which the new sociality brings.

The construction and maintenance of a self is a constant struggle 'won only provisionally and always entailing expenditure of considerable amounts of psychological energy' (Frosh, 1991, p. 187). It is clear that for many of the young women of our research the speed of societal change and the instabilities of the social world are turned inward to be experienced as instabilities of the self. This inner turmoil is particularly intense for educationally successful girls and young women. How, then, do working-class girls and young women inhabit the phantasmatic spaces accorded to them of the complex subject positions through which they are regulated? How are they supposed to remake themselves as workers and as women in the new sociality? In particular, how do working-class girls who succeed in education manage to negotiate hybrid subjectivities, or other kinds of self-invention and regulation?

Project 4 : 21 transitions to womanhood

Project 4:21 is a longitudinal study of two groups of working-class and middle-class girls and young women who were born in the 1970s and who grew up through a turbulent period of British history. One group of 30 middle-class and working-class girls, born in 1972–73, was studied when they were four years old, at home with their mothers and at nursery school (Tizard and Hughes, 1984) and then in school when they were 10 years old (Walkerdine and Lucey, 1989). Another smaller group of girls, born in 1978, also took part in the study when they were six years old. Ten years later we followed up both groups when they were 16 and 21 years old.[1]

Of the 21 working-class young women who took part in the last phase of Project 4 : 21, only five (27 per cent) had stayed on past compulsory schooling to A level and were applying to study, were already studying or had completed courses of study at higher education level. This was compared to 15 (93 per cent) of the middle-class young women. In the following section we focus on two of these working-class young women: Holly, a 'mixed-race' 21-year-old who lives with her partner and their two children, and Nicky, a single, white 21-year-old. Both lived in large towns within an hour's train journey to London. We are using the particularities of their biographies to highlight not only their uniqueness, but also to pick out and trace the threads of similarity that run through and across the narratives of the educationally successful working-class young women.

Into the family

The inseparability of home and school in the success and failure of working-class children has long been taken as read. Although this is also the case for the production of middle-class educational success, middle-class families are discursively positioned in a positive way and they are not subject to the kind of pathologisations which historically inform regulative and interventionist educational policies aimed at raising the achievement of working-class children (Finch, 1984; David, 1993; Vincent and Warren, 1999). While we wanted to retain the significance of the family in explanations of educational achievement, we felt that we were in danger of becoming trapped by available discourses which we felt to be inadequate on two counts. First, a deficit model underpins conceptions of working-class families. That is, since middle-class children do vastly better in school than working-class children, the everyday practices of working-class families must somehow be lacking that which ensures success in middle-class families. Policies and initiatives designed to improve working-class children's educational performance have focused on precisely those interior spaces of family interaction; spaces that have been inevitably pathologised when set against the obsessively 'normalised' interior family spaces of the middle classes. Furthermore, this serves to push responsibility further and further into the family and away from considerations of sociality (Vincent and Warren, 1999).

Second, existing sociological work which attempts to theorise connections between the individual and society (between agency and structure) is limited by an unwillingness to work with the notion of unconscious processes. In addition to this, traditional sociology invests much in an individual/society dualism (Henriques *et al.*, 1997) so that the social and the psychic are understood as twin but opposite poles or forces. The psychoanalytically informed post-structuralism that guides our work assumes what Althusser (1969) called a position of 'absolute interiority' between the subject and the social.

While the educational pathways from primary school to university for the vast majority of the middle-class girls were so smooth and similar it was almost as if they were on educational 'conveyor belts', there were contradictions and anomalies at every turn when we looked at the production of working-class educational success. Although we could not come up with any convenient typologies of the successful working-class girl, we can point to some complex trends in this subgroup. Powerfully present in all of their narratives was the notion of 'independence', and an identification of themselves as 'strong and independent', a self-identification which, throughout their narratives, is closely linked to their parents' struggle and the desire for 'escape'.

Nicky

Nicky, a white working-class 21-year-old young woman, was in the last year of her undergraduate course. She hoped to continue her studies to Master's level. When she was 10 years old Nicky's primary school teacher described her as 'a steady, competent little worker...she's quietly motivated, she's not one of these that makes a great fuss about anything' (Walkerdine and Lucey, 1989). This resonates clearly with the adolescent Nicky, who quietly got on with her work and never made a fuss about being bullied because she did not want to worry her parents and because she wanted 'to try and sort things out for myself'. 'Never asking for anything' and 'never making a fuss' were common themes in these young women's narratives and in their parents' descriptions of them.

Nicky went to a mixed comprehensive which she describes as 'very rough' and which she 'couldn't wait' to leave. After achieving two As, two Bs, four Cs and one D at General Certificate of Secondary Education (GCSE), she went on to study science A levels at the local further education college. Having firmly decided that she wanted to go to university, which she describes as her 'big aim in life', she was also aware that competition was tough and she needed to get good A level results. Feminist accounts have highlighted how even the most basic information about the education system is simply not available to working-class children (Plummer, 2000). Even those young women who were considered 'bright', who were able to apply themselves at school and whose parents wanted them to do well educationally were given little advice on how to move into higher education.

> Well I talked to my parents about it, but my parents never went to college or anything, they finished school early, so. They always wanted me to get a good education, but they weren't able to give much practical advice... I had to make them on my own, and when I actually applied for my university degree, I didn't really know what I wanted to do at the time, apart from science. So I was a bit in the dark.

When Nicky didn't get the grades she needed to get into university she took a year out. This wasn't a gap year characterised by the kind of travel and 'experience' (often through paid or voluntary work overseas) which many of the middle-class young women describe. Instead Nicky took an Open University course to get the entrance qualifications she needed and worked in a shop in order to save enough money so that she would not have to ask her parents for any when she began her undergraduate studies.

Unlike the professional middle-class parents, who have a wealth of knowledge about higher education, as well as providing considerable financial support and stability, the working-class girls know that the only path to university is likely to be a lonely one. For some parents who attempted to provide the kind of continuity between home and school which was so firmly in place in the middle-class families, this meant going back to school themselves. Most working-class parents, however, whose own experiences of schooling were characterised by failure, only felt able to help their children in the early primary school years. It is probably difficult for some to imagine the complex emotions caught up in that relationship, of a parent who feels inadequate to help their child, especially as they progress through education. The parent may feel shame and the child equally shame and anger and pain. This is lived as psychic but it is produced socially and needs to be understood as profoundly psychosocial.

> I mean they've always been there. I knew they would have helped me if they were able to, and they did, sort of, like when I got my prospectus for university, they sat down and went through them with me and I sort of told them what I was looking for, and they tried to help me out that way. But apart from that there wasn't really much practical advice they could give, 'cos they hadn't been in the same situation themselves. They've been good.

Drawing on their longitudinal study of young people, Thomson *et al.* (2003) look at the relationship between resources, location, families, ability and ambition in the educational biographies of working-class young women. They maintain that 'theories of individualisation tend to underplay the importance of relationships and forms of reciprocity and obligation that are embedded within them for understanding the identities and practices in which individuals engage' (p. 44). Working-class girls like Nicky have found great inner resources in order to achieve their goals, but their unwillingness to seek help from parents, to never 'make a fuss about anything' also speaks of a massive psychic defence. Such defences are necessary to cope with the pain of family deprivation and poverty. It is not uncommon for working-class women who have gone through higher education to speak of the fact that their parents went without in order that the children might have something, often continually throughout their childhood (Walkerdine, 1996).

> I try and help my parents a bit I suppose. I try not to ask too much. 'Cos I know they can't afford it, but they don't like that, they don't like me knowing that they can't afford it, which is fair enough...I wanted to make sure that when I went to university I had enough money. I mean, I get a full grant, but I wanted to make sure that I had enough money, so I never came out of it in debt. I'm the same now, I mean, it's really tough trying to survive on my grant.
>
> (Nicky)

Oppositions between play and hard work are not so stark in the middle-class families, where going to university is often a rite of passage that most family members have undertaken. For them, there is an expectation that student life should be both a time of serious study and a youthful sabbatical in which to experience and experiment with the new. In contrast, the working-class young women at or planning to go to university often encountered negative perceptions of students from wider family.

> My uncle...He's very biased about a lot of things and one of them is students so he doesn't believe I do anything at university except go out and get drunk...a lot of people in my family just think I'm playing at things. I'm going nowhere and that I just don't have what it takes to hold down a job. And that has been the view from a few of my uncles and aunts and one or two of my cousins and I've just given up trying to explain it.
>
> (Nicky)

Working-class young women, however, have on some level introjected the notion that students do indeed do what they want, which is usually taken to mean that they do very little. And indeed, the young women are enjoying themselves at university; they are having fun and doing what they want; they do not have the kinds of responsibilities that their parents had when they were the same age, and they are looking forward to a better life than their parents had. Not only this, but there is guilt in the knowledge that their parents are supporting something which is having an unforeseen consequence in pushing them further apart from one another. 'Survival guilt' is a common experience amongst people who have survived a great trauma or genocide, for example, when others died. While the families of these young women have not perished, of course, there is a sense in which their new lives as upwardly mobile women have been produced on the back of the sometimes self-imposed deprivations of their parents.

While parents give the strong message that this better life is exactly what they want for their children, envy is sometimes aroused, an emotion with such negative connotations that few will give voice to it. Nicky's mother says, 'I must admit I get jealous sometimes, you know, and thinking, 'cos I wish we'd had the chance to do that when we were younger'. Whether envy and anger are spoken or not, the knowledge that they are being given a chance that their parents (or siblings) never had is embedded in the experience of educational success for working-class children. The recognition that one might be the object of others' envy may not exist on a conscious, rational level, precisely because it is so irrational to think that a parent with whom we share a loving relationship could harbour such negative feelings towards us. However, on an unconscious level, the fear that this envy may cause us to be the target of parents' aggressive feelings continues to operate and may in turn provoke our own aggression. In an object relations model (Klein, 1959), aggression towards the parent (typically the mother) can be notoriously difficult for the child to express or even acknowledge because of intense fears that the parent will retaliate by an equally aggressive rejection of the child.

Holly

Holly, a mixed-race 21-year-old, had two young children of her own and lived with her partner who was the children's father. For her, being strong and independent and not having to rely on other people is articulated through a powerful identification with her mother, who escaped a violent relationship with their father to bring Holly and her siblings up alone.

> I don't know, I think my mum's like a really strong woman and I think she's made us – like all of us are really strong and independent and we can just stand by ourselves, we don't need anybody else. And I think it's the way she's brought us up, so that we don't need to rely on other people.

The idea for Holly that life is a struggle, that, as her mother told her, 'we're gonna have to work twice as hard as anybody else' because she is 'mixed race', together with a reliance on the self and a strong identification with her mother is the emotional and discursive mix which has driven her educational career. Mirza argues that a preoccupation with subculture, in particular 1980s subcultures of resistance, had a major effect on the study of black women. What emerged in this work was a core romantic idea that young black women were motivated mostly by and through an identification with strong black mothers. For Holly, the overlapping discursive categories of 'strong woman' and 'black woman', while there may indeed be mythical aspects to them (Mirza, 1992), have nevertheless been ones that are complexly meaningful to her. A recurring theme throughout her narrative is her mother's strength in having to do everything for and by herself and she consistently identifies with this. For herself, Holly has constructed a coherent self-identity as a 'strong black mother' even though her own mother is white.

Recent debates on cultural identity have stressed, variously, the fluidity, fragmentation and multiplicity of subjectivity in these post-modern and post-colonial times (Donald and Rattansi, 1992). Post-structuralist and feminist accounts of ethnicity question the fixed binary of black/white in previous models of race and racism, partly by paying attention to the ways in which differences such as those articulated around culture, gender, social class and locality are articulated (Blair and Holland, 1995; Brah, 1996). A further move towards breaking down those dualisms has been the critical examination of white ethnicities (Rattansi, 1993; Back, 1995; Nayak, 2001).

Holly's narrative articulates the uneasy hybrid position of the mixed-race girl, the pain as well as pleasure in the occupation of 'liminal' spaces, the borderlands of black/white where racism is also fluid and breaches boundaries. She was required to walk a very thin and fluid line in relation to her colour identity, particularly when she moved school at age 11. At this time she transferred from a predominantly white primary school where: 'I was getting beaten up, called nigger, coolie you know, and they didn't see me as white at all. 'Cos me and my sister were the only black kids in the whole of the school.'

She then moved to a much more racially mixed secondary school, where, in order to fit in, she was required to perform a completely different kind of racial identification.

> I can remember everybody used to call me white girl because I'd grown up in...and we went to an all white school, I'd become like whitified, you know what I mean? So when I started the school I was very white, but they didn't like that because I wasn't being black enough. So then I went for a good few years trying to be as black as I could be, do you know what I mean? Talking in slang and just really hard and beating up white girls just for being white girls you know.

Holly highlights clearly that identifications are rarely straightforward and much more likely to be cross-cut by contradictory dis-identifications. Her shifting subjectivity could only be played out at school, while careful attempts were made to protect her white mother from her rejection of whiteness. Holly had to perform major feats of binary demarcations: between home and school, black and white, conformity and resistance. For instance, she managed to be both rebellious *and* resistant to the school's culture at a public level, while privately conforming to the demands and discipline of academic work.

> Well I was quite smart actually, because I was doing all this at school, so that's probably why the teachers thought I wouldn't get anything, but then I'd go home and study. So I was having all the fun in the day and then I'd go home and do my work. I wasn't that stupid not to do any work.
>
> (Holly)

These were painful years for Holly, partly because of the ambivalence she clearly held, but was unable to acknowledge, towards her mother as a white woman. Perhaps she was also disowning a part of herself; her own whiteness – no wonder when it is this aspect of her subjectivity that is most problematic to and denied by others: white people only see her blackness and black people want to attack her whiteness:

> but it's a case of if I'm walking down the street, I'm seen as black, I'm not seen as being white, if I'd committed a crime it's just another black person committing the crime. Not a white person, but people can't seem to see that.
>   And I think also because I was like suffering abuse from black people as well for being part white, so I was like getting it from all directions.

The development of 'racial', ethnic and class identities depends upon processes of inclusion and exclusion:

> the positing of boundaries in relation to who can and cannot belong according to certain parameters which are extremely heterogeneous, ranging from the credentials of being born in the right place, conforming to cultural or other symbolic practices, language, and very centrally behaving in sexually appropriate ways.
>
> (Anthias and Yuval-Davies, 1992, p. 4)

Discussions of hybridisation stress fluidity and the possibilities contained in liminal spaces. What is less explored in those debates, but arises continually in the stories of our subjects, is that the creation of hybrid subjectivities also involves the construction and the constant policing of internal and external 'boundaries', where competing and conflictual people, behaviour, identifications and ideas must be kept apart. Holly kept her hatred of white girls away from her mother, whom she loved, through a series of complex emotional defences such as denial, projection and splitting. Object relations theory suggests ways in which boundaries are constructed, separating the 'good' and the 'bad' (Winnicott, 1957; Klein, 1959), 'the stereotypical representations of others which inform social practices of exclusion and inclusion but which, at the same time, define the self' (Sibley, 1995, p. 5). Internal demarcations are shored up and articulated through the development of external boundaries which help to keep things, people, emotions, activities in their 'proper' place. Psychoanalytically informed approaches, for instance, those drawing on the work of the psychiatrist Franz Fanon, have revealed how racial or ethnic identities are formed in a relational dynamic of power, fear and desire (Fanon, 1969). While we may desperately want to banish troublesome aspects of our own identities, this is no easy task. We are not only deeply attached to them, but also psychologically dependent on them; 'It is for this reason that what is socially peripheral is so frequently symbolically central' (Stallybrass and White, 1986).

> So this process of rejection is not a neat, clinical method of expulsion. Like a shadow cast by a moving figure, the sublimated identity is ever present in the act of subjectivity, operating in the dark margins of the unconscious.
>
> (Nayak, 2001, p. 142)

Belonging and escape

Nicky and Holly both state that they have 'always wanted to go to university'. This desire certainly seems to be connected to their determination to embark and remain on their educational journeys and to actively divert, if not halt, the process of social reproduction. As Nicky says:

> I've always wanted to go to 'uni'. I don't know why. I have to do a bit better for myself. 'Cos a lot of people my own age in my family, a bit younger, a bit older or, all they've done is, well a lot of them have dropped out of school early and gone and got themselves a job that's got absolutely no prospects to it, like working in a Burger Bar or something. And I just did not want that for myself. I couldn't see myself spending the rest of my life stuck in a Burger Bar. I just knew I had to get out and do something a bit better.

It is interesting to note that Holly was the only young woman who was able to sustain her educational career despite twice becoming pregnant in the middle of her studies: she had her first child during her A levels and her second child while she was studying for her first degree. But for Holly who, ironically, was the most highly qualified young woman in the entire sample at this point in her life, the spectre of such poverty and racial pathologisation had in part, at least, provoked and promoted the kind of motivation needed to stay on educational course and not, as she says, 'be another case of another black girl being on social security'.

All of the working-class young women who have done well at school share a fantasy of escape in their drive towards higher education, one which can be closely connected to their parents' explicitly articulated wish for their children to have better lives than they did. One mother says, 'All we want is for our children to do better than we did. I think that's what everyone wants'. Indeed, Holly expresses the same thing when she talks of her own educational career, and hopes for her children when she says she 'just want[s] things to be better for them'. But this is not what everyone wants or needs: it is not a desire articulated by the middle-class parents. For these working-class families, higher education and the possibilities it offers of entrance into a profession represents escape from the grinding facts of ordinary working-class life. These working-class mothers and fathers do not want their daughters to have to do the kinds of work they have to do: boring, repetitive, dirty and hard, with little pay, status or security. As Pilling (1990) suggests, working-class parents' desires and dreams of a better life for their children act as a powerful engine which drives their positive motivation towards education and helps to maintain them on the path to higher education. But the provenance of this motivation means that other, equally powerful messages are transferred in the emotional interchange between working-class parent and child. For the middle-class families, educational success is the theme around which the reproduction of social class position revolves (Walkerdine *et al.*, 2001; Lucey and Reay, 2002). Within this scenario, what is aimed at is to become like your parents in the sense of having the same kind of career as them, the same levels of income, material comfort and lifestyle. For the working-class daughters of aspirational parents, the message is quite different; it is clearly about *not* becoming like them and it is this which is central to both their daughters' drive to higher education and the deep ambivalences which beset some of them. They are, as Caroline Knowles observes in the context of her discussion on 'race, identities and lives', 'caught in the dynamic of belonging and escape' (1999, p. 128).

In order to improve on their parents' lives they have had to differentiate themselves from those who did not or could not improve (Skeggs, 1997, p. 82; Thomson *et al.*, 2003). Wanting something different, something more than your parents, not only implies that there is something wrong with your parents' life, but that there is something wrong with *them*. This kind of dis-identification with one's parents and family can engender a deep sense of shame – itself so shameful that it must be psychically regulated through repressive mechanisms.

Perhaps most importantly, and which we think explains why so many of the working-class young women give up, these dis-identifications with their parents mean that the leaving involved in going to university and perhaps becoming a professional hits on a very deep level. These are separations on a grand scale which the middle-class young women simply do not have to tackle. Of course, psychic separation from parents is an issue for everyone to a greater or lesser extent. But for able working-class girls who do well at school, what is so clearly at stake is the loss of identity, control, status (within the family perhaps), the community, belonging, safety: all major ego losses, any one of which can unconsciously constitute a threat to our very survival. Nicky made a very clear and conscious decision to 'get away' to a university far from her home town. Perhaps less conscious was her decision to go to one in a city where there were strong family connections. Her rational choices about which university offered her the best course, had the best reputation, facilities etc. may have been powerfully informed by her unconscious desire to put in place some bridges between her old and new world. Holly, like Nicky, articulates clear, conscious desires for independence and escape, and yet by becoming a teenage mother, not once, but twice, both at crucial junctions on her educational pathway, she did the very thing guaranteed to keep her close to and dependent on her mother. We could therefore view teenage motherhood as a complex attempt to maintain present status in the face of overwhelming change and loss.

Going it alone

As Nicky points out, nobody seems to know anything that can help her and she has no financial resources to fall back on if she gets into debt. In this view, nobody is psychically or economically there to help her: there is no strong bounded autonomous ego (as in the picture painted of the normal middle-class four-year-old, *pace* Walkerdine and Lucey, 1989), but a painful separation which wards off the anger, the pain and loneliness with a defence that she needs no one, can do it all by herself. Actually, underneath all this pain may be a powerful anger that her parents have nothing to give her, or a fear that there is nothing to stop her falling apart other than her 'outer armour' (Trevithick, 1988).

The going alone protects her and them from the pain and the anger. Freud posited that we are all in a state of conflict with our loved ones as we try to reconcile the love we feel for them with our sense of disappointment and resulting anger over their inevitable failings. It is this conflict which lies at the heart of ambivalence and the reason why it can be very hard, even impossible, to accept such a conflict. Unconsciously, we may 'substitute a conflict within themselves for a conflict with the other' (Hoggett, 2001, p. 46). At times like these, when parts of ourselves are at war with other parts, we are clearly not unitary subjects – we may even be actively engaged in a destructive relationship towards other parts. Anger directed against the external world, but which remains unspeakable, is turned upon the self, turned inwards with its full and destructive force, to produce self-denigration, feelings of worthlessness, blame and accusation.

It would be easy to argue that such defences are pathological, and we could muster many a theory to sing a song of inadequate parenting. But in our view, such analyses would be wildly wrong. The defences Nicky and Holly exhibit are the very things that ensure that they get to and succeed in higher education. The double bind is that they may have aspects that are harmful to them emotionally but they are also essential to them practically. Just as it is completely inappropriate to assume that working-class copies of middle-class family practices would make for educational success, so it is equally inappropriate to assume that working-class psychic processes should, in the best of all worlds, mirror those of the middle classes. As Pheterson (1993) argues, systems of domination bring their own defences to dominator and dominated. We might argue further that the kind of dissociation which allows Nicky and Holly to succeed is a way of coping with the terrifying differences in practices, subject positions, modes of discourse, performance and regulation which the two worlds provide. This kind of split and fragmented subjectivity in this analysis is necessary to cross the divide. Whether a new position, that of hybrid, is formed in the process is no simple matter, either psychically or socially. It would be all too easy to suggest that these two worlds that Nicky and Holly keep so defensively apart could be easily integrated for them. This is not to say that they could not be integrated with a great deal of hard emotional work. But to suggest otherwise would be to deny the massive social inequalities which are at their foundation.

Conclusion

Liberal discourses ask, 'what can we do to make working-class children succeed at school?' and focus on pedagogy and practice, of teachers and parents, particularly mothers. The Left is, in the meantime, hooked on theories of reproduction.

None of these frameworks can really address how or why some working-class children succeed. The more recent 'conformist' literature on working-class children who do well at school is replete with problems, with the 'conformist' category set up as an opposition to the 'resistance' literature (e.g. Willis, 1977). We are advocating an understanding of working-class girls' success as not a simple conformity at all, but then neither could it be understood as an easy rebellion or resistance. Why some girls would long for something different and be able to make this happen through what is an emotionally and socially terrifying shift while others feel safer staying within the well-understood and maintained practices of school failure is a question which demands to be asked, but is not the question which is usually addressed within the educational literature.

The twin shafts of education and professional status on which many strands of middle-class subjectivity rest mean that the children of the professional middle classes receive strong messages from early childhood that it is their destiny to go to university and become professionals, a destiny which is pushed hard and has its own real constraints and costs (Lucey and Reay, 2002). This is certainly not the destiny of the working-class girls, nor is it presented as such by those who have achieved examination success at school. Is this why so many of them give up, even when they have a relatively sure footing on that path (see Walkerdine et al., 2001)? Because it is not the working-class girls' destiny, the motivation to remain on that path must be generated from within. There are no structural reasons why they should succeed and therefore they have to rely on their own inner resources. However, we also wish to stress that, should that success be achieved by the working-class girl, the hopes and aspirations of her and her parents become intertwined with the pain of separation and therefore loss and shift of identity (Reay, 1997). The girls who have not done so well at school at least do not have to face the difficulties that choice can bring. How, then, do any working-class girls at all succeed in education when they are regulated to be produced as 'docile subjects' who in the present 'government of freedom' must remake themselves as autonomous, reflexive subjects? We argue that the regulation is double-edged. It is precisely the strong boundaries between work and play which are crucial for understanding the production of a subject who is capable of recognising the absolute separation of home and school (Walkerdine, 1991) and coping with it psychically by complex defences. These very inner resources which are necessary to success can also be self-destructive and this contradiction needs to be understood in order to assist children and adults in this transition.

There are no easy hybrids. Hybridity may be a cultural and social fact but it is never lived easily in a psychic economy. Not only are working-class girls who do well at school and go on to higher education moving into intellectual and occupational spheres traditionally seen to be masculine, they are also moving out of their class sphere, beyond the wildest dreams of anyone in their families, into clean, professional, interesting jobs. Just moving into the intellectual domain is a massive shift for them, requiring a complete internal and external 'makeover', where complex unconscious defences, put in place as protection, can also act as 'deep obstacles to the exercise of choice, and to the fulfilment of consciously held goals' (Rustin, 1991, p. 23). It is not just worthwhile but essential to explore these psychosocial processes if we are serious about the project of equality in education. Without a consideration of the psychodynamic processes involved, the deep and enduring failure of the majority of working-class girls and boys will continue unabated.

NOTE

1   The majority of the young women were white, though there was one Afro-Caribbean, one Asian and one 'mixed-race' young woman in the overall sample. A subsidiary sample of six black and Asian 21-year-old young women was added to the original sample.

REFERENCES

Adkins, L. (1995) *Gendered Work: Sexuality, Family and the Labour Market* (Buckingham, Open University Press).
Adkins, L. (2001) 'Cultural feminisation: "money, sex and power" for (wo)men', *Signs*, 26: 31–57.
Althusser, L. (1969) *For Marx* (London, New Left Books).
Anthias, F. and Yuval-Davies, N. (1992) *Racialized Boundaries: Race, Nation, Gender, Colour and Class and The Anti-racist Struggle* (London, Routledge).
Anzaldua, G. (1987) *Borderlands/La Frontera: The New Mestiza* (San Francisco, CA, Spinsters/Aunt Lute).
Back, L. (1995) *New Ethnicities and Urban Culture* (London, UCL Press).
Beck, U. (1992) *Risk Society: Towards a New Modernity* (London, Sage).
Bhabha, H. (1984) 'The other question: the stereotype and colonial discourse', *Screen*, 24: 18–36.
Bhabha, H. (1990) 'The third space', in J. Rutherford (ed.), *Identity* (London, Lawrence & Wishart).
Bhabha, H. (1996) 'Cultures in-between', in S. Hall and P. Du Gay (eds), *Questions of Cultural Identity* (London, Sage).
Blair, M. and Holland, J. (eds) (1995) *Identity and Diversity* (Clevedon, Multilingual Matters).
Bradley, H. (1996) *Fractured Identities: Changing Patterns of Inequality* (Cambridge, Polity Press).
Brah, A. (1996) *Cartographies of Diaspora: Contesting Identities* (London, Routledge).
Coleman, J. (1988) 'Social capital in the creation of human capital', *American Journal of Sociology*, 94: 95–120.
Cowie, E. (1997) *Representing the Woman: Cinema and Psychoanalysis* (London, Macmillan).
David, M.E. (1993) *Parents, Gender and Education Reform* (Cambridge, Polity Press).
Donald, J. and Rattansi, A. (eds) (1992) *'Race', Culture and Difference* (London, Sage).
Fanon, F. (1969) *Black Skin, White Mask* (Harmondsworth, Penguin).
Finch, J. (1984) *Education as Social Policy* (London, Longman).
Frosh, S. (1991) *Identity Crisis: Modernity, Psychoanalysis and The Self* (London, Macmillan).
Frosh, S. (1997) *For and Against Psychoanalysis* (London, Routledge).
Frosh, S., Phoenix, A. and Pattman, R. (2002) *Young Masculinities* (Basingstoke, Palgrave).
Fukuyama, F. (1999) *Trust: The Social Virtues and the Creation of Prosperity* (London, Penguin).
Giddens, A. (1991) *Modernity and Self Identity: Self and Society in The Late Modern Age* (Cambridge, Polity Press).
Gilroy, P. (1993) *The Black Atlantic* (London, Verso).
Grossberg, L. (1996) 'Identity and cultural studies – is that all there is?', in S. Hall and P. Du Gay (eds), *Questions of Cultural Identity* (London, Sage).
Hall, S. (1993) 'New ethnicities', in J. Donald and A. Rattansi (eds), *'Race', Culture and Difference* (London, Sage).
Henriques, J., Hollway, W., Urwin, C., Venn, C. and Walkerdine, V. (1997) *Changing the Subject: Psychology, Social Regulation and Subjectivity*, 2nd edn (London, Routledge).
Hoggett, P. (2001) 'Agency, rationality and social policy', *Journal of Social Policy*, 30: 37–56.
Hollway, W. and Jefferson, T. (2000) *Doing Qualitative Research Differently: Free Associations, Narrative and The Interview Method* (London, Sage).

Klein, M. (1959) 'Our adult world and its roots in infancy', in M. Klein (ed.), *Envy and Gratitude and Other Works; 1946–1963* (London, Virago Press).

Knowles, C. (1999) 'Race, identities and lives', *Sociological Review*, 47: 111–135.

Lucey, H. and Reay, D. (2000) 'Social class and the psyche', *Soundings*, 15: 139–154.

Lucey, H. and Reay, D. (2002) 'Carrying the beacon of excellence: social class differentiation and anxiety at a time of transition', *Journal of Educational Policy*, 17: 321–336.

Lucey, H., Melody, J. and Walkerdine, V. (2003) 'Developing a psycho-social method in one longitudinal study', *International Journal of Social Research Methodology, Theory and Practice*, 6 (in press).

Mirza, H. (1992) *Young, Female and Black* (London, Routledge).

Modood, T. (1992) *Not Easy Being British* (Stoke-on-Trent, Trentham Books).

Nayak, A. (2001) 'Ice white and ordinary', in B. Francis and C. Skelton (eds), *Investigating Gender: Contemporary Perspectives in Education* (Buckingham, Open University Press).

Pheterson, G. (1993) 'Historical and material determinants of psychodynamic development', in J. Adleman and G. Enguidanos (eds), *Racism in the Lives of Women in New York* (New York, Haworth Press).

Phoenix, A. (1991) *Young Mothers?* (Cambridge, Polity Press).

Phoenix, A. (1996) 'Social constructions of lone motherhood: a case of competing discourses', in E. Bortolaia Silva (ed.), *Good Enough Mothering? Feminist Perspectives on Lone Motherhood* (London, Routledge).

Pilling, D. (1990) *Escape from Disadvantage* (London, Falmer Press).

Plummer, G. (2000) *Failing Working-class Girls* (Stoke-on-Trent, Trentham Books).

Putnam, R. (2000) *Bowling Alone: The Collapse and Revival of American Community* (Boston, MA, Simon & Schuster).

Rattansi. A. (1993) 'Changing the subject? Racism, culture and education', in J. Donald and A. Rattansi (eds), *'Race', Culture and Difference* (London, Sage).

Reay, D. (1997) 'The double bind of the working class feminist academic: the success of failure or the failure of success?', in P. Mahony and C. Zmroczek (eds), *Class Matters: Working Class Women's Perspectives on Social Class* (London, Taylor & Francis).

Reay, D. (2001) 'The paradox of contemporary femininities', in B. Francis and C. Skelton (eds), *Investigating Gender: Contemporary Perspectives in Education* (Buckingham, Open University Press).

Rustin, M. (1991) *The Good Society and the Inner World: Psychoanalysis, Politics and Culture* (New York, Verso).

Shaw, J. (1995) *Education, Gender and Anxiety* (London, Taylor & Francis).

Sibley, D. (1995) *Geographies of Exclusion* (London, Routledge).

Skeggs, B. (1997) *Formations of Class and Gender* (London, Sage).

Stallybrass, P. and White, A. (1986) *The Politics and Poetics of Transgression* (London, Methuen).

Thomson, R., Henderson, S. and Holland, J. (2003) 'Making the most of what you've got? Resources, values and inequalities in young women's transitions to adulthood', *Educational Review*, 55: 33–46.

Tizard, B. and Hughes, M. (1984) *Young Children Learning* (London, Fontana).

Tokarczyk, M. and Fay, E. (eds) (1995) *Working Class Women in the Academy: Labourers in The Knowledge Factory* (Amherst, MA, University of Massachusetts Press).

Trevithick, P. (1988) 'Unconsciousness raising with working-class women', in S. Krzowski and P. Land (eds), *In Our Experience* (London, The Women's Press).

Vincent, C. and Warren, S. (1999) 'Becoming a "better" parent? Motherhood, education and transition', *British Journal of Sociology of Education*, 19: 177–193.

Walkerdine, V. (1991) *Schoolgirl Fictions* (London, Verso).

Walkerdine, V. (1996) *Daddy's Girl: Young Girls and Popular Culture* (London, Macmillan).

Walkerdine, V. and Lucey, H. (1989) *Democracy in the Kitchen: Regulating Mothers and Socialising Daughters* (London, Virago).

Walkerdine, V., Lucey, H. and Melody, J. (2001) *Growing up Girl: Psychosocial Explorations of Gender and Class* (Basingstoke, Palgrave).

Willis, P. (1977) *Learning to Labour* (Farnborough, Saxon House).

Winnicott, D.W. (1957) *The Child and the Family: First Relationships* (London, Tavistock).